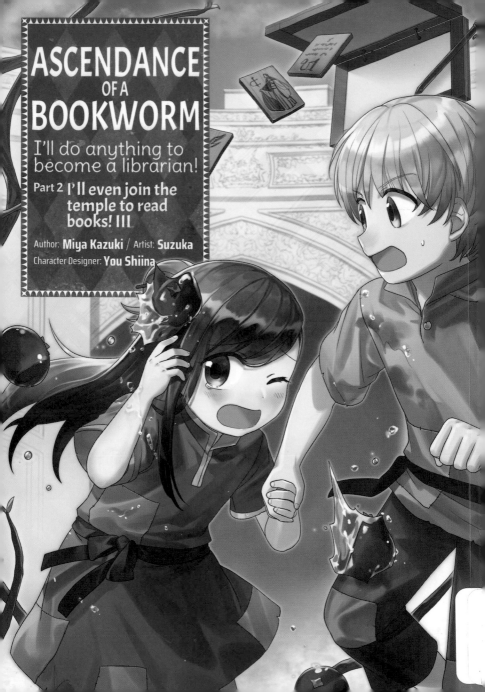

ASCENDANCE OF A BOOKWORM

I'll do anything to become a librarian!

Part 2 **I'll even join the temple to read books! III**

Author: **Miya Kazuki** / Artist: **Suzuka**

Character Designer: **You Shiina**

ASCENDANCE OF A BOOKWORM

I'll do anything to become a librarian!

Part 2 I'll even join the temple to read books!

Volume 3

Author: **Miya Kazuki** / Artist: **Suzuka**

Character Designer: **You Shiina**

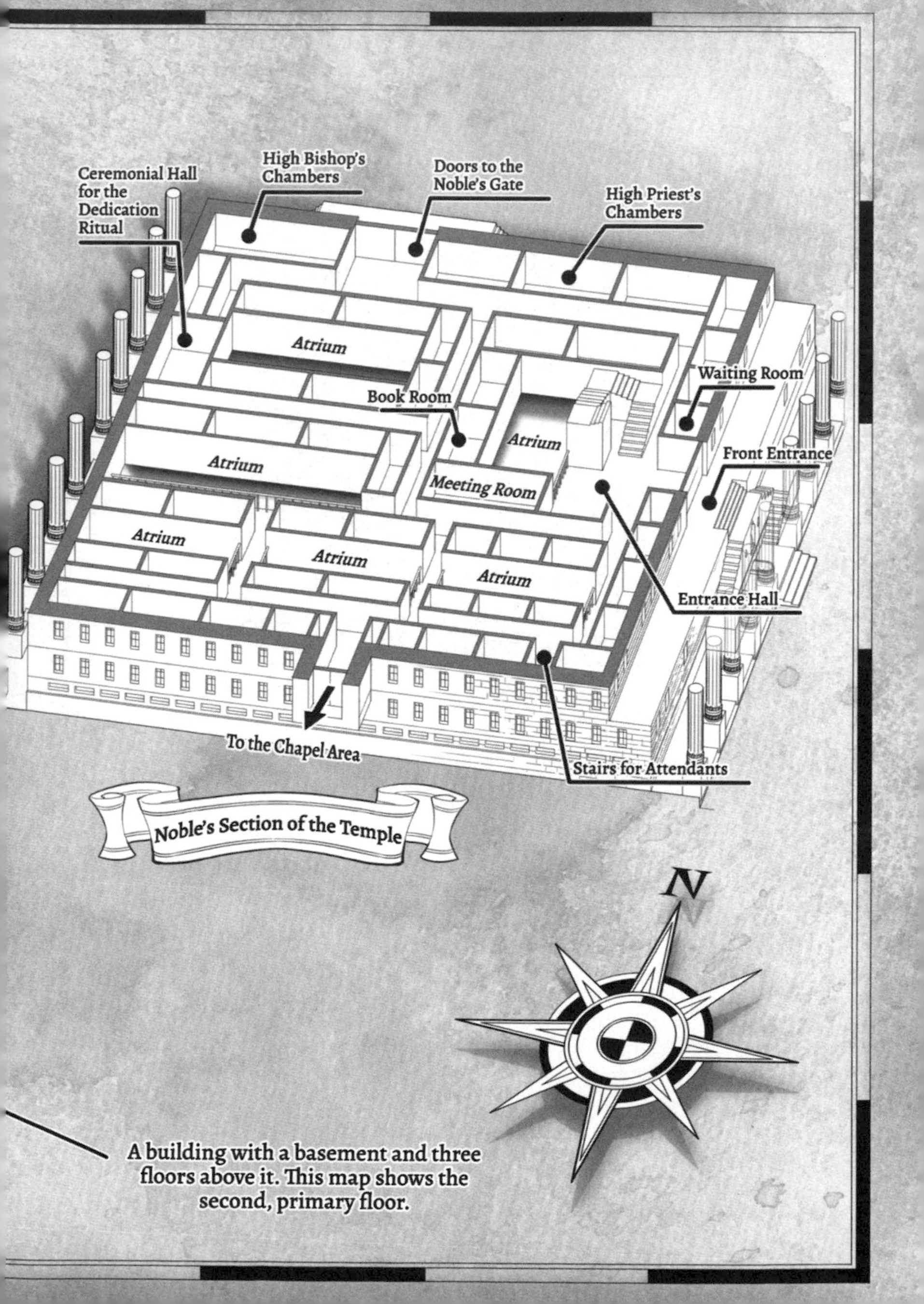
High Bishop's Chambers
Ceremonial Hall for the Dedication Ritual
Doors to the Noble's Gate
High Priest's Chambers
Atrium
Waiting Room
Book Room
Atrium
Atrium
Front Entrance
Meeting Room
Atrium
Atrium
Atrium
Entrance Hall
To the Chapel Area
Stairs for Attendants
Noble's Section of the Temple
N
A building with a basement and three floors above it. This map shows the second, primary floor.

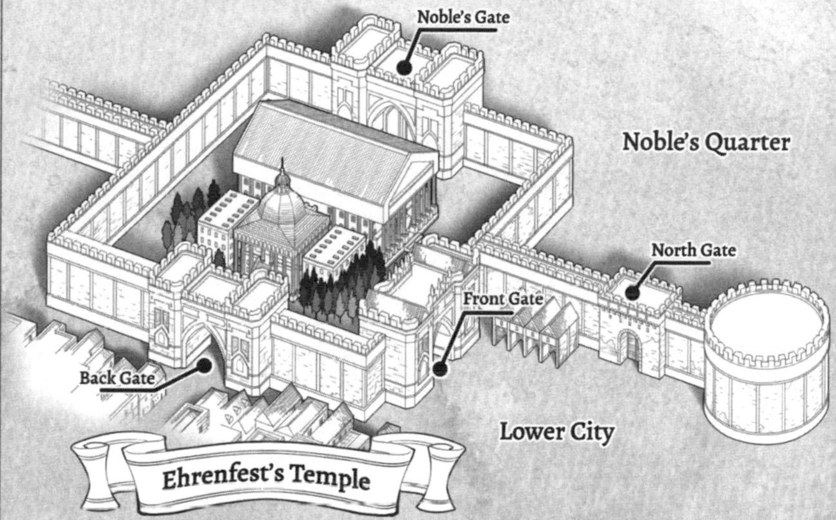
Noble's Gate
Noble's Quarter
North Gate
Front Gate
Back Gate
Lower City
Ehrenfest's Temple

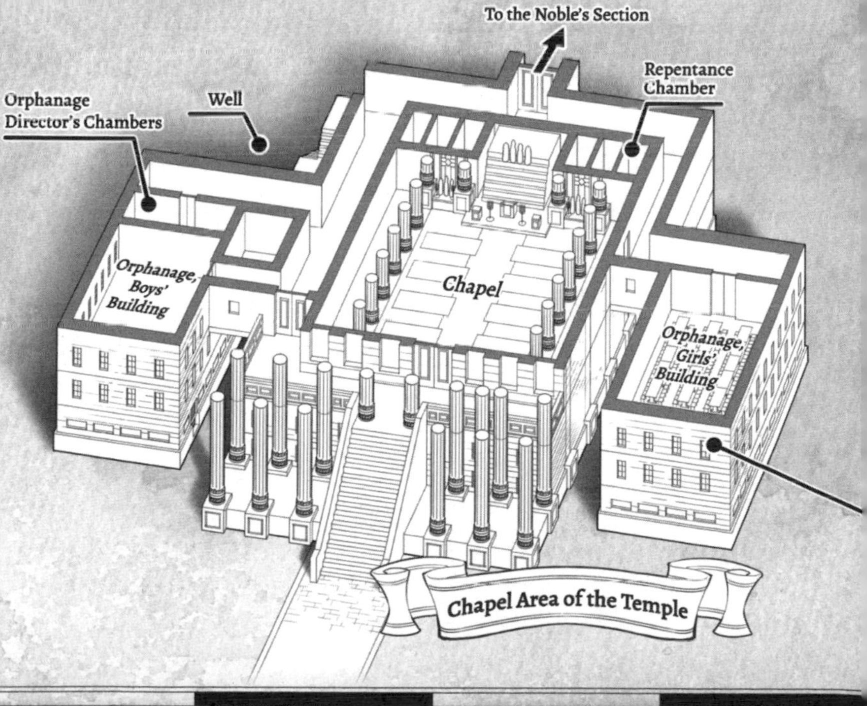
To the Noble's Section
Repentance Chamber
Orphanage Director's Chambers
Well
Orphanage, Boys' Building
Chapel
Orphanage, Girls' Building
Chapel Area of the Temple

ASCENDANCE OF A BOOKWORM
I'll do anything to become a librarian!
Part 2 I'll even join the temple to read books!
Volume III

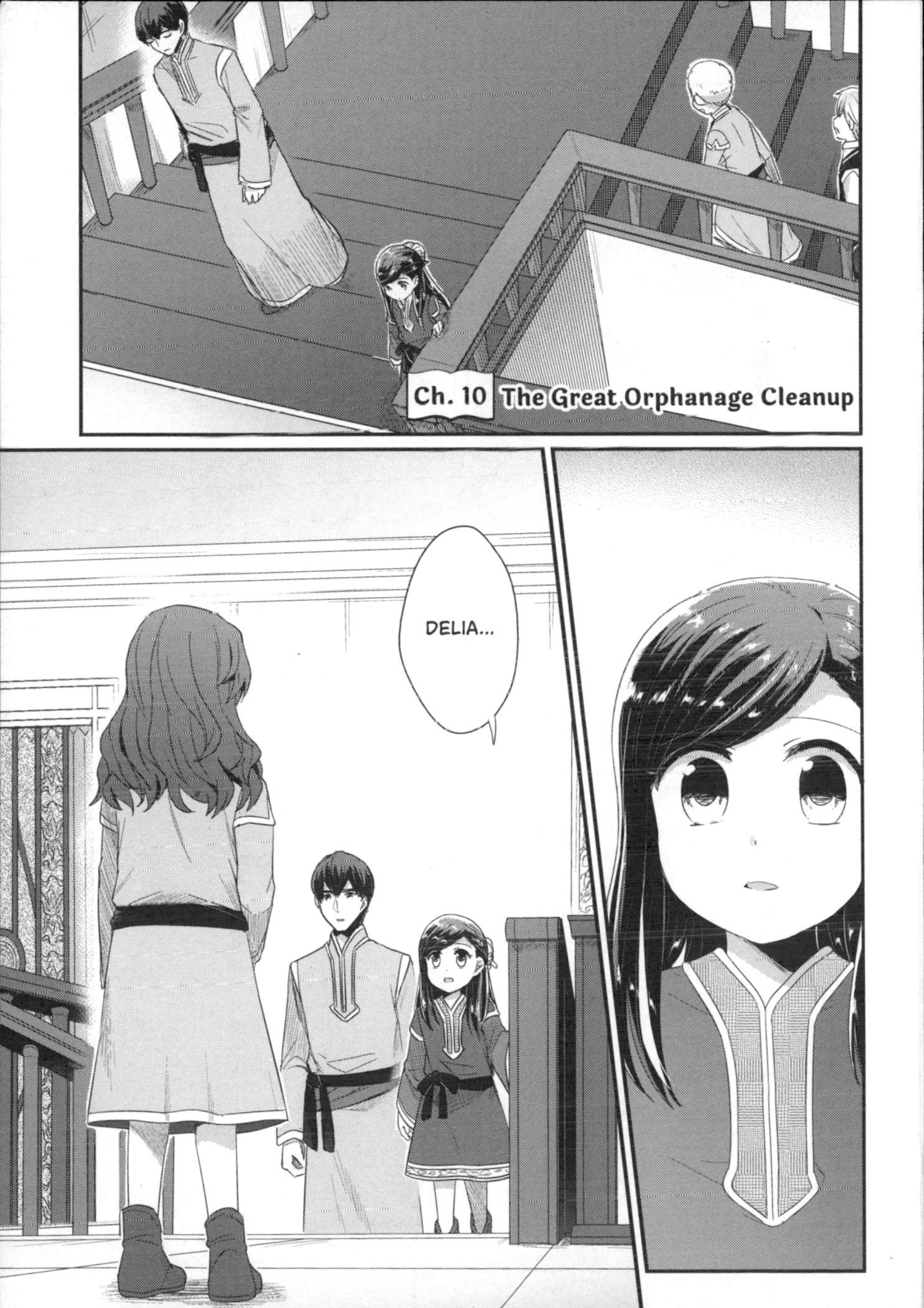
Ch. 10 The Great Orphanage Cleanup
DELIA...

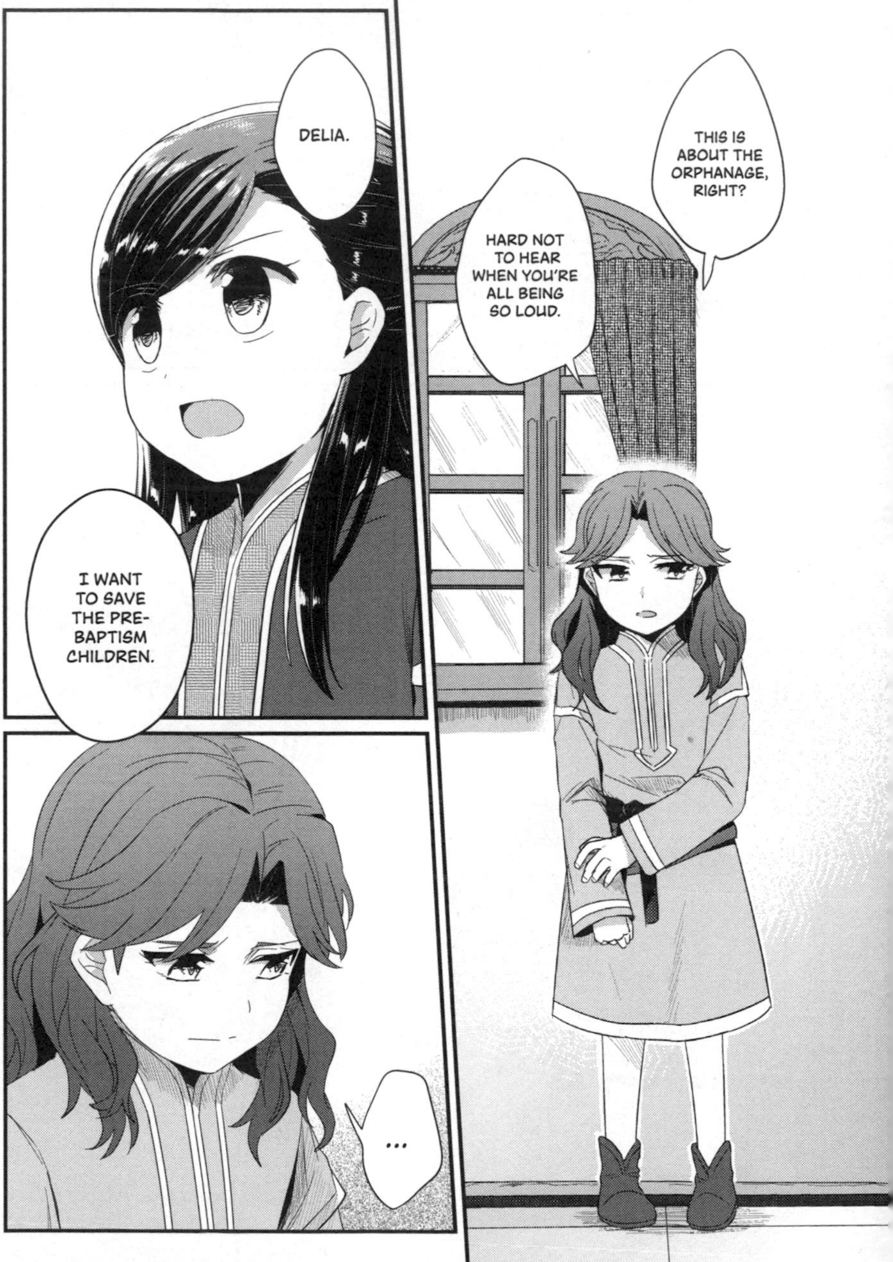
THIS IS ABOUT THE ORPHANAGE, RIGHT?
HARD NOT TO HEAR WHEN YOU'RE ALL BEING SO LOUD.
DELIA.
I WANT TO SAVE THE PRE-BAPTISM CHILDREN.
...

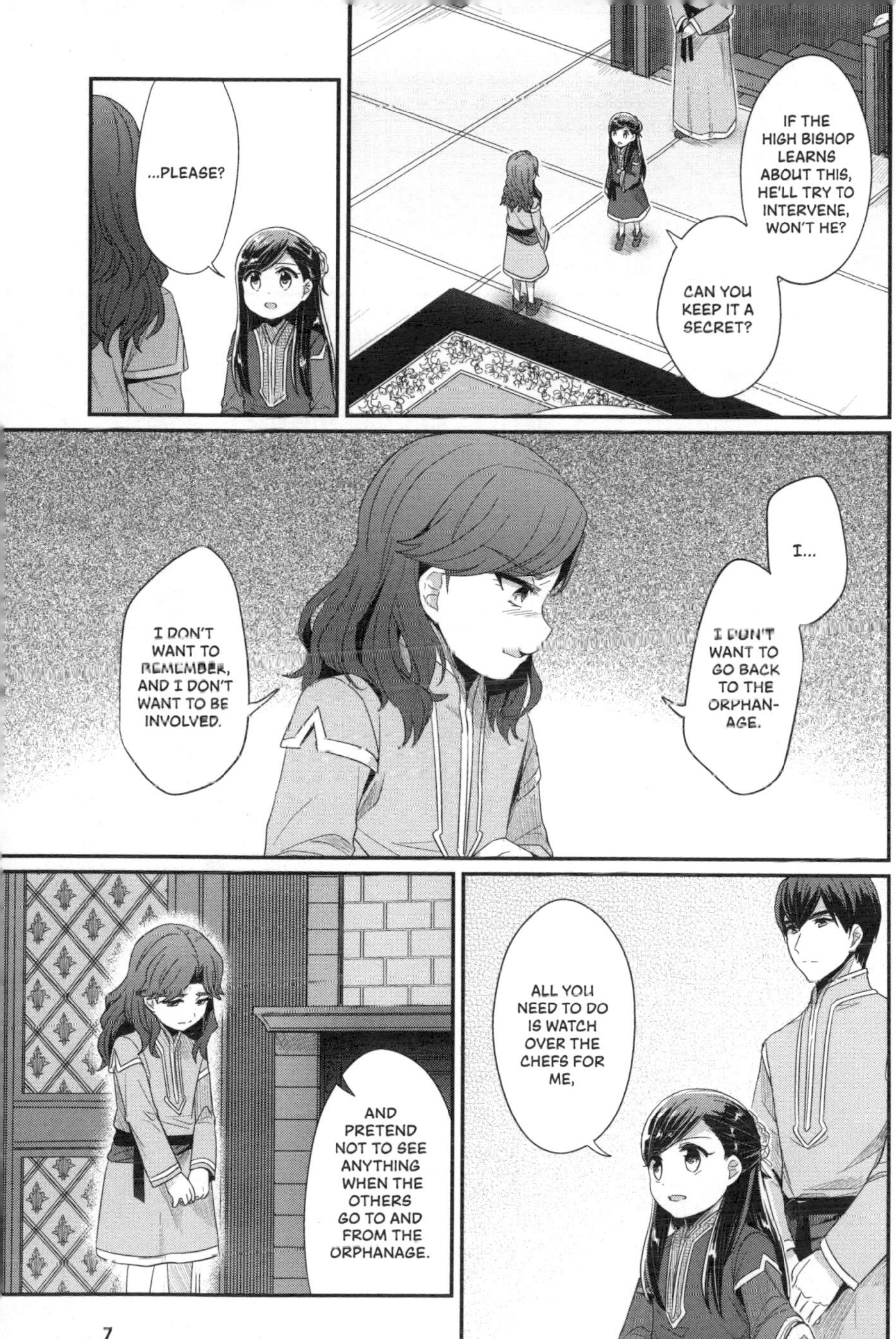
IF THE HIGH BISHOP LEARNS ABOUT THIS, HE'LL TRY TO INTERVENE, WON'T HE?
CAN YOU KEEP IT A SECRET?
...PLEASE?
I...
I DON'T WANT TO GO BACK TO THE ORPHANAGE.
I DON'T WANT TO REMEMBER, AND I DON'T WANT TO BE INVOLVED.
ALL YOU NEED TO DO IS WATCH OVER THE CHEFS FOR ME,
AND PRETEND NOT TO SEE ANYTHING WHEN THE OTHERS GO TO AND FROM THE ORPHANAGE.

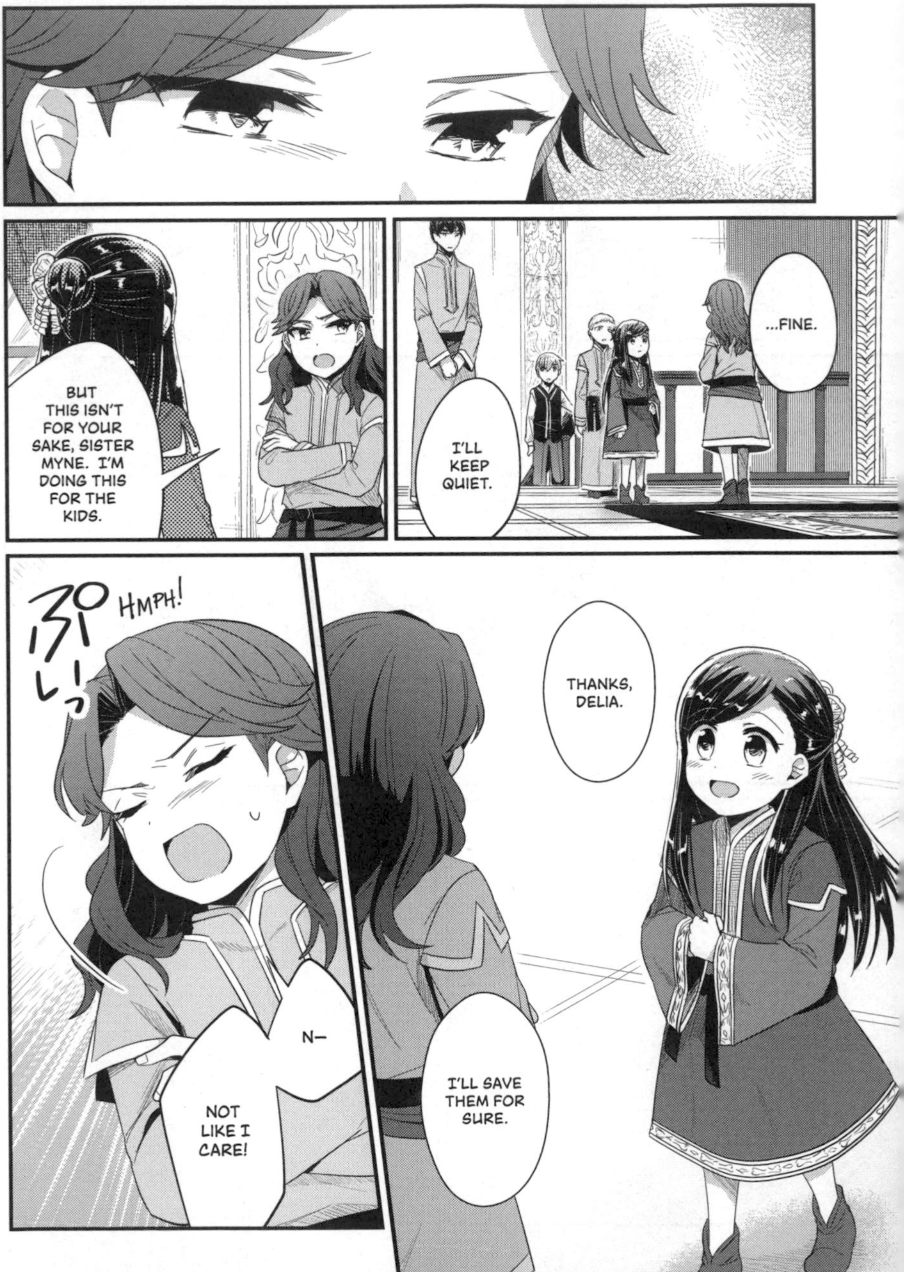

...FINE.
I'LL KEEP QUIET.
BUT THIS ISN'T FOR YOUR SAKE, SISTER MYNE. I'M DOING THIS FOR THE KIDS.
THANKS, DELIA.
I'LL SAVE THEM FOR SURE.
ぷいっ
HMPH!
N—
NOT LIKE I CARE!

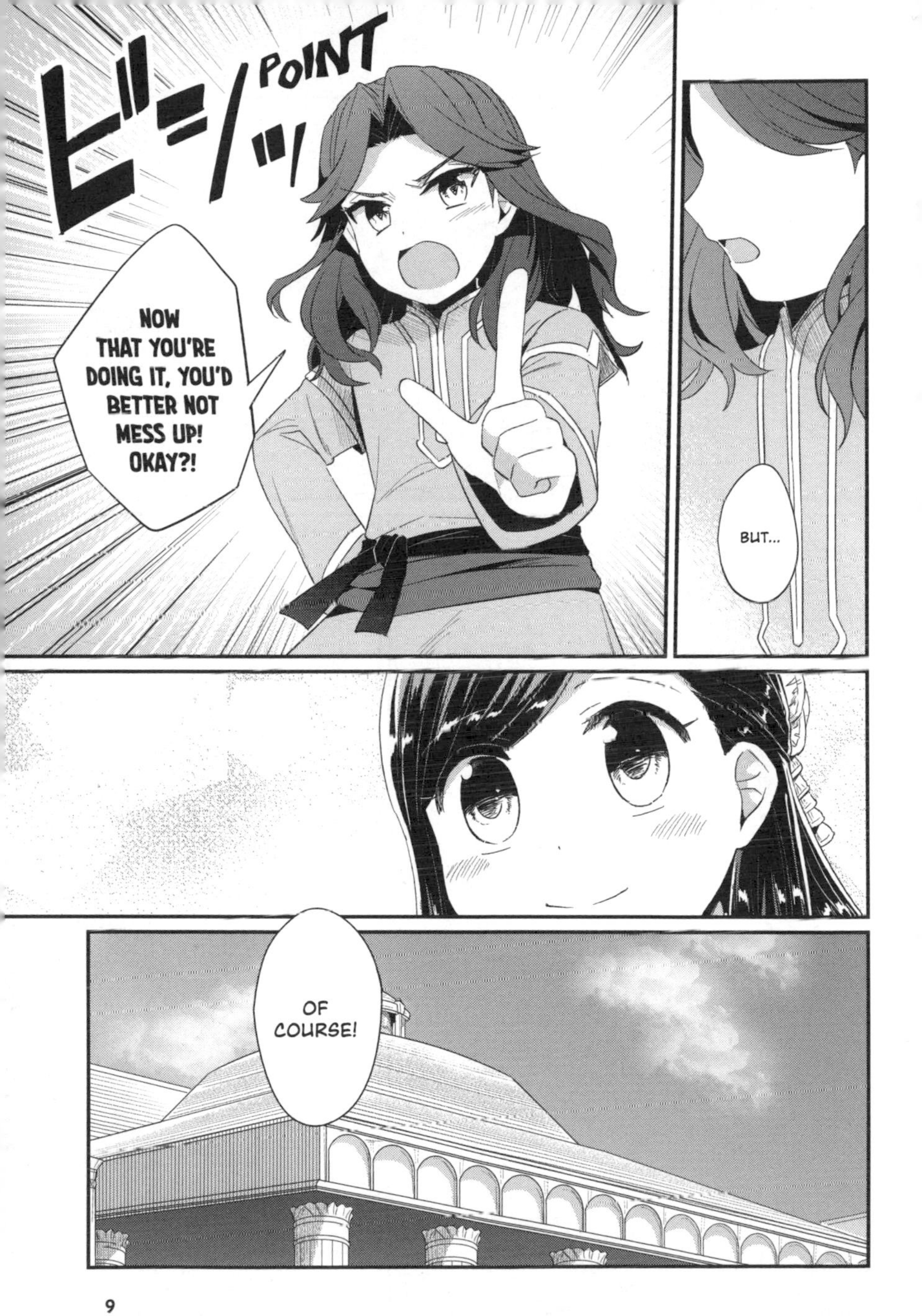
BUT...
POINT
NOW THAT YOU'RE DOING IT, YOU'D BETTER NOT MESS UP! OKAY?!
OF COURSE!

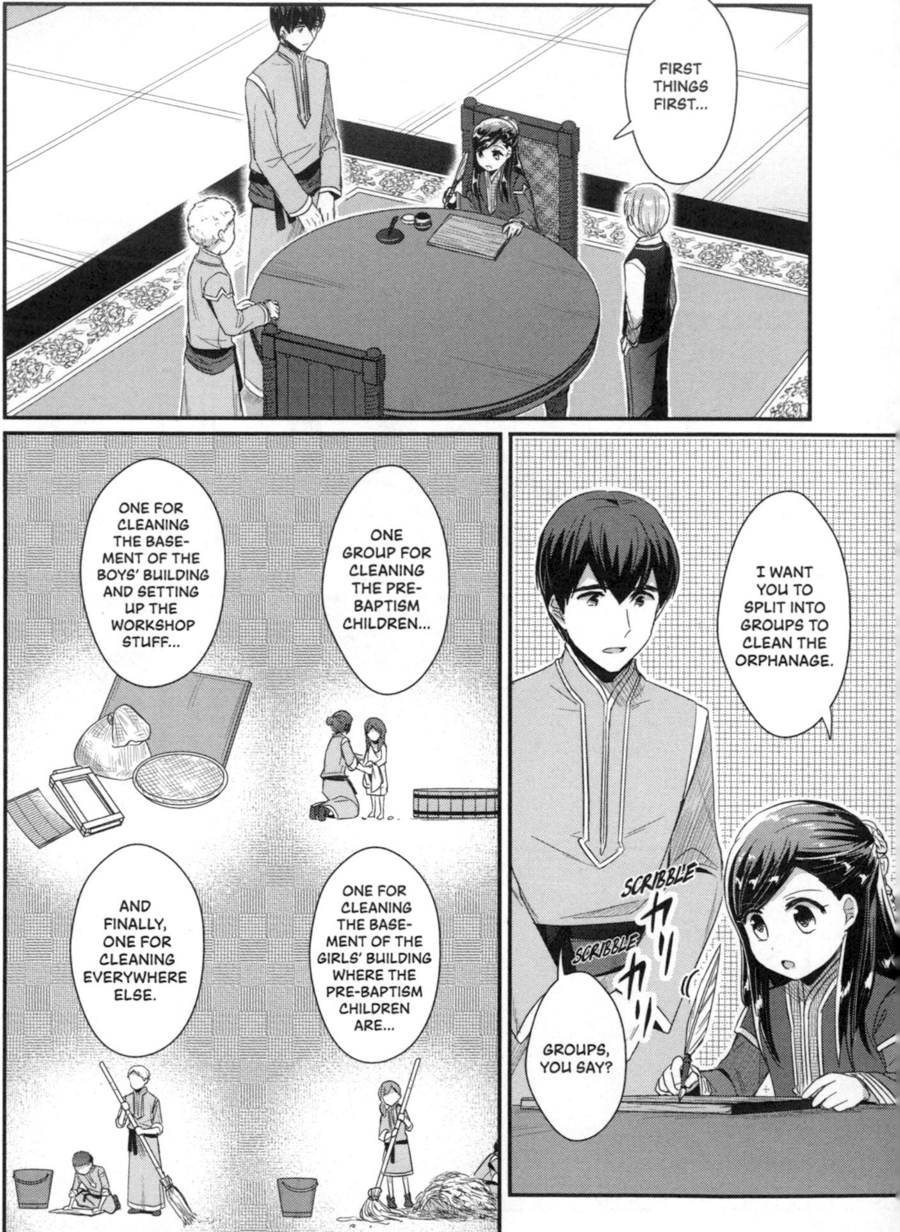
FIRST THINGS FIRST...
I WANT YOU TO SPLIT INTO GROUPS TO CLEAN THE ORPHANAGE.
SCRIBBLE
カリ
SCRIBBLE
カリ
GROUPS, YOU SAY?
ONE GROUP FOR CLEANING THE PRE-BAPTISM CHILDREN...
ONE FOR CLEANING THE BASEMENT OF THE BOYS' BUILDING AND SETTING UP THE WORKSHOP STUFF...
ONE FOR CLEANING THE BASEMENT OF THE GIRLS' BUILDING WHERE THE PRE-BAPTISM CHILDREN ARE...
AND FINALLY, ONE FOR CLEANING EVERYWHERE ELSE.

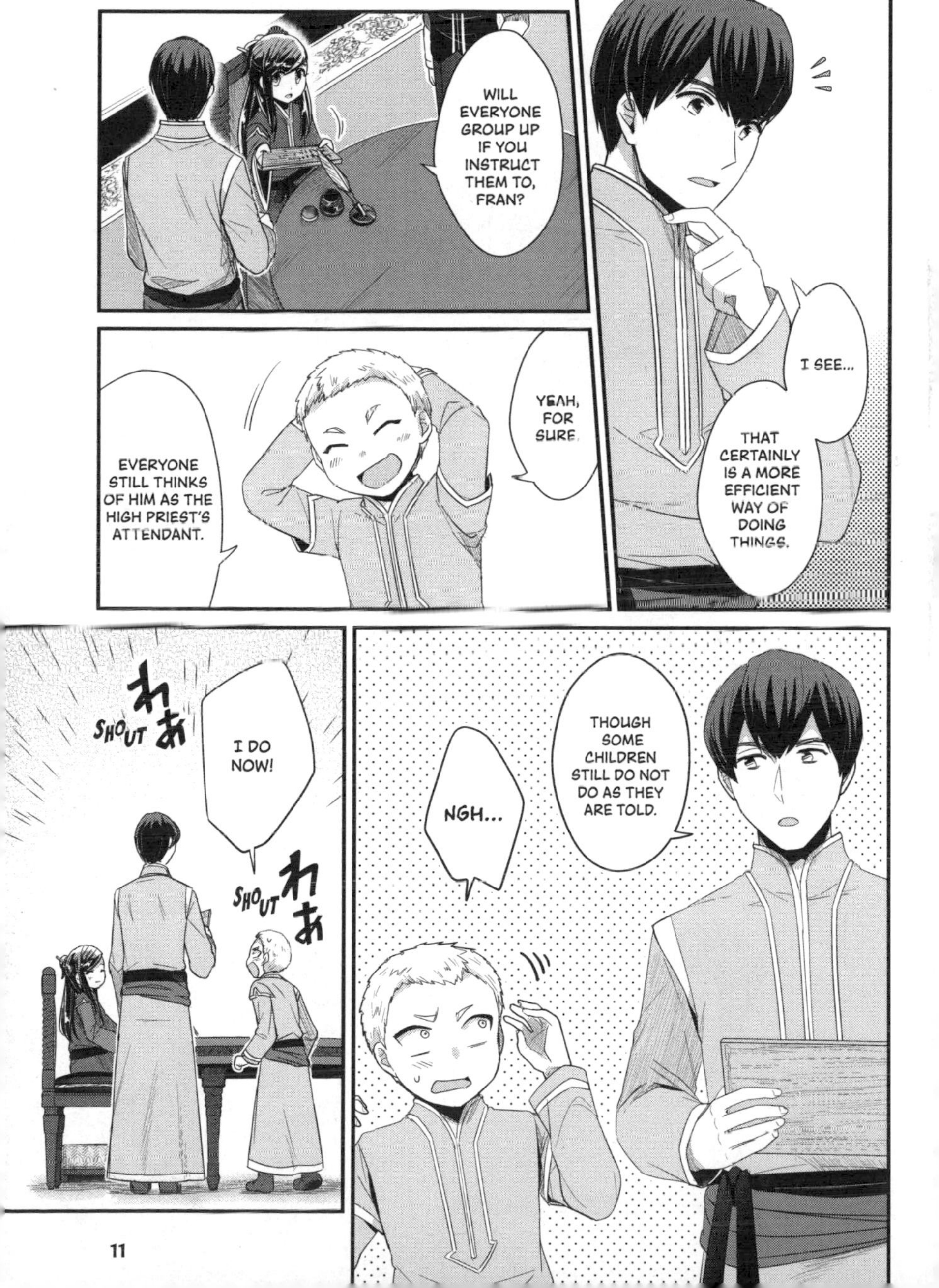
I SEE...
THAT CERTAINLY IS A MORE EFFICIENT WAY OF DOING THINGS.
WILL EVERYONE GROUP UP IF YOU INSTRUCT THEM TO, FRAN?
YEAH, FOR SURE.
EVERYONE STILL THINKS OF HIM AS THE HIGH PRIEST'S ATTENDANT.
THOUGH SOME CHILDREN STILL DO NOT DO AS THEY ARE TOLD.
NGH...
SHOUT わあ
I DO NOW!
SHOUT わあ

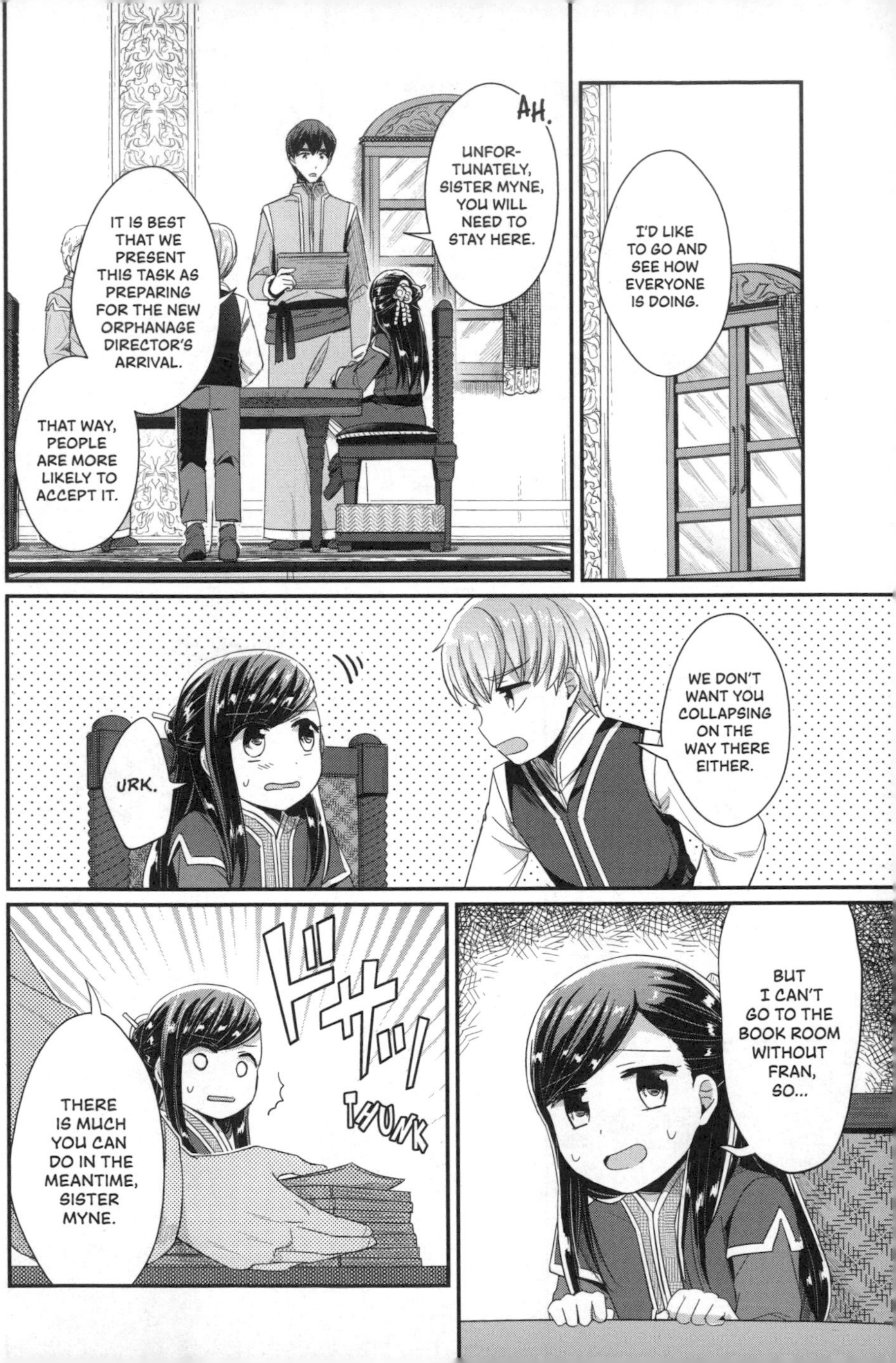
I'D LIKE TO GO AND SEE HOW EVERYONE IS DOING.
AH.
UNFOR-TUNATELY, SISTER MYNE, YOU WILL NEED TO STAY HERE.
IT IS BEST THAT WE PRESENT THIS TASK AS PREPARING FOR THE NEW ORPHANAGE DIRECTOR'S ARRIVAL.
THAT WAY, PEOPLE ARE MORE LIKELY TO ACCEPT IT.
WE DON'T WANT YOU COLLAPSING ON THE WAY THERE EITHER.
URK.
BUT I CAN'T GO TO THE BOOK ROOM WITHOUT FRAN, SO...
ドサッ
THUNK
THERE IS MUCH YOU CAN DO IN THE MEANTIME, SISTER MYNE.

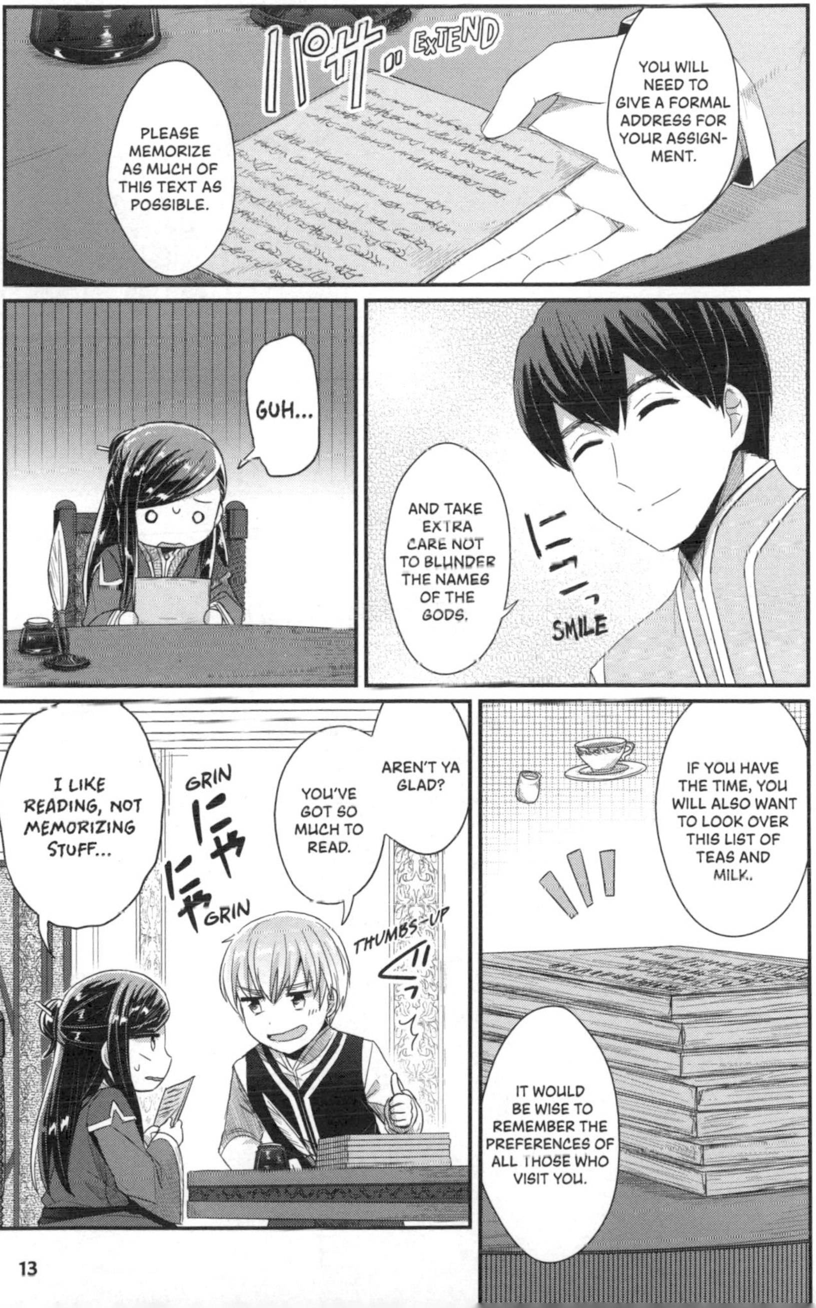
YOU WILL NEED TO GIVE A FORMAL ADDRESS FOR YOUR ASSIGNMENT.
EXTEND
PLEASE MEMORIZE AS MUCH OF THIS TEXT AS POSSIBLE.
AND TAKE EXTRA CARE NOT TO BLUNDER THE NAMES OF THE GODS.
SMILE
GUH...
IF YOU HAVE THE TIME, YOU WILL ALSO WANT TO LOOK OVER THIS LIST OF TEAS AND MILK.
IT WOULD BE WISE TO REMEMBER THE PREFERENCES OF ALL THOSE WHO VISIT YOU.
AREN'T YA GLAD?
YOU'VE GOT SO MUCH TO READ.
GRIN
GRIN
THUMBS-UP
I LIKE READING, NOT MEMORIZING STUFF...

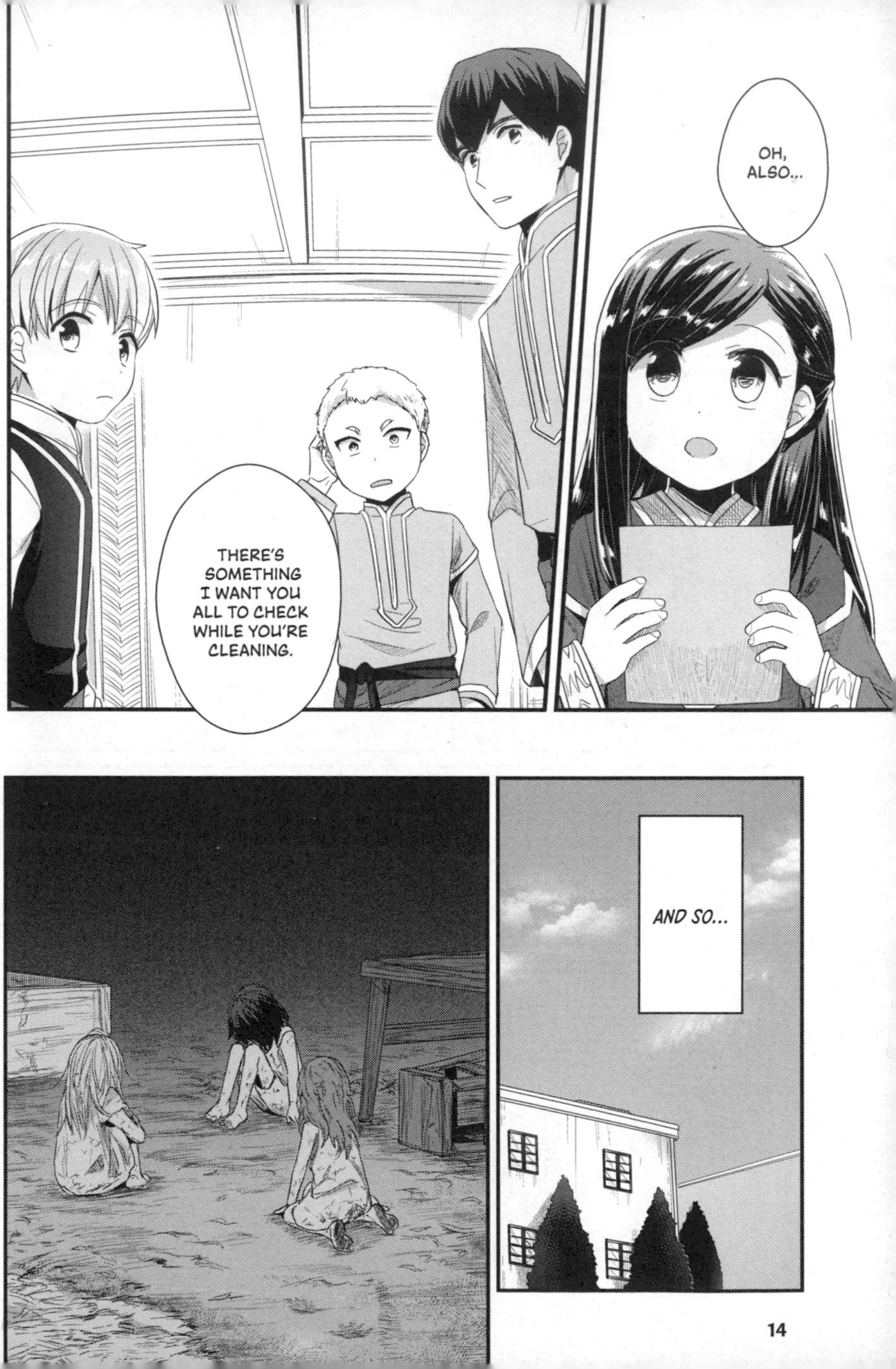
OH, ALSO...
THERE'S SOMETHING I WANT YOU ALL TO CHECK WHILE YOU'RE CLEANING.
AND SO...

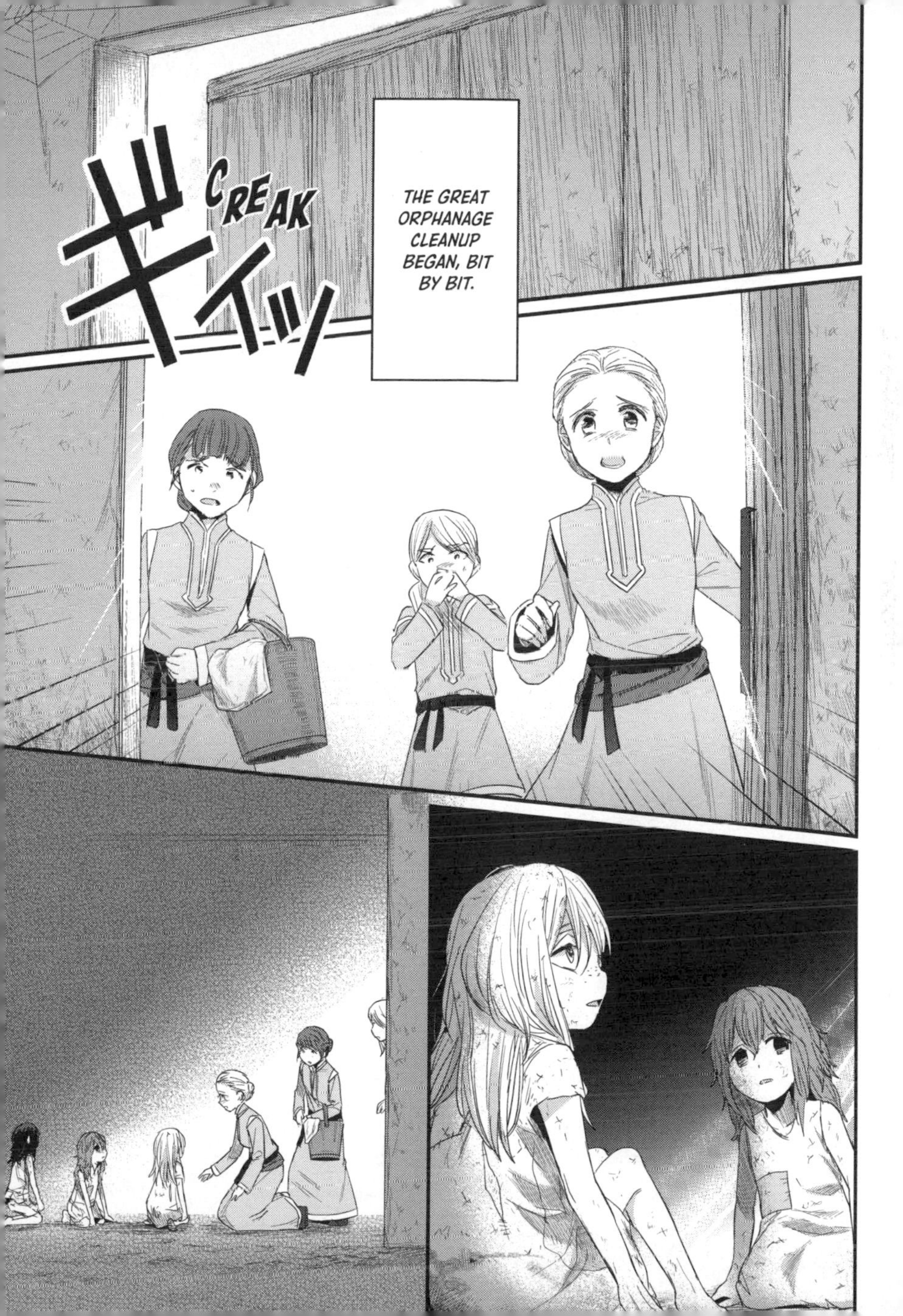
ギイッ
CREAK
THE GREAT ORPHANAGE CLEANUP BEGAN, BIT BY BIT.

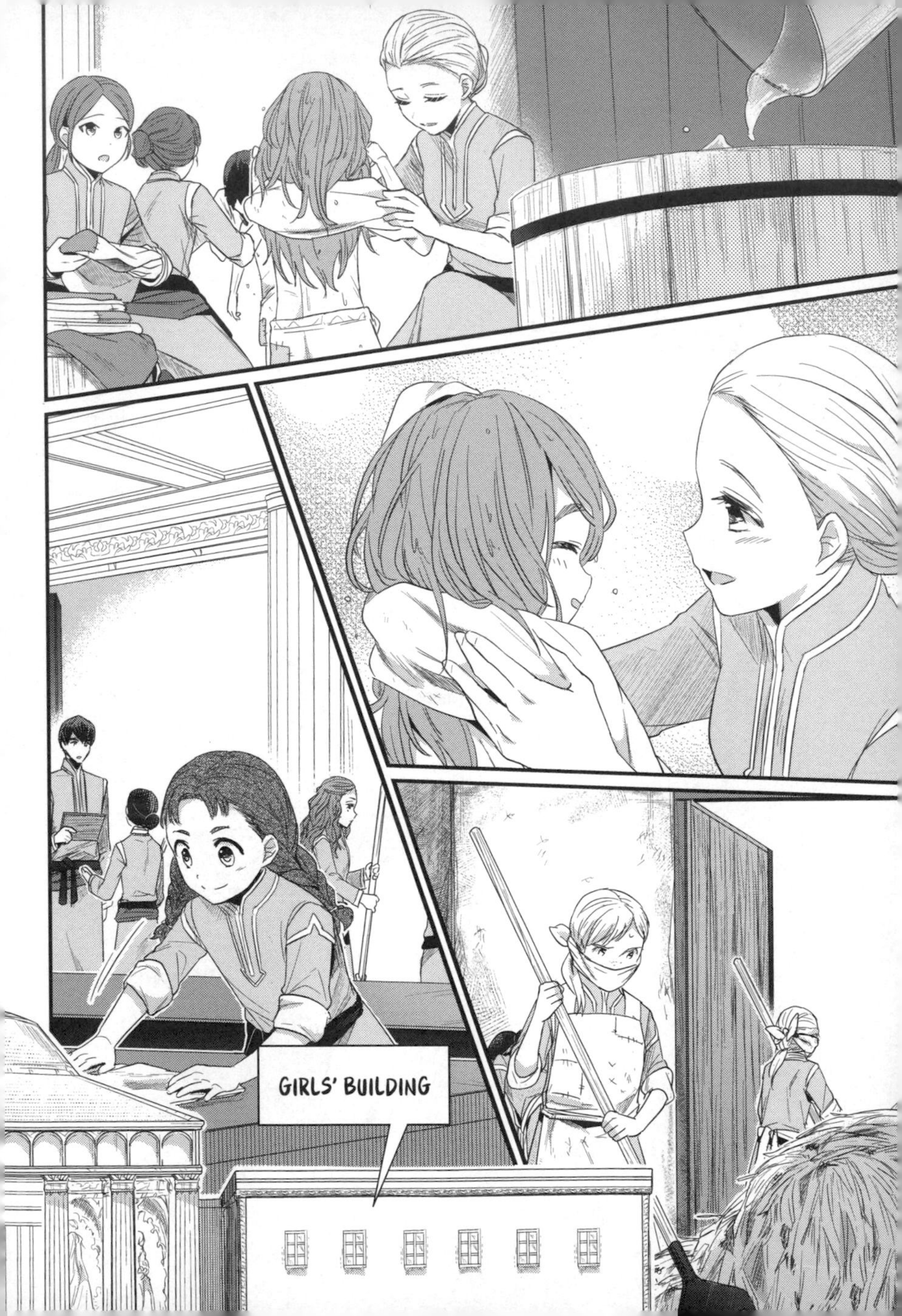
GIRLS' BUILDING

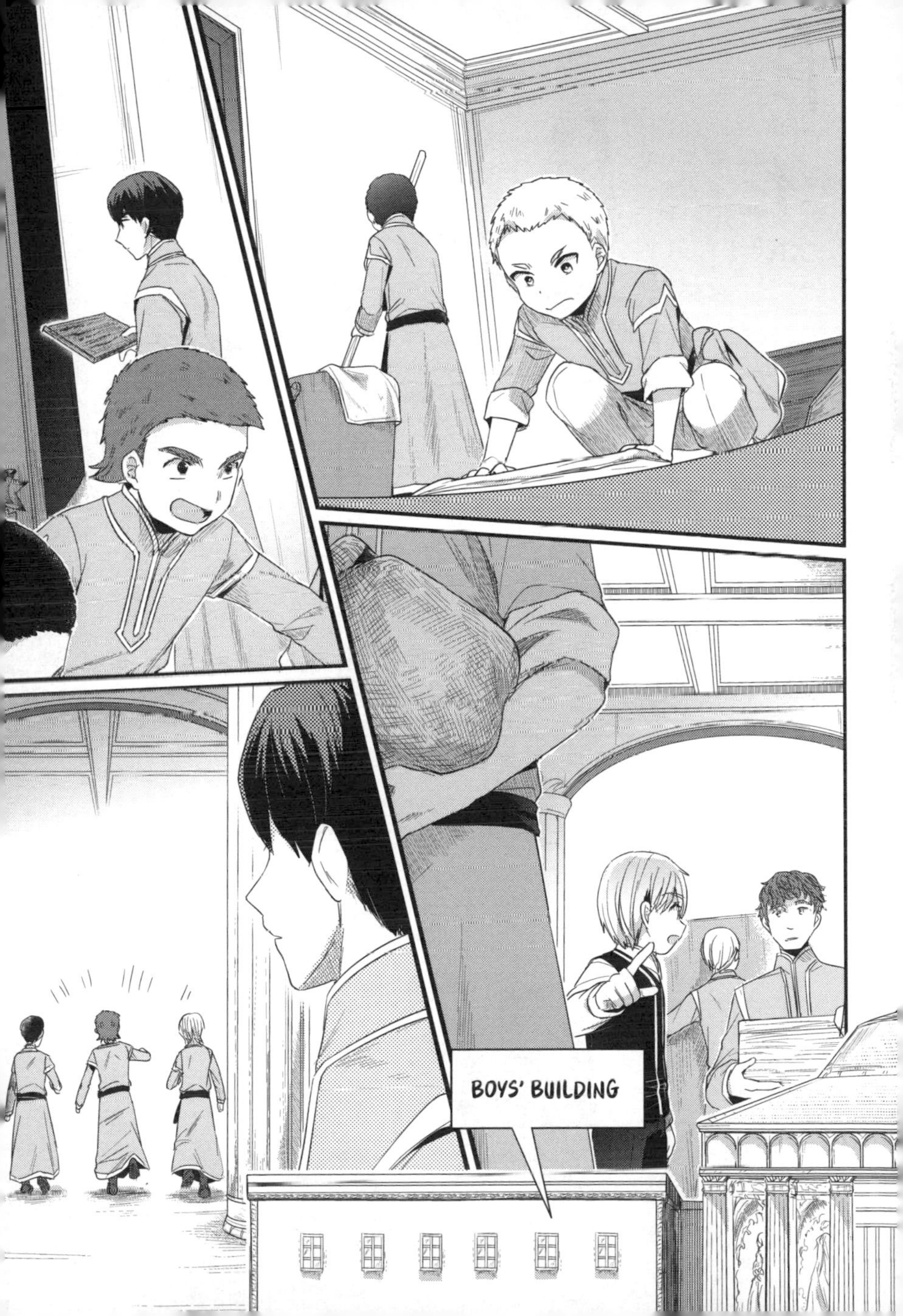
BOYS' BUILDING

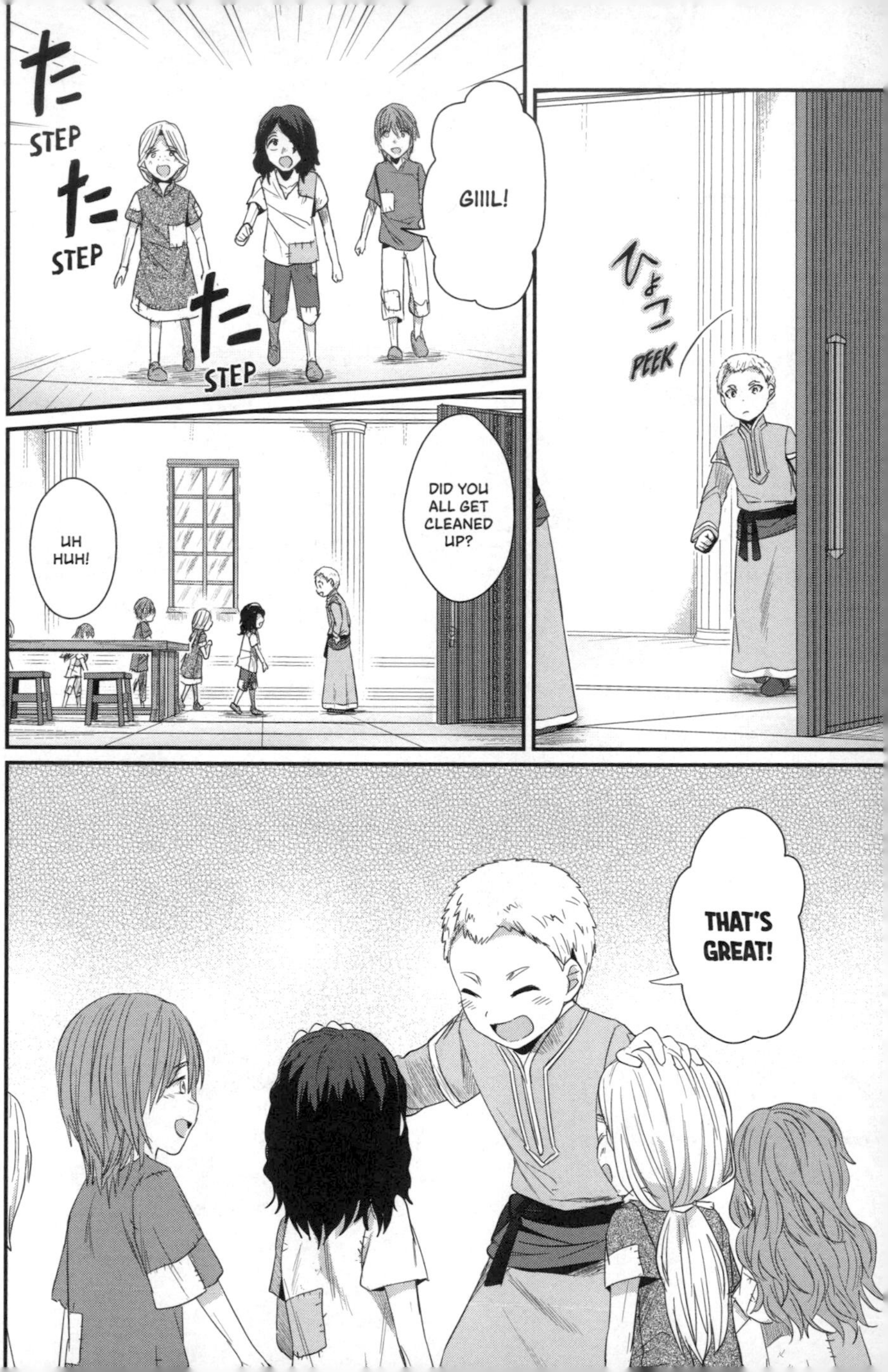

ひょこ
PEEK
GIIIL!
た
STEP
た
STEP
た
STEP
DID YOU ALL GET CLEANED UP?
UH HUH!
THAT'S GREAT!

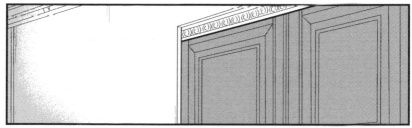

ARE THERE ANY KIDS WHO ARE SICK, OR TOO WEAK TO MOVE?

FRAN.

NO DOUBT DUE TO GIL BRINGING THEM FOOD IN THE INTERIM.

THEY ALL BUT WORSHIP HIM AS THEIR SAVIOR.

NONE AT ALL.

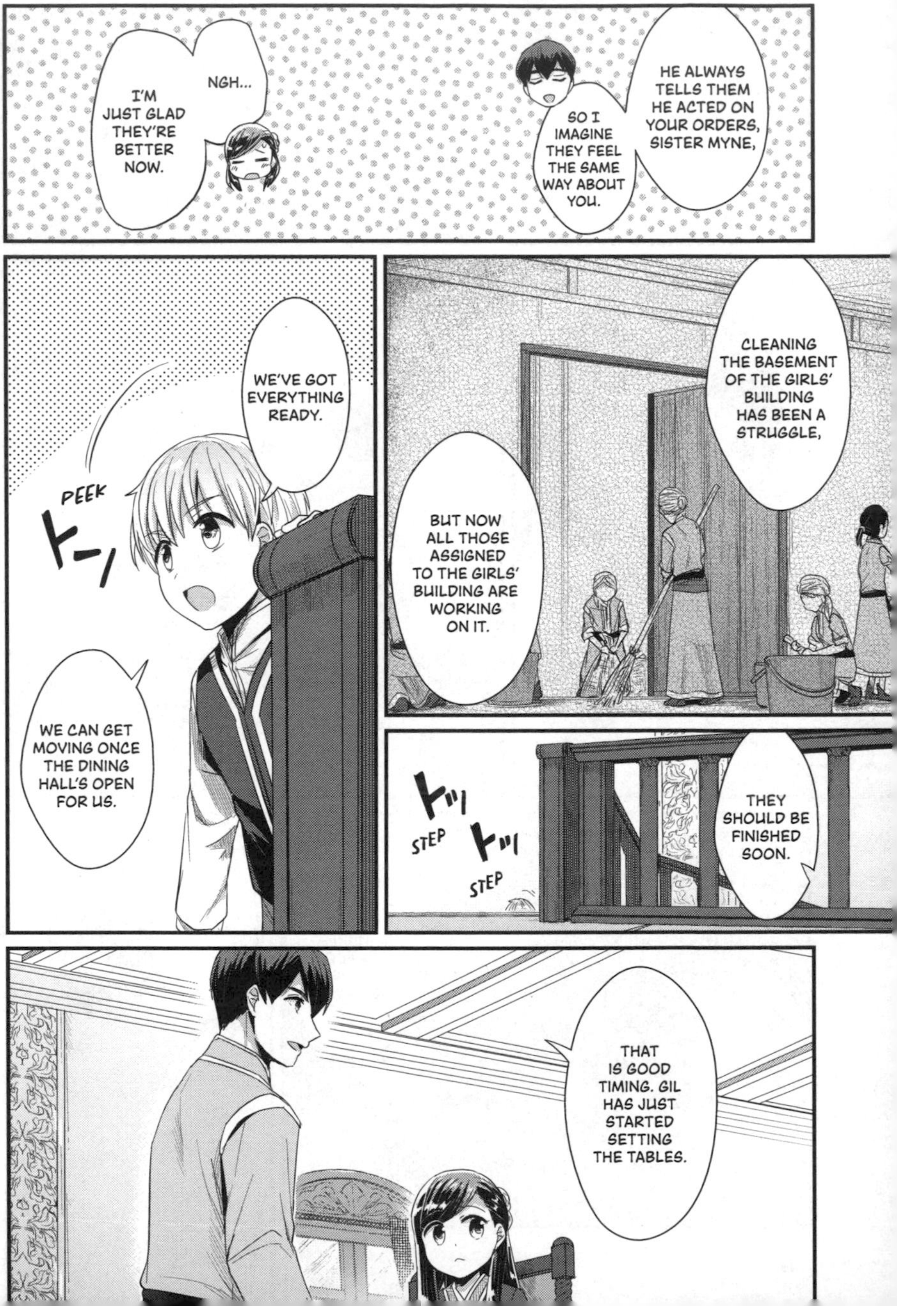
HE ALWAYS TELLS THEM HE ACTED ON YOUR ORDERS, SISTER MYNE,
SO I IMAGINE THEY FEEL THE SAME WAY ABOUT YOU.
NGH...
I'M JUST GLAD THEY'RE BETTER NOW.
CLEANING THE BASEMENT OF THE GIRLS' BUILDING HAS BEEN A STRUGGLE,
BUT NOW ALL THOSE ASSIGNED TO THE GIRLS' BUILDING ARE WORKING ON IT.
THEY SHOULD BE FINISHED SOON.
STEP
STEP
PEEK
WE'VE GOT EVERYTHING READY.
WE CAN GET MOVING ONCE THE DINING HALL'S OPEN FOR US.
THAT IS GOOD TIMING. GIL HAS JUST STARTED SETTING THE TABLES.

SISTER MYNE, HAVE YOU FINISHED MEMORIZING THE WELCOMING ADDRESS?

MORE OR LESS...

CAN I BRING THE PAPER, JUST TO BE SAFE?

CHUCKLE

CERTAINLY.

IN ANY CASE, WE SHALL SEND WORD WHEN WE ARE READY.

DELIA WILL PREPARE YOU FOR YOUR VISIT.

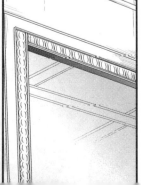

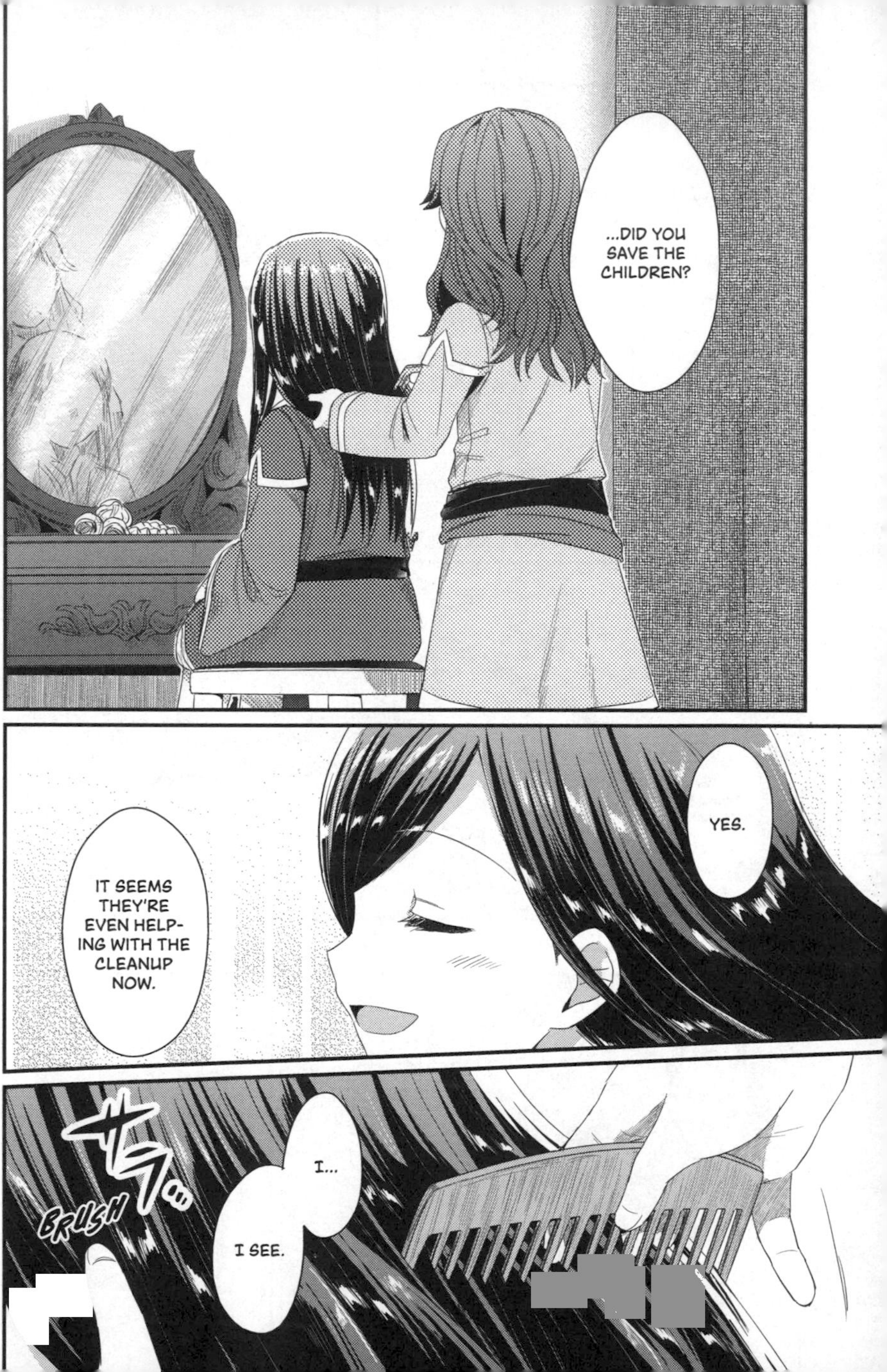
...DID YOU SAVE THE CHILDREN?
YES.
IT SEEMS THEY'RE EVEN HELPING WITH THE CLEANUP NOW.
I...
I SEE.
BRUSH

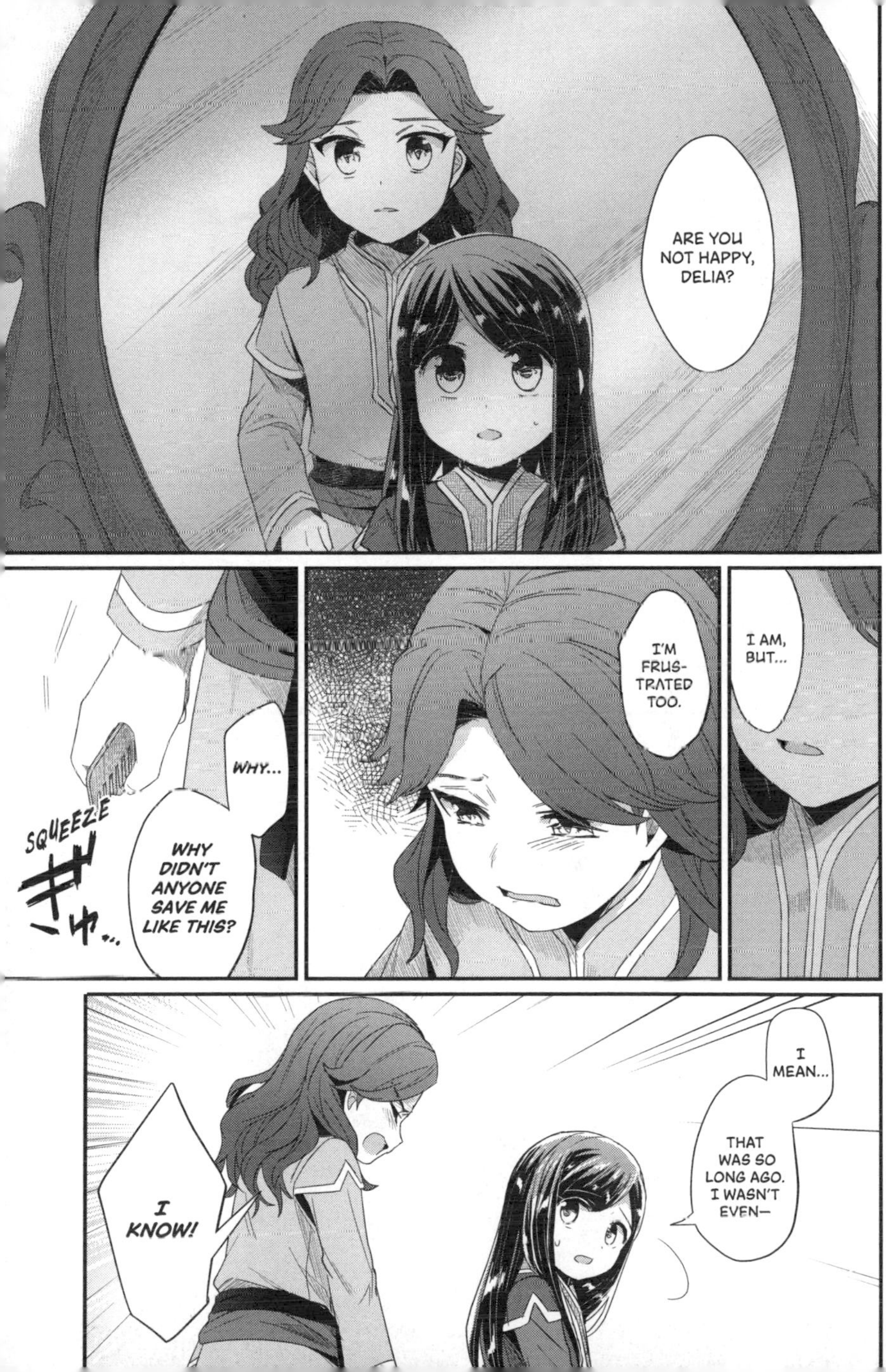
ARE YOU NOT HAPPY, DELIA?
I AM, BUT...
I'M FRUS-TRATED TOO.
WHY...
WHY DIDN'T ANYONE SAVE ME LIKE THIS?
SQUEEZE
I MEAN...
THAT WAS SO LONG AGO. I WASN'T EVEN—
I KNOW!

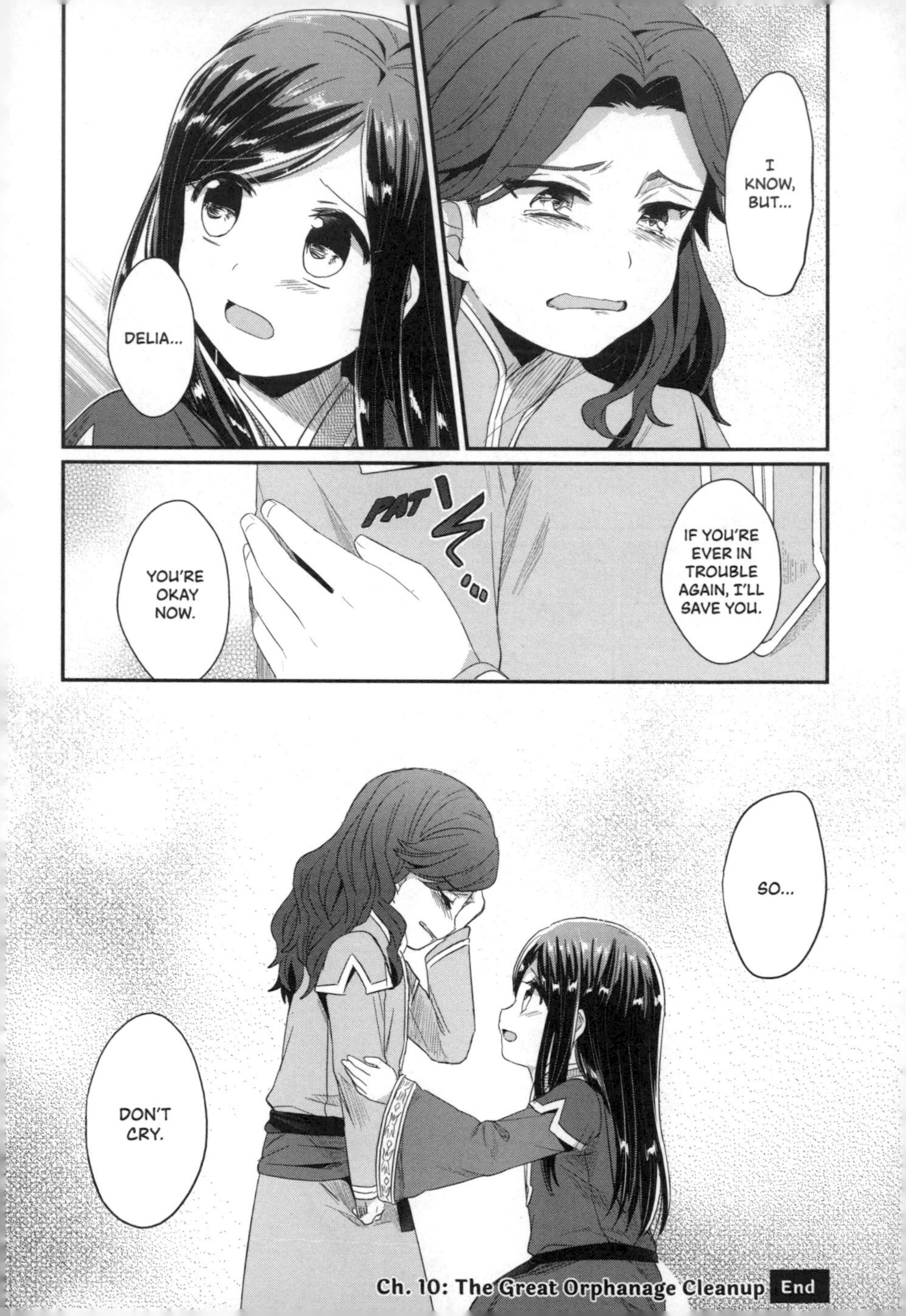
I KNOW, BUT...
DELIA...
IF YOU'RE EVER IN TROUBLE AGAIN, I'LL SAVE YOU.
PAT
YOU'RE OKAY NOW.
SO...
DON'T CRY.
Ch. 10: The Great Orphanage Cleanup End

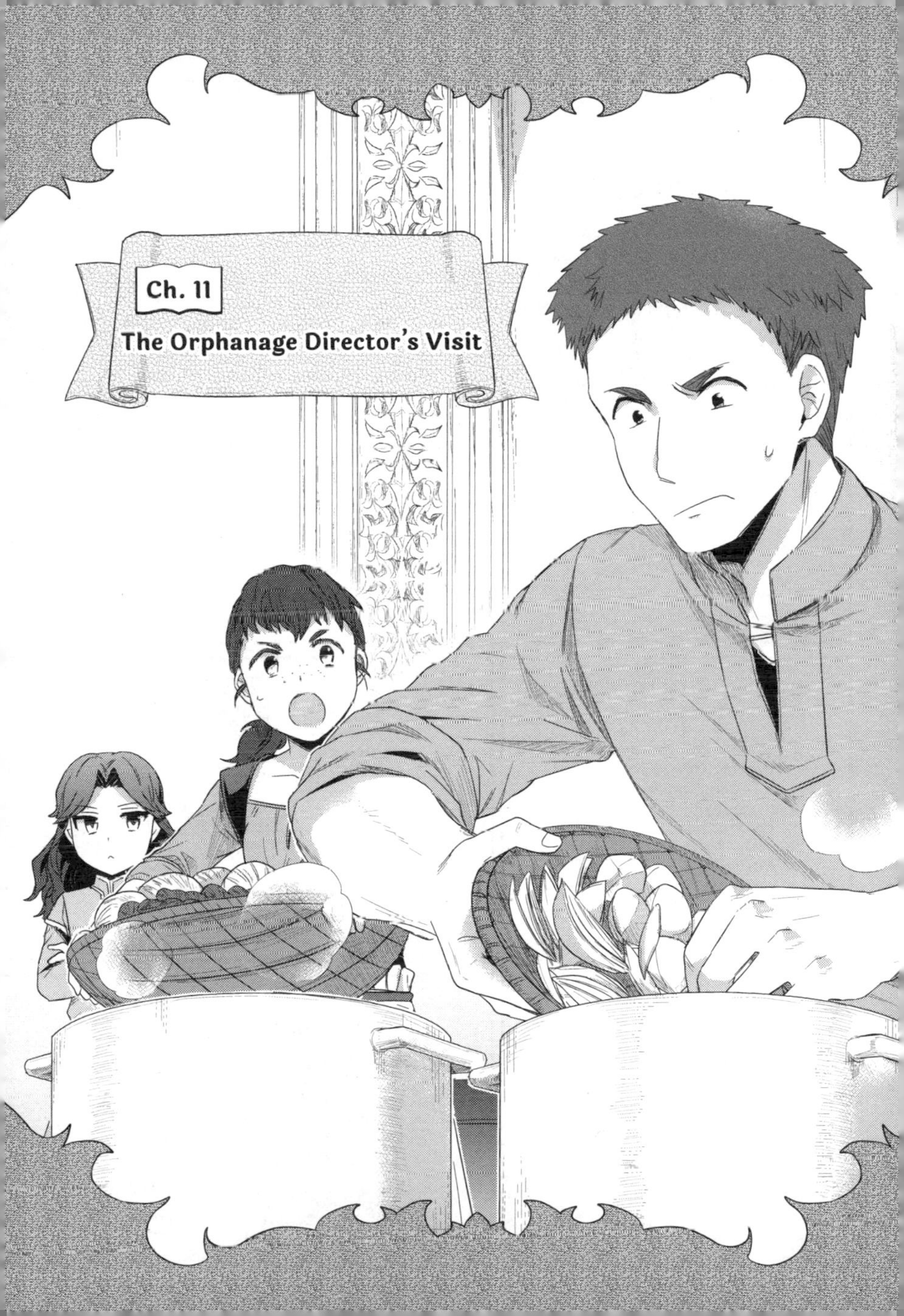
Ch. 11
The Orphanage Director's Visit

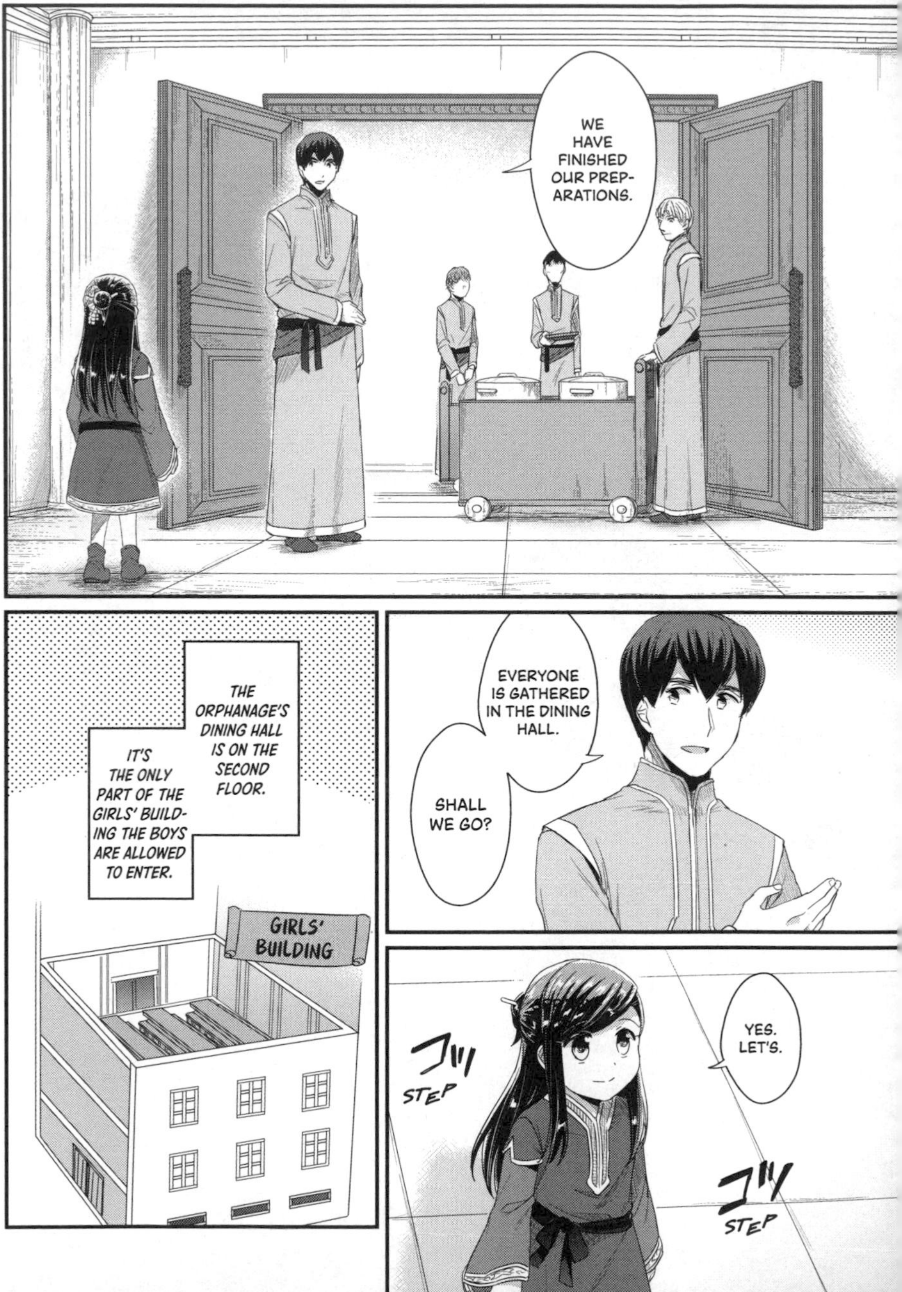
WE HAVE FINISHED OUR PREP-ARATIONS.
EVERYONE IS GATHERED IN THE DINING HALL.
SHALL WE GO?
YES. LET'S.
ゴッ
STEP
ゴッ
STEP
THE ORPHANAGE'S DINING HALL IS ON THE SECOND FLOOR.
IT'S THE ONLY PART OF THE GIRLS' BUILD-ING THE BOYS ARE ALLOWED TO ENTER.
GIRLS' BUILDING

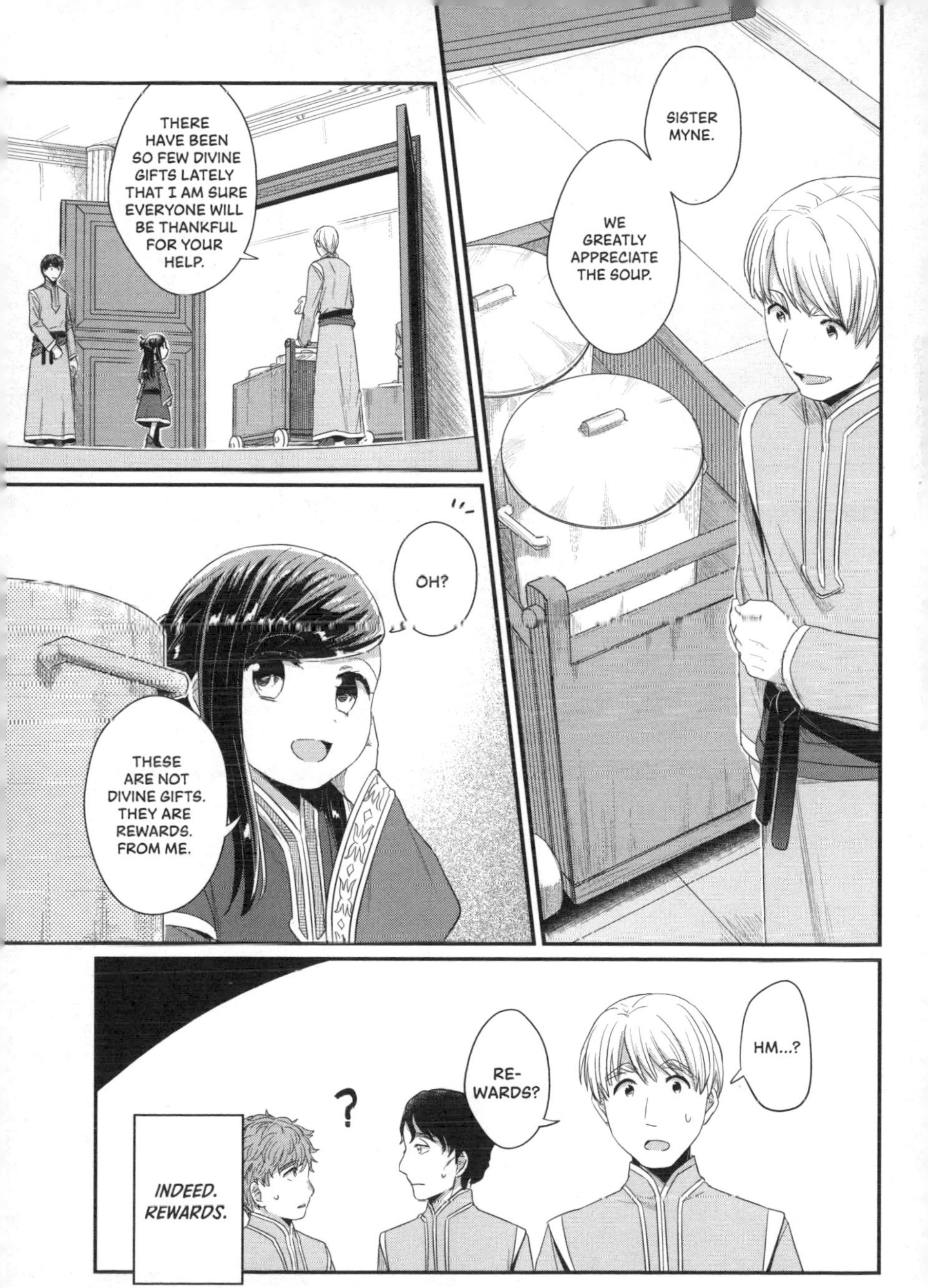
SISTER MYNE.
WE GREATLY APPRECIATE THE SOUP.
THERE HAVE BEEN SO FEW DIVINE GIFTS LATELY THAT I AM SURE EVERYONE WILL BE THANKFUL FOR YOUR HELP.
OH?
THESE ARE NOT DIVINE GIFTS. THEY ARE REWARDS. FROM ME.
HM...?
RE-WARDS?
?
INDEED. REWARDS.

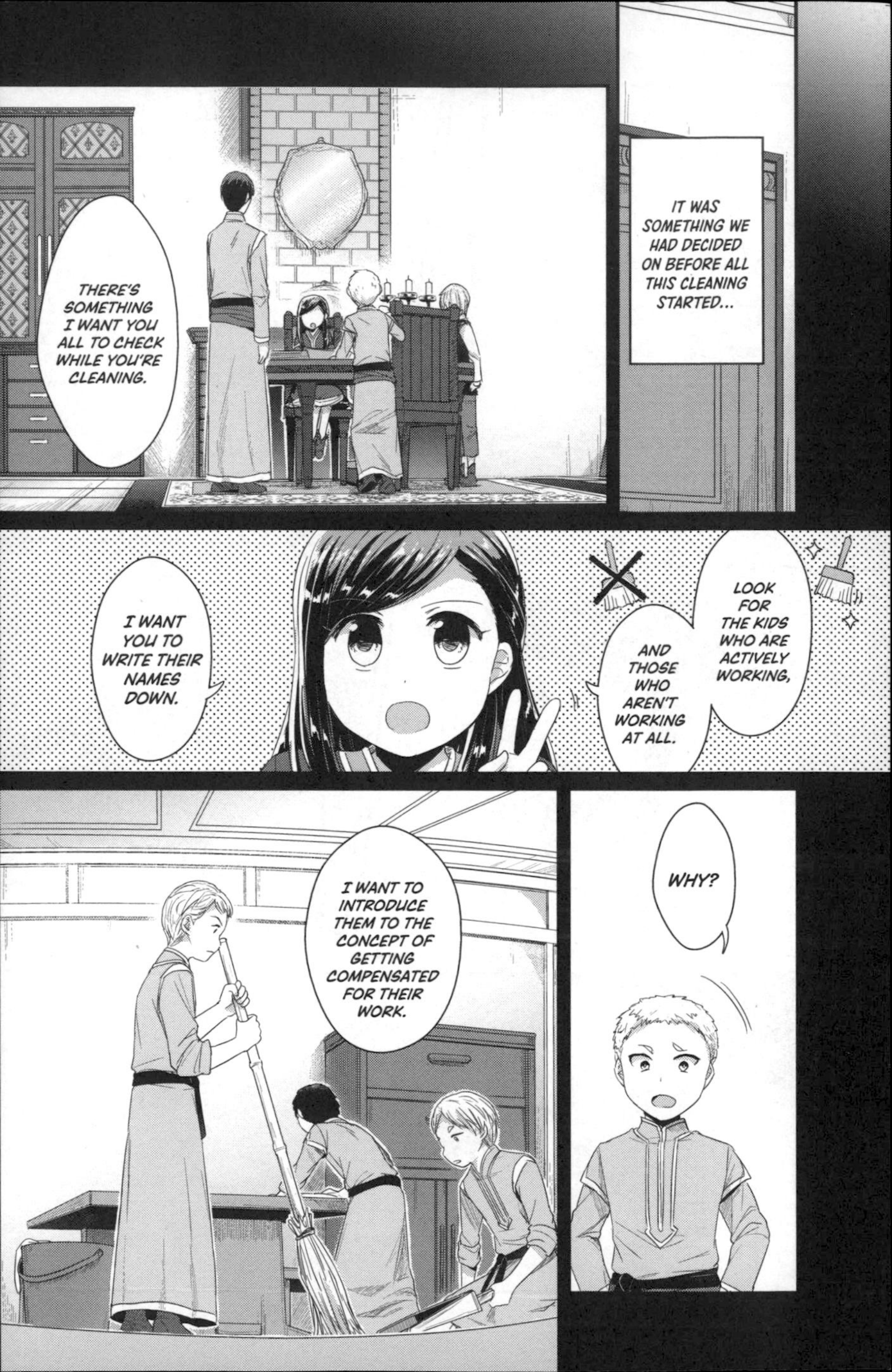
IT WAS SOMETHING WE HAD DECIDED ON BEFORE ALL THIS CLEANING STARTED...
THERE'S SOMETHING I WANT YOU ALL TO CHECK WHILE YOU'RE CLEANING.
LOOK FOR THE KIDS WHO ARE ACTIVELY WORKING,
AND THOSE WHO AREN'T WORKING AT ALL.
I WANT YOU TO WRITE THEIR NAMES DOWN.
WHY?
I WANT TO INTRODUCE THEM TO THE CONCEPT OF GETTING COMPENSATED FOR THEIR WORK.

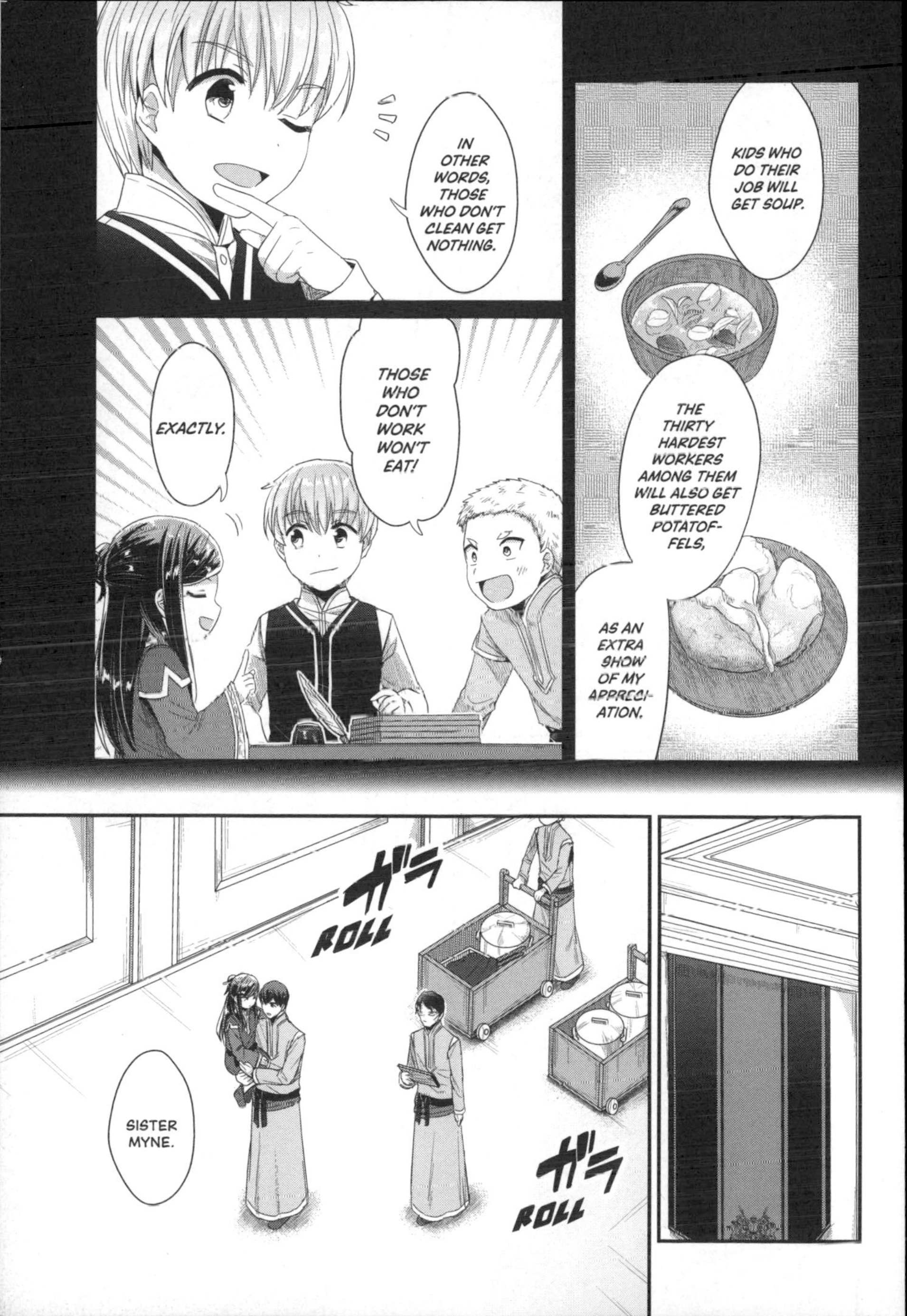
KIDS WHO DO THEIR JOB WILL GET SOUP.
THE THIRTY HARDEST WORKERS AMONG THEM WILL ALSO GET BUTTERED POTATOFFELS,
AS AN EXTRA SHOW OF MY APPRECIATION.
IN OTHER WORDS, THOSE WHO DON'T CLEAN GET NOTHING.
THOSE WHO DON'T WORK WON'T EAT!
EXACTLY.
ガラ
ROLL
SISTER MYNE.
ガラ
ROLL

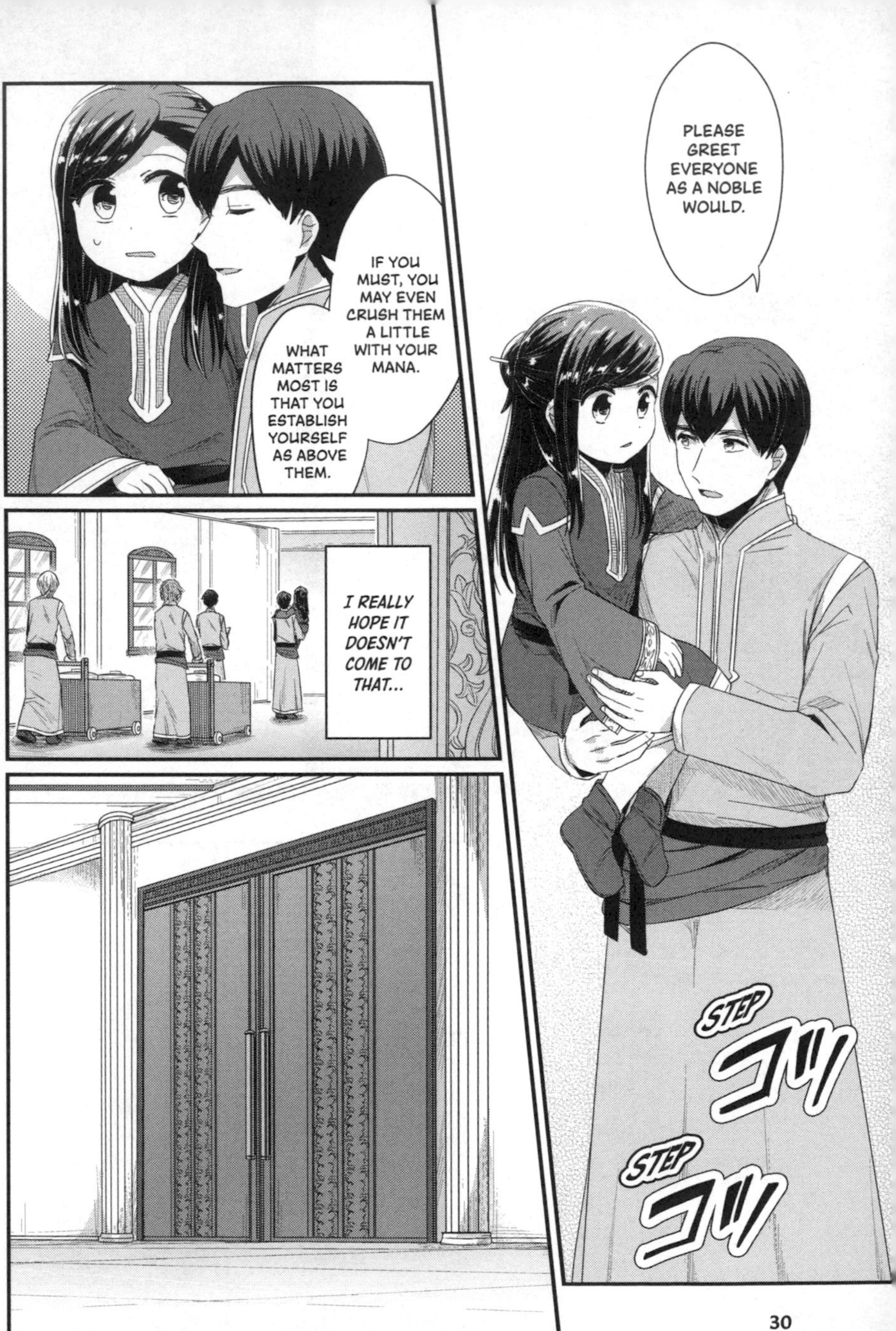
PLEASE GREET EVERYONE AS A NOBLE WOULD.
STEP
コツ
STEP
コツ
IF YOU MUST, YOU MAY EVEN CRUSH THEM A LITTLE WITH YOUR MANA.
WHAT MATTERS MOST IS THAT YOU ESTABLISH YOURSELF AS ABOVE THEM.
I REALLY HOPE IT DOESN'T COME TO THAT...

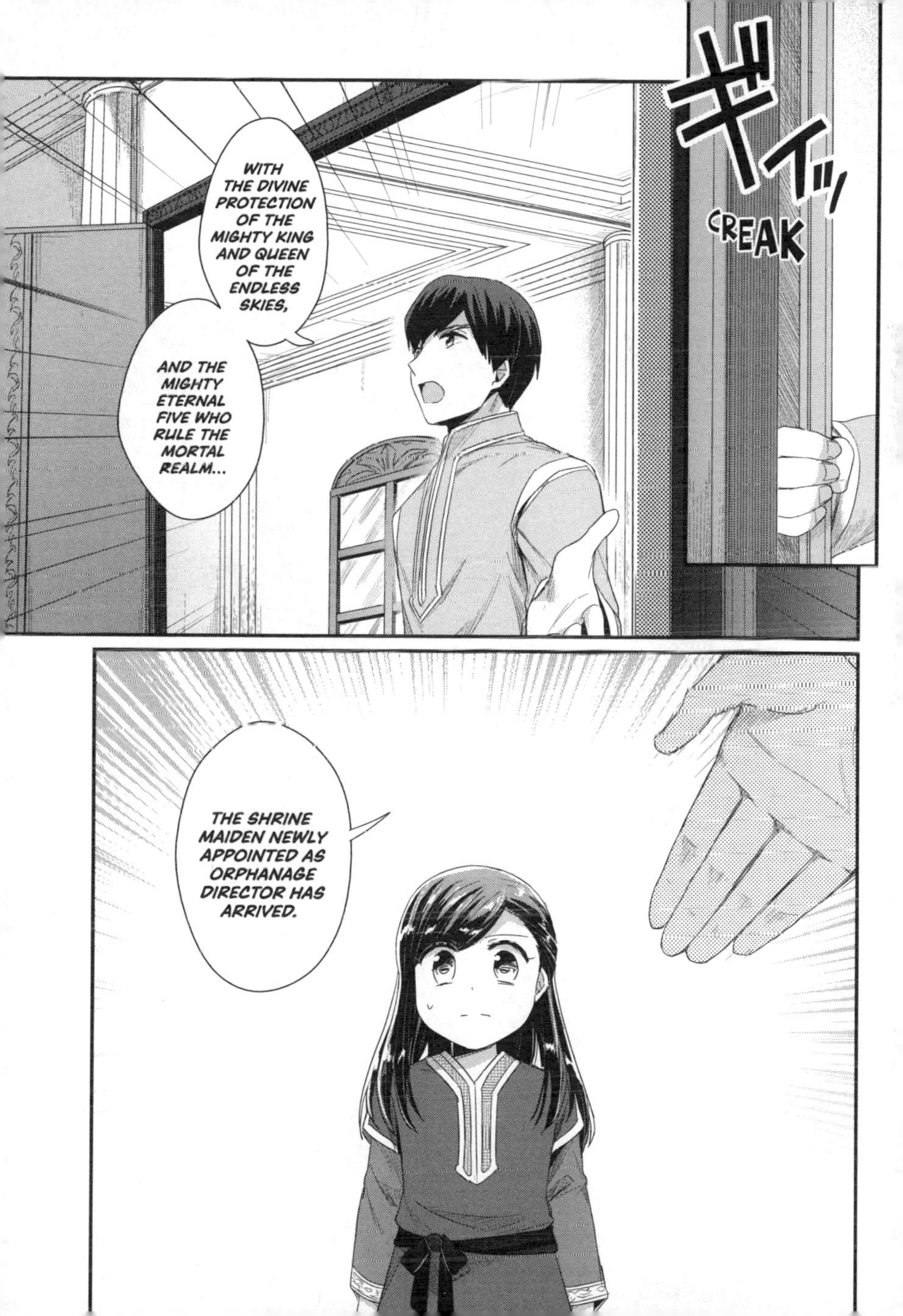
ギイッ
CREAK
WITH THE DIVINE PROTECTION OF THE MIGHTY KING AND QUEEN OF THE ENDLESS SKIES,
AND THE MIGHTY ETERNAL FIVE WHO RULE THE MORTAL REALM...
THE SHRINE MAIDEN NEWLY APPOINTED AS ORPHANAGE DIRECTOR HAS ARRIVED.

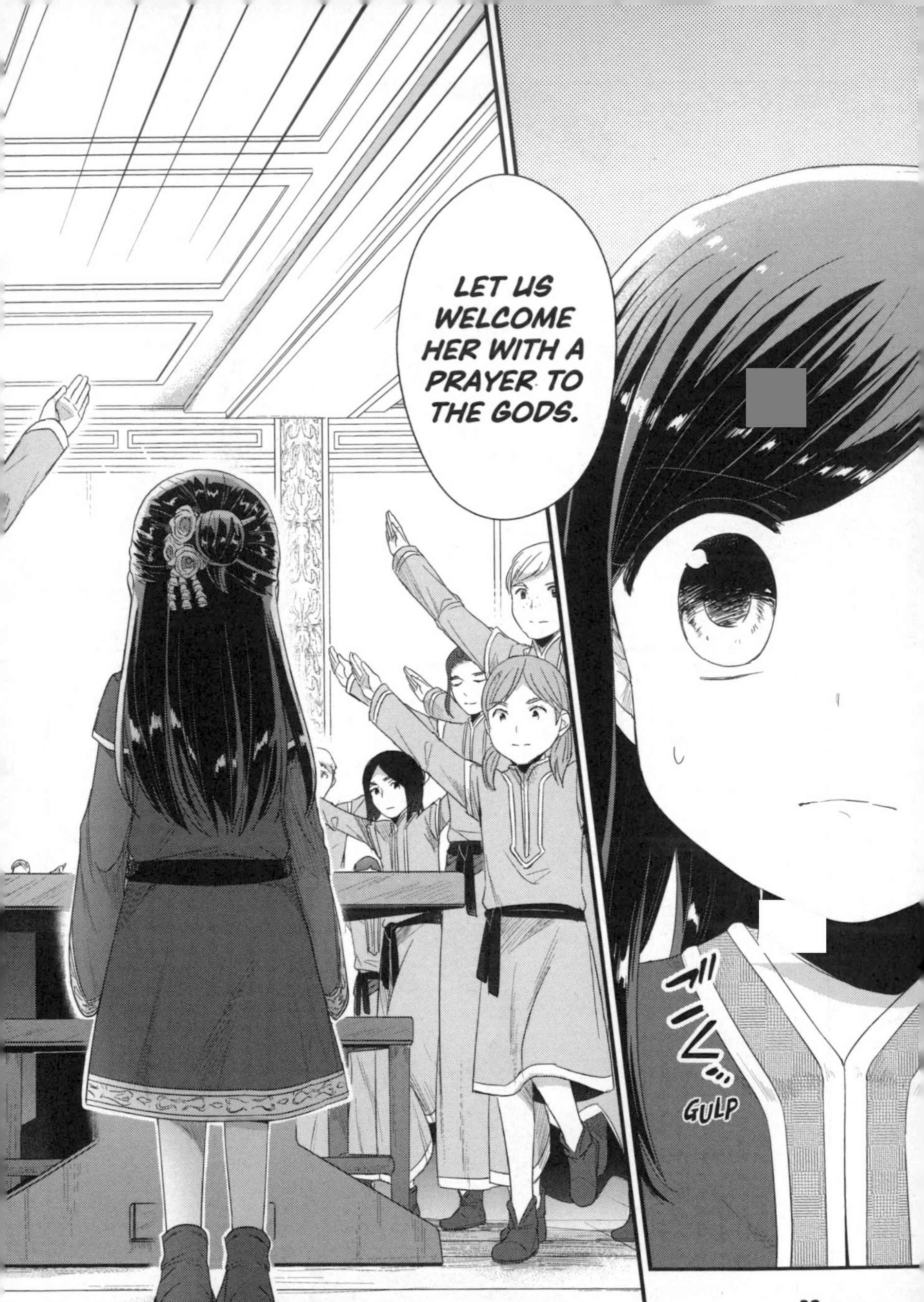
LET US WELCOME HER WITH A PRAYER TO THE GODS.
GULP

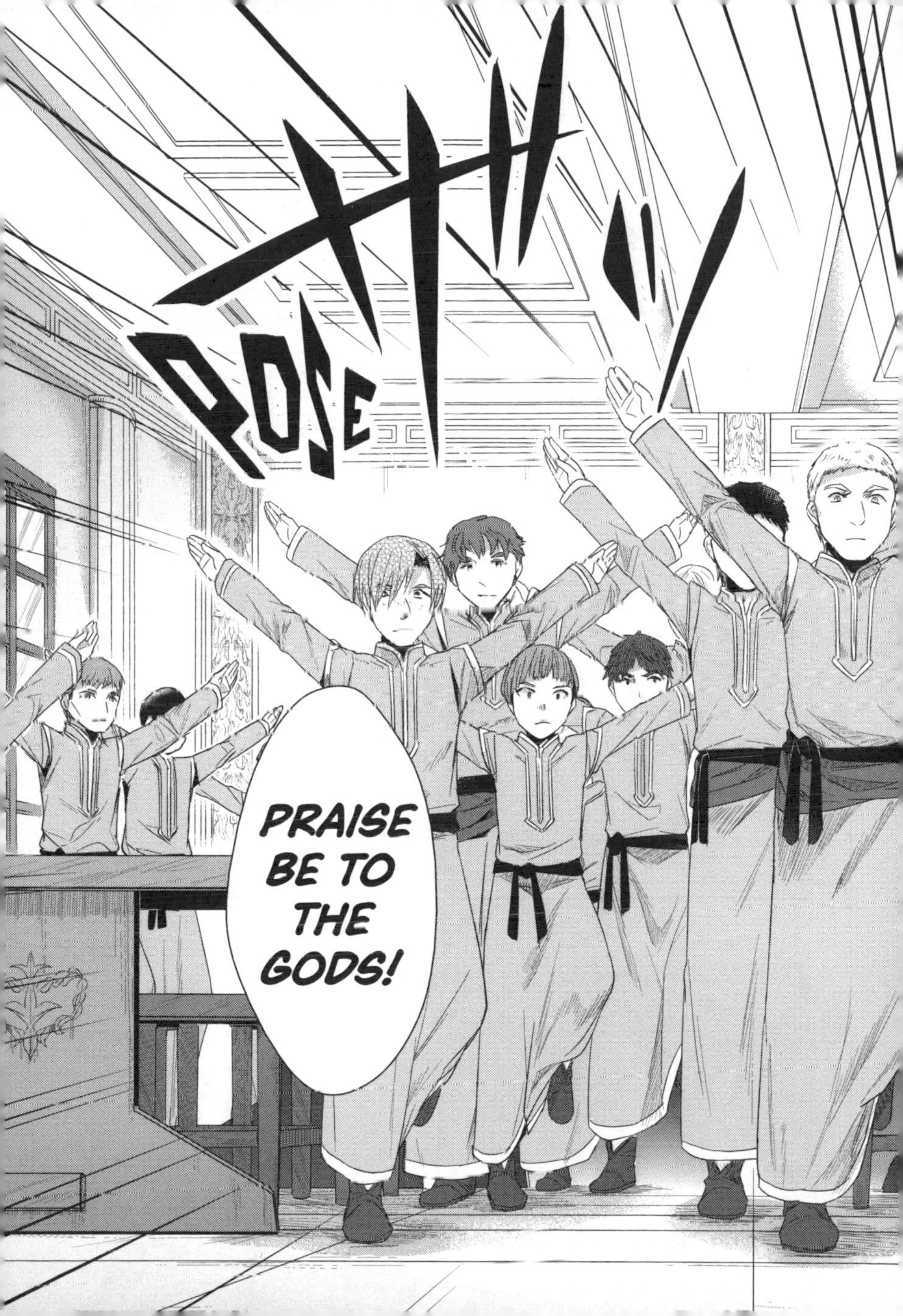
ザッ
POSE
PRAISE BE TO THE GODS!

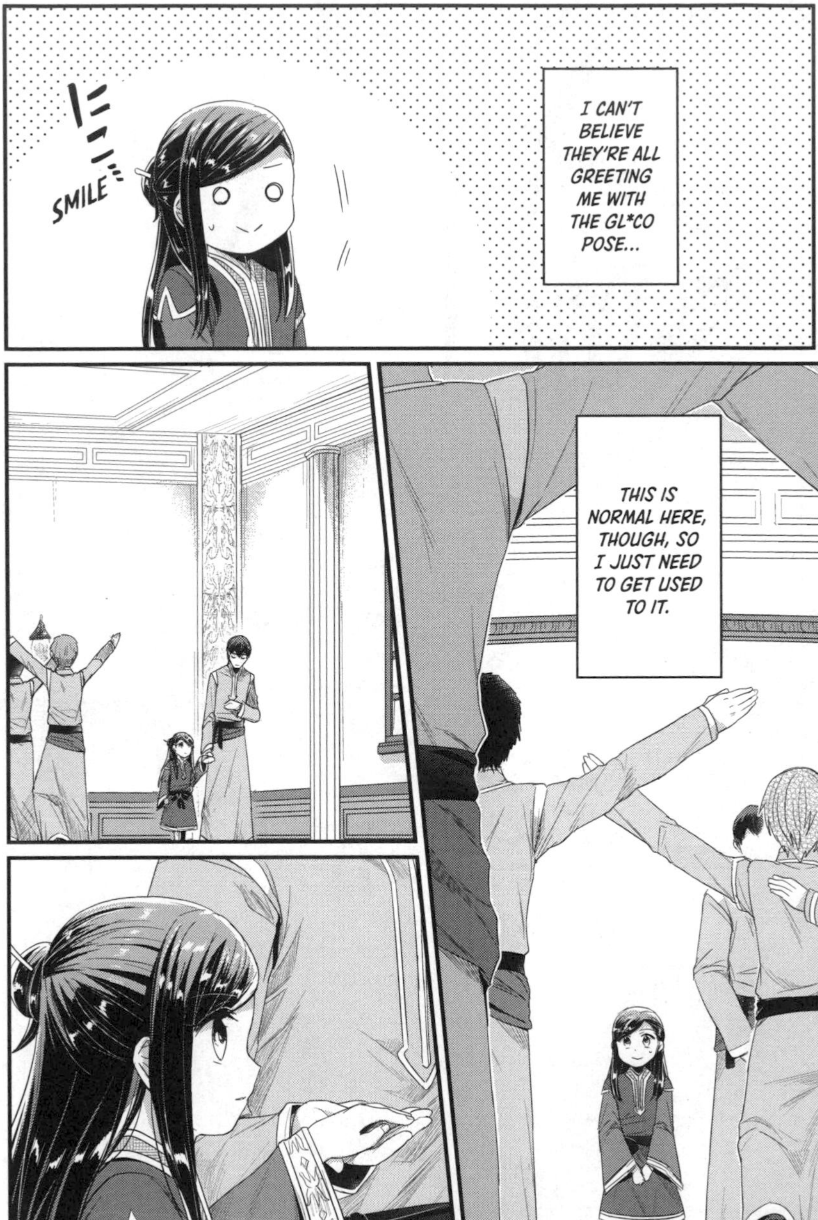
I CAN'T BELIEVE THEY'RE ALL GREETING ME WITH THE GL*CO POSE...
SMILE
THIS IS NORMAL HERE, THOUGH, SO I JUST NEED TO GET USED TO IT.

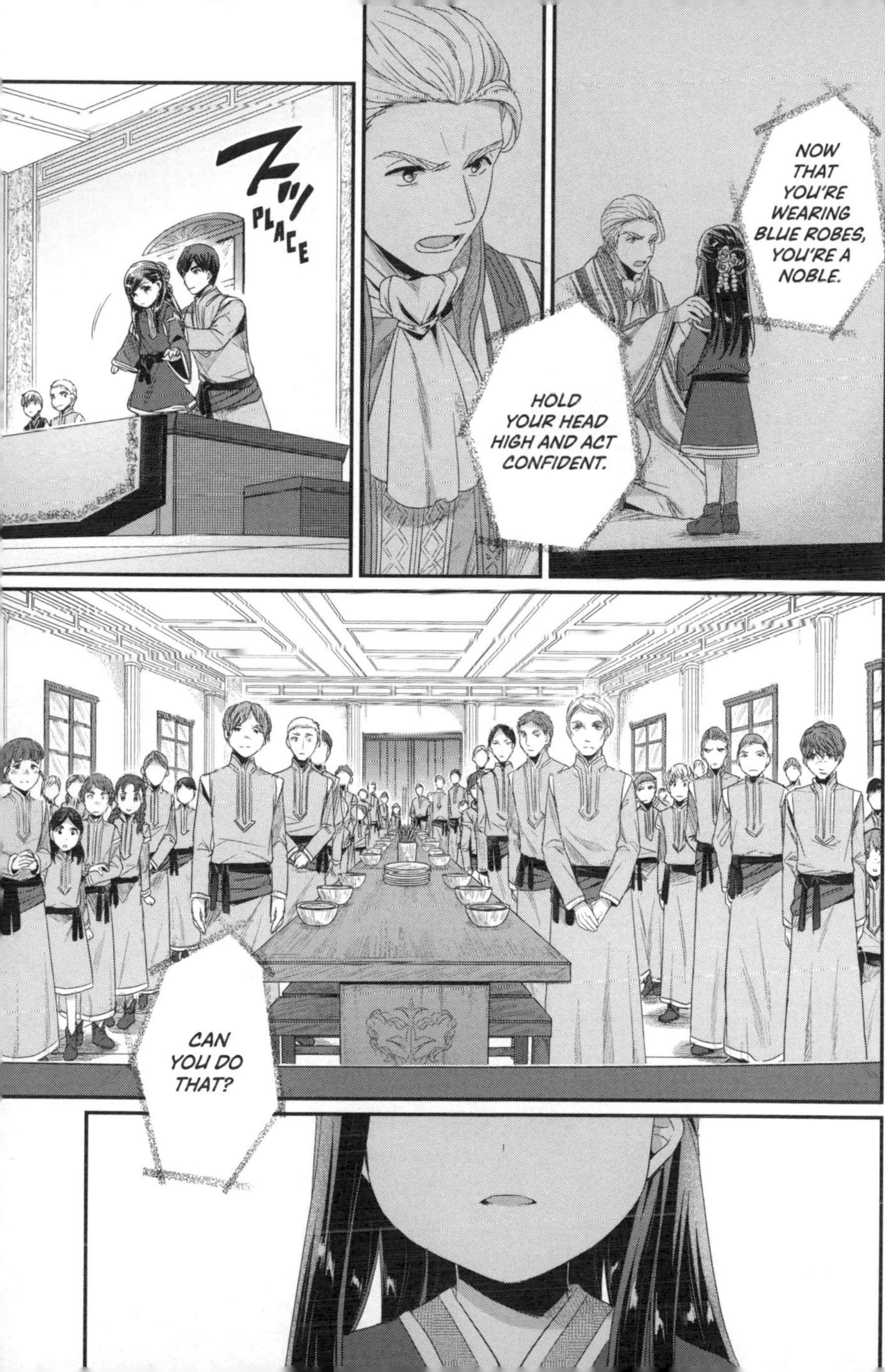
NOW THAT YOU'RE WEARING BLUE ROBES, YOU'RE A NOBLE.
HOLD YOUR HEAD HIGH AND ACT CONFIDENT.
PLACE
CAN YOU DO THAT?

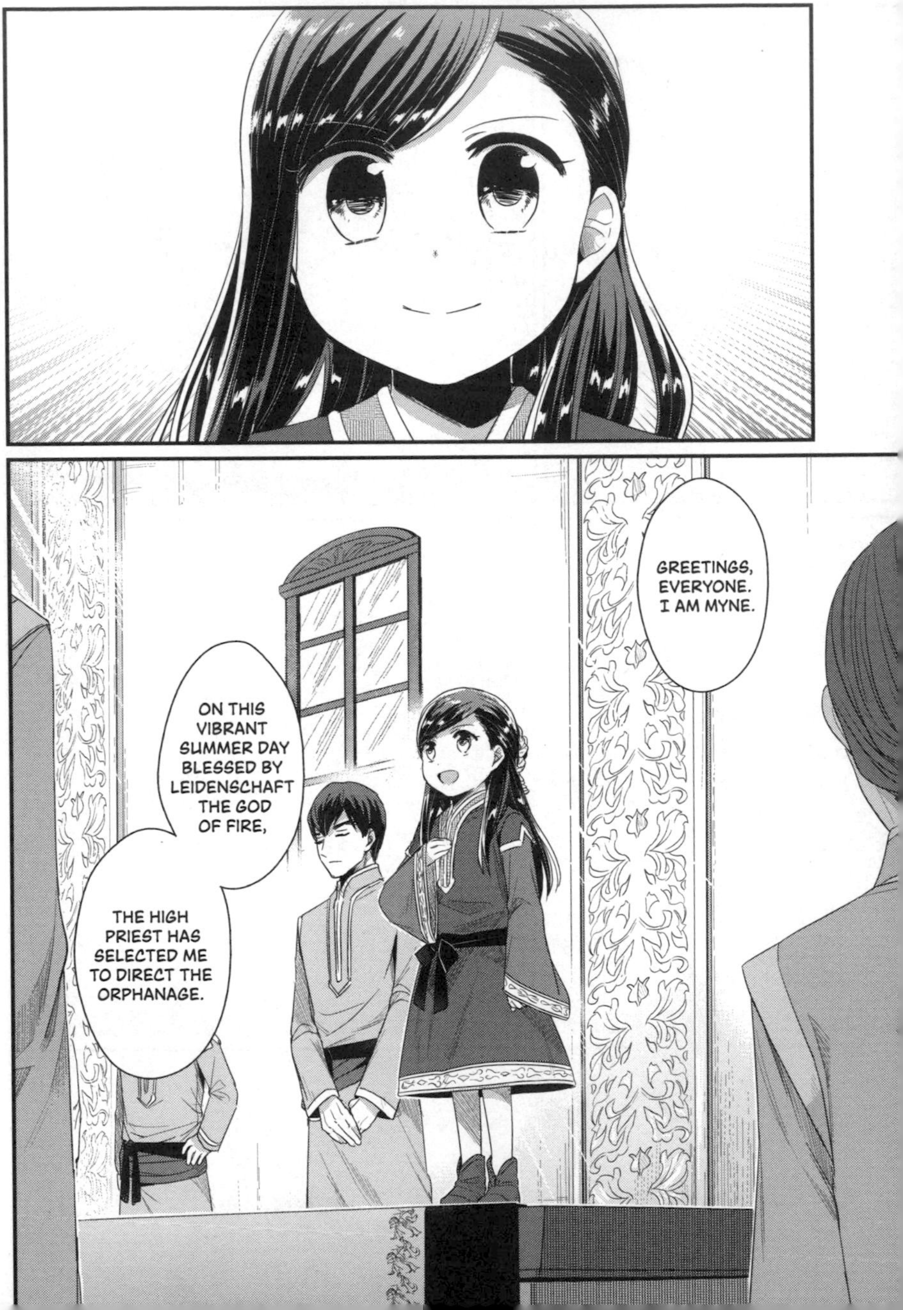
GREETINGS, EVERYONE. I AM MYNE.
ON THIS VIBRANT SUMMER DAY BLESSED BY LEIDENSCHAFT THE GOD OF FIRE,
THE HIGH PRIEST HAS SELECTED ME TO DIRECT THE ORPHANAGE.

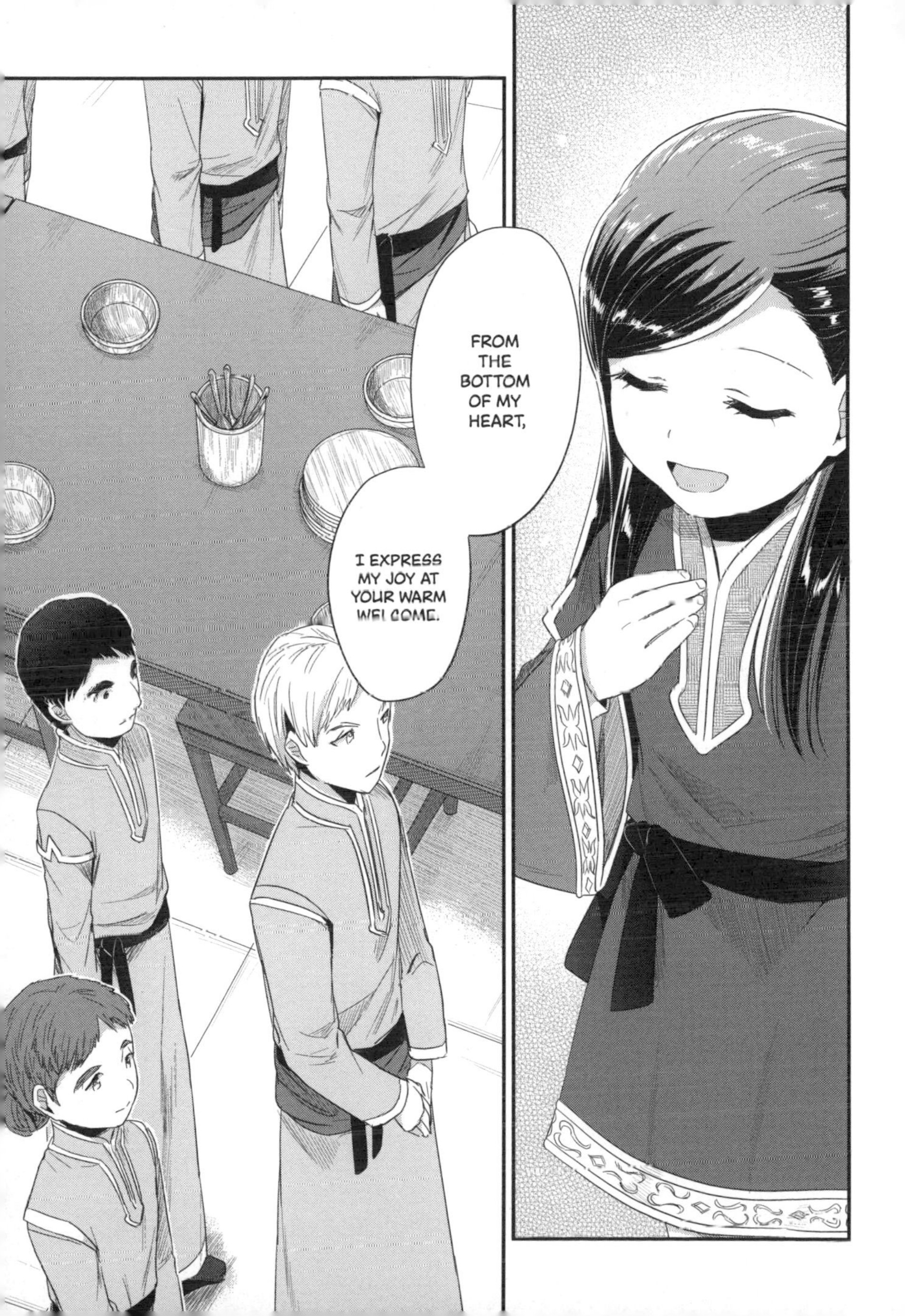
FROM THE BOTTOM OF MY HEART,
I EXPRESS MY JOY AT YOUR WARM WELCOME.

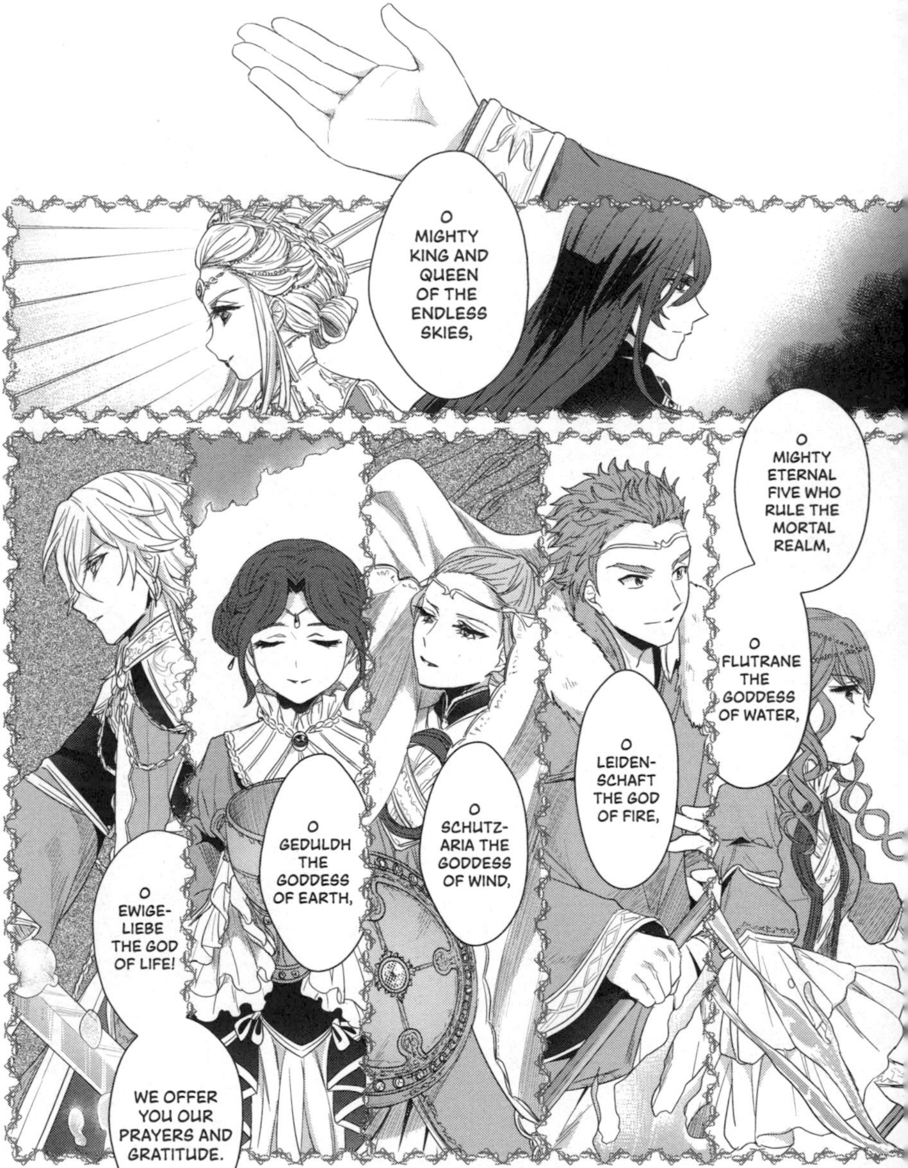
O MIGHTY KING AND QUEEN OF THE ENDLESS SKIES,
O MIGHTY ETERNAL FIVE WHO RULE THE MORTAL REALM,
O FLUTRANE THE GODDESS OF WATER,
O LEIDENSCHAFT THE GOD OF FIRE,
O SCHUTZARIA THE GODDESS OF WIND,
O GEDULDH THE GODDESS OF EARTH,
O EWIGELIEBE THE GOD OF LIFE!
WE OFFER YOU OUR PRAYERS AND GRATITUDE.

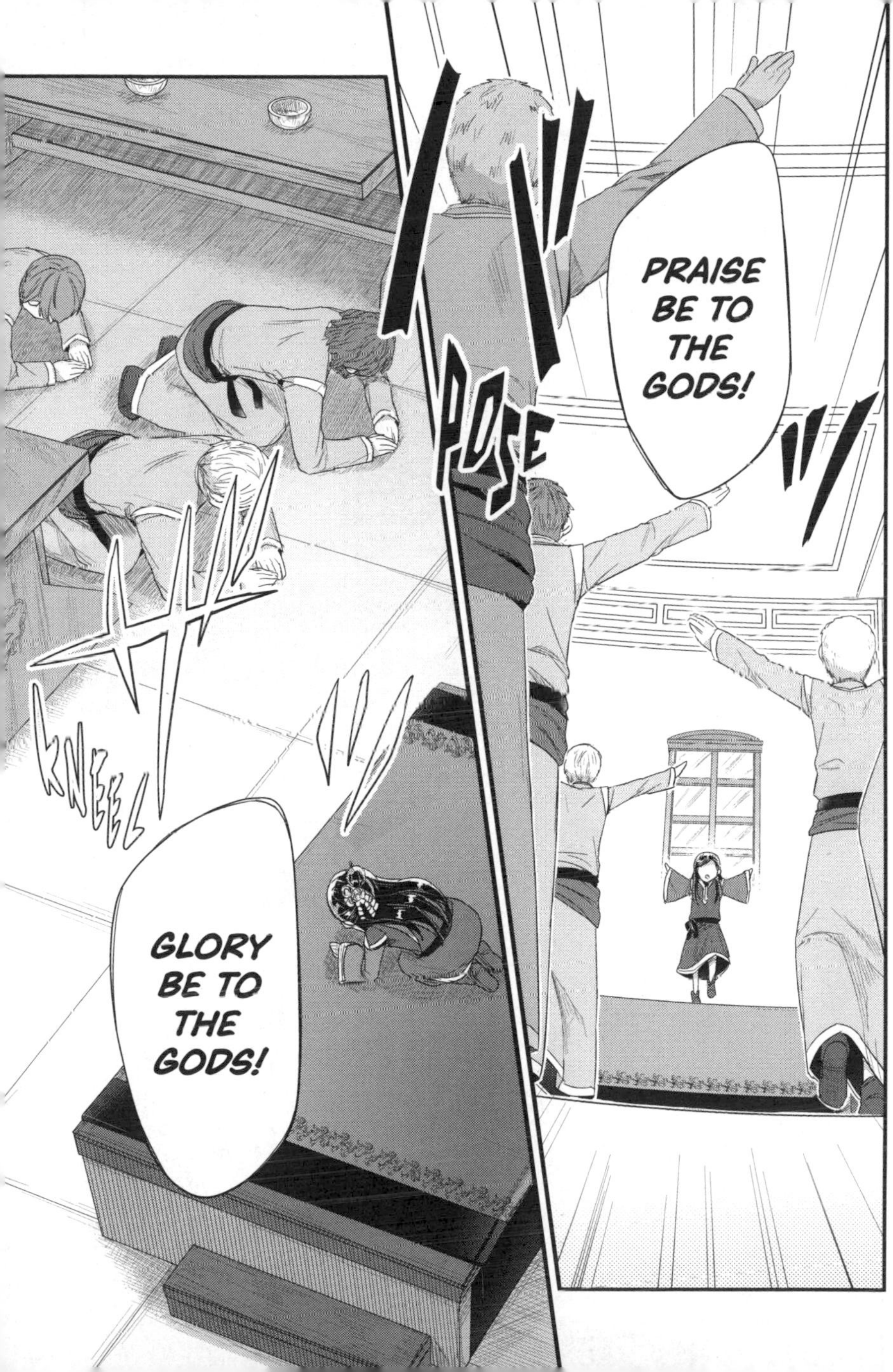
PRAISE BE TO THE GODS!
POSE
GLORY BE TO THE GODS!
KNEEL

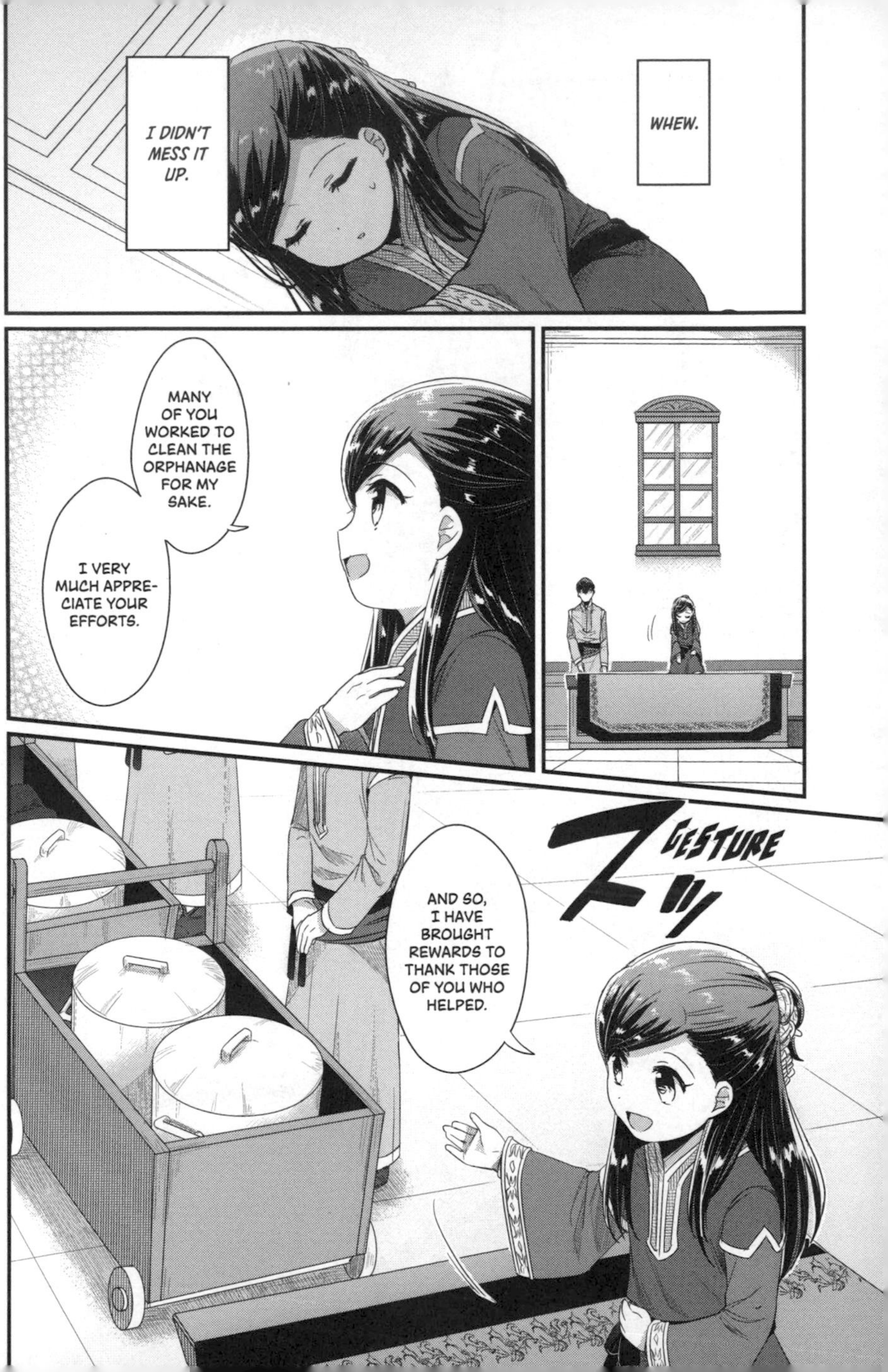
WHEW.
I DIDN'T MESS IT UP.
MANY OF YOU WORKED TO CLEAN THE ORPHANAGE FOR MY SAKE.
I VERY MUCH APPRE-CIATE YOUR EFFORTS.
GESTURE
AND SO, I HAVE BROUGHT REWARDS TO THANK THOSE OF YOU WHO HELPED.

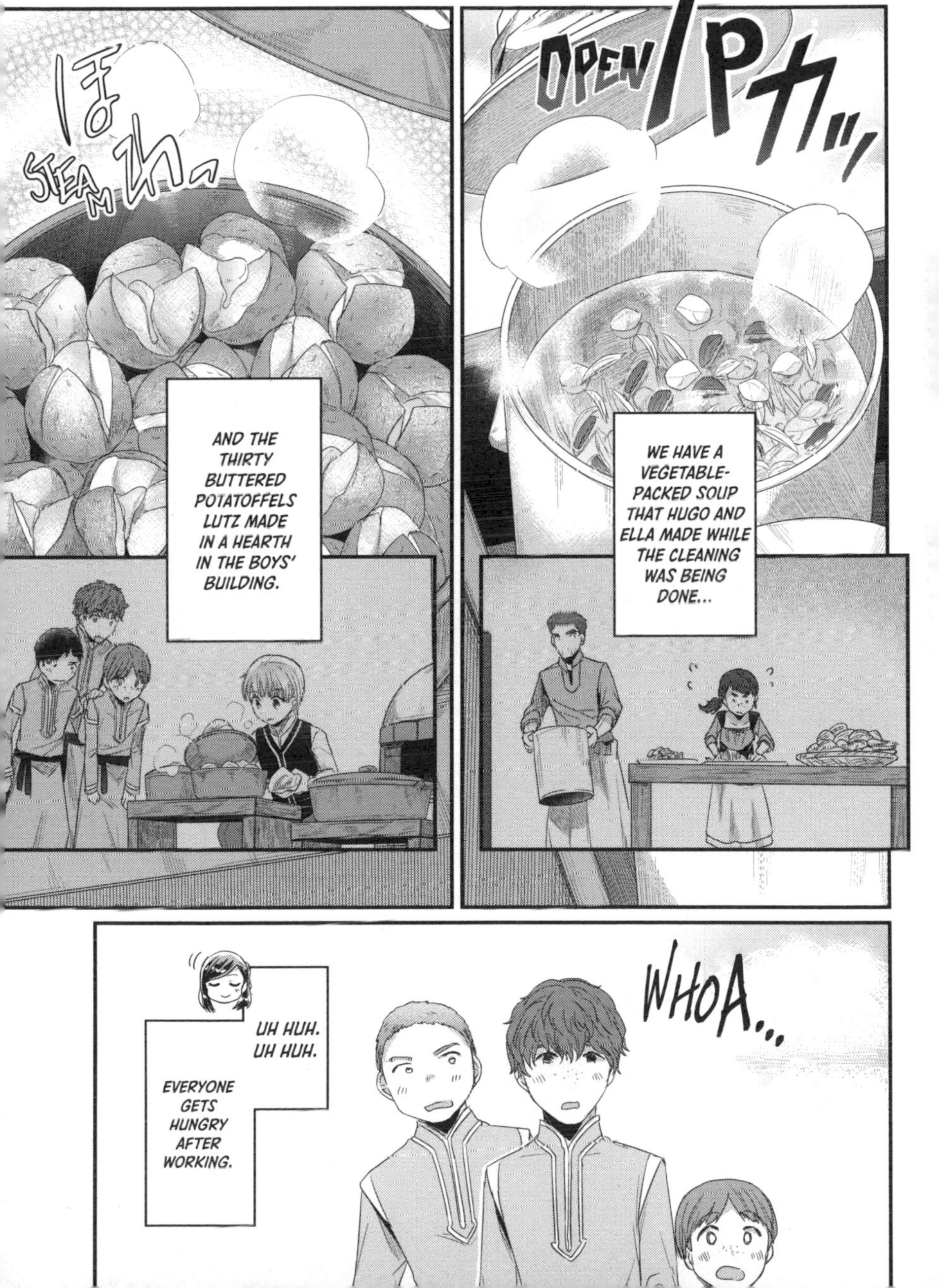
OPEN
WE HAVE A VEGETABLE-PACKED SOUP THAT HUGO AND ELLA MADE WHILE THE CLEANING WAS BEING DONE...
STEAM
AND THE THIRTY BUTTERED POTATOFFELS LUTZ MADE IN A HEARTH IN THE BOYS' BUILDING.
WHOA...
UH HUH. UH HUH.
EVERYONE GETS HUNGRY AFTER WORKING.

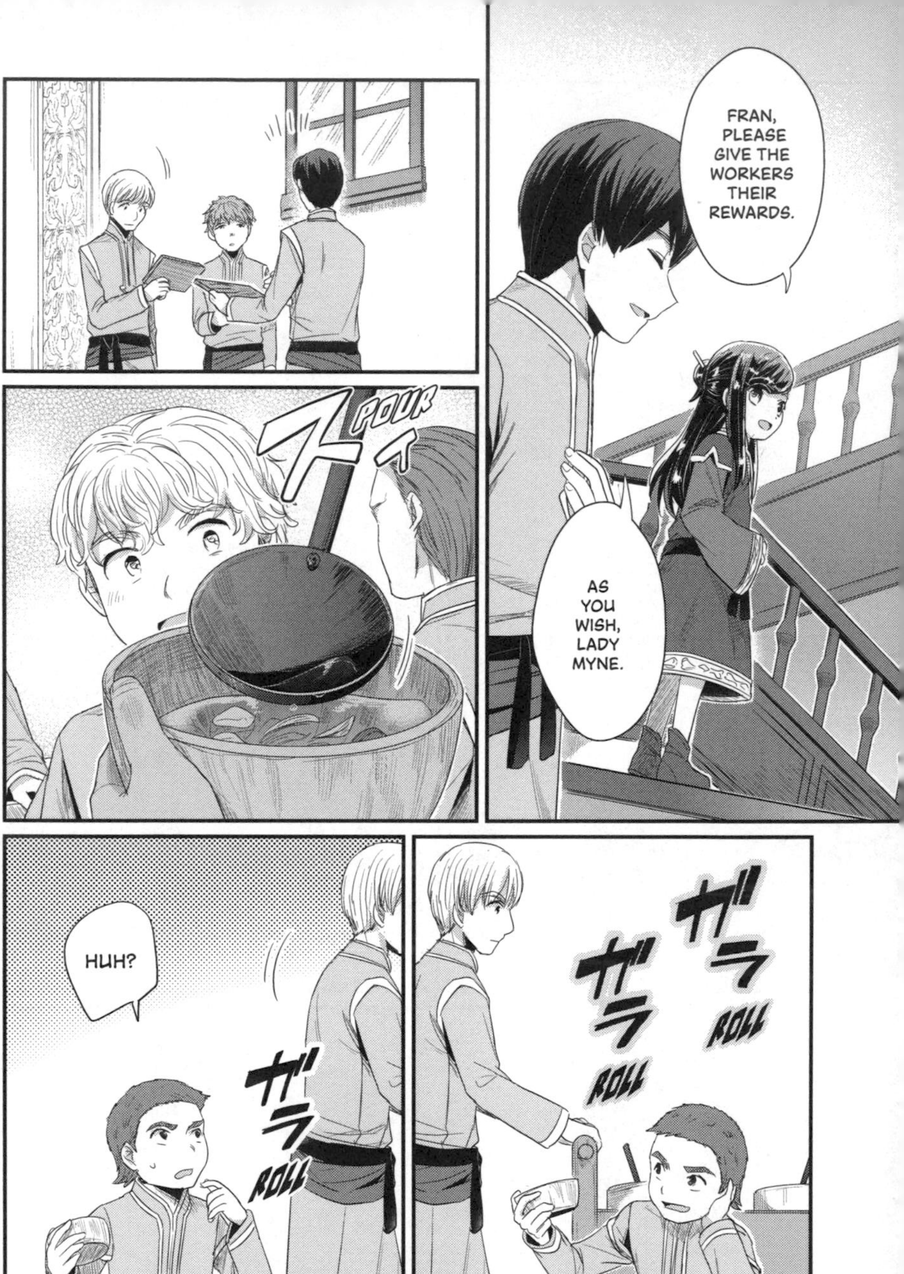
FRAN, PLEASE GIVE THE WORKERS THEIR REWARDS.
AS YOU WISH, LADY MYNE.
スイ
POUR
ガラガラ
ROLL
ROLL
HUH?
ガラ
ROLL

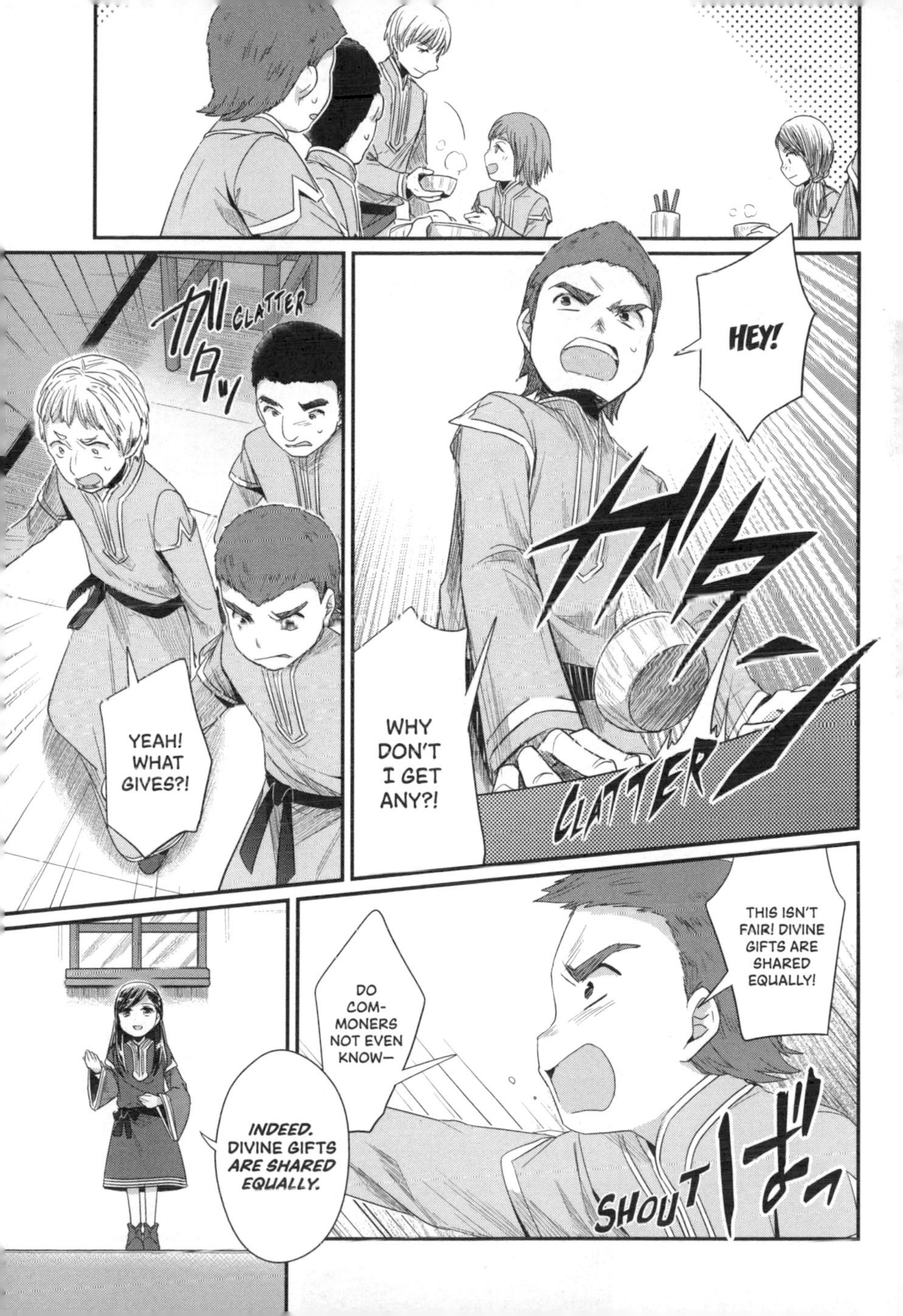
HEY!
WHY DON'T I GET ANY?!
CLATTER
CLATTER
YEAH! WHAT GIVES?!
THIS ISN'T FAIR! DIVINE GIFTS ARE SHARED EQUALLY!
DO COM-MONERS NOT EVEN KNOW—
SHOUT
INDEED. DIVINE GIFTS ARE SHARED EQUALLY.

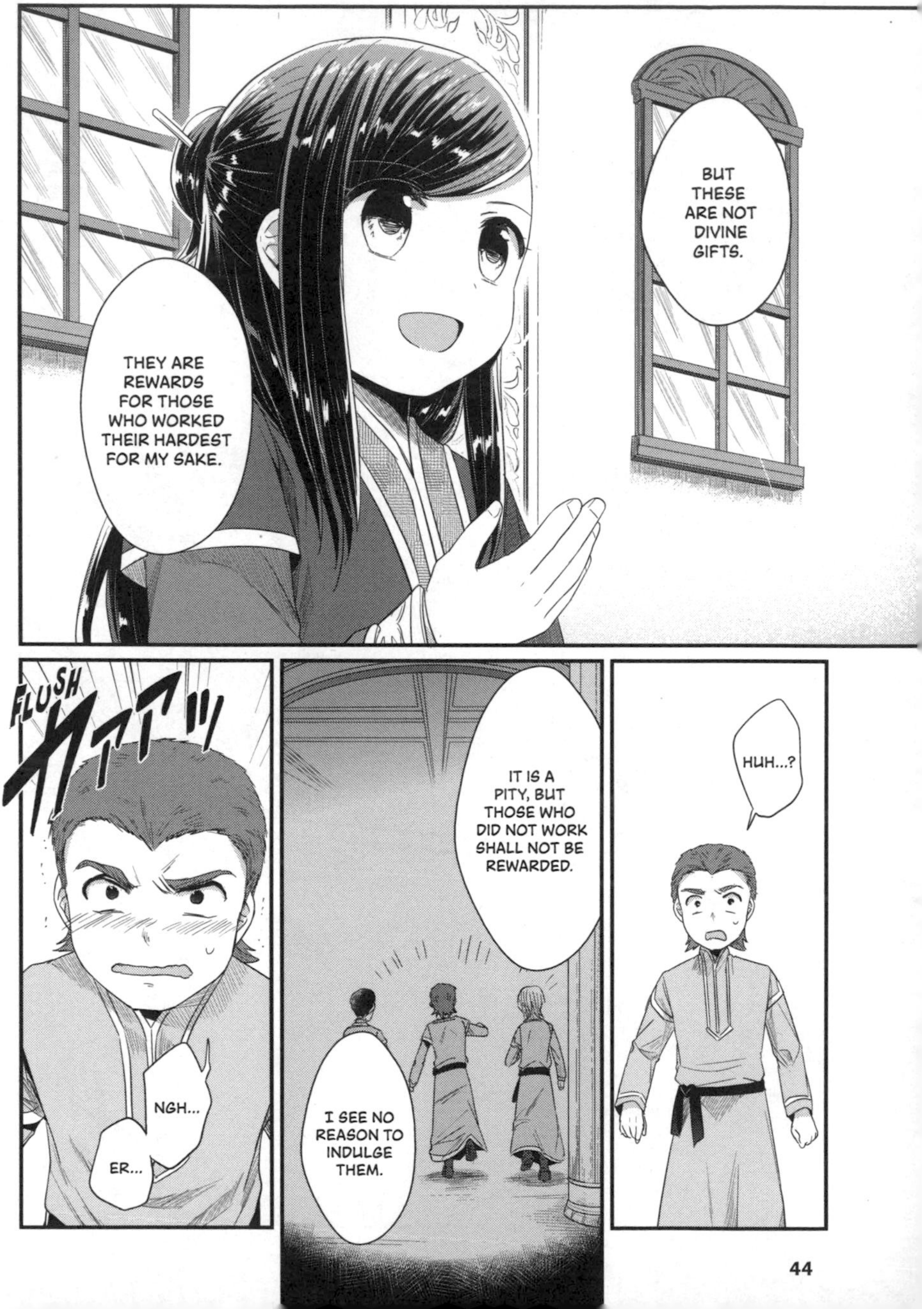
BUT THESE ARE NOT DIVINE GIFTS.
THEY ARE REWARDS FOR THOSE WHO WORKED THEIR HARDEST FOR MY SAKE.
HUH...?
IT IS A PITY, BUT THOSE WHO DID NOT WORK SHALL NOT BE REWARDED.
I SEE NO REASON TO INDULGE THEM.
FLUSH
NGH...
ER...

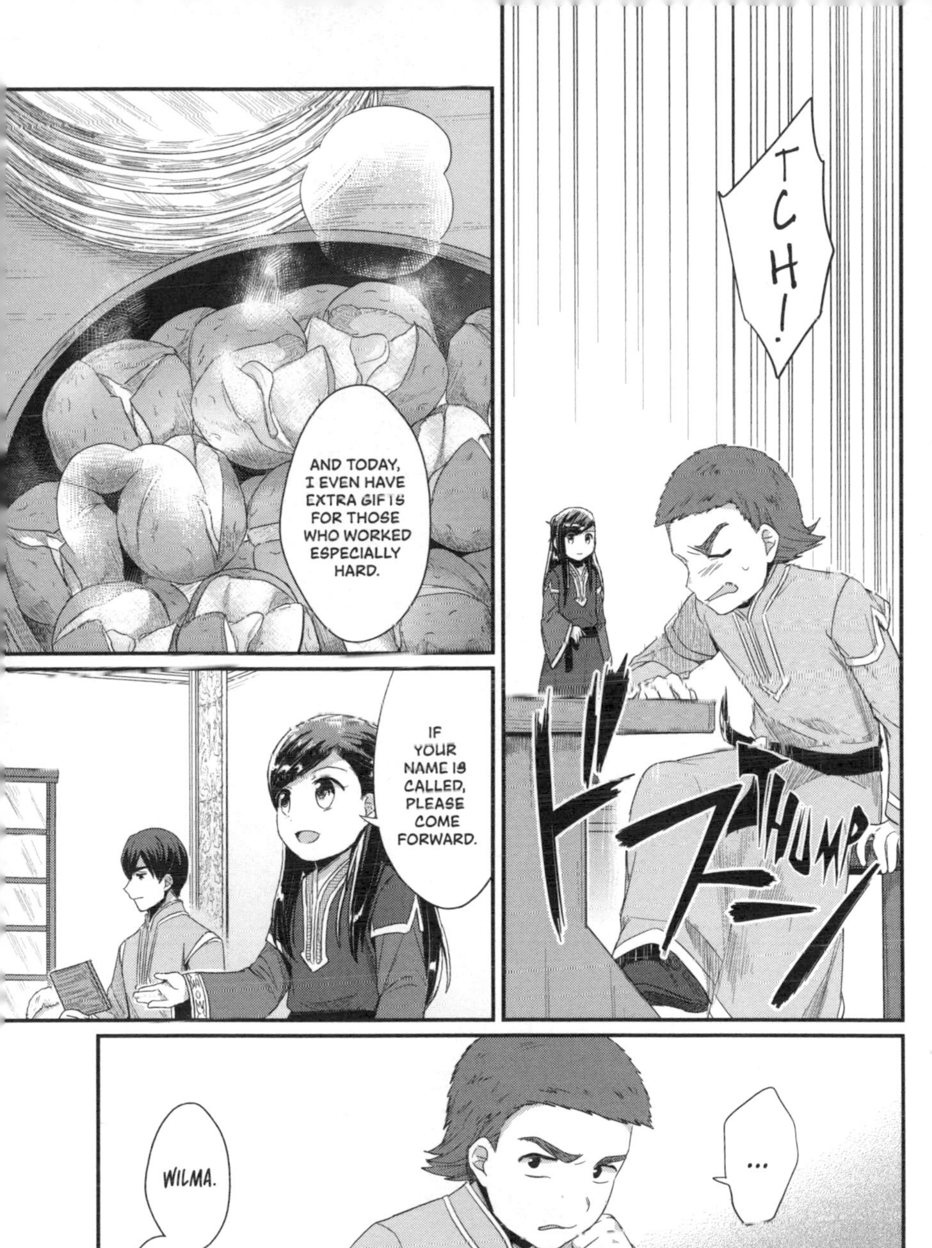
TCH!
THUMP
AND TODAY, I EVEN HAVE EXTRA GIFTS FOR THOSE WHO WORKED ESPECIALLY HARD.
IF YOUR NAME IS CALLED, PLEASE COME FORWARD.
...
WILMA.
MONIKA

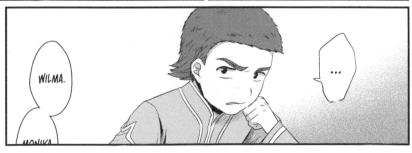

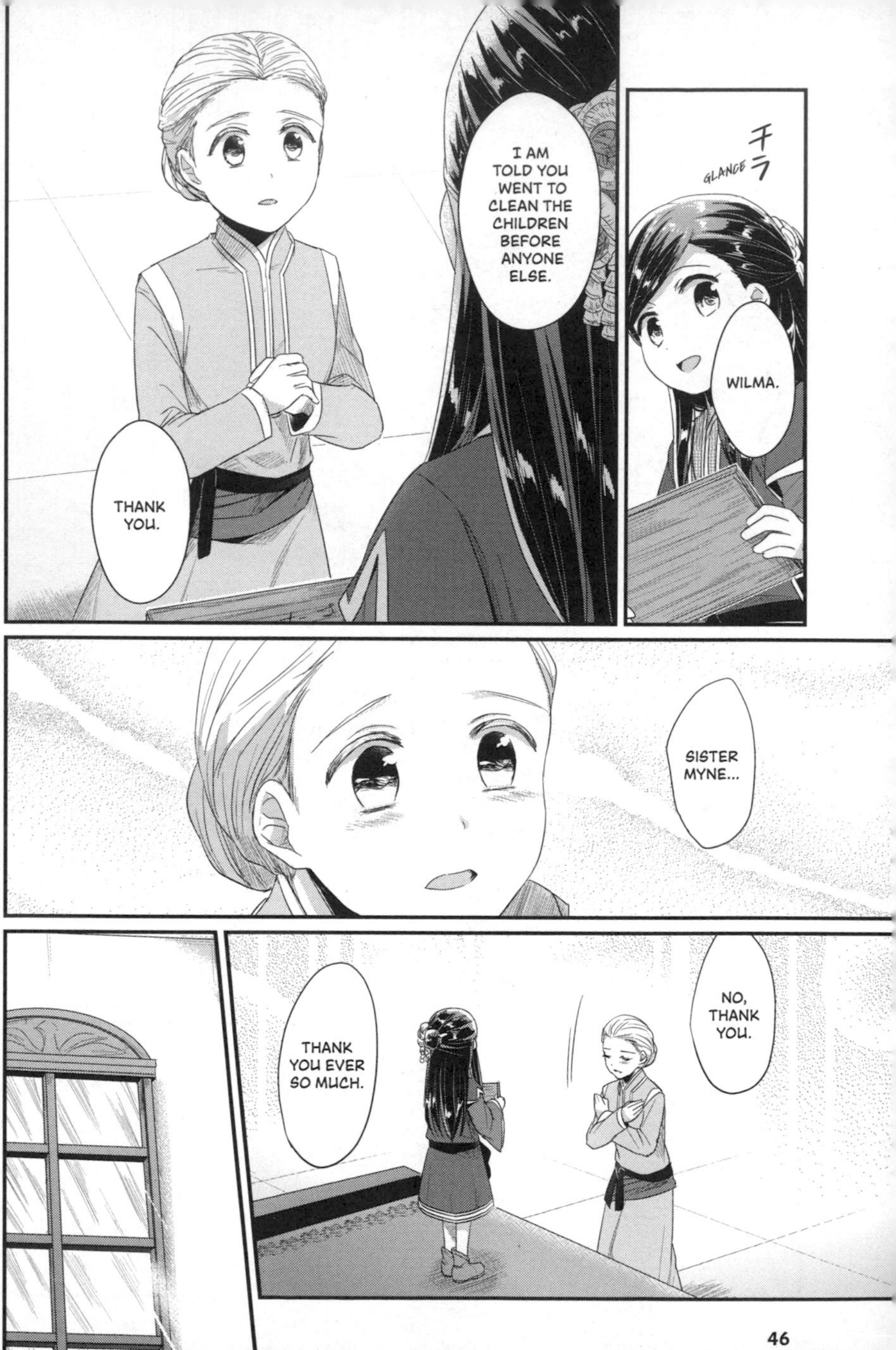
チラ
GLANCE
WILMA.
I AM TOLD YOU WENT TO CLEAN THE CHILDREN BEFORE ANYONE ELSE.
THANK YOU.
SISTER MYNE...
NO, THANK YOU.
THANK YOU EVER SO MUCH.

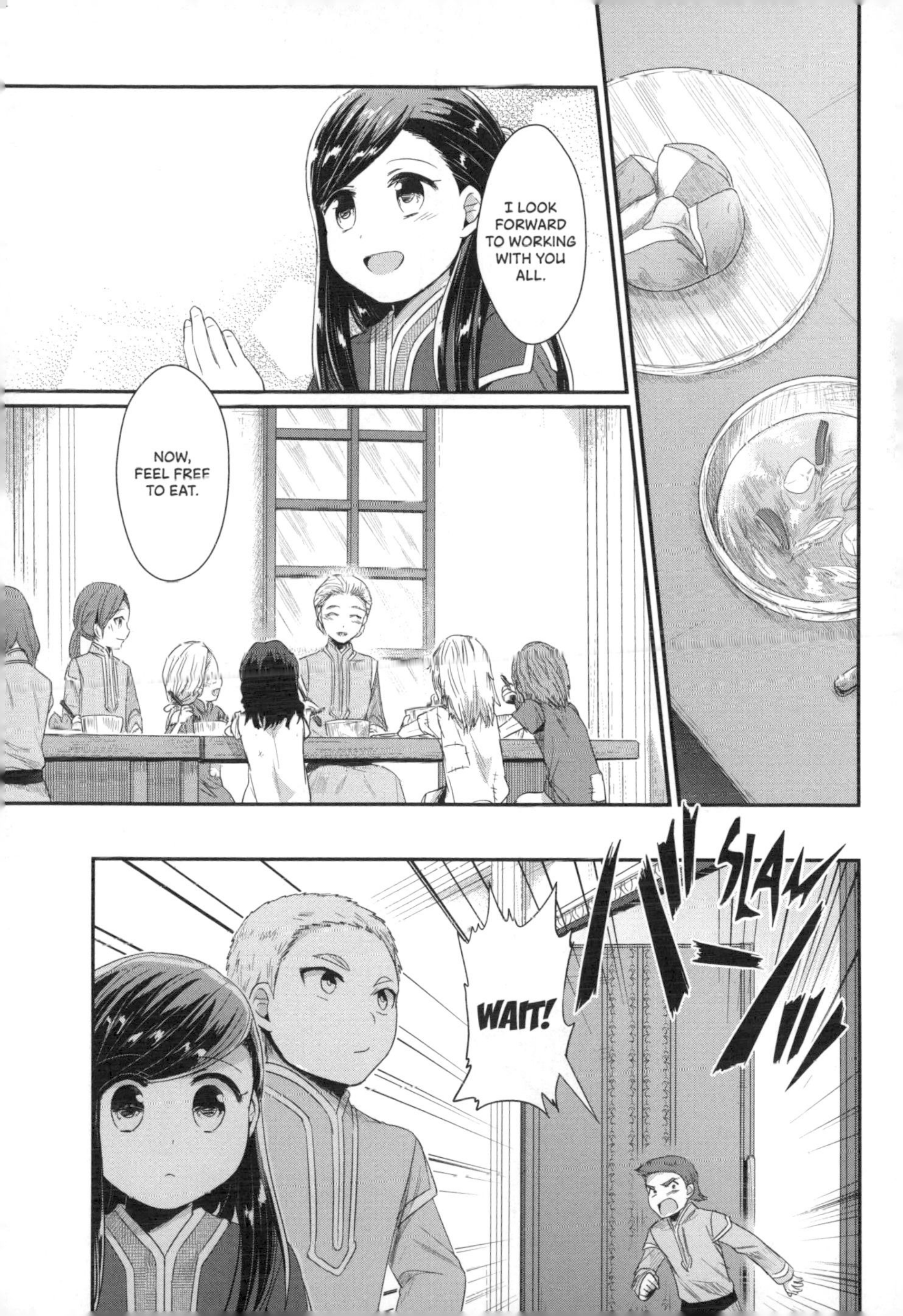
I LOOK FORWARD TO WORKING WITH YOU ALL.
NOW, FEEL FREE TO EAT.
SLAM
WAIT!

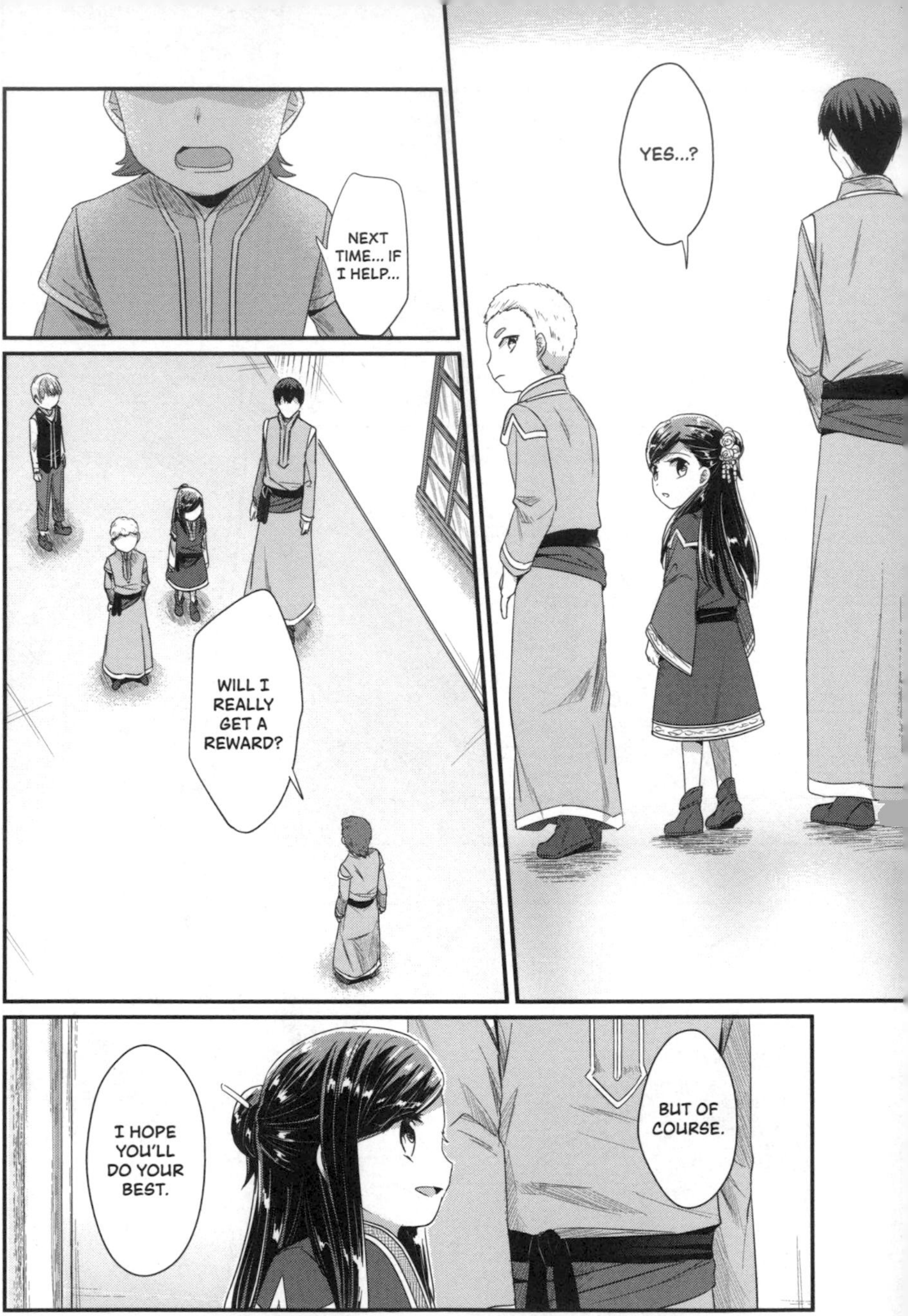
YES...?
NEXT TIME... IF I HELP...
WILL I REALLY GET A REWARD?
BUT OF COURSE.
I HOPE YOU'LL DO YOUR BEST.

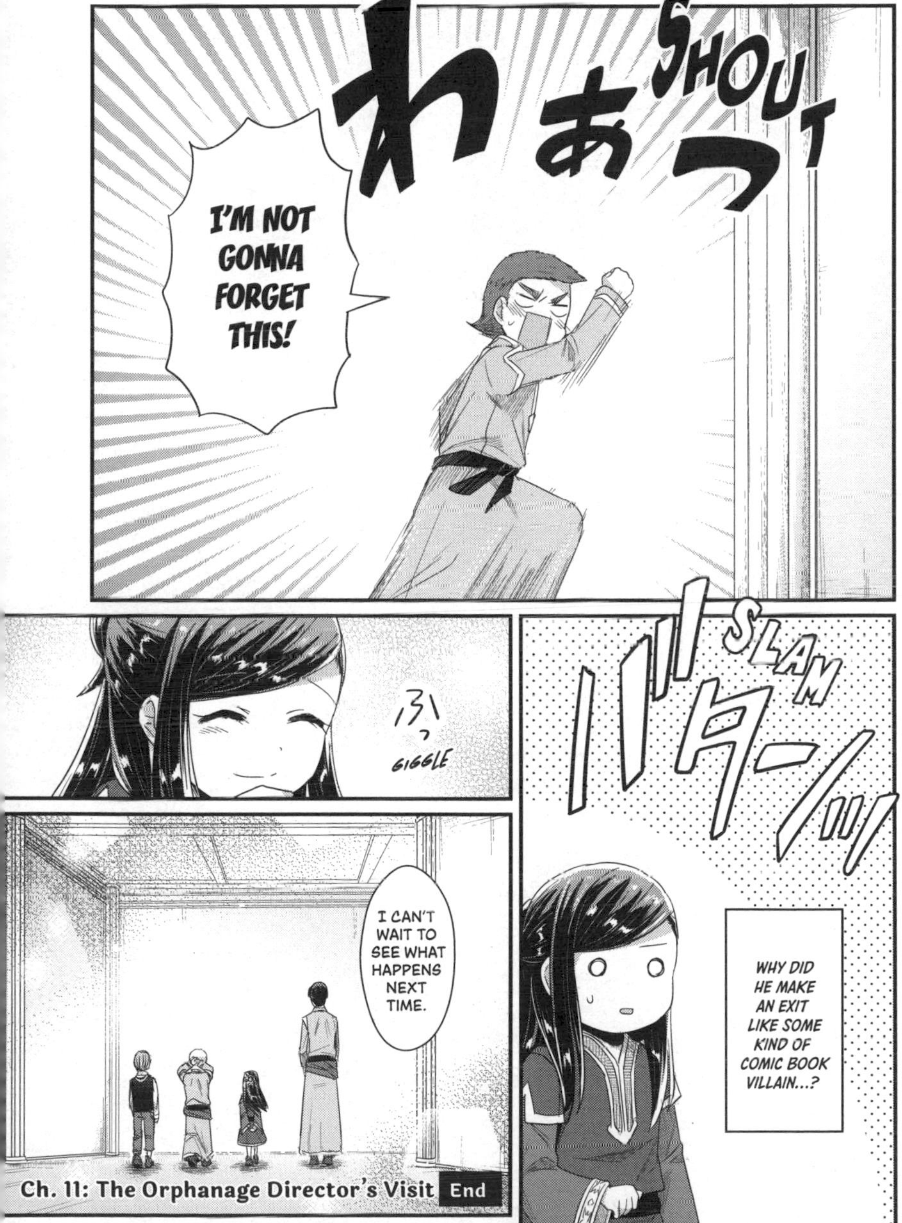
わあっ
SHOUT
I'M NOT GONNA FORGET THIS!
バターン
SLAM
WHY DID HE MAKE AN EXIT LIKE SOME KIND OF COMIC BOOK VILLAIN...?
ふっ
GIGGLE
I CAN'T WAIT TO SEE WHAT HAPPENS NEXT TIME.

Ch. 11: The Orphanage Director's Visit End

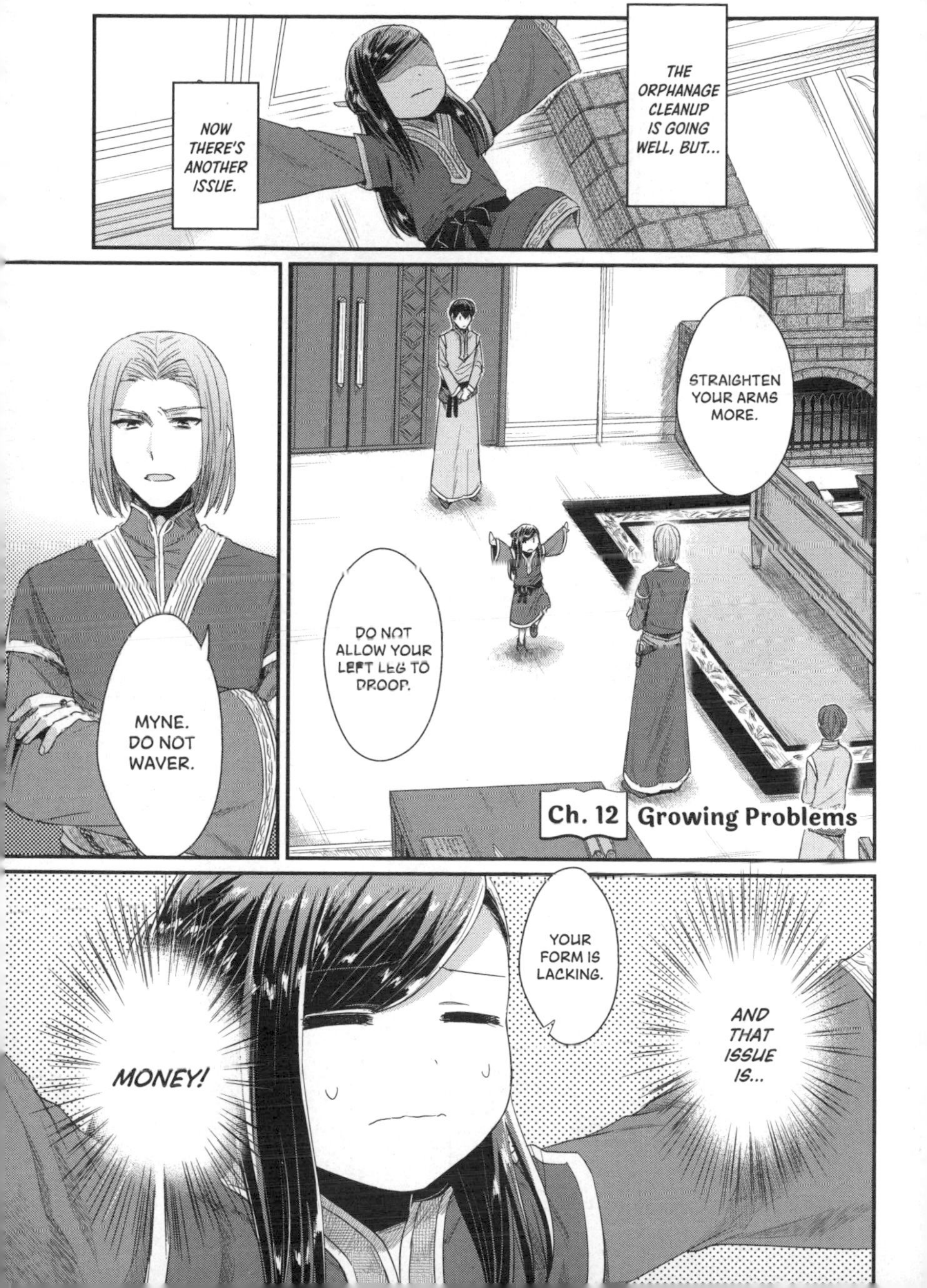
THE ORPHANAGE CLEANUP IS GOING WELL, BUT...
NOW THERE'S ANOTHER ISSUE.
STRAIGHTEN YOUR ARMS MORE.
DO NOT ALLOW YOUR LEFT LEG TO DROOP.
Ch. 12 Growing Problems
MYNE. DO NOT WAVER.
YOUR FORM IS LACKING.
AND THAT ISSUE IS...
MONEY!

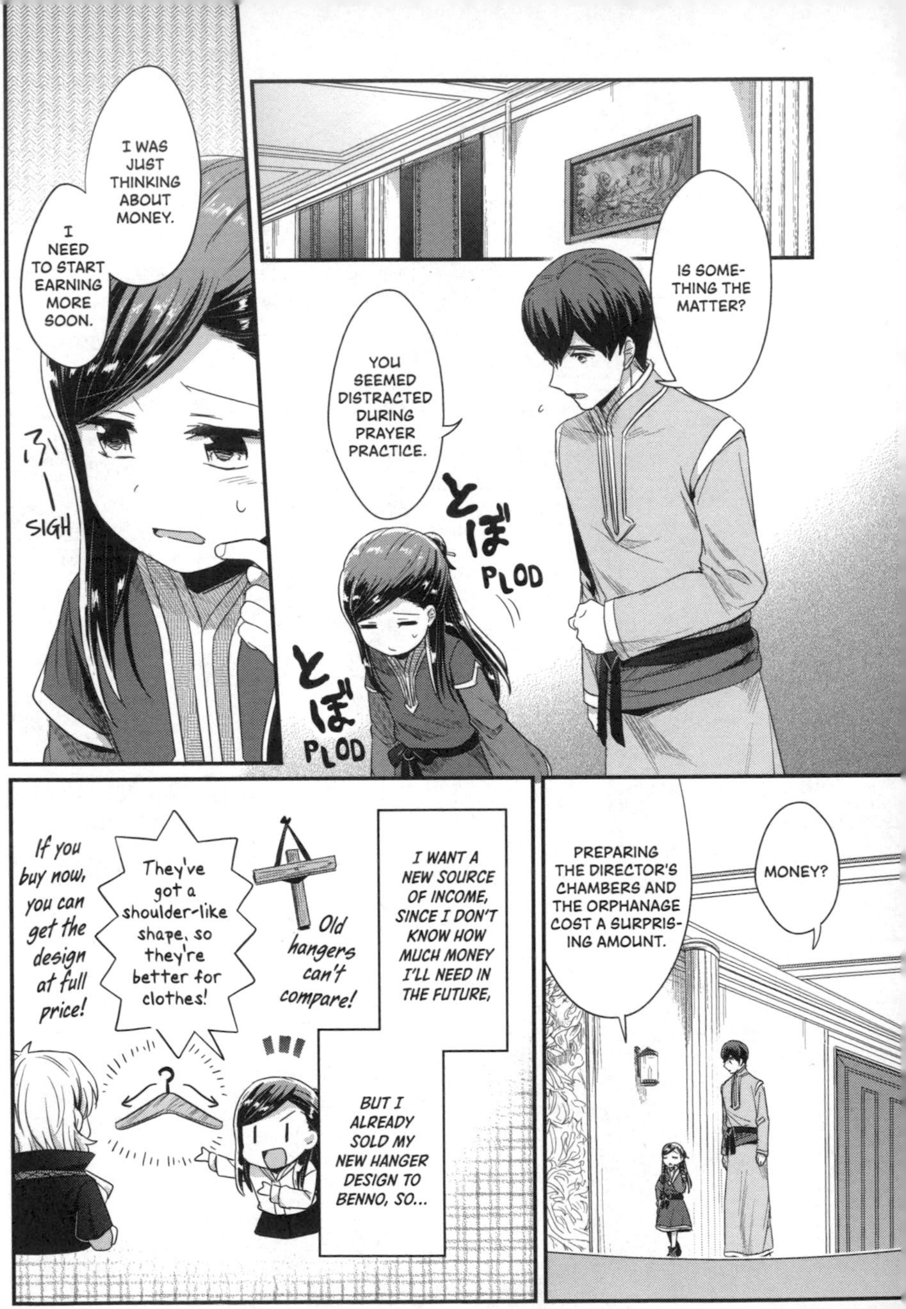
IS SOME-THING THE MATTER?
YOU SEEMED DISTRACTED DURING PRAYER PRACTICE.
とぼ PLOD
とぼ PLOD
I WAS JUST THINKING ABOUT MONEY.
I NEED TO START EARNING MORE SOON.
ふー SIGH
MONEY?
PREPARING THE DIRECTOR'S CHAMBERS AND THE ORPHANAGE COST A SURPRIS-ING AMOUNT.
I WANT A NEW SOURCE OF INCOME, SINCE I DON'T KNOW HOW MUCH MONEY I'LL NEED IN THE FUTURE,
BUT I ALREADY SOLD MY NEW HANGER DESIGN TO BENNO, SO...
Old hangers can't compare!
They've got a shoulder-like shape, so they're better for clothes!
If you buy now, you can get the design at full price!

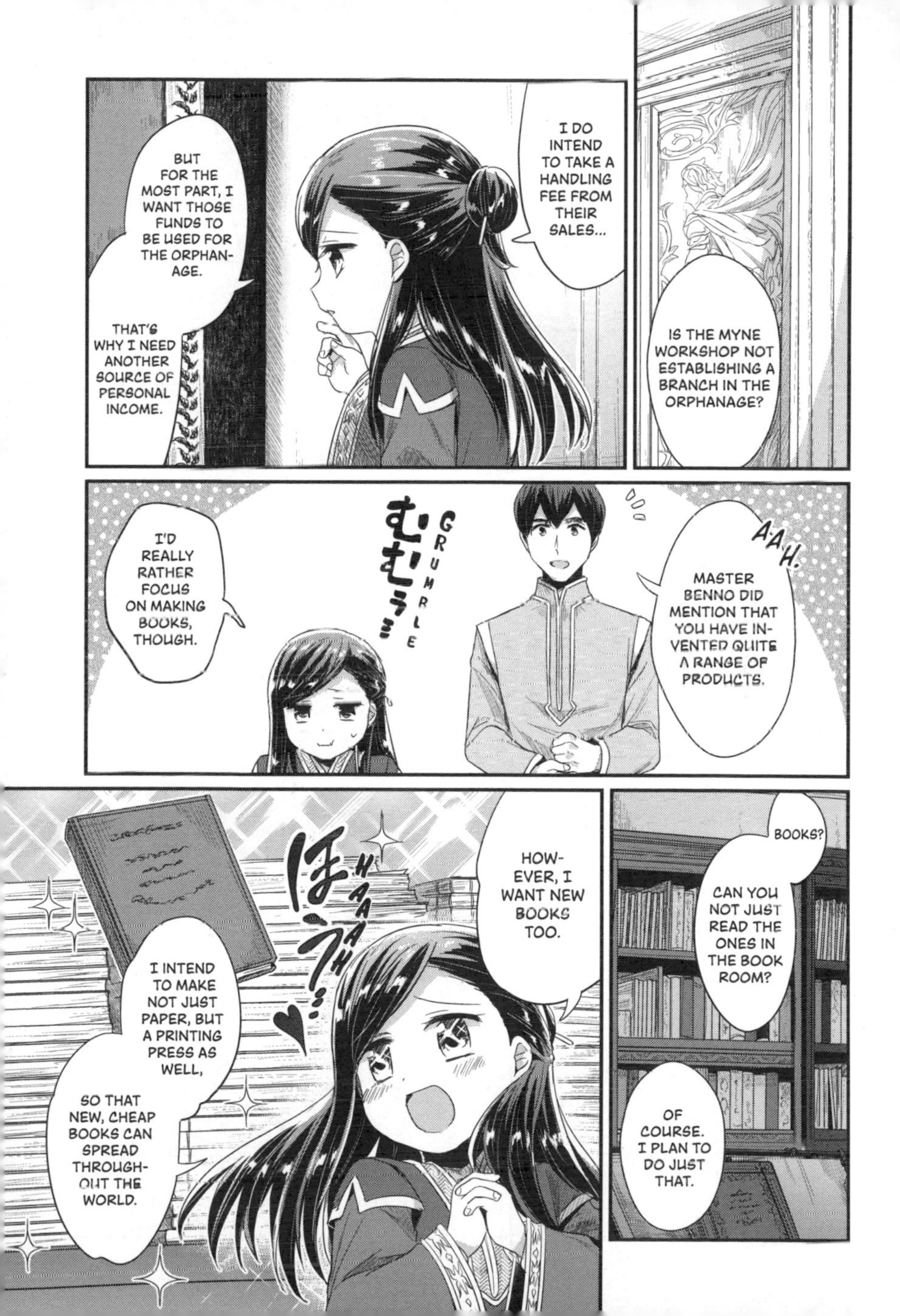
IS THE MYNE WORKSHOP NOT ESTABLISHING A BRANCH IN THE ORPHANAGE?
I DO INTEND TO TAKE A HANDLING FEE FROM THEIR SALES...
BUT FOR THE MOST PART, I WANT THOSE FUNDS TO BE USED FOR THE ORPHANAGE.
THAT'S WHY I NEED ANOTHER SOURCE OF PERSONAL INCOME.
AAH.
MASTER BENNO DID MENTION THAT YOU HAVE INVENTED QUITE A RANGE OF PRODUCTS.
GRUMBLE
I'D REALLY RATHER FOCUS ON MAKING BOOKS, THOUGH.
BOOKS?
CAN YOU NOT JUST READ THE ONES IN THE BOOK ROOM?
OF COURSE. I PLAN TO DO JUST THAT.
HOWEVER, I WANT NEW BOOKS TOO.
HAAAAH
I INTEND TO MAKE NOT JUST PAPER, BUT A PRINTING PRESS AS WELL,
SO THAT NEW, CHEAP BOOKS CAN SPREAD THROUGHOUT THE WORLD.

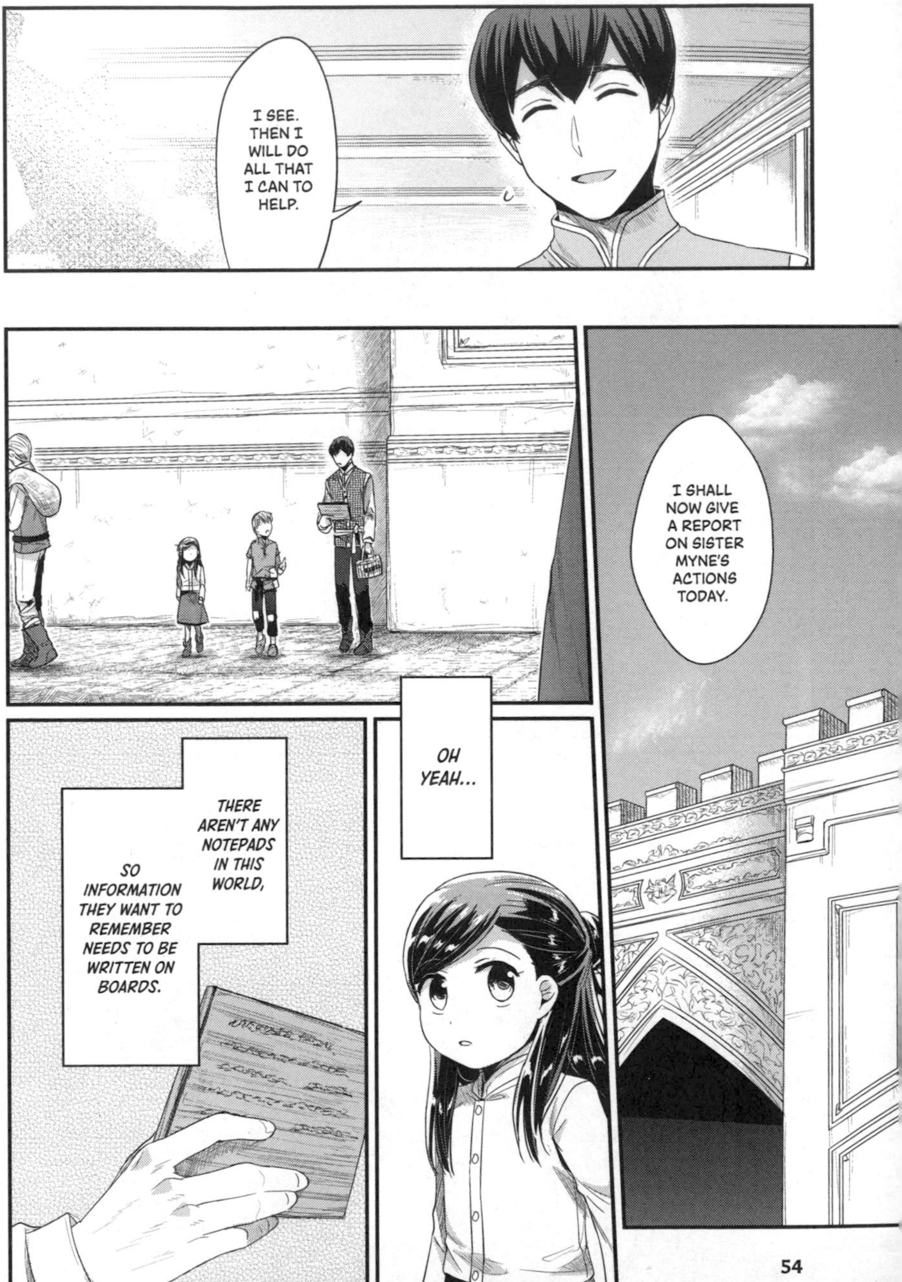
I SEE. THEN I WILL DO ALL THAT I CAN TO HELP.
I SHALL NOW GIVE A REPORT ON SISTER MYNE'S ACTIONS TODAY.
OH YEAH...
THERE AREN'T ANY NOTEPADS IN THIS WORLD,
SO INFORMATION THEY WANT TO REMEMBER NEEDS TO BE WRITTEN ON BOARDS.

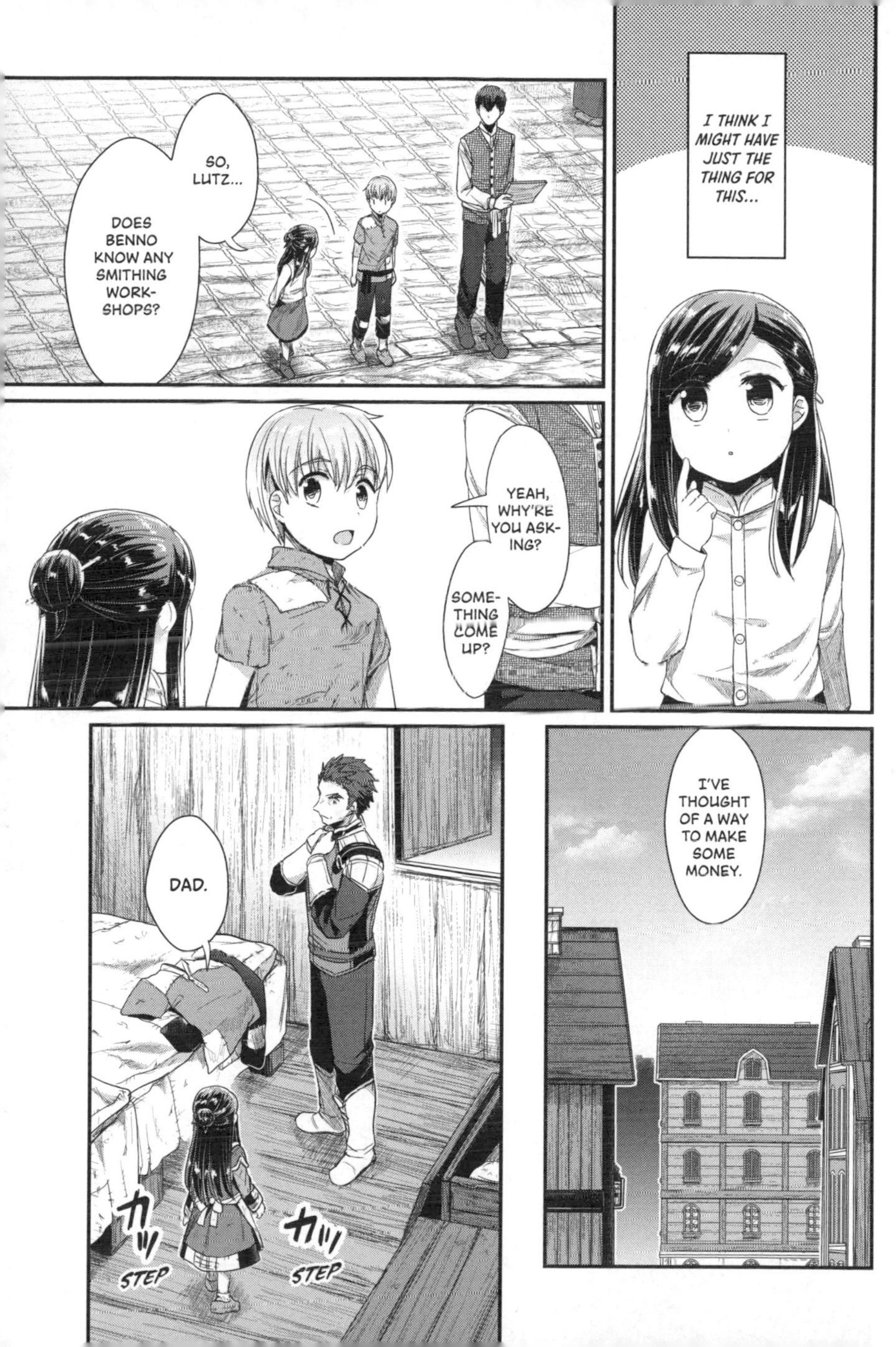
I THINK I MIGHT HAVE JUST THE THING FOR THIS...
SO, LUTZ...
DOES BENNO KNOW ANY SMITHING WORK-SHOPS?
YEAH, WHY'RE YOU ASK-ING?
SOME-THING COME UP?
I'VE THOUGHT OF A WAY TO MAKE SOME MONEY.
DAD.
STEP
STEP

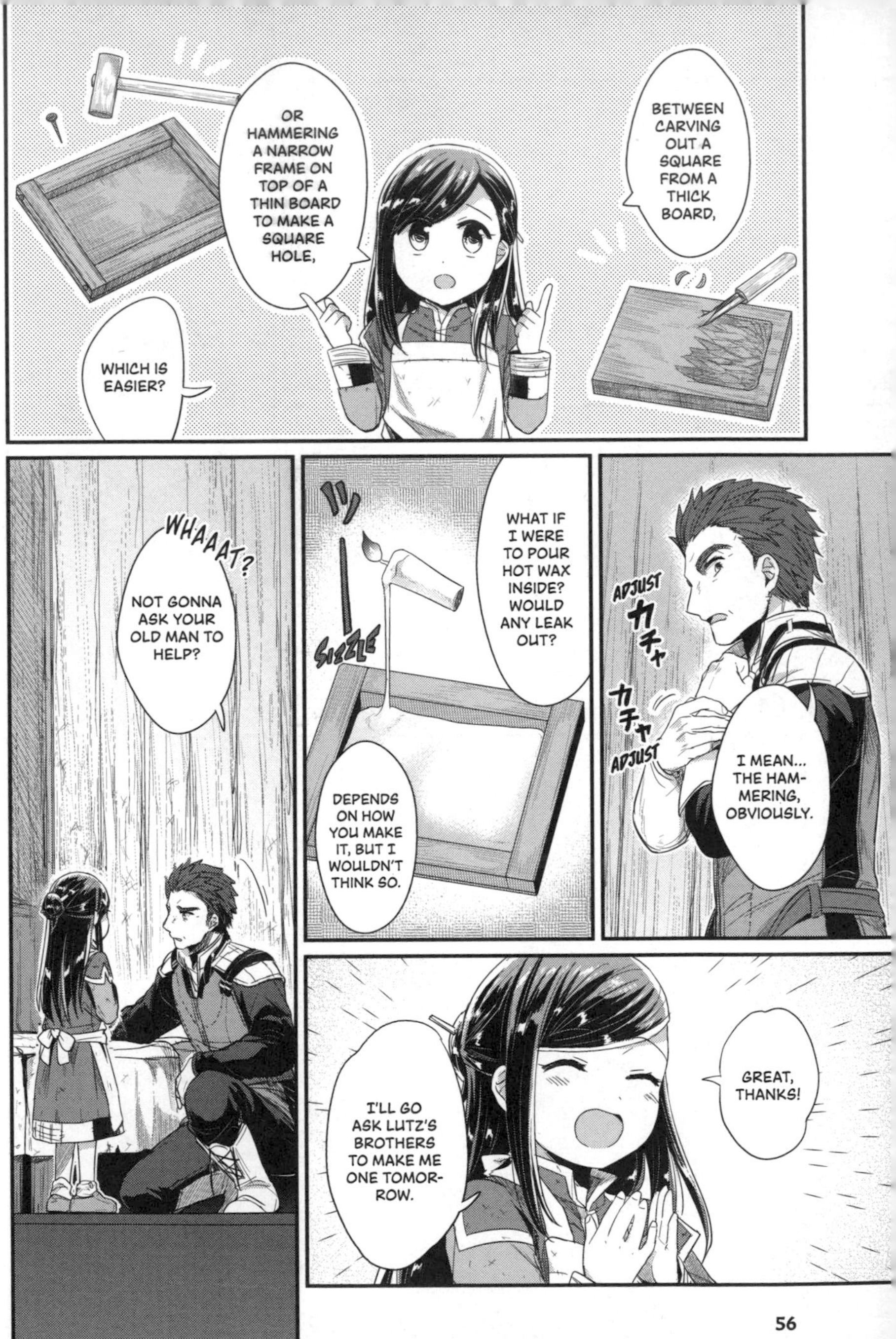
BETWEEN CARVING OUT A SQUARE FROM A THICK BOARD,
OR HAMMERING A NARROW FRAME ON TOP OF A THIN BOARD TO MAKE A SQUARE HOLE,
WHICH IS EASIER?
ADJUST
カチャ
カチャ
ADJUST
I MEAN... THE HAM-MERING, OBVIOUSLY.
WHAT IF I WERE TO POUR HOT WAX INSIDE? WOULD ANY LEAK OUT?
SIZZLE
DEPENDS ON HOW YOU MAKE IT, BUT I WOULDN'T THINK SO.
GREAT, THANKS!
I'LL GO ASK LUTZ'S BROTHERS TO MAKE ME ONE TOMOR-ROW.
WHAAAT?
NOT GONNA ASK YOUR OLD MAN TO HELP?

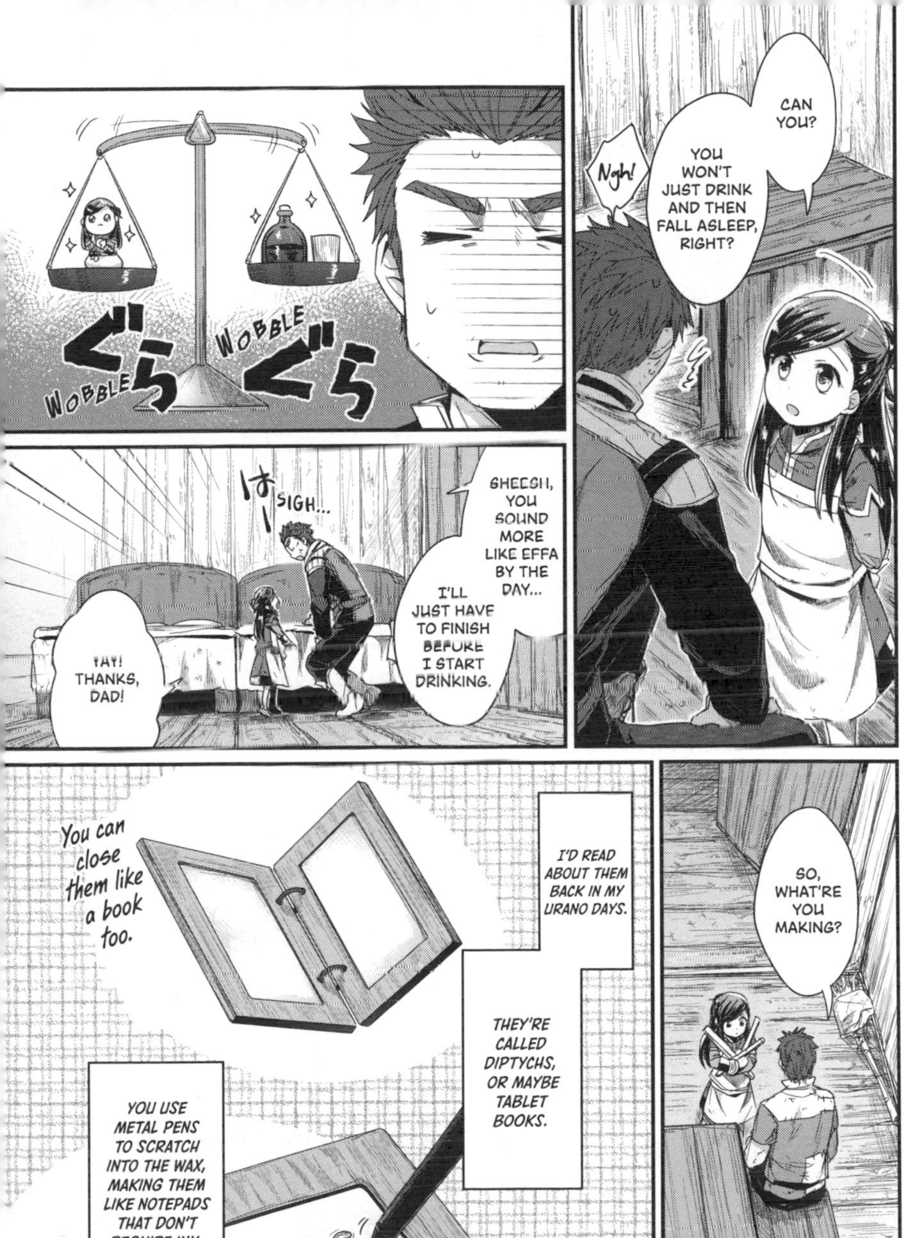
CAN YOU?
YOU WON'T JUST DRINK AND THEN FALL ASLEEP, RIGHT?
Ngh!
WOBBLE ぐら
WOBBLE ぐら
はぁ SIGH...
GHEESH, YOU SOUND MORE LIKE EFFA BY THE DAY...
I'LL JUST HAVE TO FINISH BEFORE I START DRINKING.
YAY! THANKS, DAD!
SO, WHAT'RE YOU MAKING?
I'D READ ABOUT THEM BACK IN MY URANO DAYS.
You can close them like a book too.
THEY'RE CALLED DIPTYCHS, OR MAYBE TABLET BOOKS.
YOU USE METAL PENS TO SCRATCH INTO THE WAX, MAKING THEM LIKE NOTEPADS THAT DON'T REQUIRE INK.
ABC

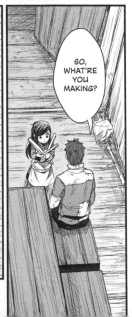

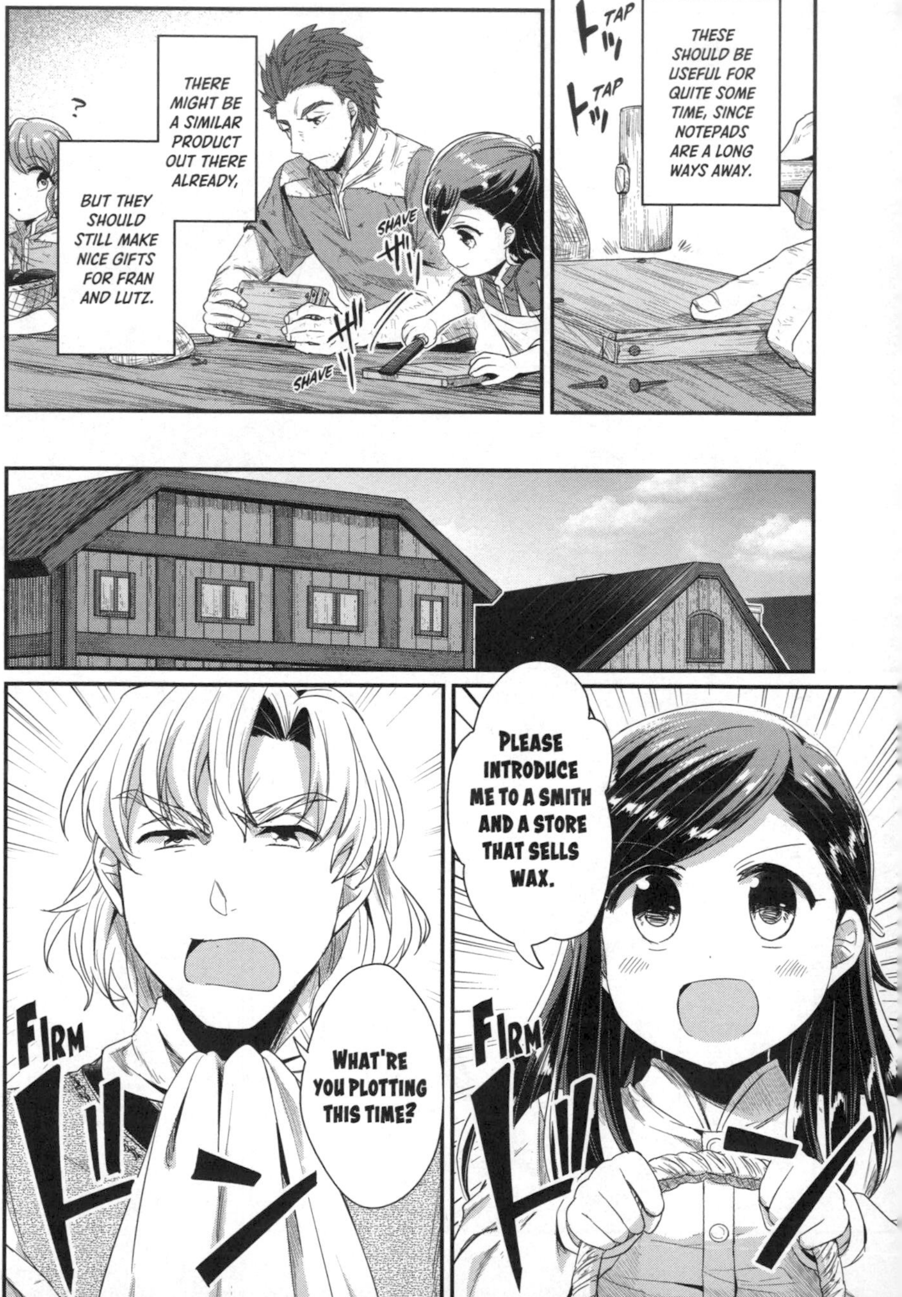
TAP
TAP
THESE SHOULD BE USEFUL FOR QUITE SOME TIME, SINCE NOTEPADS ARE A LONG WAYS AWAY.
THERE MIGHT BE A SIMILAR PRODUCT OUT THERE ALREADY,
BUT THEY SHOULD STILL MAKE NICE GIFTS FOR FRAN AND LUTZ.
?
SHAVE
SHAVE
PLEASE INTRODUCE ME TO A SMITH AND A STORE THAT SELLS WAX.
FIRM
WHAT'RE YOU PLOTTING THIS TIME?
FIRM

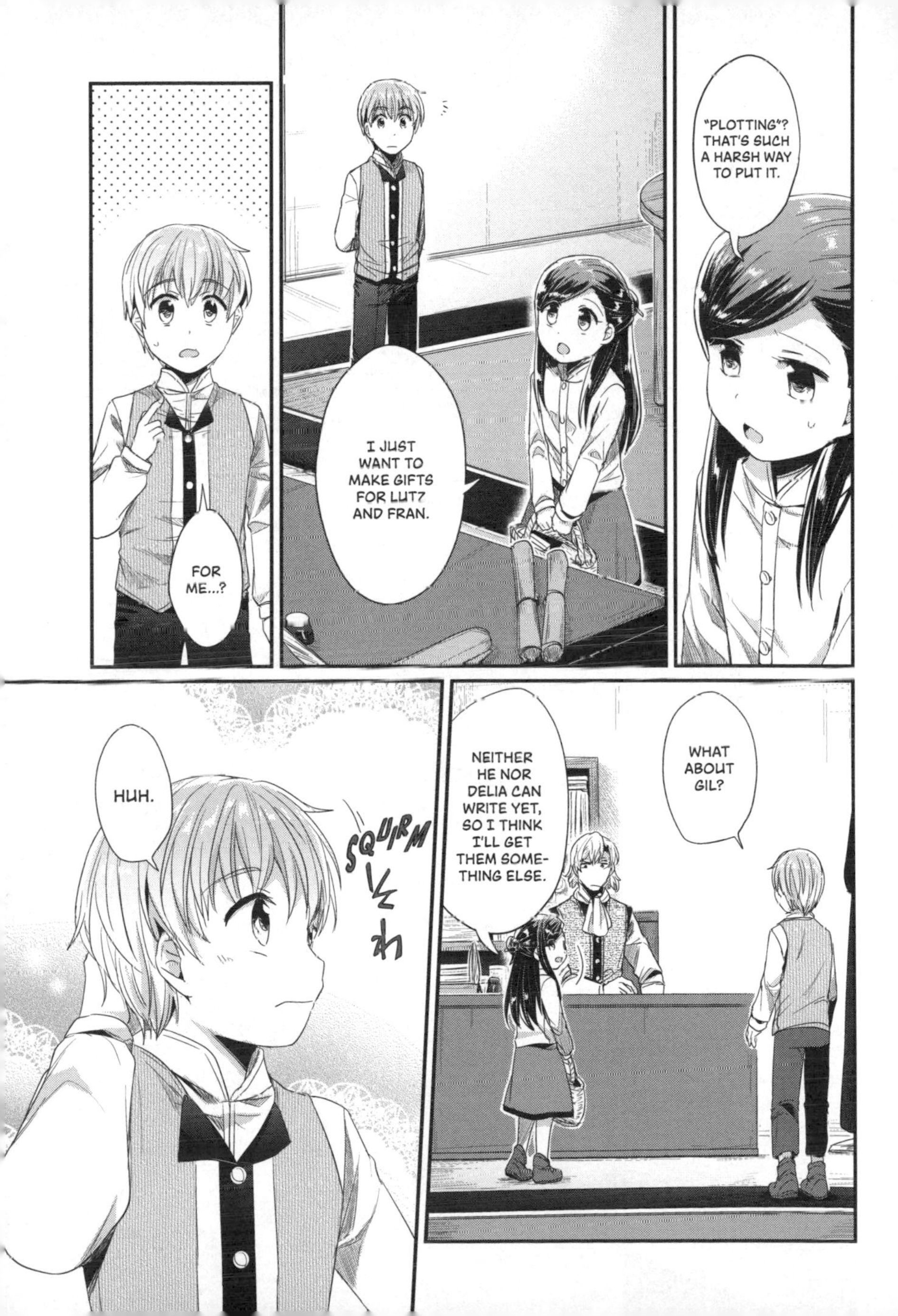
"PLOTTING"? THAT'S SUCH A HARSH WAY TO PUT IT.
I JUST WANT TO MAKE GIFTS FOR LUTZ AND FRAN.
FOR ME...?
WHAT ABOUT GIL?
NEITHER HE NOR DELIA CAN WRITE YET, SO I THINK I'LL GET THEM SOMETHING ELSE.
HUH.
SQUIRM

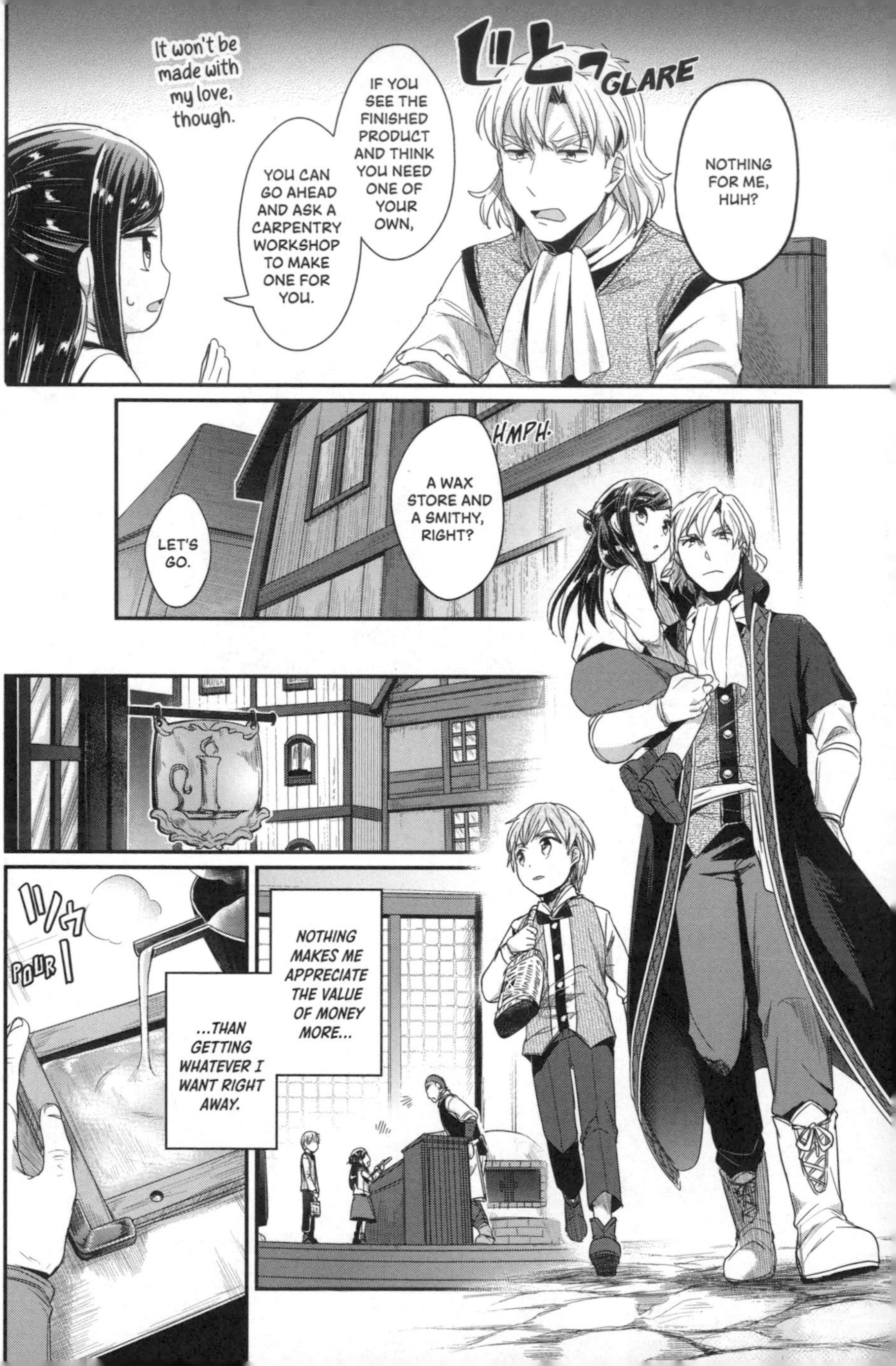
じとっ GLARE
NOTHING FOR ME, HUH?
IF YOU SEE THE FINISHED PRODUCT AND THINK YOU NEED ONE OF YOUR OWN,
YOU CAN GO AHEAD AND ASK A CARPENTRY WORKSHOP TO MAKE ONE FOR YOU.
It won't be made with my love, though.
HMPH.
A WAX STORE AND A SMITHY, RIGHT?
LET'S GO.
NOTHING MAKES ME APPRECIATE THE VALUE OF MONEY MORE...
...THAN GETTING WHATEVER I WANT RIGHT AWAY.
POUR

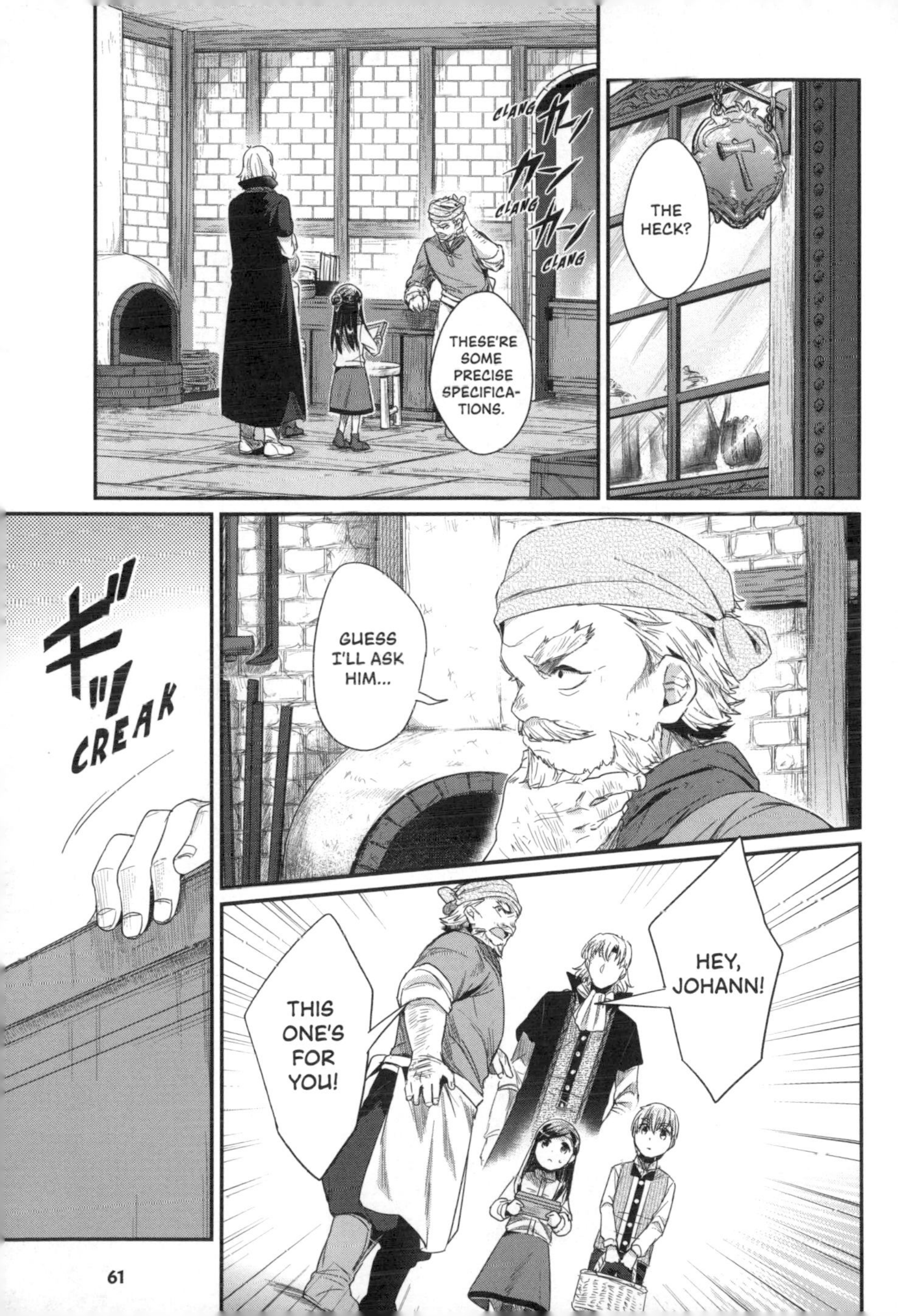
THE HECK?
CLANG
CLANG
CLANG
THESE'RE SOME PRECISE SPECIFICA-TIONS.
GUESS I'LL ASK HIM...
HEY, JOHANN!
THIS ONE'S FOR YOU!
CREAK

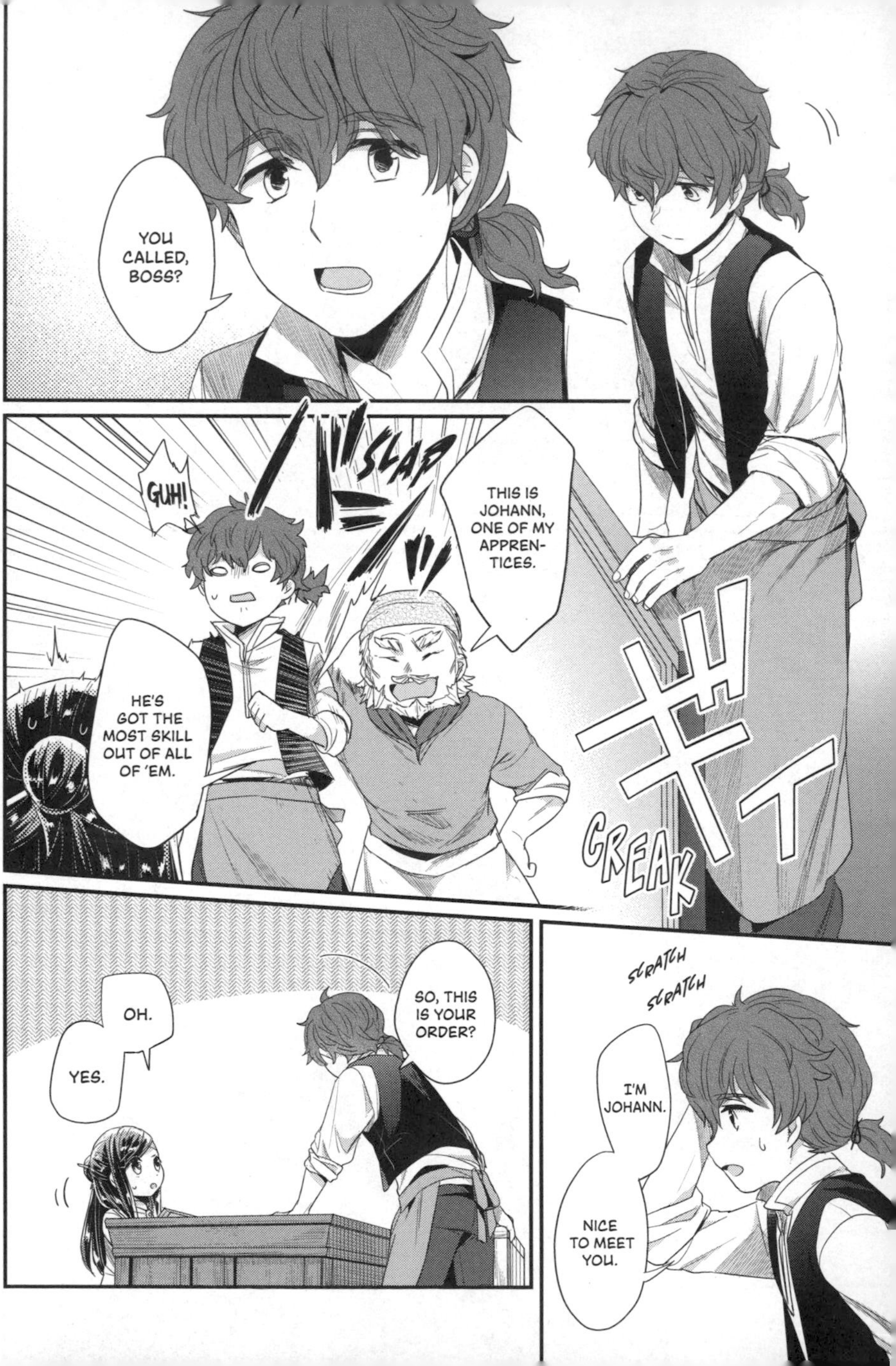
CREAK
YOU CALLED, BOSS?
THIS IS JOHANN, ONE OF MY APPRENTICES.
SLAP
GUH!
HE'S GOT THE MOST SKILL OUT OF ALL OF 'EM.
SCRATCH SCRATCH
I'M JOHANN.
NICE TO MEET YOU.
SO, THIS IS YOUR ORDER?
OH.
YES.

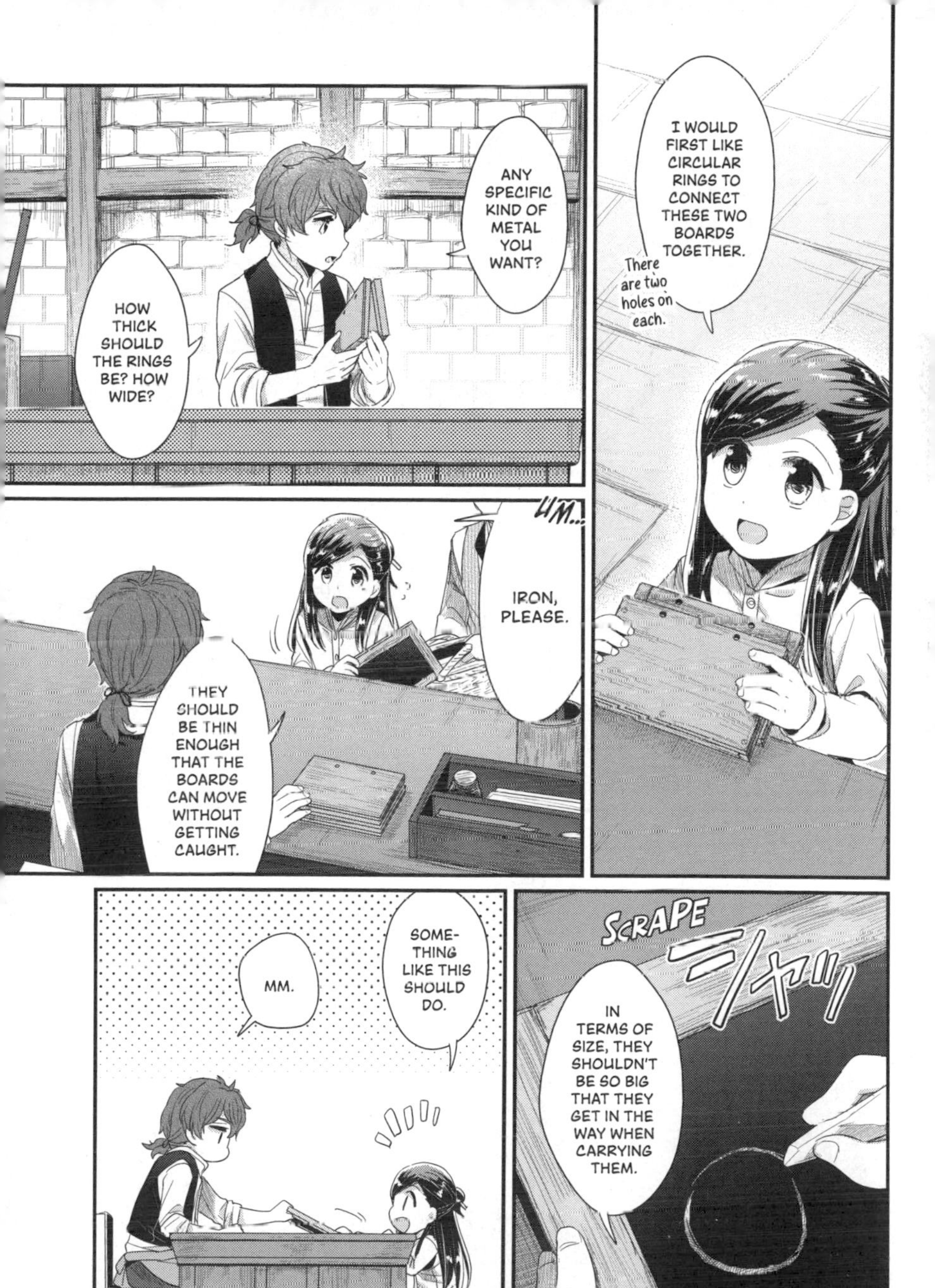
I WOULD FIRST LIKE CIRCULAR RINGS TO CONNECT THESE TWO BOARDS TOGETHER.
There are two holes on each.
ANY SPECIFIC KIND OF METAL YOU WANT?
HOW THICK SHOULD THE RINGS BE? HOW WIDE?
UM...
IRON, PLEASE.
THEY SHOULD BE THIN ENOUGH THAT THE BOARDS CAN MOVE WITHOUT GETTING CAUGHT.
SCRAPE
IN TERMS OF SIZE, THEY SHOULDN'T BE SO BIG THAT THEY GET IN THE WAY WHEN CARRYING THEM.
SOME-THING LIKE THIS SHOULD DO.
MM.

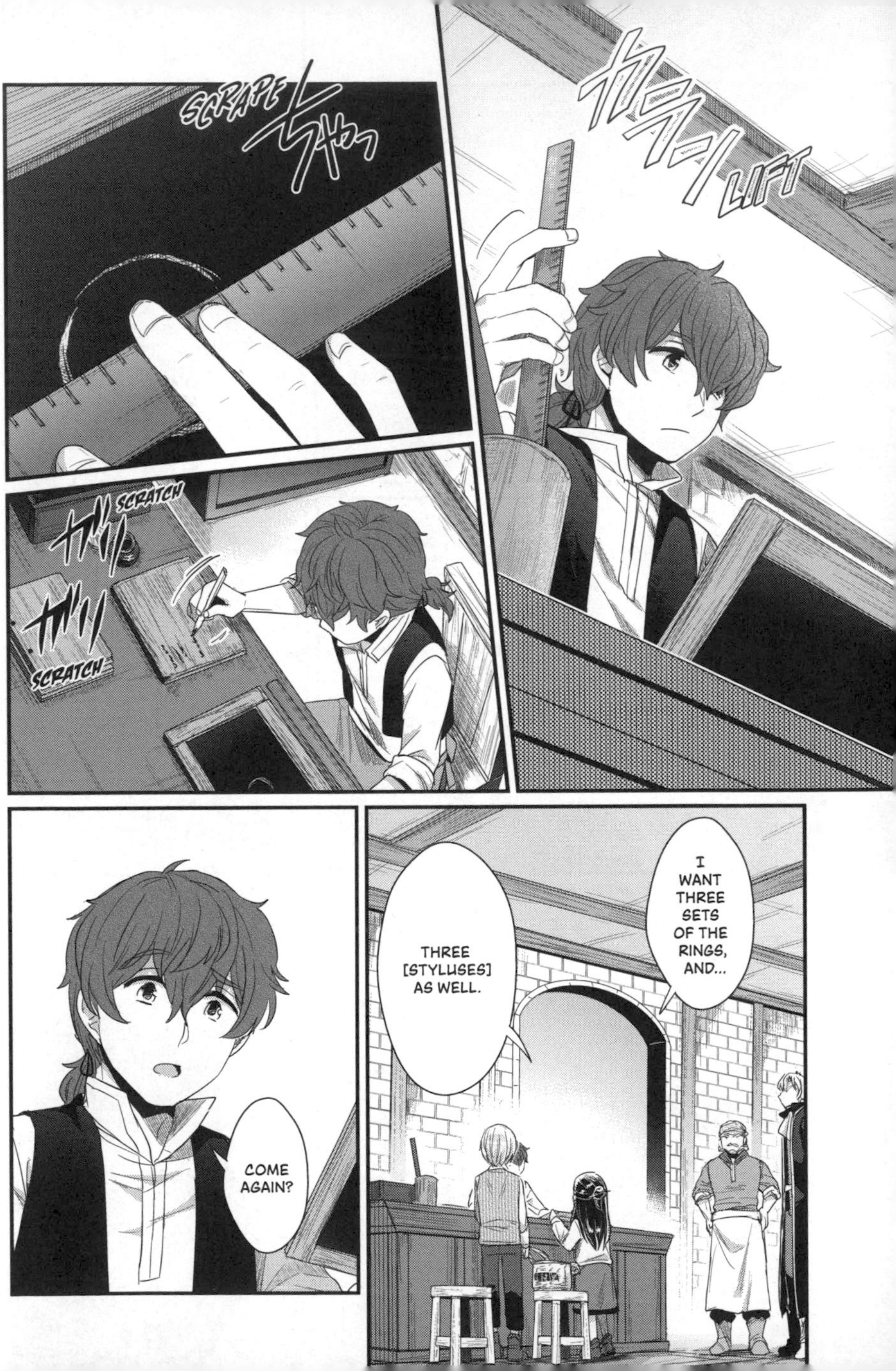
カラーン
LIFT
SCRAPE
ちゃっ
SCRATCH
ガリッ
ガリッ
SCRATCH
I WANT THREE SETS OF THE RINGS, AND...
THREE [STYLUSES] AS WELL.
COME AGAIN?

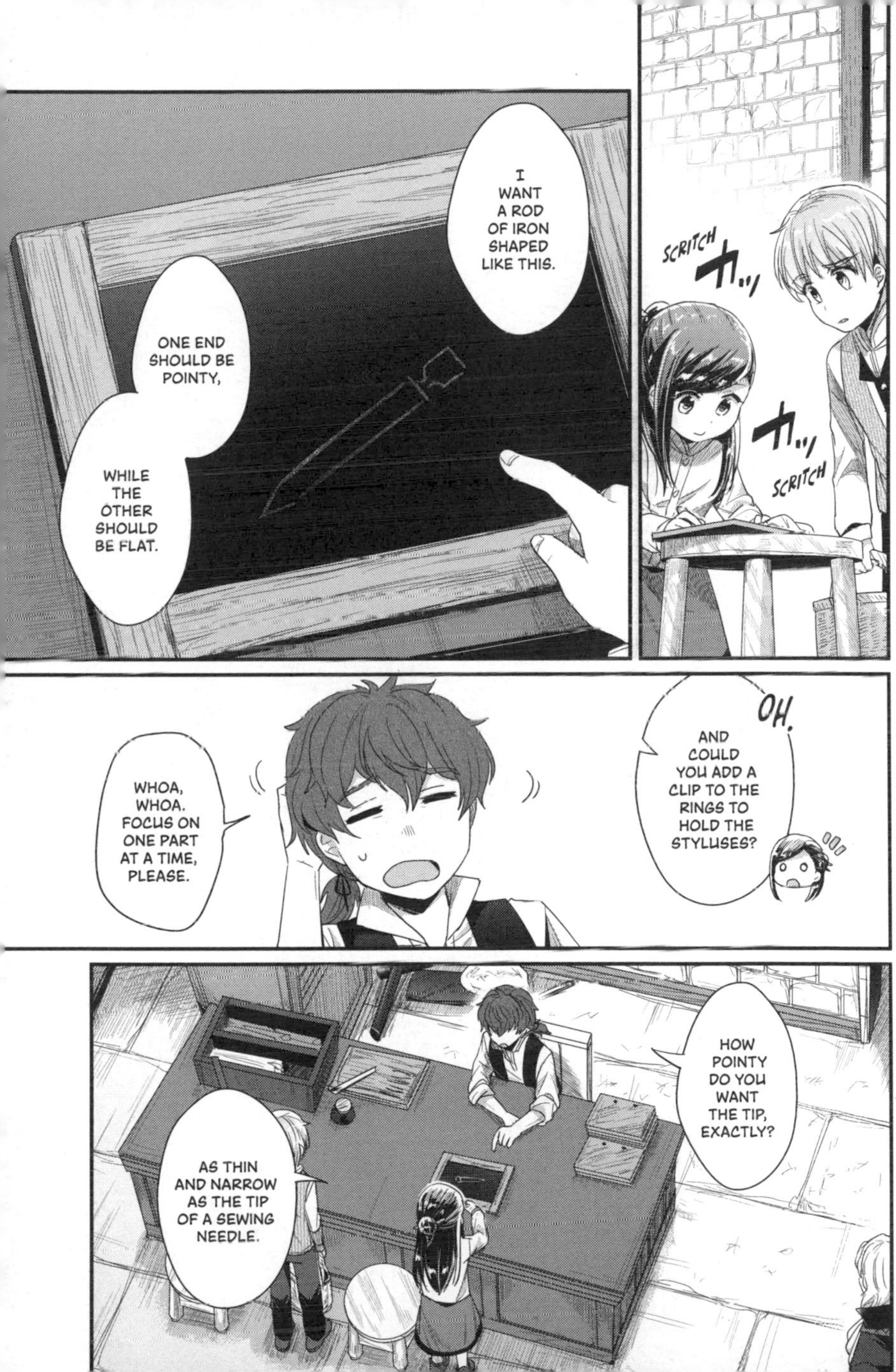
SCRITCH
カッ
カッ
SCRITCH
I WANT A ROD OF IRON SHAPED LIKE THIS.
ONE END SHOULD BE POINTY,
WHILE THE OTHER SHOULD BE FLAT.
OH.
AND COULD YOU ADD A CLIP TO THE RINGS TO HOLD THE STYLUSES?
WHOA, WHOA. FOCUS ON ONE PART AT A TIME, PLEASE.
HOW POINTY DO YOU WANT THE TIP, EXACTLY?
AS THIN AND NARROW AS THE TIP OF A SEWING NEEDLE.

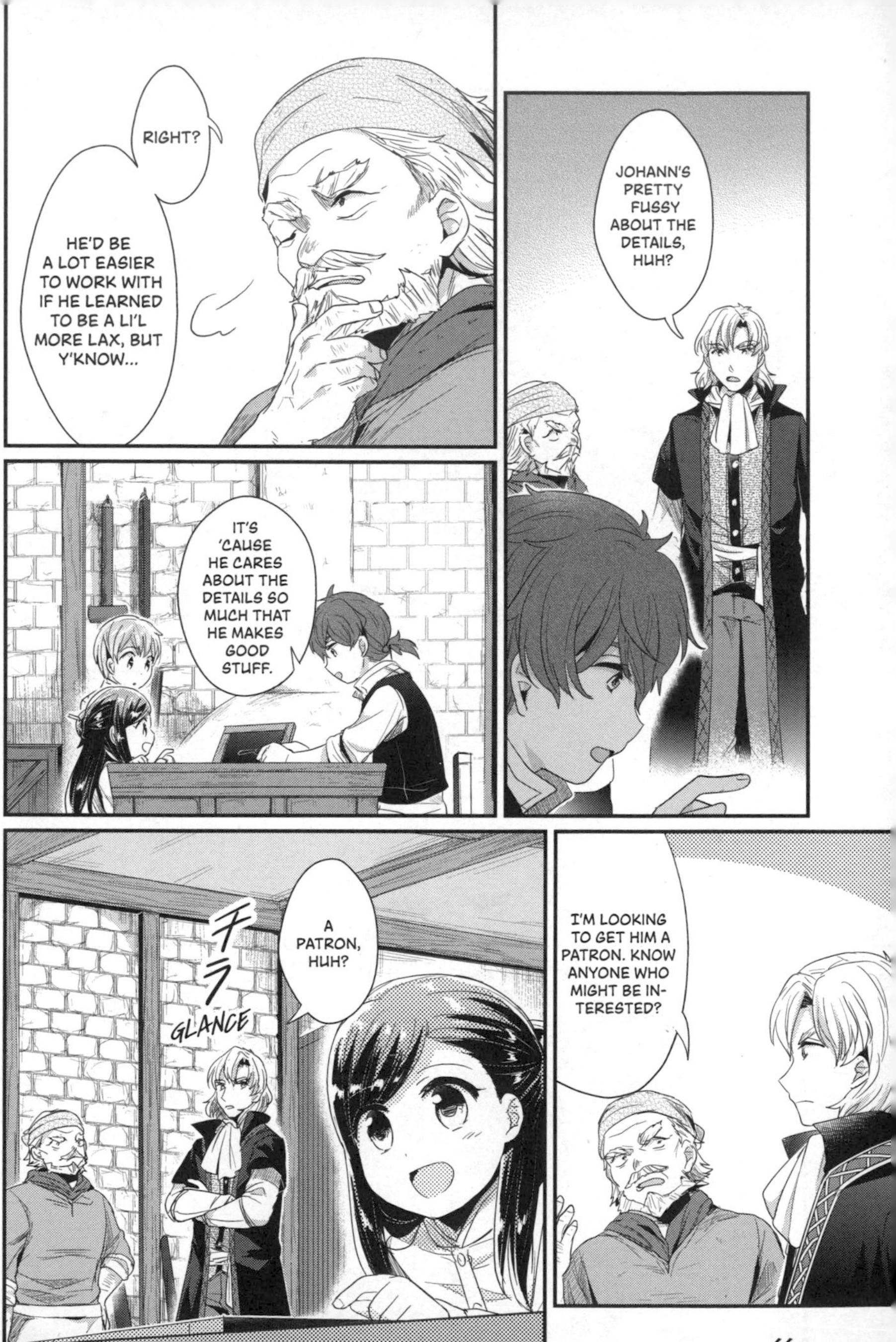
JOHANN'S PRETTY FUSSY ABOUT THE DETAILS, HUH?
RIGHT?
HE'D BE A LOT EASIER TO WORK WITH IF HE LEARNED TO BE A LI'L MORE LAX, BUT Y'KNOW...
IT'S 'CAUSE HE CARES ABOUT THE DETAILS SO MUCH THAT HE MAKES GOOD STUFF.
I'M LOOKING TO GET HIM A PATRON. KNOW ANYONE WHO MIGHT BE INTERESTED?
A PATRON, HUH?
チラ
GLANCE

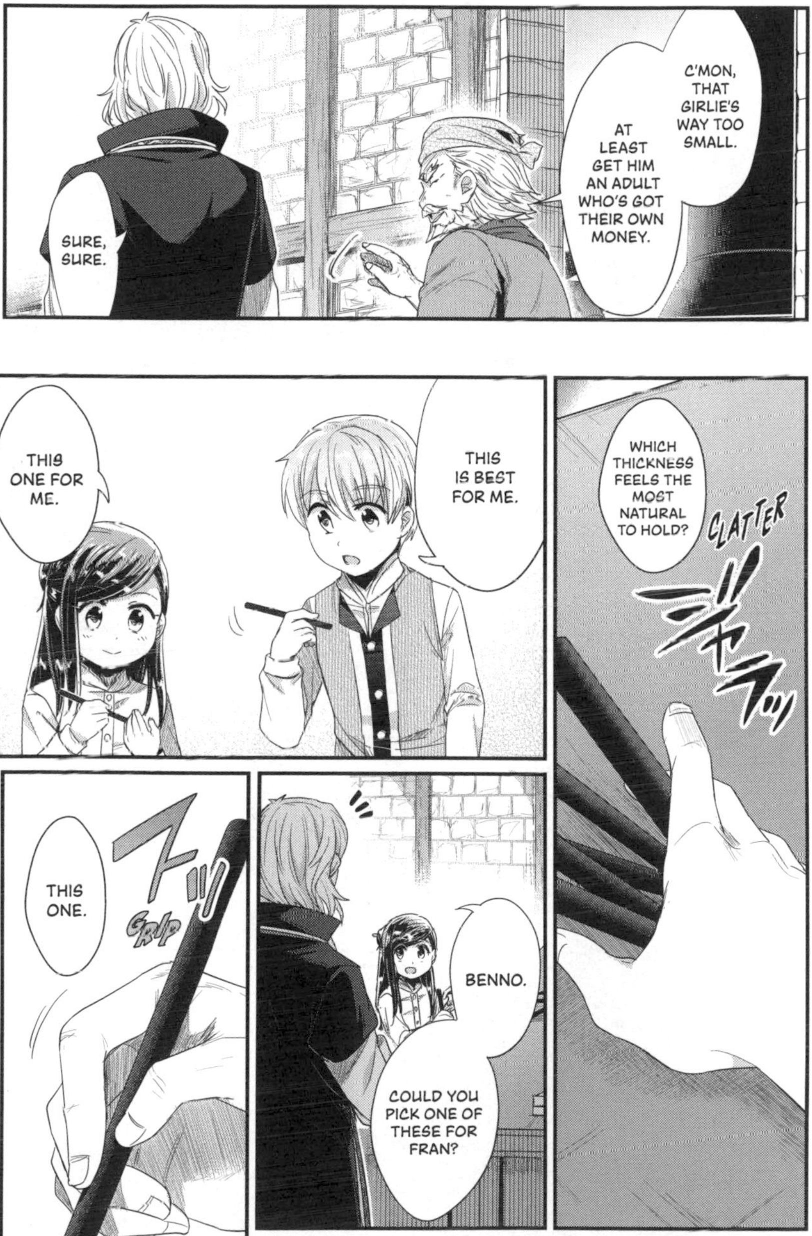
C'MON, THAT GIRLIE'S WAY TOO SMALL.
AT LEAST GET HIM AN ADULT WHO'S GOT THEIR OWN MONEY.
SURE, SURE.
WHICH THICKNESS FEELS THE MOST NATURAL TO HOLD?
CLATTER
THIS IS BEST FOR ME.
THIS ONE FOR ME.
BENNO.
COULD YOU PICK ONE OF THESE FOR FRAN?
THIS ONE.
GRIP

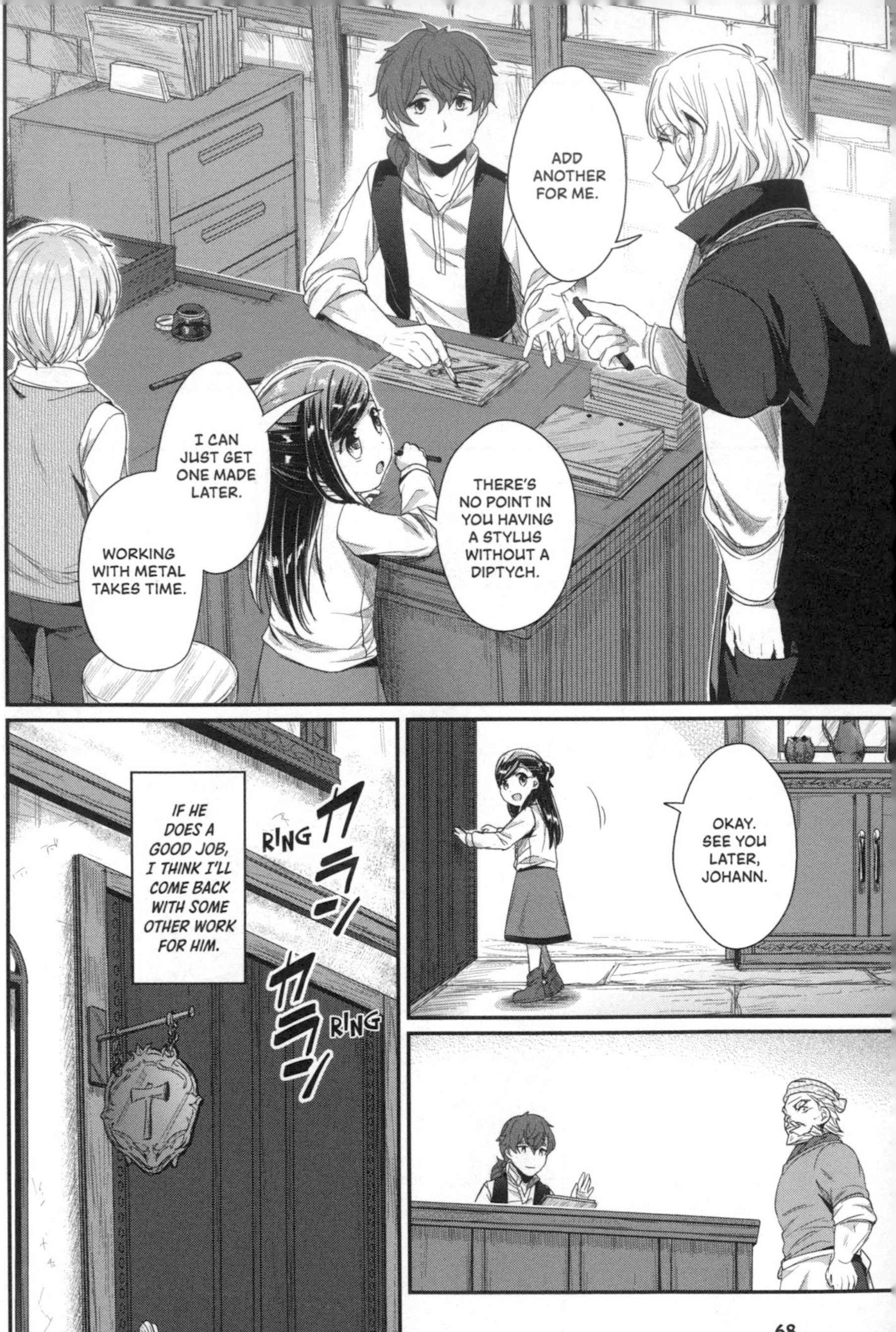
ADD ANOTHER FOR ME.
THERE'S NO POINT IN YOU HAVING A STYLUS WITHOUT A DIPTYCH.
I CAN JUST GET ONE MADE LATER.
WORKING WITH METAL TAKES TIME.
OKAY. SEE YOU LATER, JOHANN.
RING
RING
IF HE DOES A GOOD JOB, I THINK I'LL COME BACK WITH SOME OTHER WORK FOR HIM.

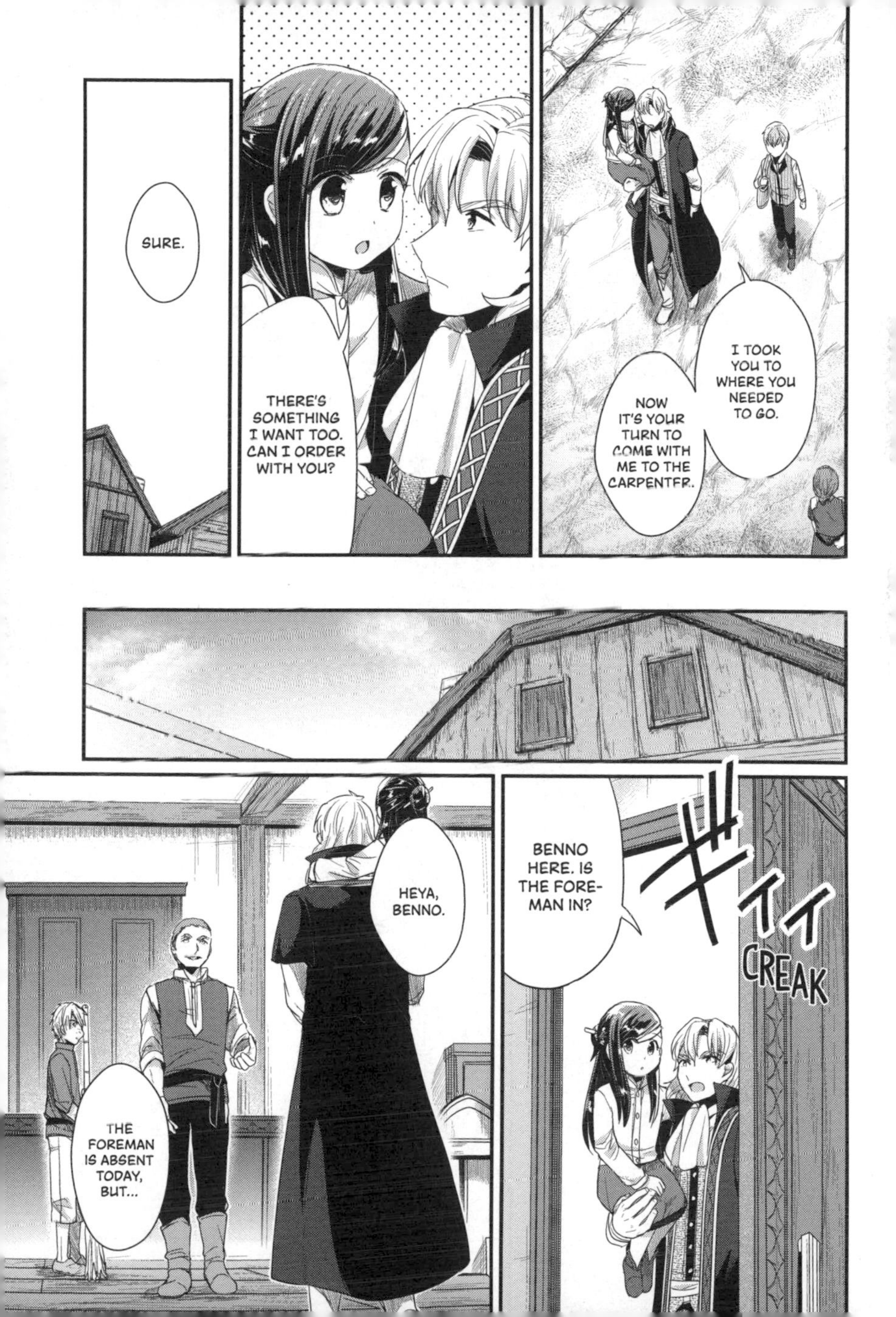
I TOOK YOU TO WHERE YOU NEEDED TO GO.
NOW IT'S YOUR TURN TO COME WITH ME TO THE CARPENTER.
THERE'S SOMETHING I WANT TOO. CAN I ORDER WITH YOU?
SURE.
ギィイ
CREAK
BENNO HERE. IS THE FORE-MAN IN?
HEYA, BENNO.
THE FOREMAN IS ABSENT TODAY, BUT...

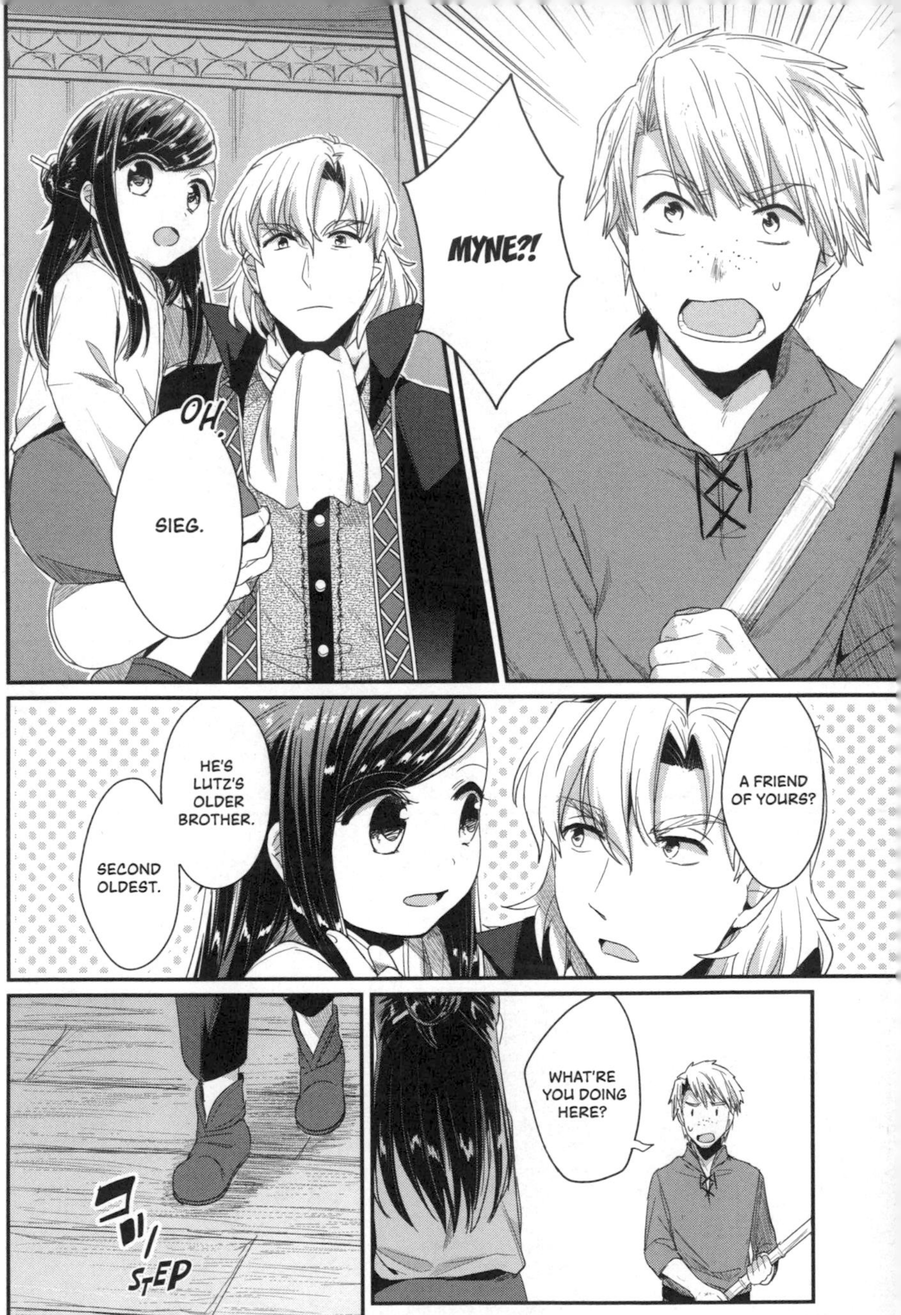
MYNE?!
OH.
SIEG.
A FRIEND OF YOURS?
HE'S LUTZ'S OLDER BROTHER.
SECOND OLDEST.
WHAT'RE YOU DOING HERE?
STEP

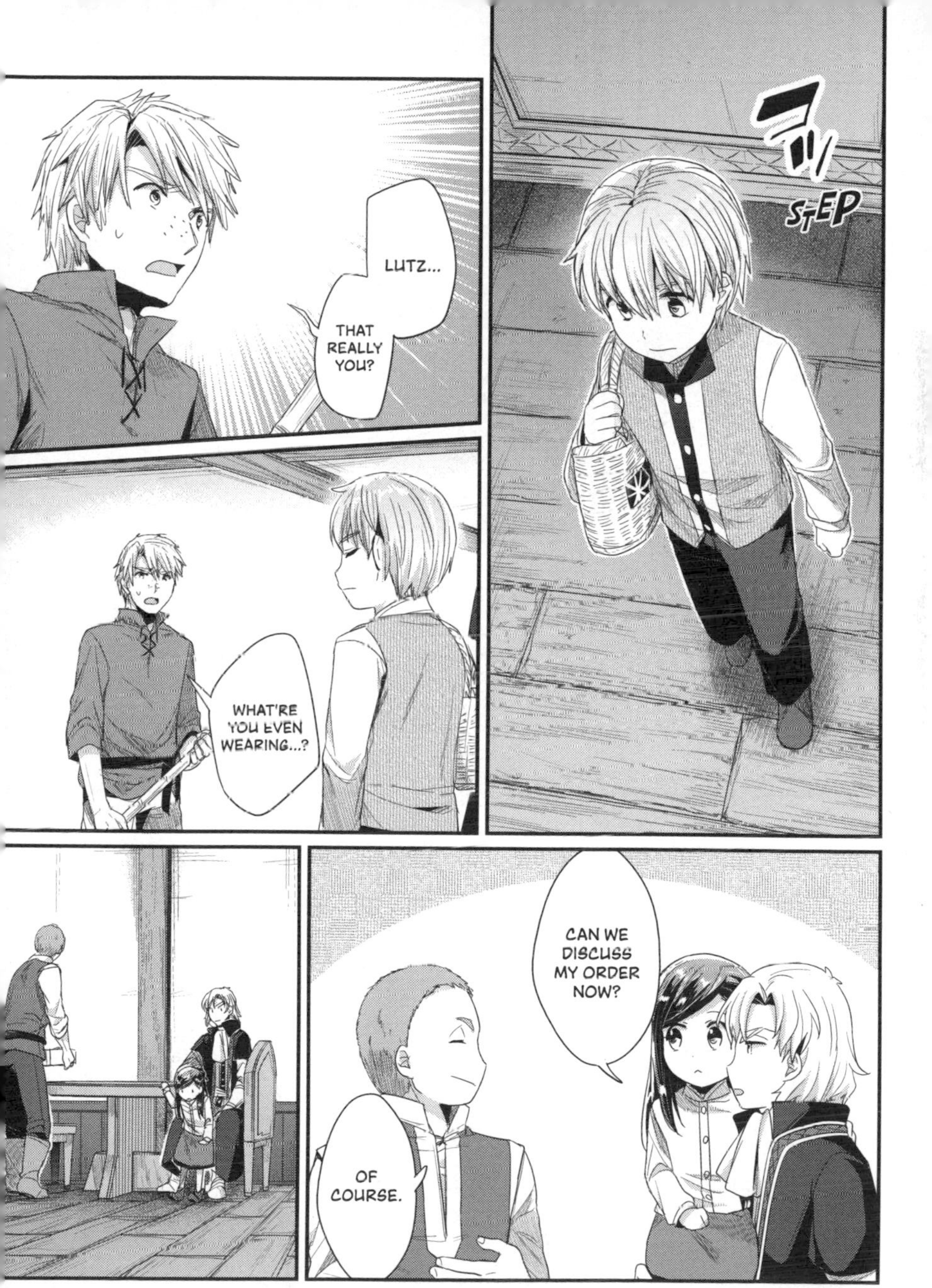
STEP
LUTZ...
THAT REALLY YOU?
WHAT'RE YOU EVEN WEARING...?
CAN WE DISCUSS MY ORDER NOW?
OF COURSE.

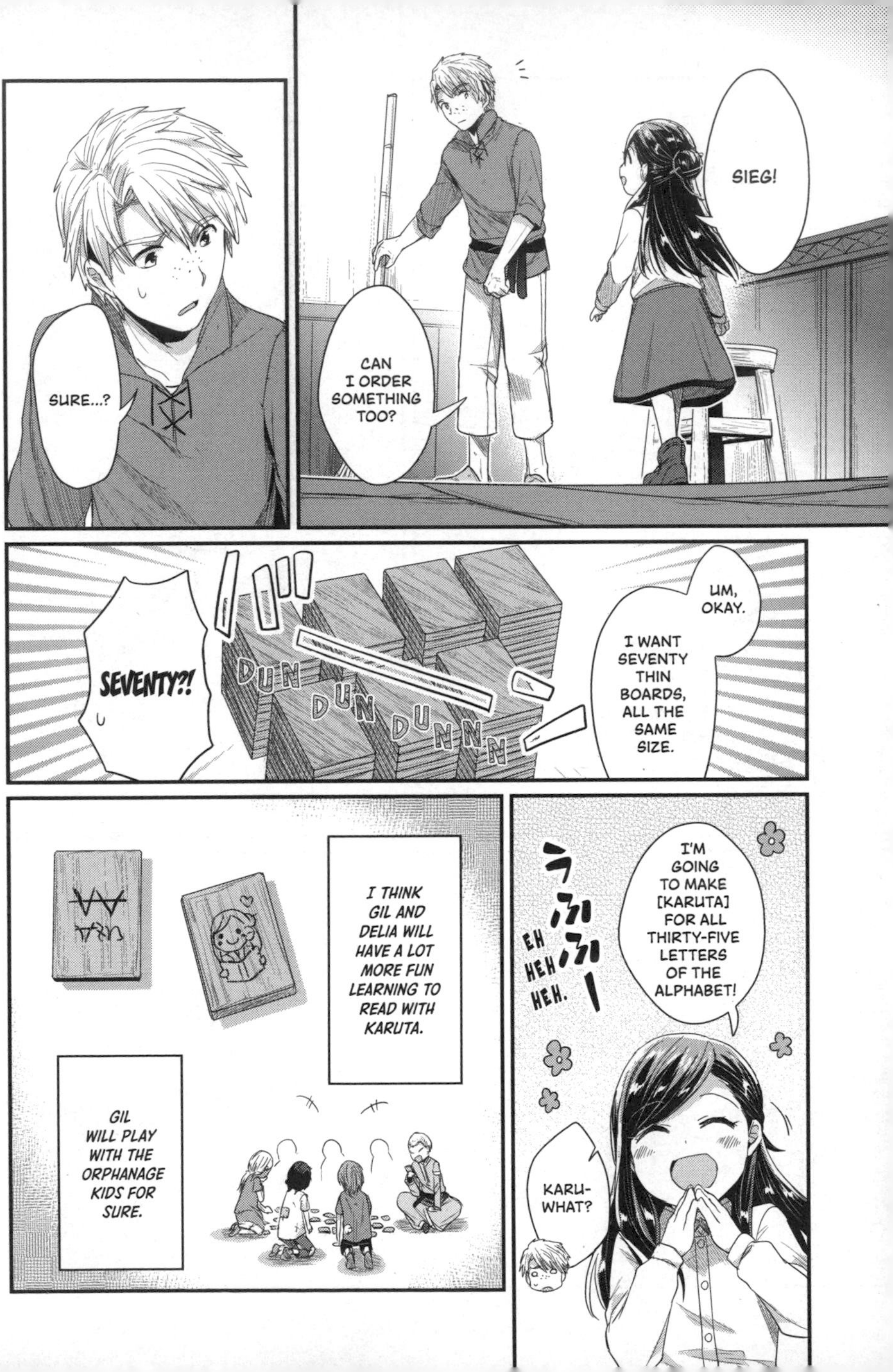
SIEG!
CAN I ORDER SOMETHING TOO?
SURE...?
UM, OKAY.
I WANT SEVENTY THIN BOARDS, ALL THE SAME SIZE.
DUN DUN DUNNN
SEVENTY?!
I'M GOING TO MAKE [KARUTA] FOR ALL THIRTY-FIVE LETTERS OF THE ALPHABET!
うふふー
EH HEH HEH.
KARU-WHAT?
I THINK GIL AND DELIA WILL HAVE A LOT MORE FUN LEARNING TO READ WITH KARUTA.
GIL WILL PLAY WITH THE ORPHANAGE KIDS FOR SURE.

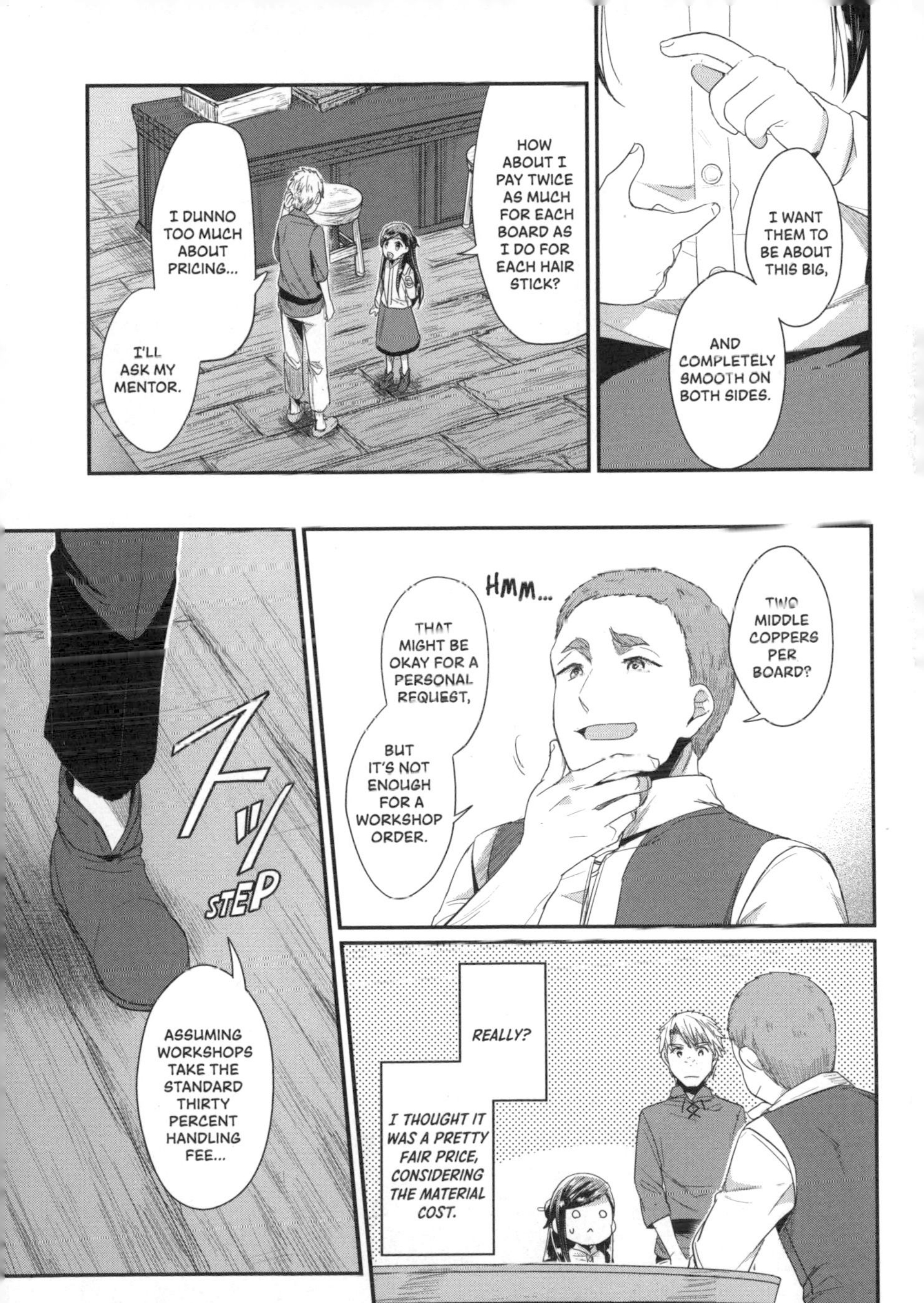
I WANT THEM TO BE ABOUT THIS BIG,
AND COMPLETELY SMOOTH ON BOTH SIDES.
HOW ABOUT I PAY TWICE AS MUCH FOR EACH BOARD AS I DO FOR EACH HAIR STICK?
I DUNNO TOO MUCH ABOUT PRICING...
I'LL ASK MY MENTOR.
TWO MIDDLE COPPERS PER BOARD?
HMM...
THAT MIGHT BE OKAY FOR A PERSONAL REQUEST,
BUT IT'S NOT ENOUGH FOR A WORKSHOP ORDER.
REALLY?
I THOUGHT IT WAS A PRETTY FAIR PRICE, CONSIDERING THE MATERIAL COST.
STEP
ASSUMING WORKSHOPS TAKE THE STANDARD THIRTY PERCENT HANDLING FEE...

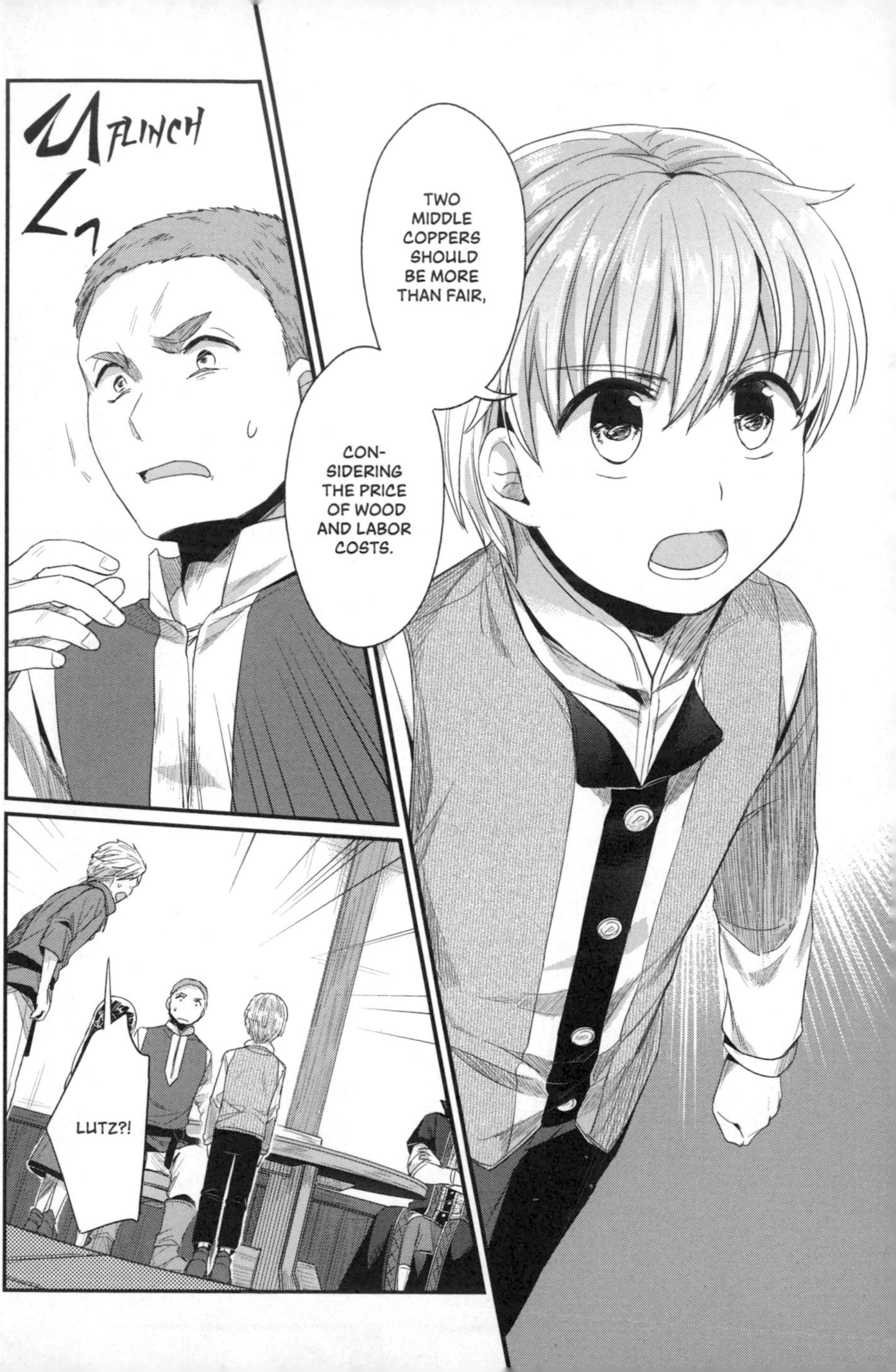
TWO MIDDLE COPPERS SHOULD BE MORE THAN FAIR,
CON-SIDERING THE PRICE OF WOOD AND LABOR COSTS.
FLINCH
LUTZ?!

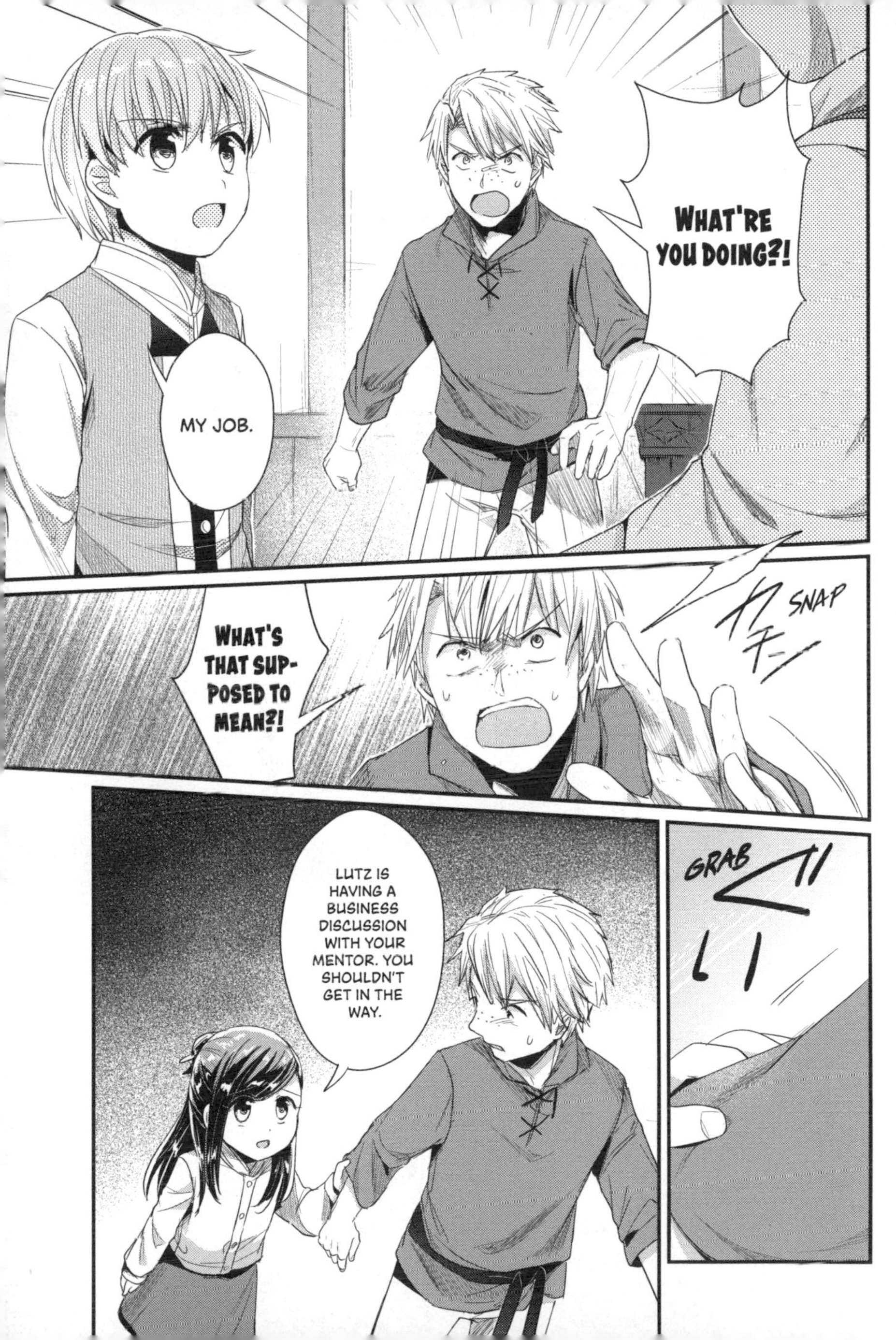
WHAT'RE YOU DOING?!
MY JOB.
SNAP
WHAT'S THAT SUP-POSED TO MEAN?!
GRAB
LUTZ IS HAVING A BUSINESS DISCUSSION WITH YOUR MENTOR. YOU SHOULDN'T GET IN THE WAY.

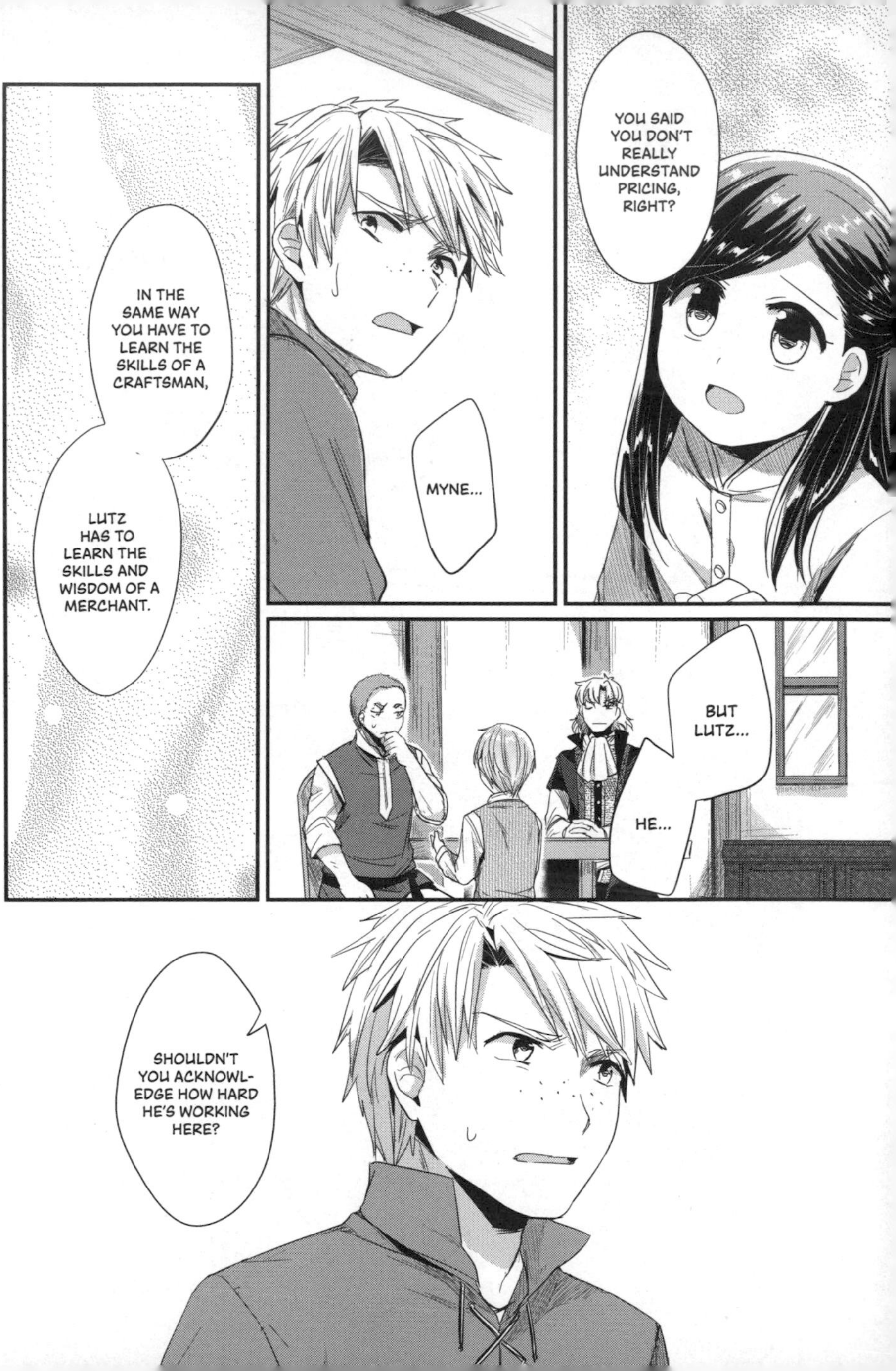
YOU SAID YOU DON'T REALLY UNDERSTAND PRICING, RIGHT?
MYNE...
BUT LUTZ...
HE...
IN THE SAME WAY YOU HAVE TO LEARN THE SKILLS OF A CRAFTSMAN,
LUTZ HAS TO LEARN THE SKILLS AND WISDOM OF A MERCHANT.
SHOULDN'T YOU ACKNOWL-EDGE HOW HARD HE'S WORKING HERE?

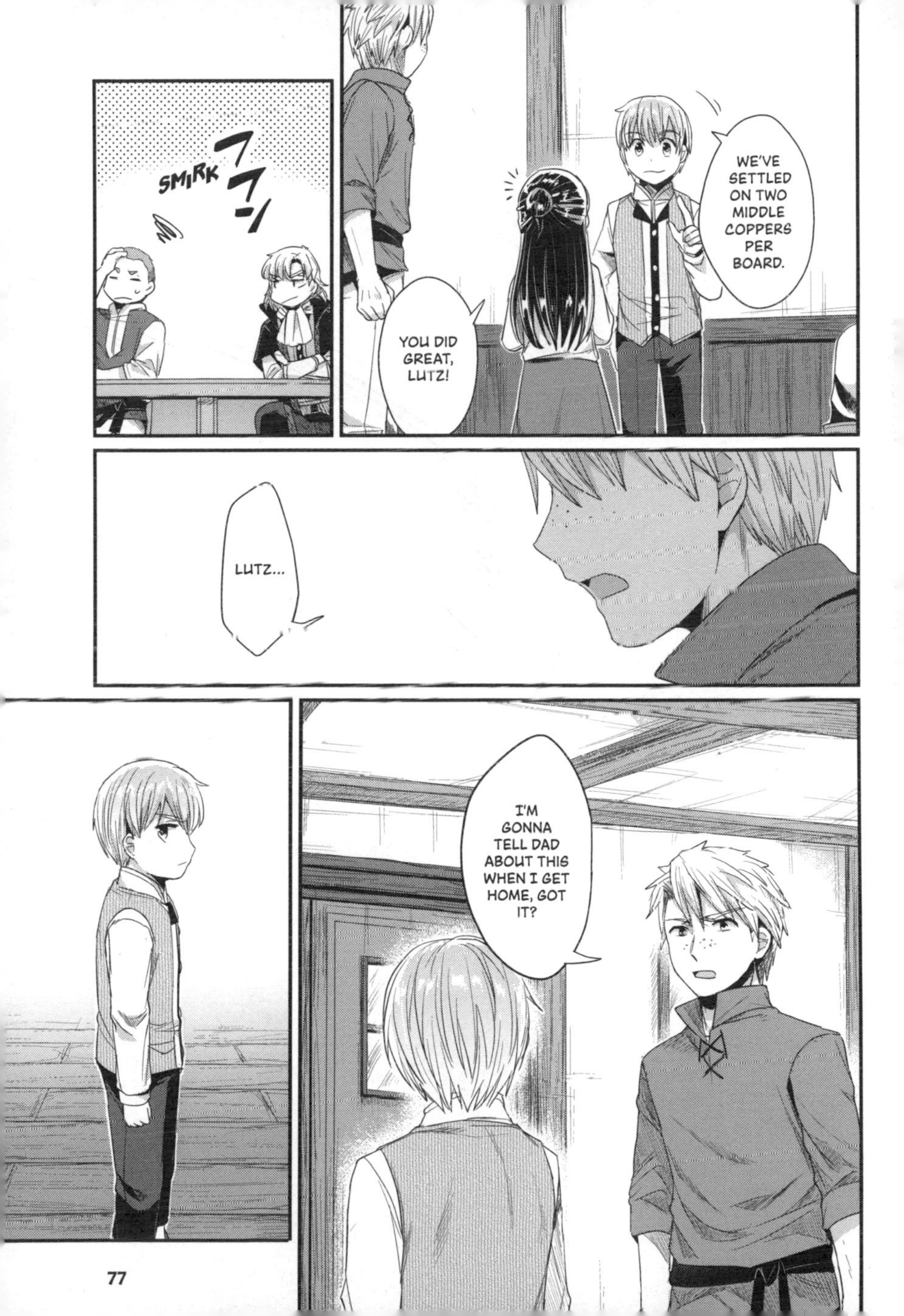
WE'VE SETTLED ON TWO MIDDLE COPPERS PER BOARD.
YOU DID GREAT, LUTZ!
SMIRK
フフン
LUTZ...
I'M GONNA TELL DAD ABOUT THIS WHEN I GET HOME, GOT IT?

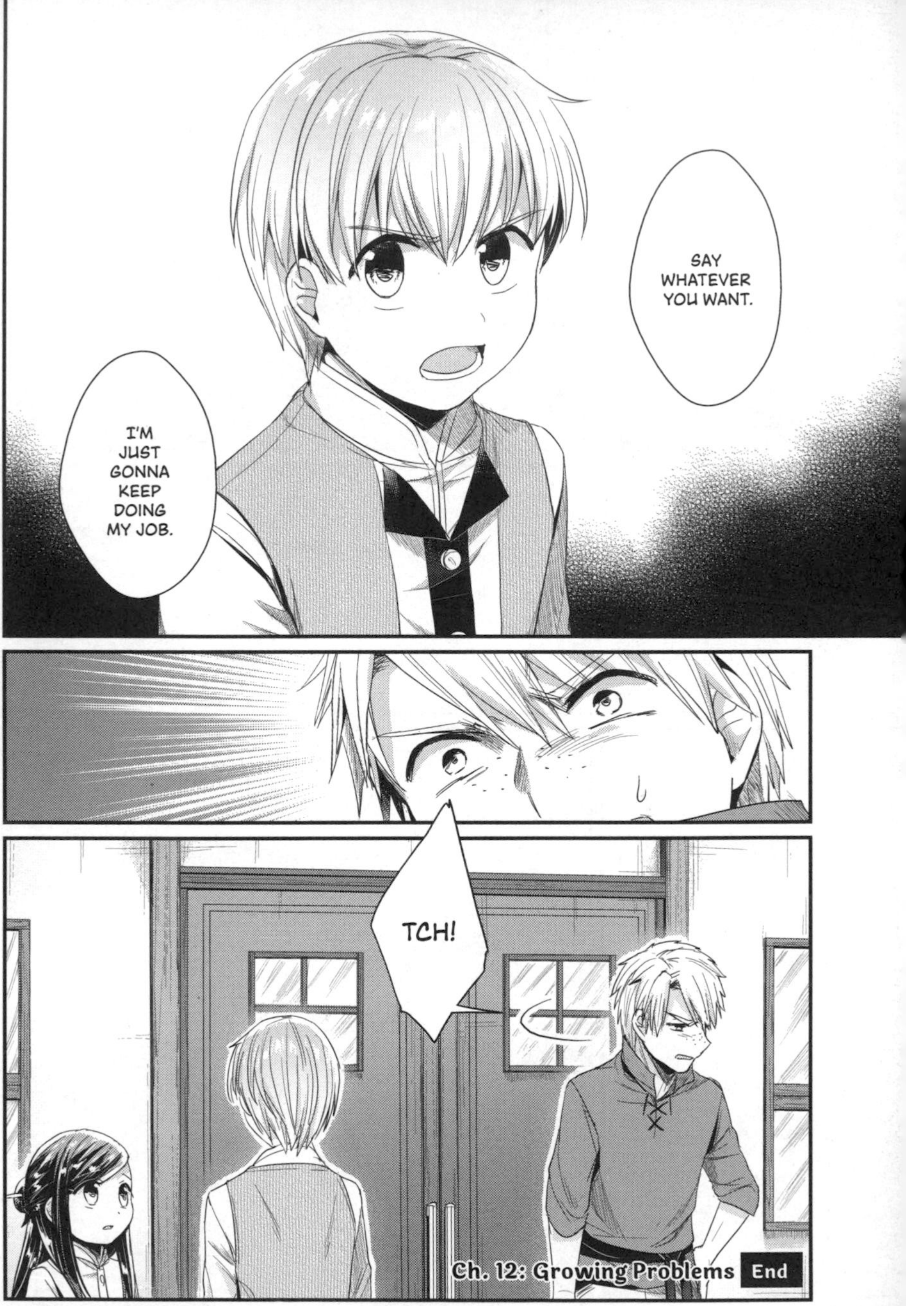
SAY WHATEVER YOU WANT.
I'M JUST GONNA KEEP DOING MY JOB.
TCH!
Ch. 12: Growing Problems End

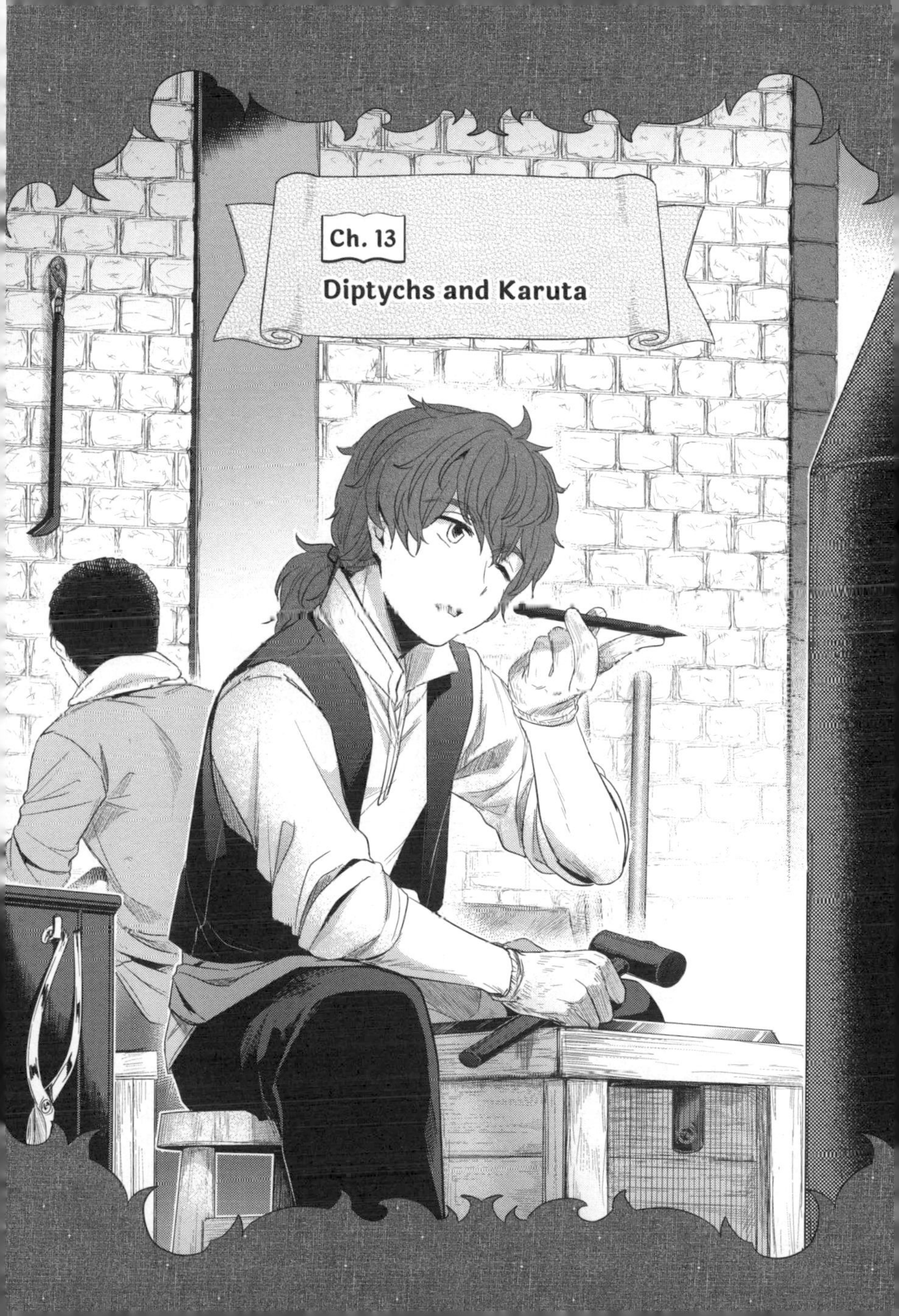
Ch. 13
Diptychs and Karuta

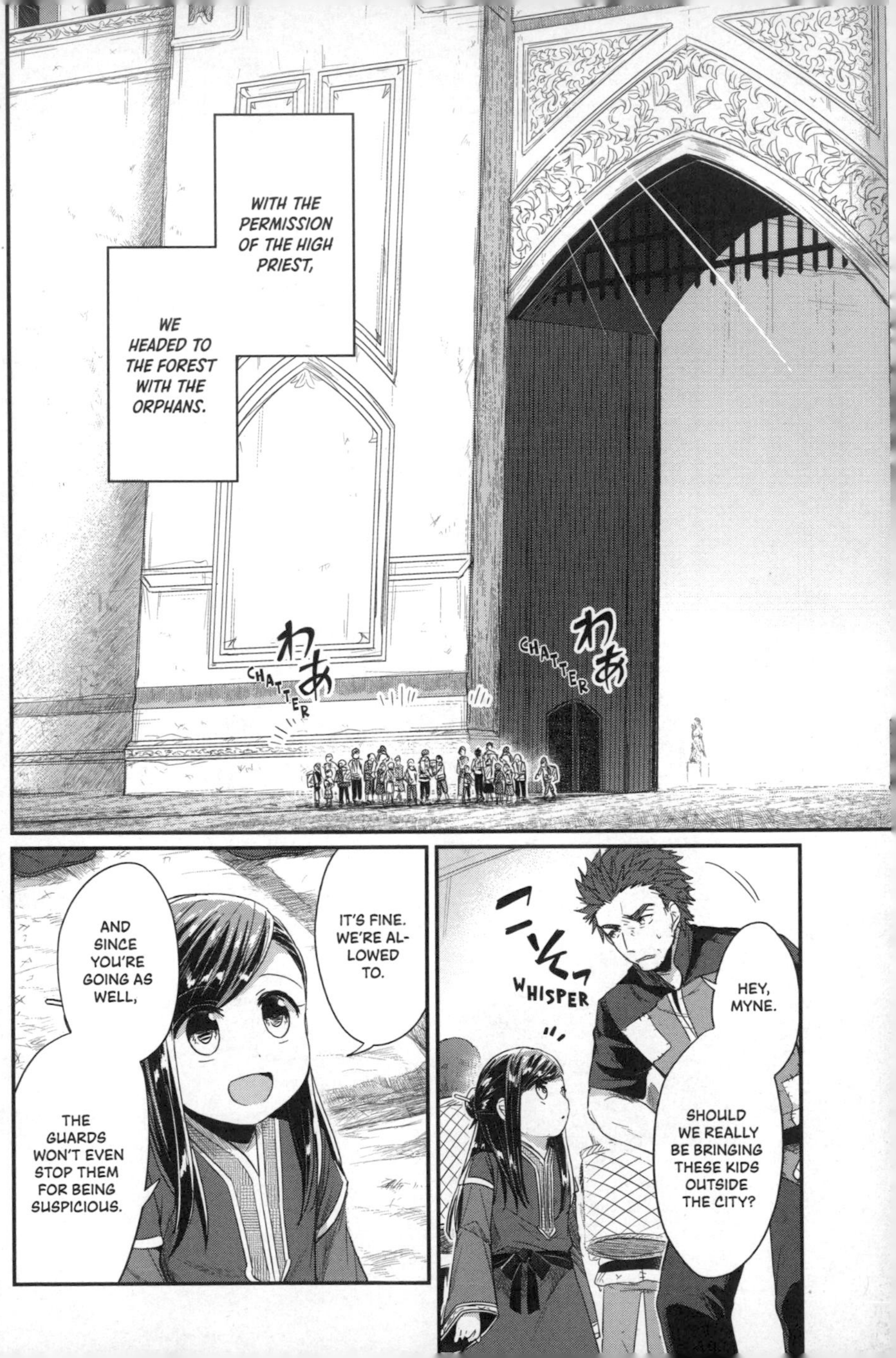
WITH THE PERMISSION OF THE HIGH PRIEST,
WE HEADED TO THE FOREST WITH THE ORPHANS.
わあ CHATTER
わあ CHATTER
WHISPER
HEY, MYNE.
SHOULD WE REALLY BE BRINGING THESE KIDS OUTSIDE THE CITY?
IT'S FINE. WE'RE ALLOWED TO.
AND SINCE YOU'RE GOING AS WELL,
THE GUARDS WON'T EVEN STOP THEM FOR BEING SUSPICIOUS.

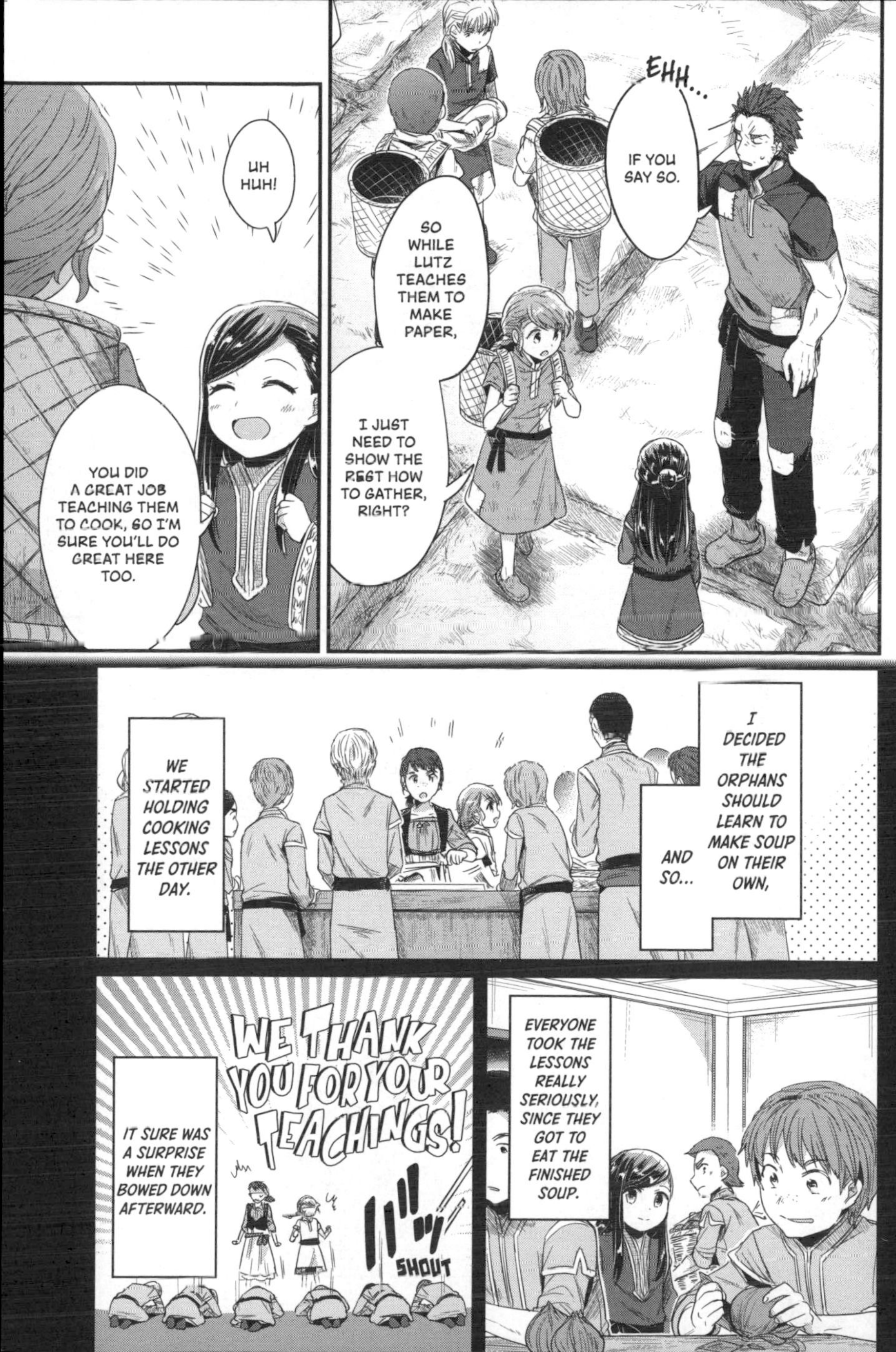
EHH...
IF YOU SAY SO.
SO WHILE LUTZ TEACHES THEM TO MAKE PAPER,
I JUST NEED TO SHOW THE REST HOW TO GATHER, RIGHT?
UH HUH!
YOU DID A GREAT JOB TEACHING THEM TO COOK, SO I'M SURE YOU'LL DO GREAT HERE TOO.
I DECIDED THE ORPHANS SHOULD LEARN TO MAKE SOUP ON THEIR OWN,
AND SO...
WE STARTED HOLDING COOKING LESSONS THE OTHER DAY.
EVERYONE TOOK THE LESSONS REALLY SERIOUSLY, SINCE THEY GOT TO EAT THE FINISHED SOUP.
WE THANK YOU FOR YOUR TEACHINGS!
IT SURE WAS A SURPRISE WHEN THEY BOWED DOWN AFTERWARD.
SHOUT

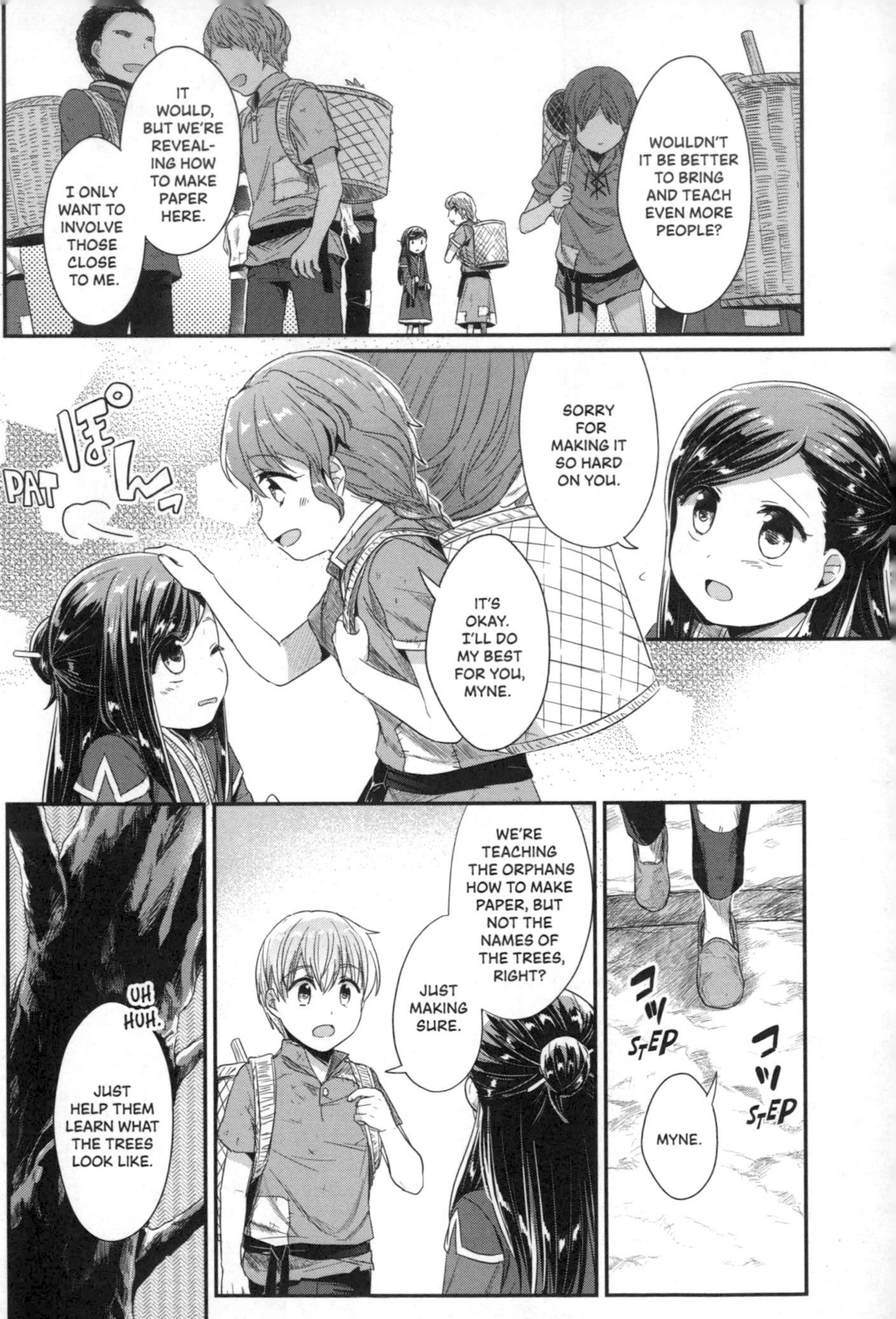
WOULDN'T IT BE BETTER TO BRING AND TEACH EVEN MORE PEOPLE?
IT WOULD, BUT WE'RE REVEAL-ING HOW TO MAKE PAPER HERE.
I ONLY WANT TO INVOLVE THOSE CLOSE TO ME.
SORRY FOR MAKING IT SO HARD ON YOU.
ぽん
PAT
IT'S OKAY. I'LL DO MY BEST FOR YOU, MYNE.
コッ
STEP
コッ
STEP
MYNE.
WE'RE TEACHING THE ORPHANS HOW TO MAKE PAPER, BUT NOT THE NAMES OF THE TREES, RIGHT?
JUST MAKING SURE.
UH HUH.
JUST HELP THEM LEARN WHAT THE TREES LOOK LIKE.

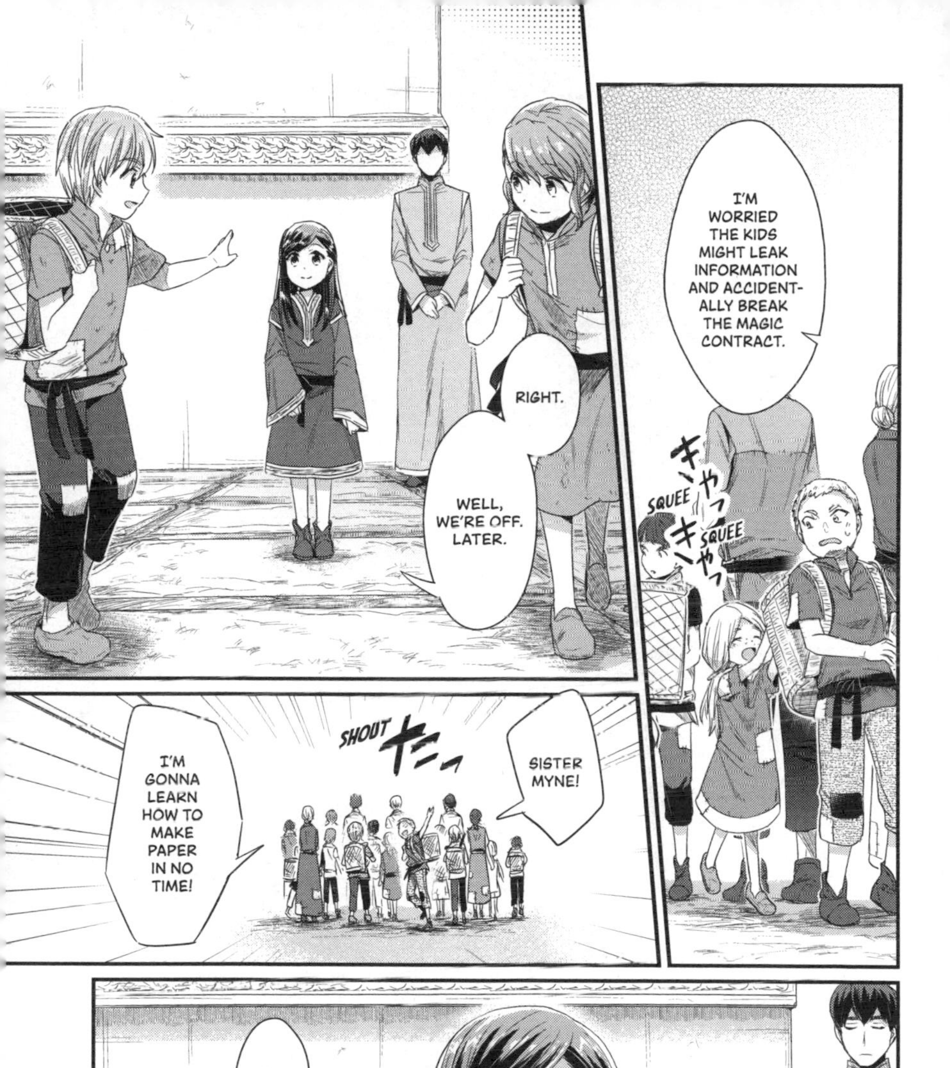
I'M WORRIED THE KIDS MIGHT LEAK INFORMATION AND ACCIDENT-ALLY BREAK THE MAGIC CONTRACT.
SQUEE
SQUEE
RIGHT.
WELL, WE'RE OFF. LATER.
SISTER MYNE!
SHOUT
I'M GONNA LEARN HOW TO MAKE PAPER IN NO TIME!
PLEASE DO.

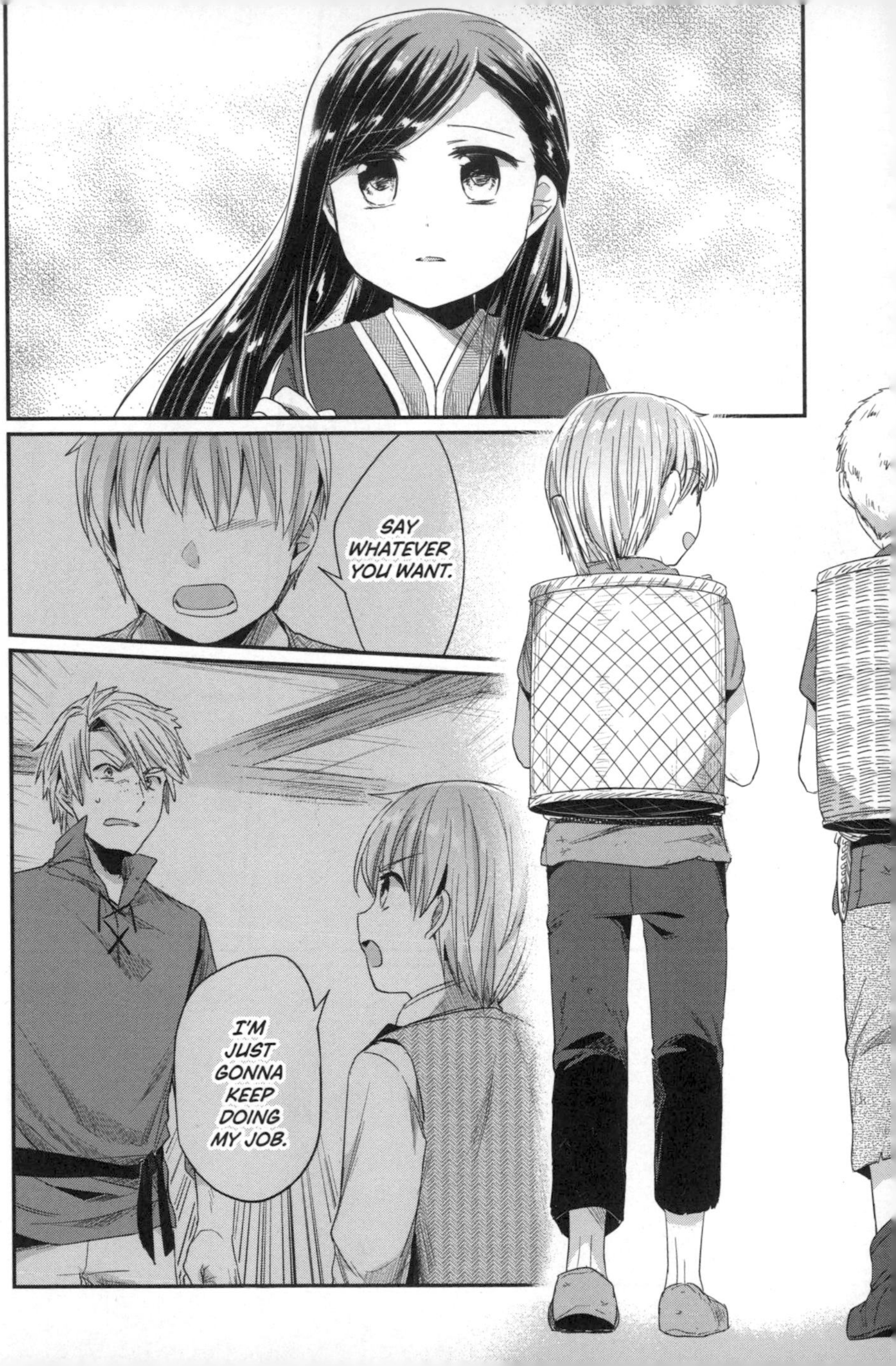
SAY WHATEVER YOU WANT.
I'M JUST GONNA KEEP DOING MY JOB.

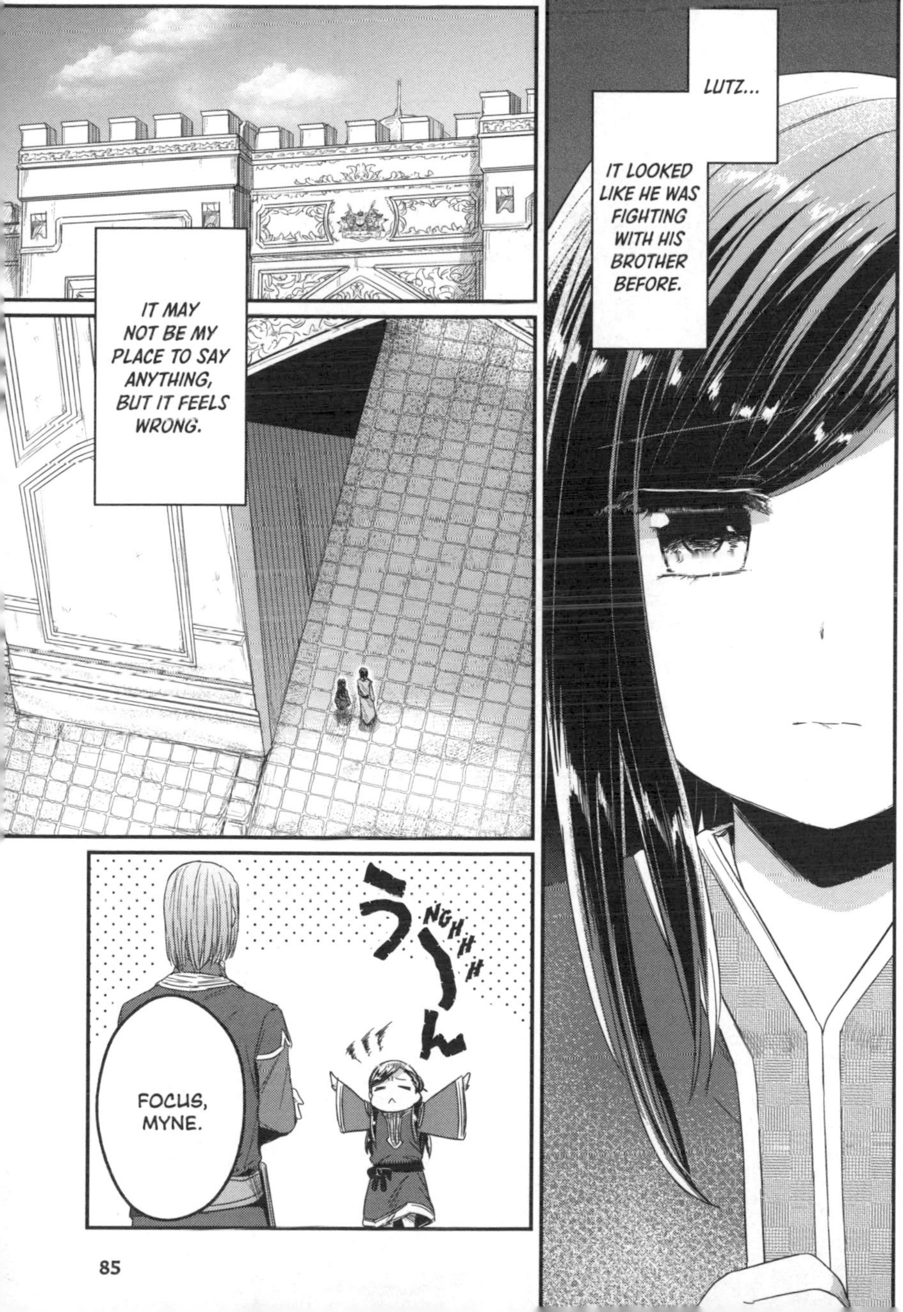
LUTZ...
IT LOOKED LIKE HE WAS FIGHTING WITH HIS BROTHER BEFORE.
IT MAY NOT BE MY PLACE TO SAY ANYTHING, BUT IT FEELS WRONG.
うーん
NGHHHH
FOCUS, MYNE.

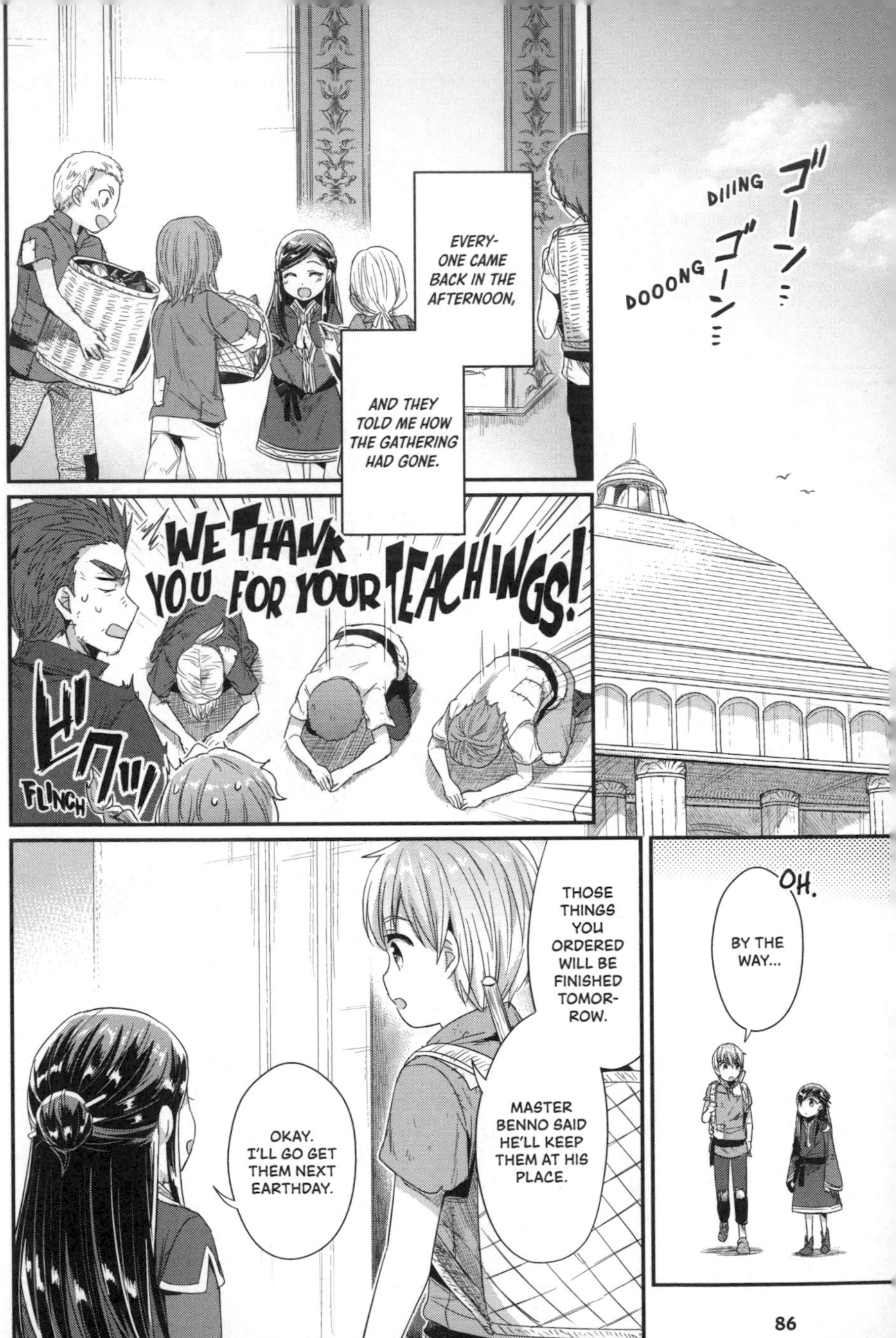
DIIING
ゴーン
DOOONG
ゴーン
EVERY-ONE CAME BACK IN THE AFTERNOON,
AND THEY TOLD ME HOW THE GATHERING HAD GONE.
WE THANK YOU FOR YOUR TEACHINGS!
ビクッ
FLINCH
OH.
BY THE WAY...
THOSE THINGS YOU ORDERED WILL BE FINISHED TOMOR-ROW.
MASTER BENNO SAID HE'LL KEEP THEM AT HIS PLACE.
OKAY. I'LL GO GET THEM NEXT EARTHDAY.

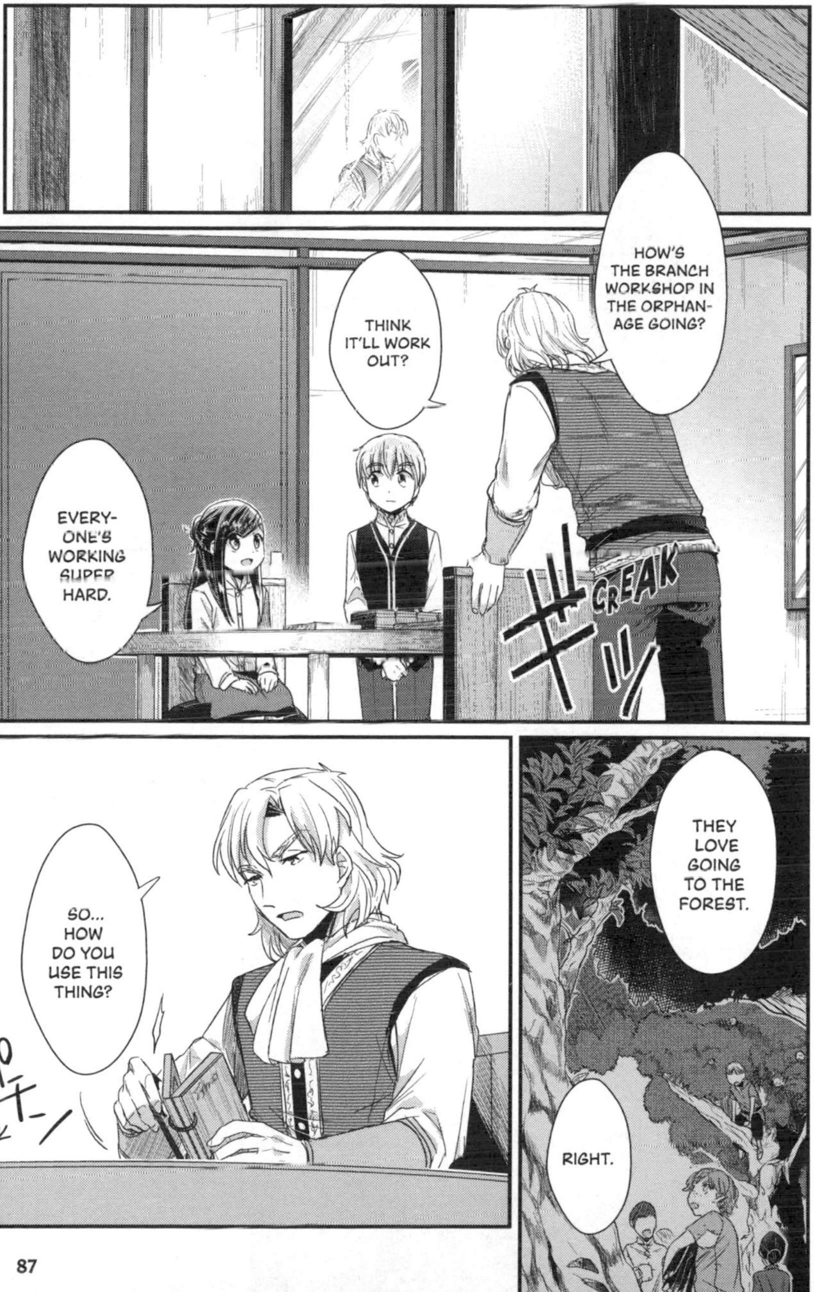
HOW'S THE BRANCH WORKSHOP IN THE ORPHANAGE GOING?
THINK IT'LL WORK OUT?
EVERYONE'S WORKING SUPER HARD.
CREAK
THEY LOVE GOING TO THE FOREST.
RIGHT.
SO... HOW DO YOU USE THIS THING?
CLICK

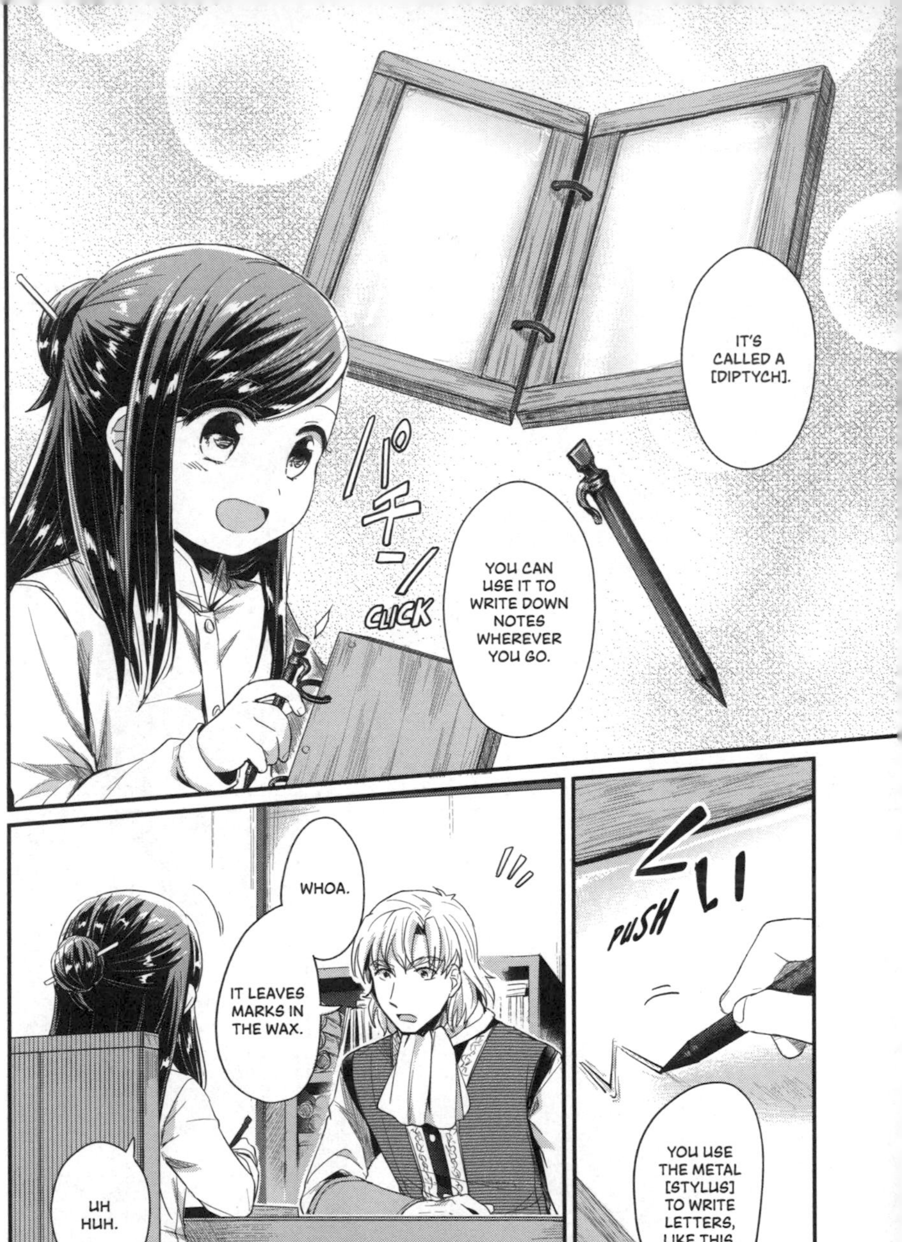
IT'S CALLED A [DIPTYCH].
YOU CAN USE IT TO WRITE DOWN NOTES WHEREVER YOU GO.
パチーン
CLICK
PUSH
YOU USE THE METAL [STYLUS] TO WRITE LETTERS, LIKE THIS.
WHOA.
IT LEAVES MARKS IN THE WAX.
UH HUH.

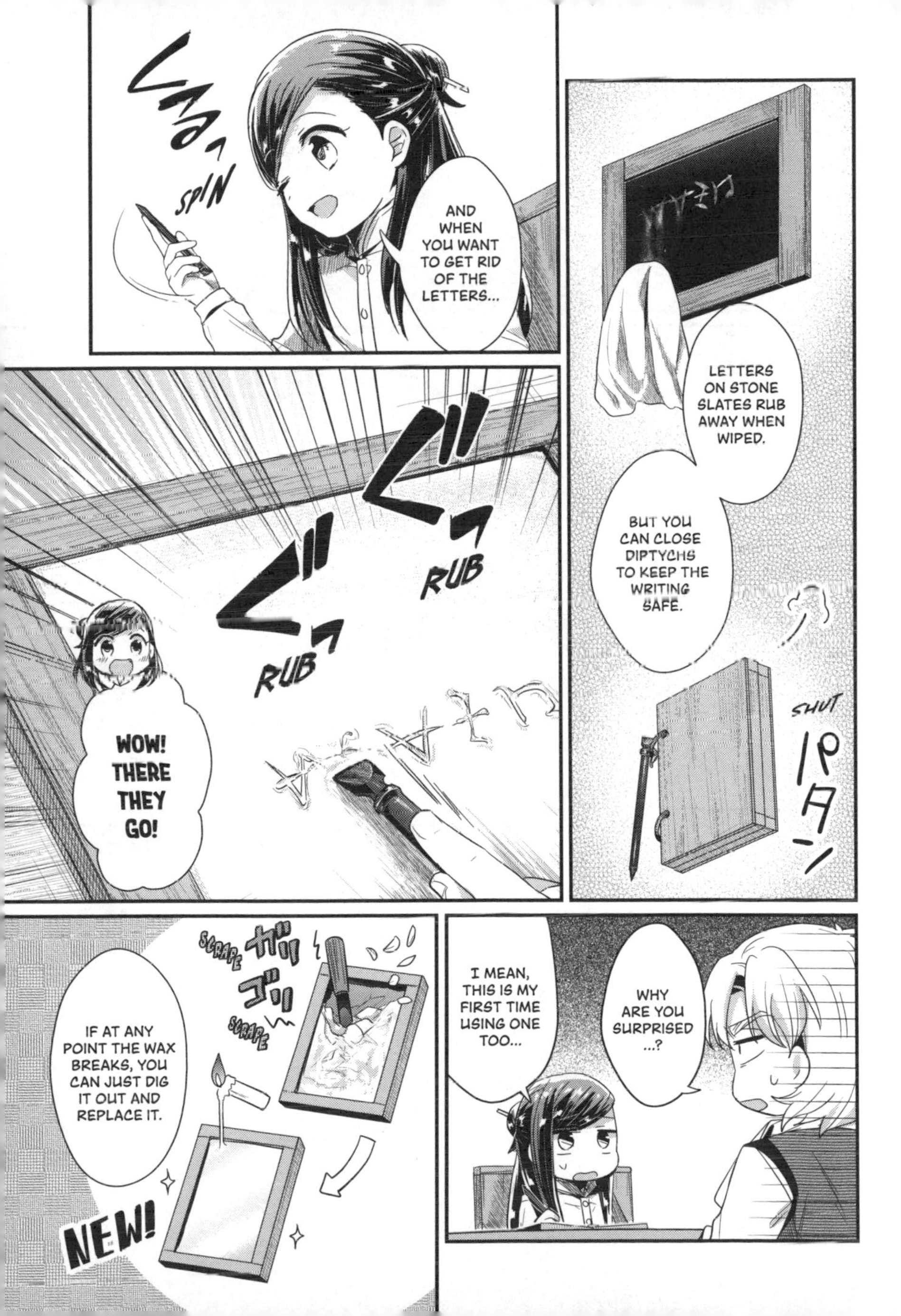
SPIN
AND WHEN YOU WANT TO GET RID OF THE LETTERS...
RUB
RUB
WOW! THERE THEY GO!
LETTERS ON STONE SLATES RUB AWAY WHEN WIPED.
BUT YOU CAN CLOSE DIPTYCHS TO KEEP THE WRITING SAFE.
SHUT
WHY ARE YOU SURPRISED ...?
I MEAN, THIS IS MY FIRST TIME USING ONE TOO...
SCRAPE
SCRAPE
IF AT ANY POINT THE WAX BREAKS, YOU CAN JUST DIG IT OUT AND REPLACE IT.
NEW!

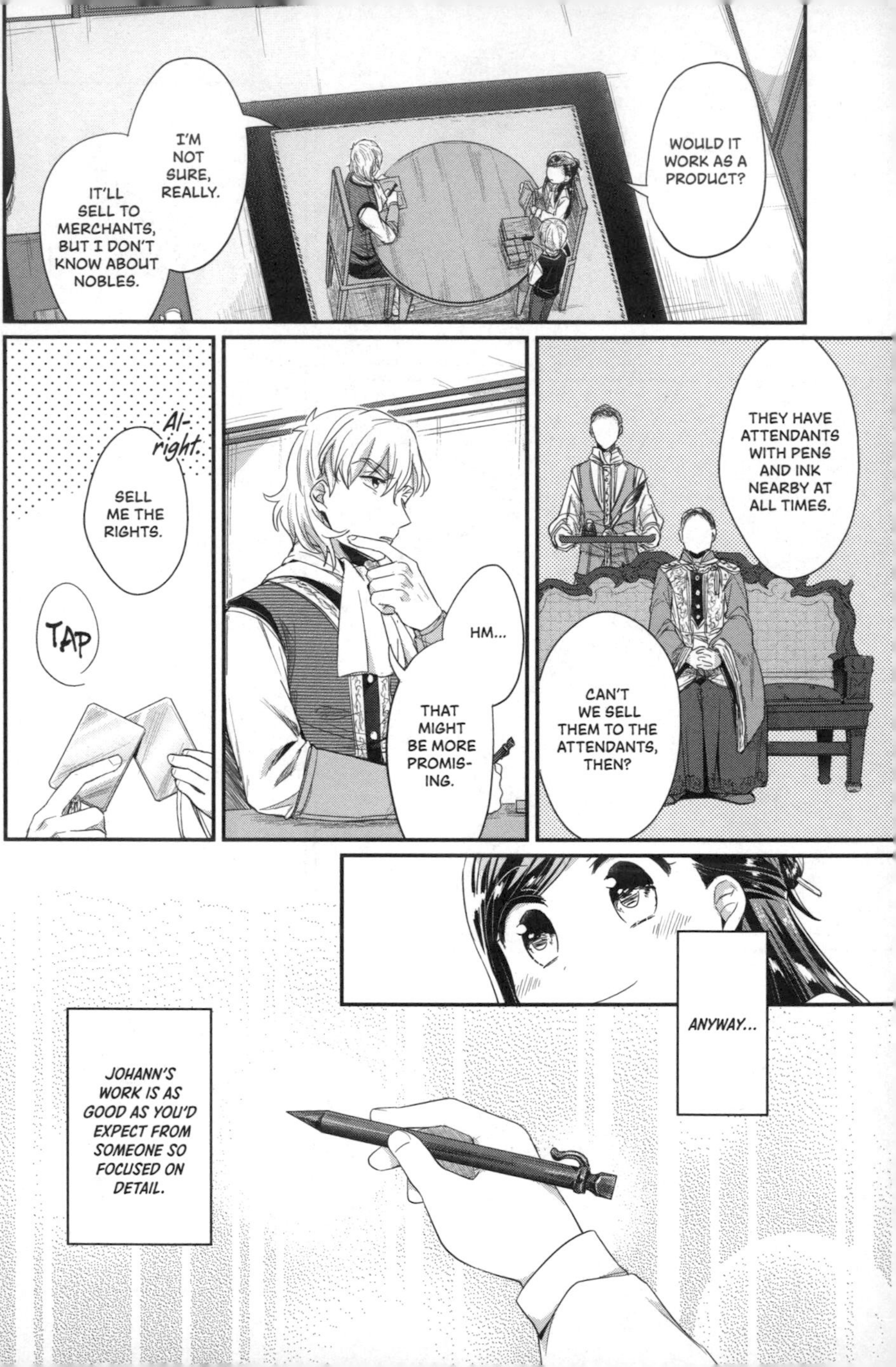
WOULD IT WORK AS A PRODUCT?
I'M NOT SURE, REALLY.
IT'LL SELL TO MERCHANTS, BUT I DON'T KNOW ABOUT NOBLES.
THEY HAVE ATTENDANTS WITH PENS AND INK NEARBY AT ALL TIMES.
CAN'T WE SELL THEM TO THE ATTENDANTS, THEN?
HM...
THAT MIGHT BE MORE PROMIS-ING.
Al-right.
SELL ME THE RIGHTS.
TAP
ANYWAY...
JOHANN'S WORK IS AS GOOD AS YOU'D EXPECT FROM SOMEONE SO FOCUSED ON DETAIL.

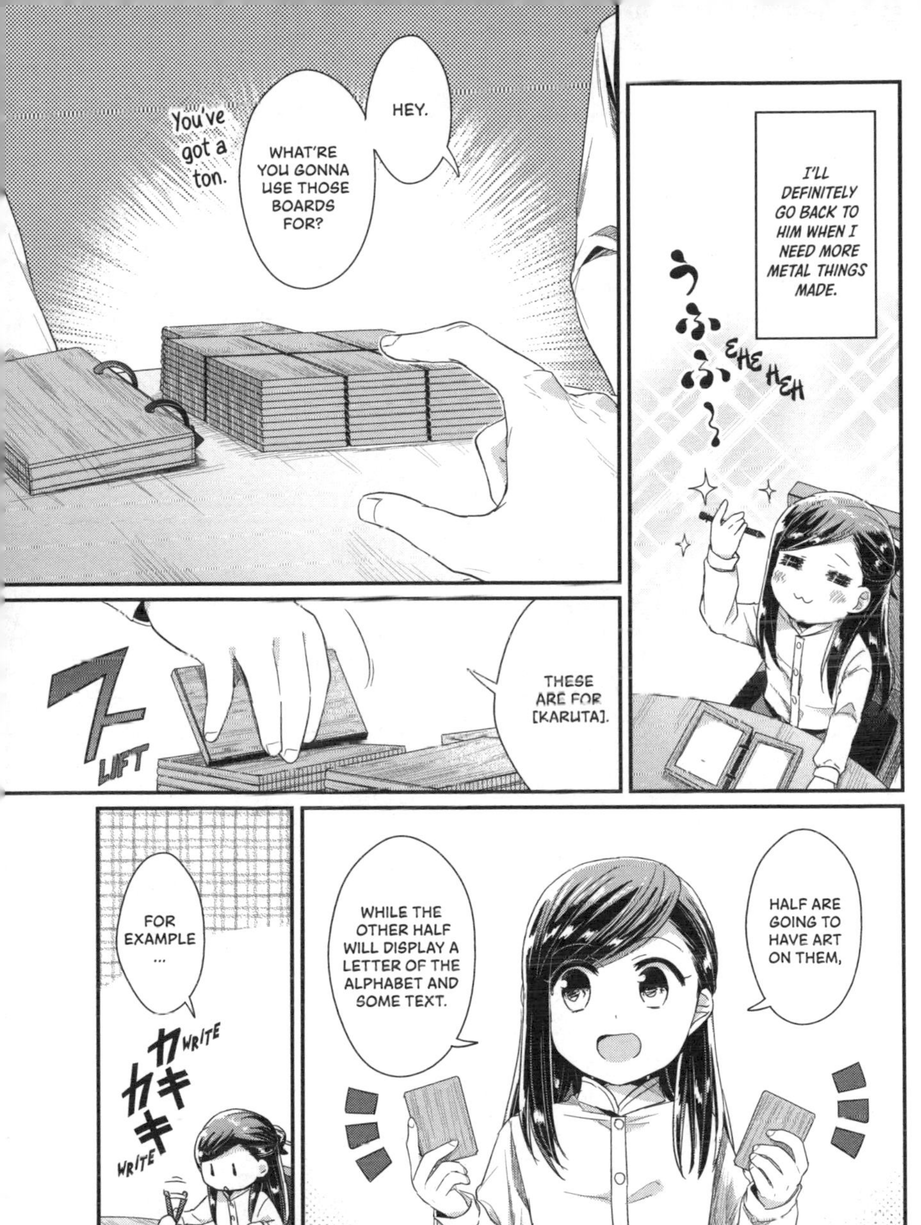
I'LL DEFINITELY GO BACK TO HIM WHEN I NEED MORE METAL THINGS MADE.
うふふ~
EHE HEH
HEY.
WHAT'RE YOU GONNA USE THOSE BOARDS FOR?
You've got a ton.
THESE ARE FOR [KARUTA].
LIFT
HALF ARE GOING TO HAVE ART ON THEM,
WHILE THE OTHER HALF WILL DISPLAY A LETTER OF THE ALPHABET AND SOME TEXT.
FOR EXAMPLE ...
カキカキ
WRITE WRITE

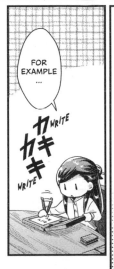

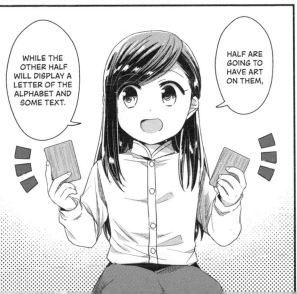

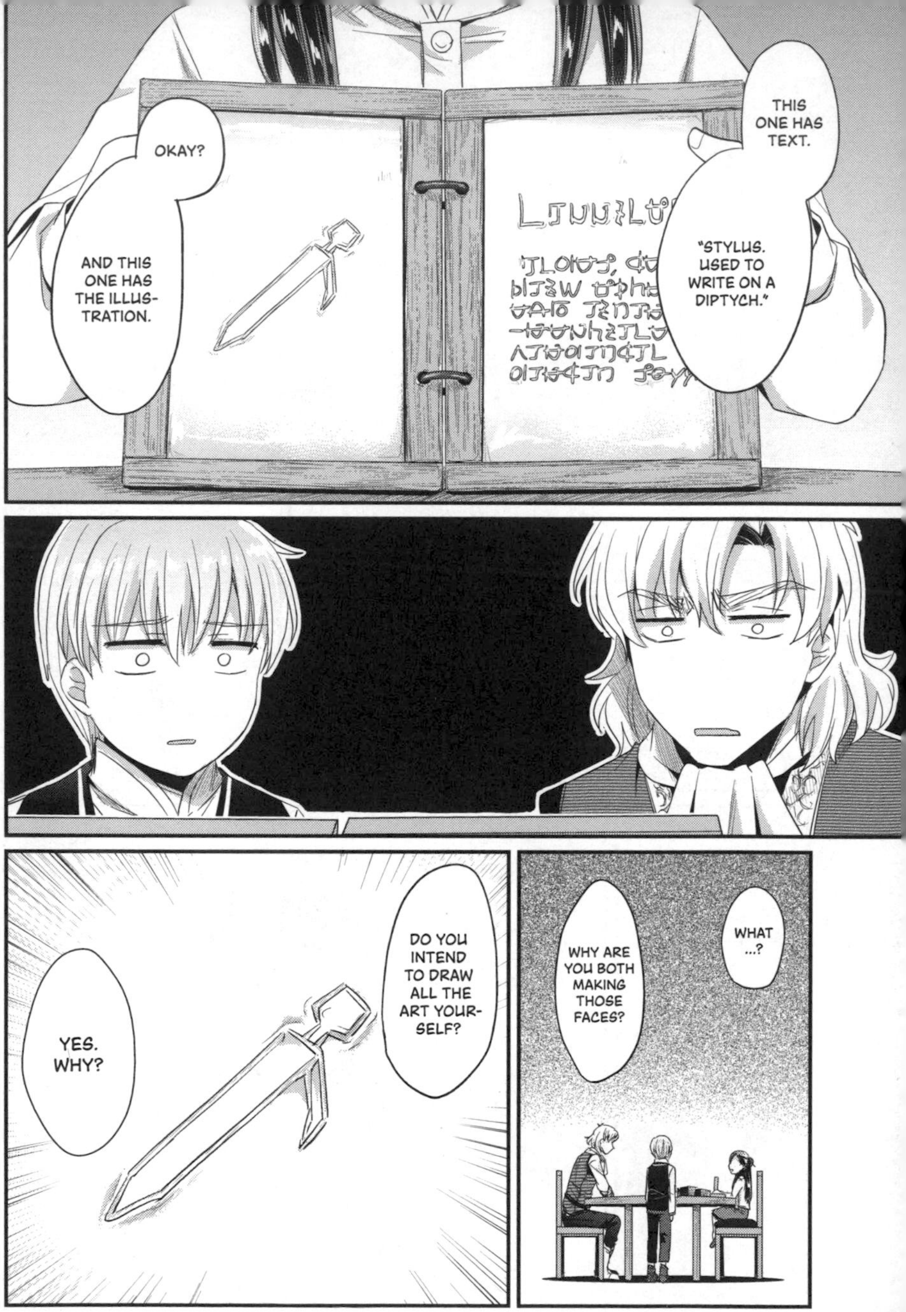
THIS ONE HAS TEXT.
"STYLUS. USED TO WRITE ON A DIPTYCH."
OKAY?
AND THIS ONE HAS THE ILLUSTRATION.
WHAT ...?
WHY ARE YOU BOTH MAKING THOSE FACES?
DO YOU INTEND TO DRAW ALL THE ART YOURSELF?
YES. WHY?

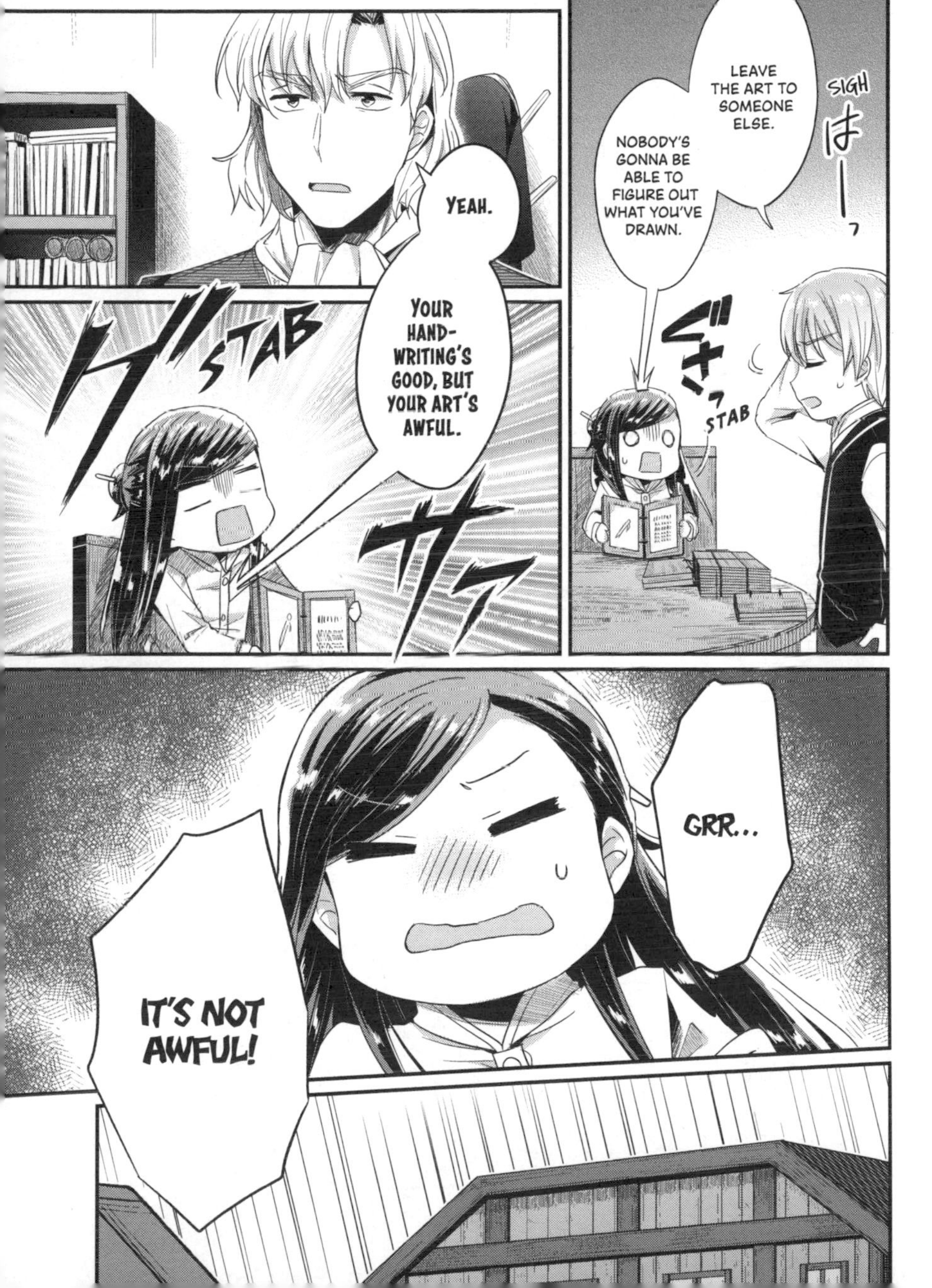
SIGH
LEAVE THE ART TO SOMEONE ELSE.
NOBODY'S GONNA BE ABLE TO FIGURE OUT WHAT YOU'VE DRAWN.
STAB
YEAH.
YOUR HAND-WRITING'S GOOD, BUT YOUR ART'S AWFUL.
STAB
GRR...
IT'S NOT AWFUL!

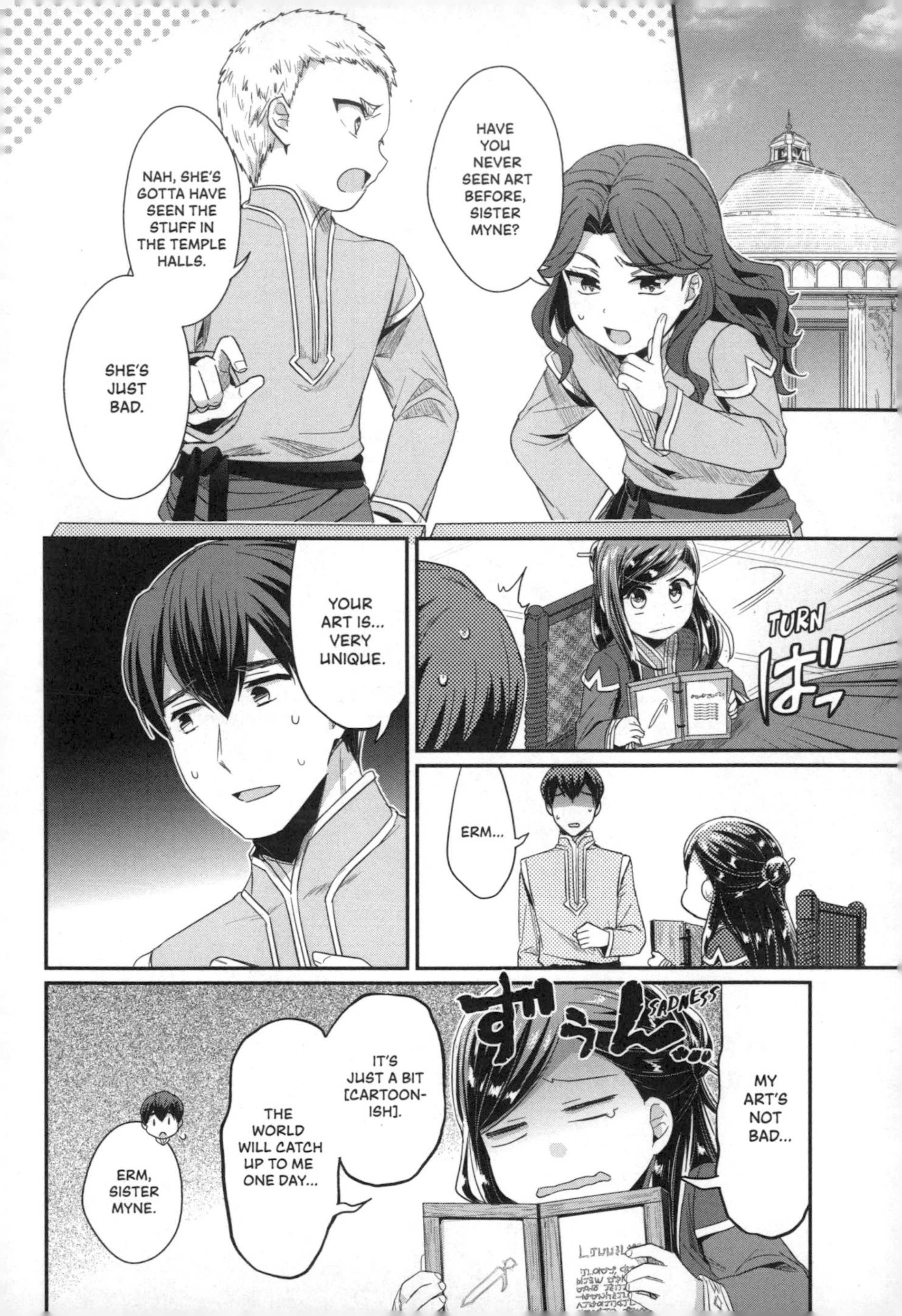
HAVE YOU NEVER SEEN ART BEFORE, SISTER MYNE?
NAH, SHE'S GOTTA HAVE SEEN THE STUFF IN THE TEMPLE HALLS.
SHE'S JUST BAD.
TURN
ばっ
ERM...
YOUR ART IS... VERY UNIQUE.
ずぅん…
SADNESS
MY ART'S NOT BAD...
IT'S JUST A BIT [CARTOON-ISH].
THE WORLD WILL CATCH UP TO ME ONE DAY...
ERM, SISTER MYNE.

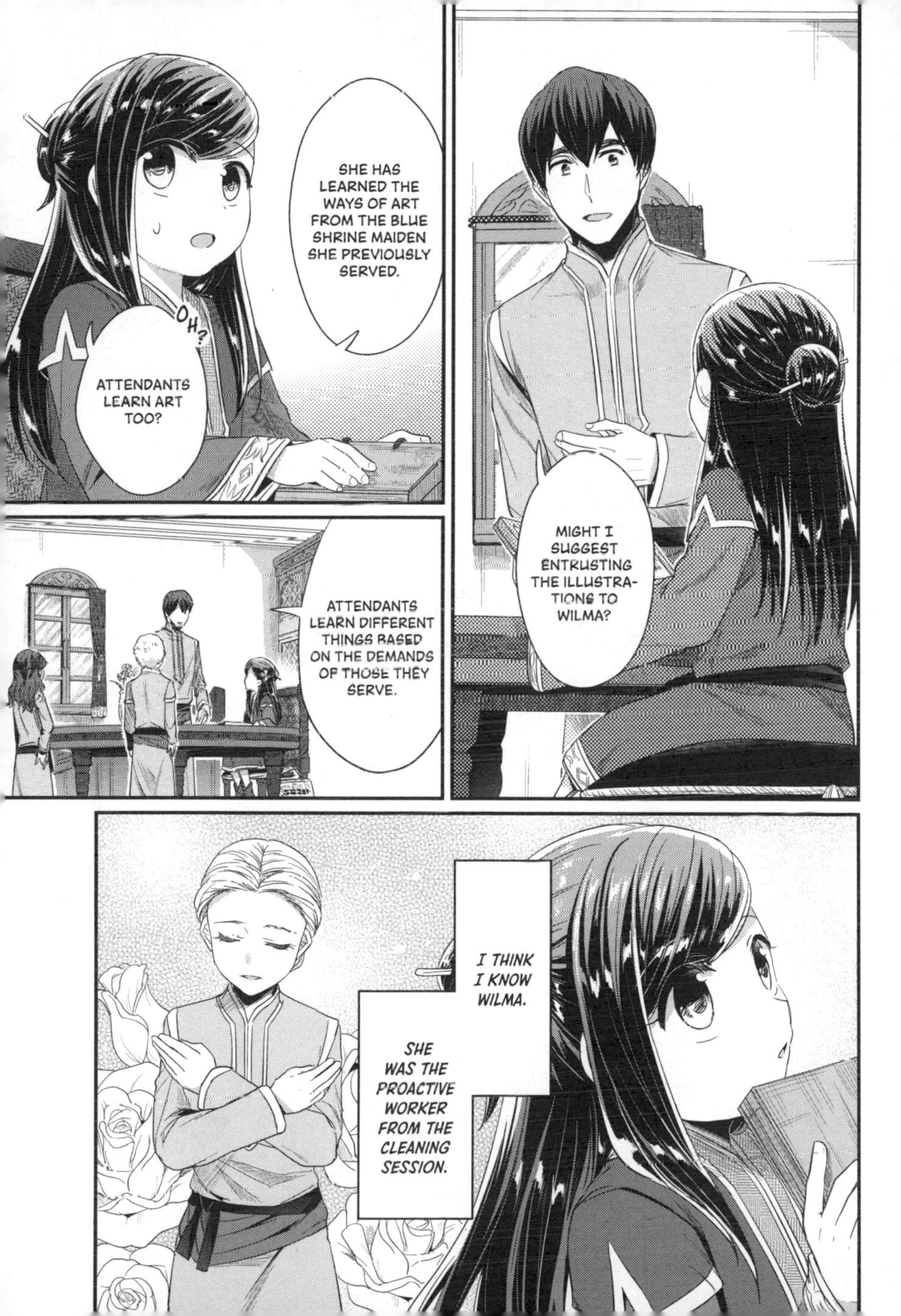
MIGHT I SUGGEST ENTRUSTING THE ILLUSTRATIONS TO WILMA?
SHE HAS LEARNED THE WAYS OF ART FROM THE BLUE SHRINE MAIDEN SHE PREVIOUSLY SERVED.
OH?
ATTENDANTS LEARN ART TOO?
ATTENDANTS LEARN DIFFERENT THINGS BASED ON THE DEMANDS OF THOSE THEY SERVE.
I THINK I KNOW WILMA.
SHE WAS THE PROACTIVE WORKER FROM THE CLEANING SESSION.

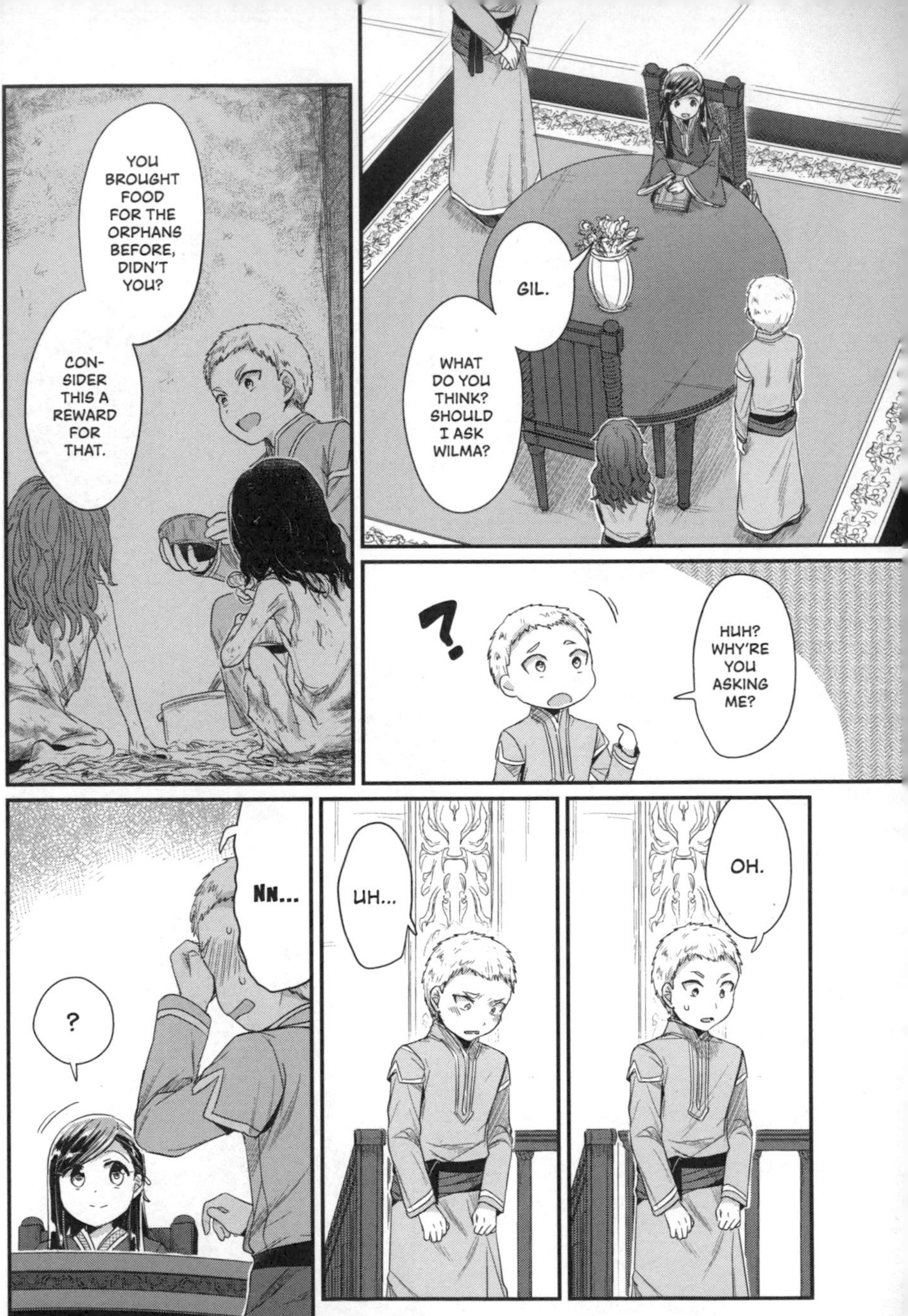
GIL.
WHAT DO YOU THINK? SHOULD I ASK WILMA?
?
HUH? WHY'RE YOU ASKING ME?
YOU BROUGHT FOOD FOR THE ORPHANS BEFORE, DIDN'T YOU?
CON-SIDER THIS A REWARD FOR THAT.
OH.
UH...
NN...
?

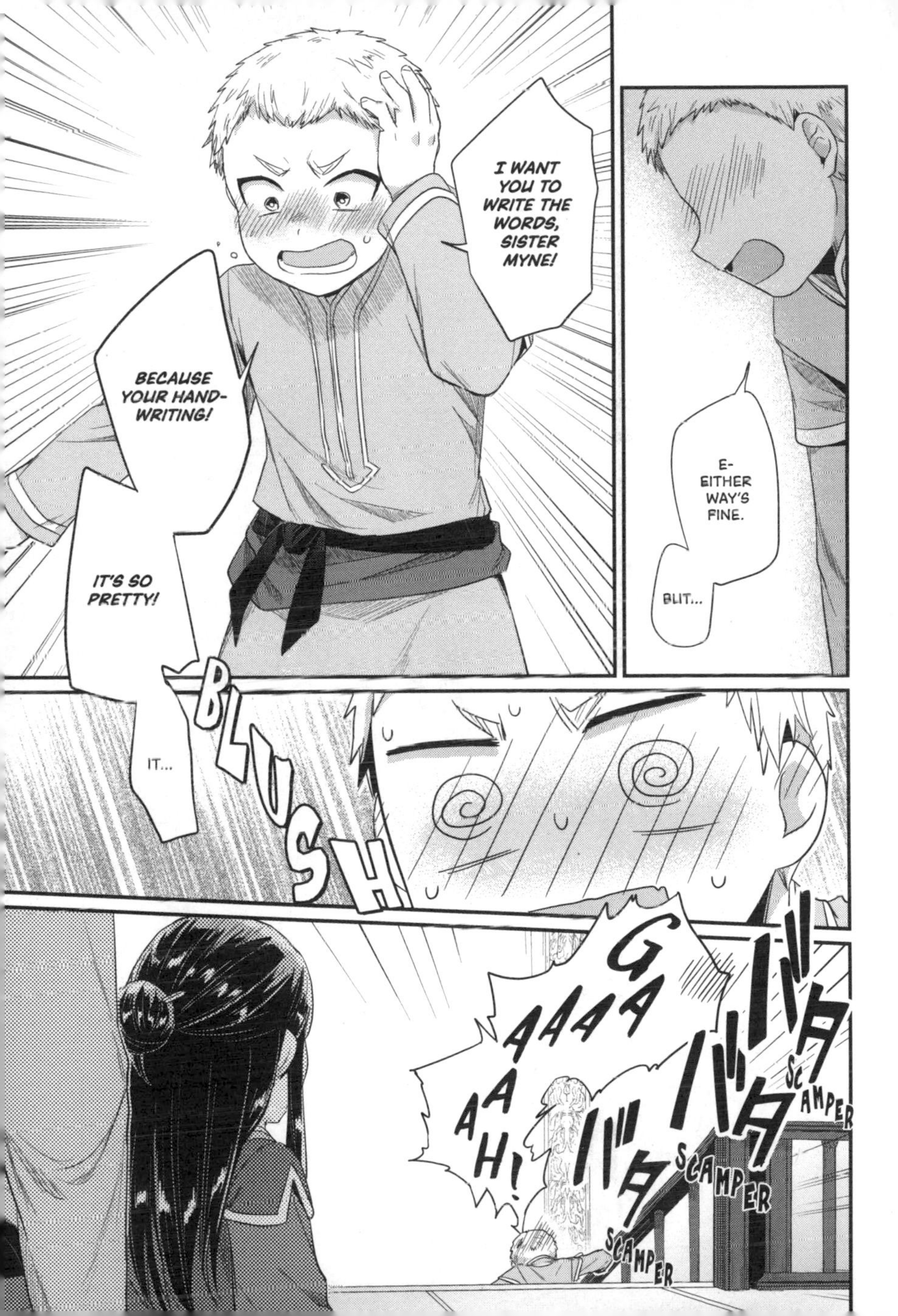
E-
EITHER
WAY'S
FINE.
BUT...
I WANT YOU TO WRITE THE WORDS, SISTER MYNE!
BECAUSE YOUR HAND-WRITING!
IT'S SO PRETTY!
IT...
BLUSH
GAAAAAAAH!
バタバタ
SCAMPER
SCAMPER
SCAMPER

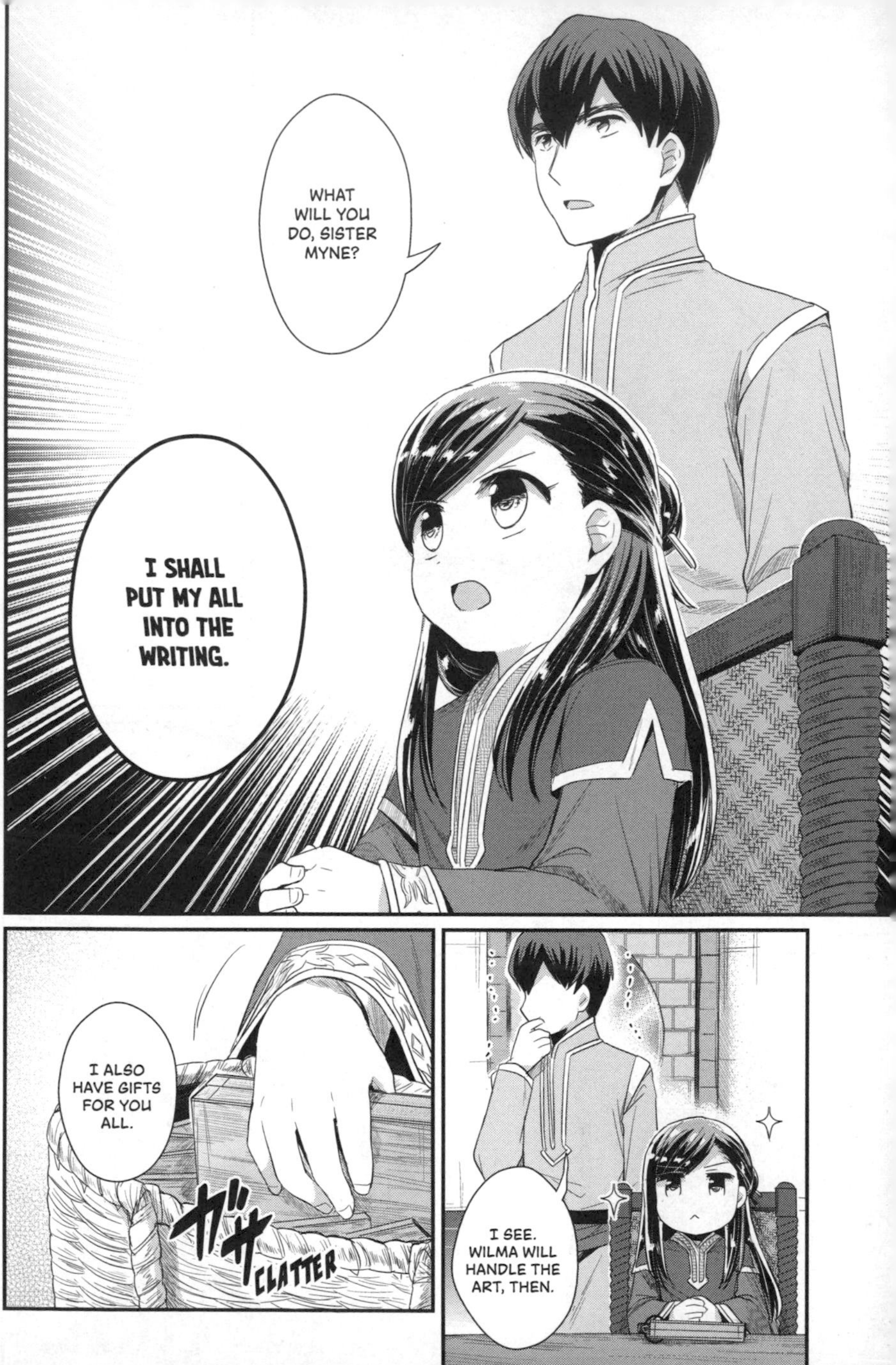
WHAT WILL YOU DO, SISTER MYNE?
I SHALL PUT MY ALL INTO THE WRITING.
I SEE. WILMA WILL HANDLE THE ART, THEN.
I ALSO HAVE GIFTS FOR YOU ALL.
ガサ
CLATTER

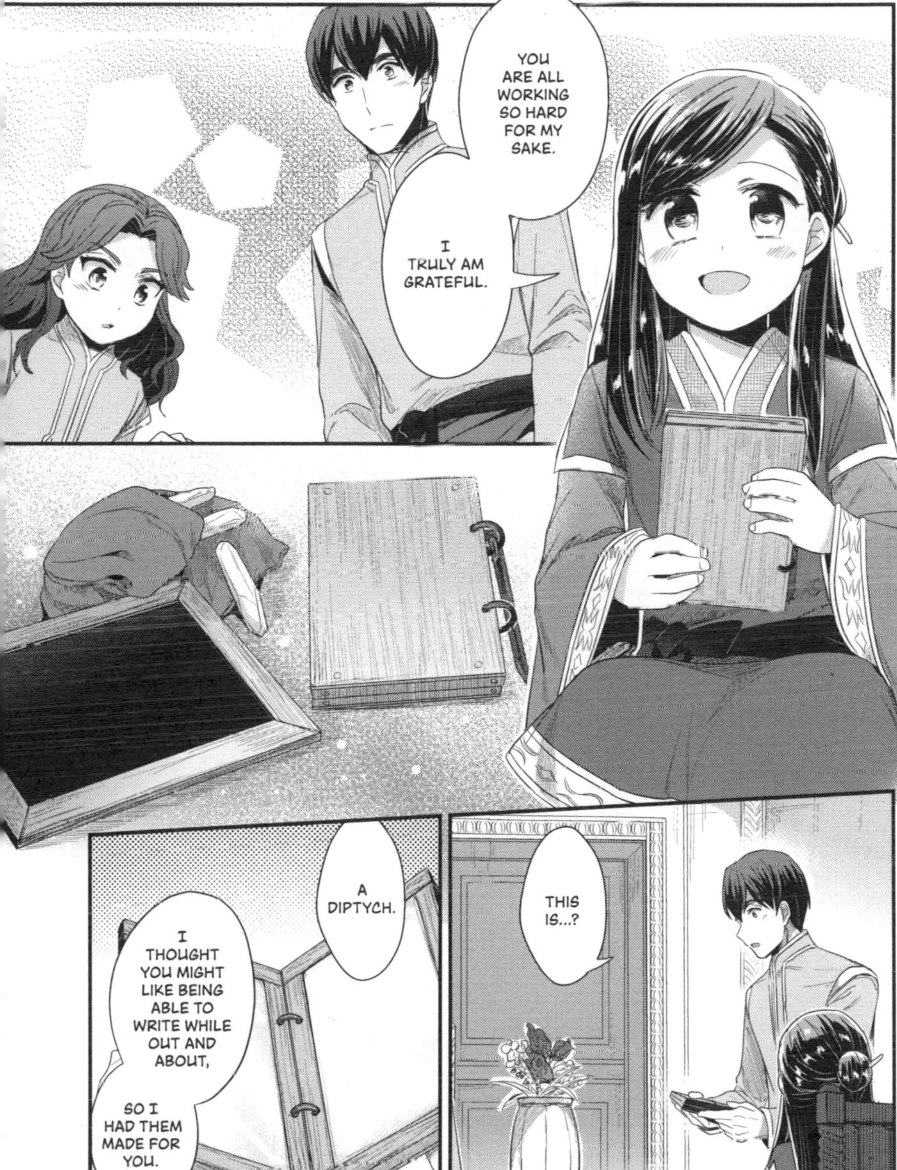
YOU ARE ALL WORKING SO HARD FOR MY SAKE.
I TRULY AM GRATEFUL.
THIS IS...?
A DIPTYCH.
I THOUGHT YOU MIGHT LIKE BEING ABLE TO WRITE WHILE OUT AND ABOUT,
SO I HAD THEM MADE FOR YOU.

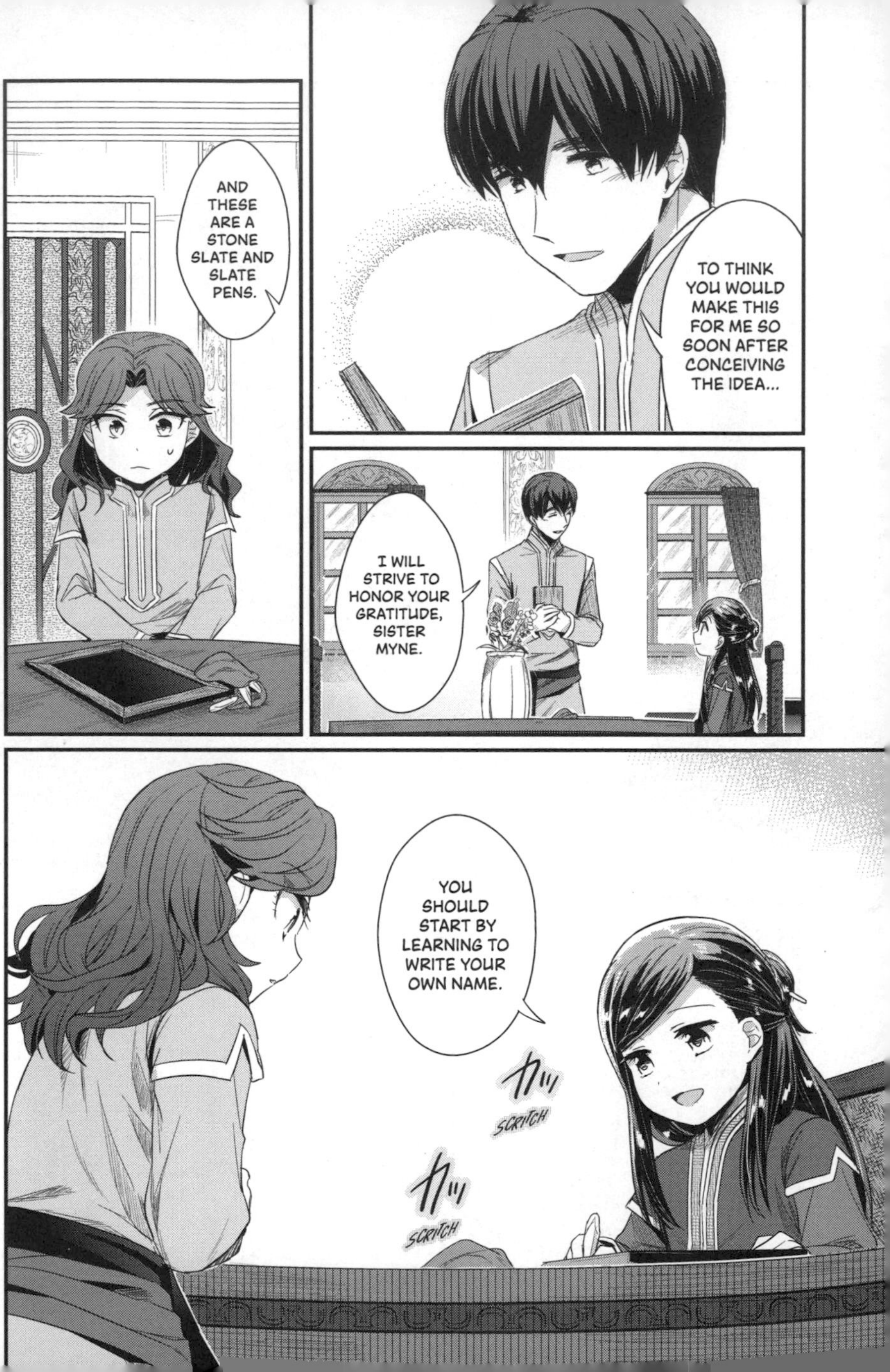
TO THINK YOU WOULD MAKE THIS FOR ME SO SOON AFTER CONCEIVING THE IDEA...
I WILL STRIVE TO HONOR YOUR GRATITUDE, SISTER MYNE.
AND THESE ARE A STONE SLATE AND SLATE PENS.
YOU SHOULD START BY LEARNING TO WRITE YOUR OWN NAME.
カッ
SCRITCH
カッ
SCRITCH

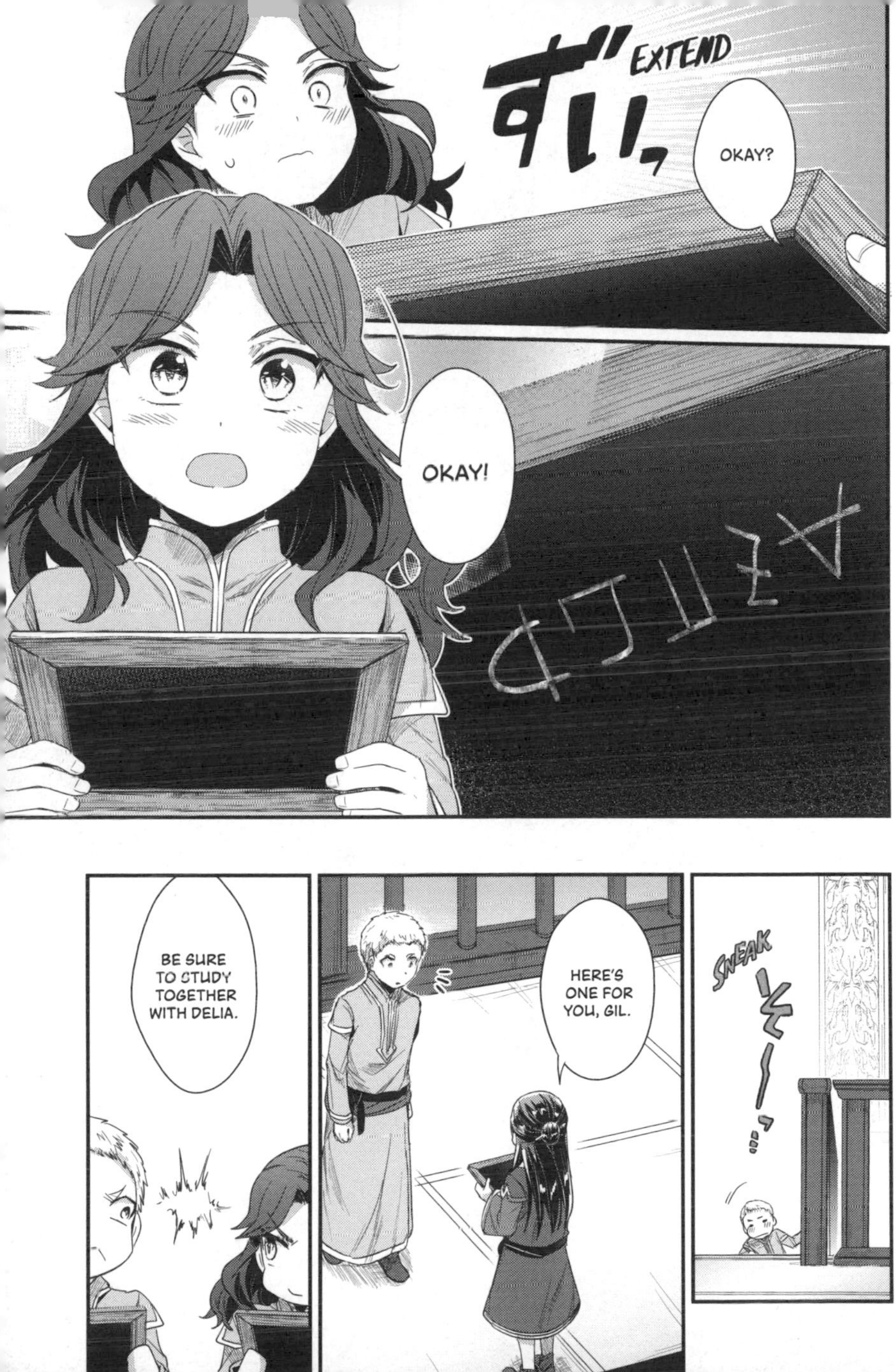
ずい
EXTEND
OKAY?
OKAY!
SNEAK
HERE'S ONE FOR YOU, GIL.
BE SURE TO STUDY TOGETHER WITH DELIA.

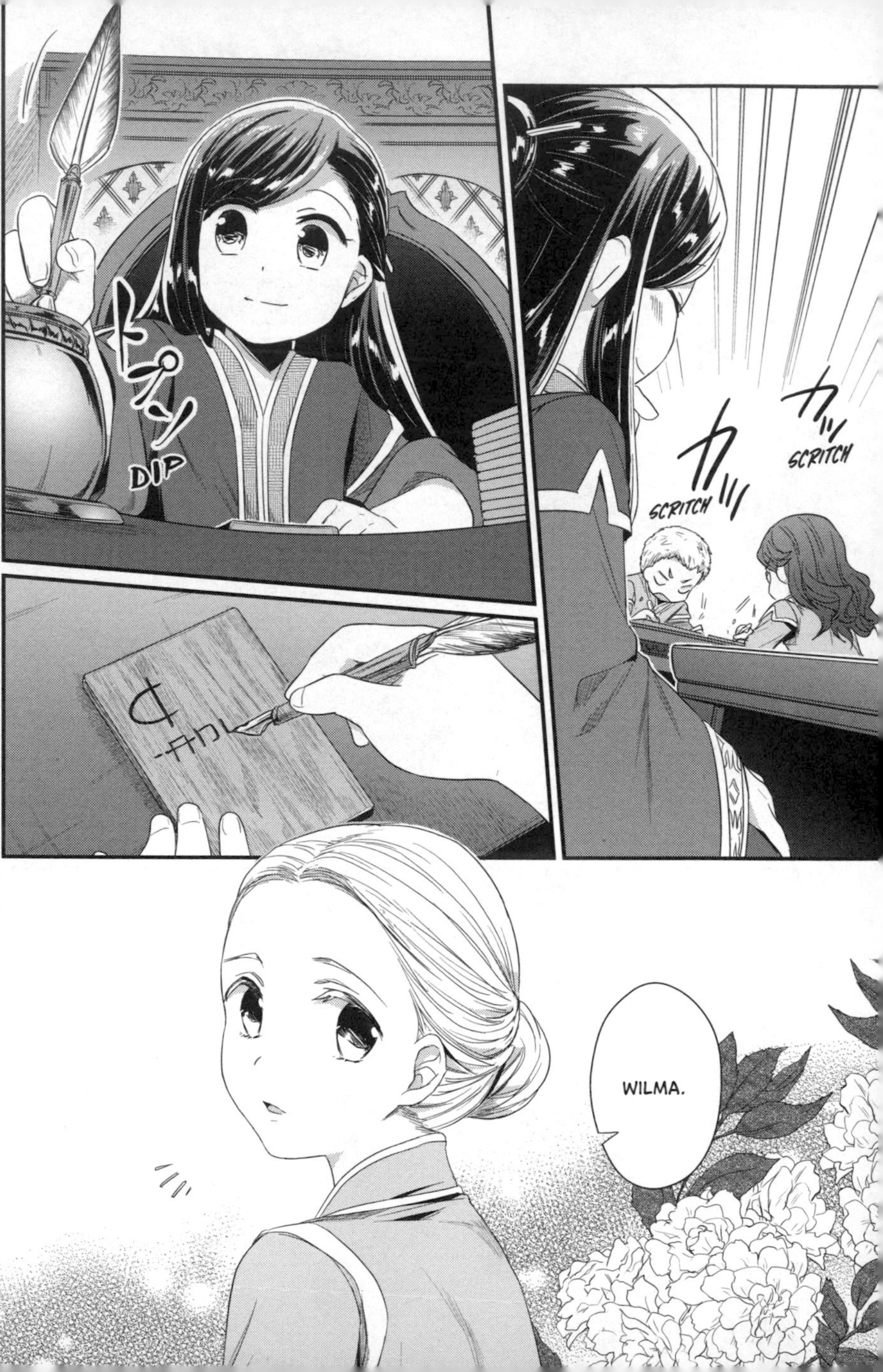
SCRITCH
SCRITCH
DIP
WILMA.

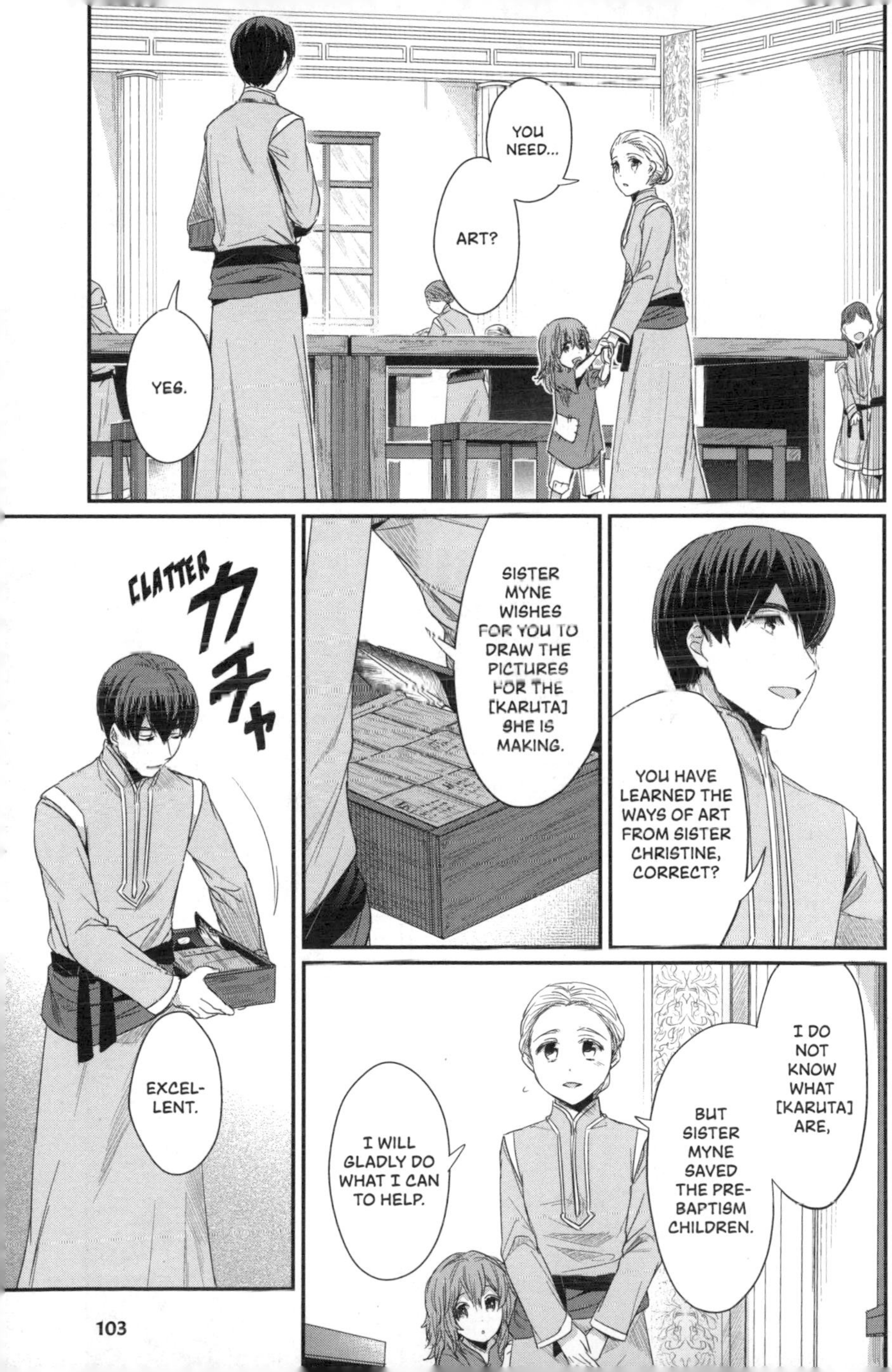
YOU NEED...
ART?
YES.
YOU HAVE LEARNED THE WAYS OF ART FROM SISTER CHRISTINE, CORRECT?
SISTER MYNE WISHES FOR YOU TO DRAW THE PICTURES FOR THE [KARUTA] SHE IS MAKING.
I DO NOT KNOW WHAT [KARUTA] ARE,
BUT SISTER MYNE SAVED THE PRE-BAPTISM CHILDREN.
I WILL GLADLY DO WHAT I CAN TO HELP.
CLATTER
カチャ
EXCEL-LENT.

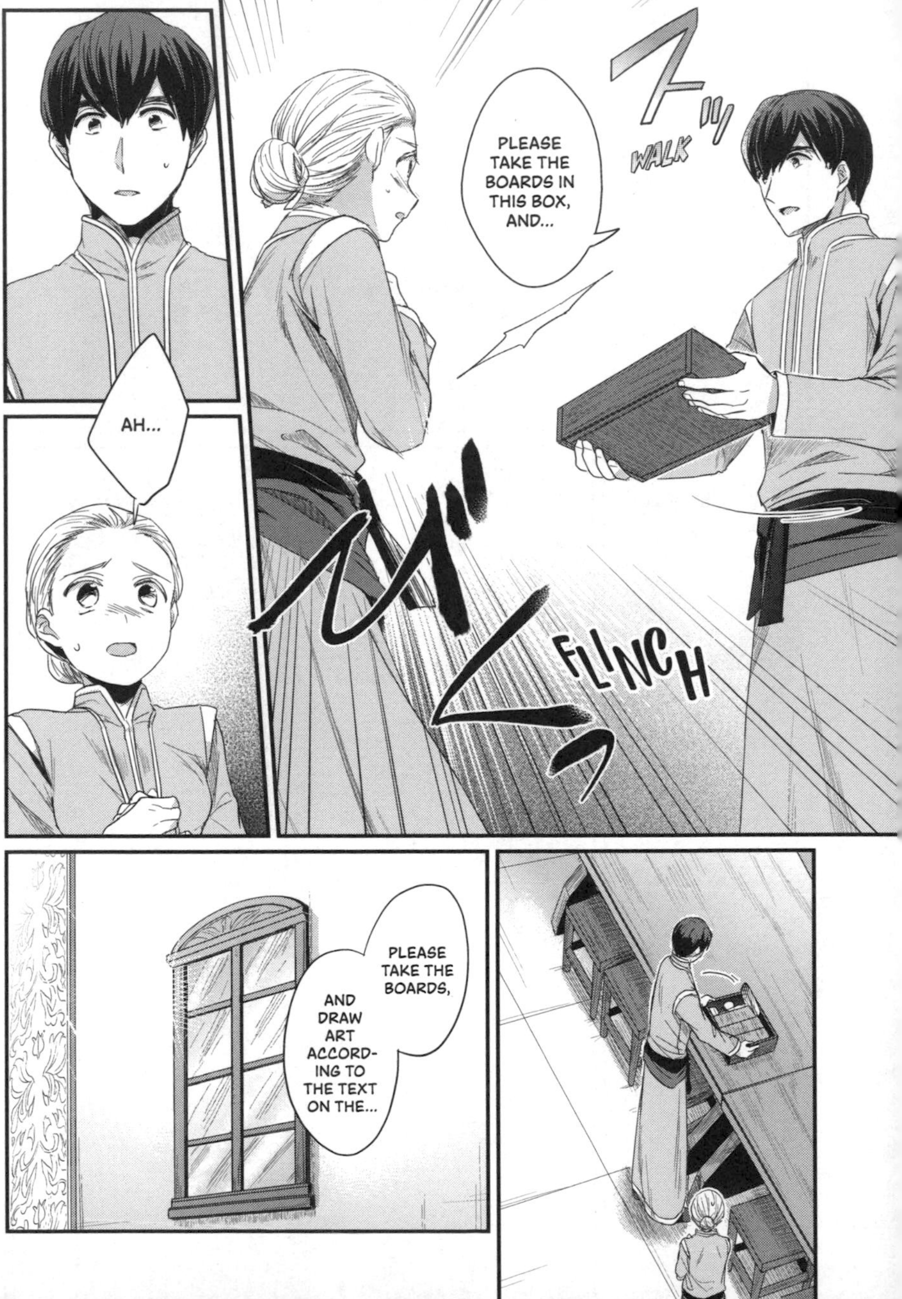
WALK
PLEASE TAKE THE BOARDS IN THIS BOX, AND...
FLINCH
AH...
PLEASE TAKE THE BOARDS, AND DRAW ART ACCORD-ING TO THE TEXT ON THE...

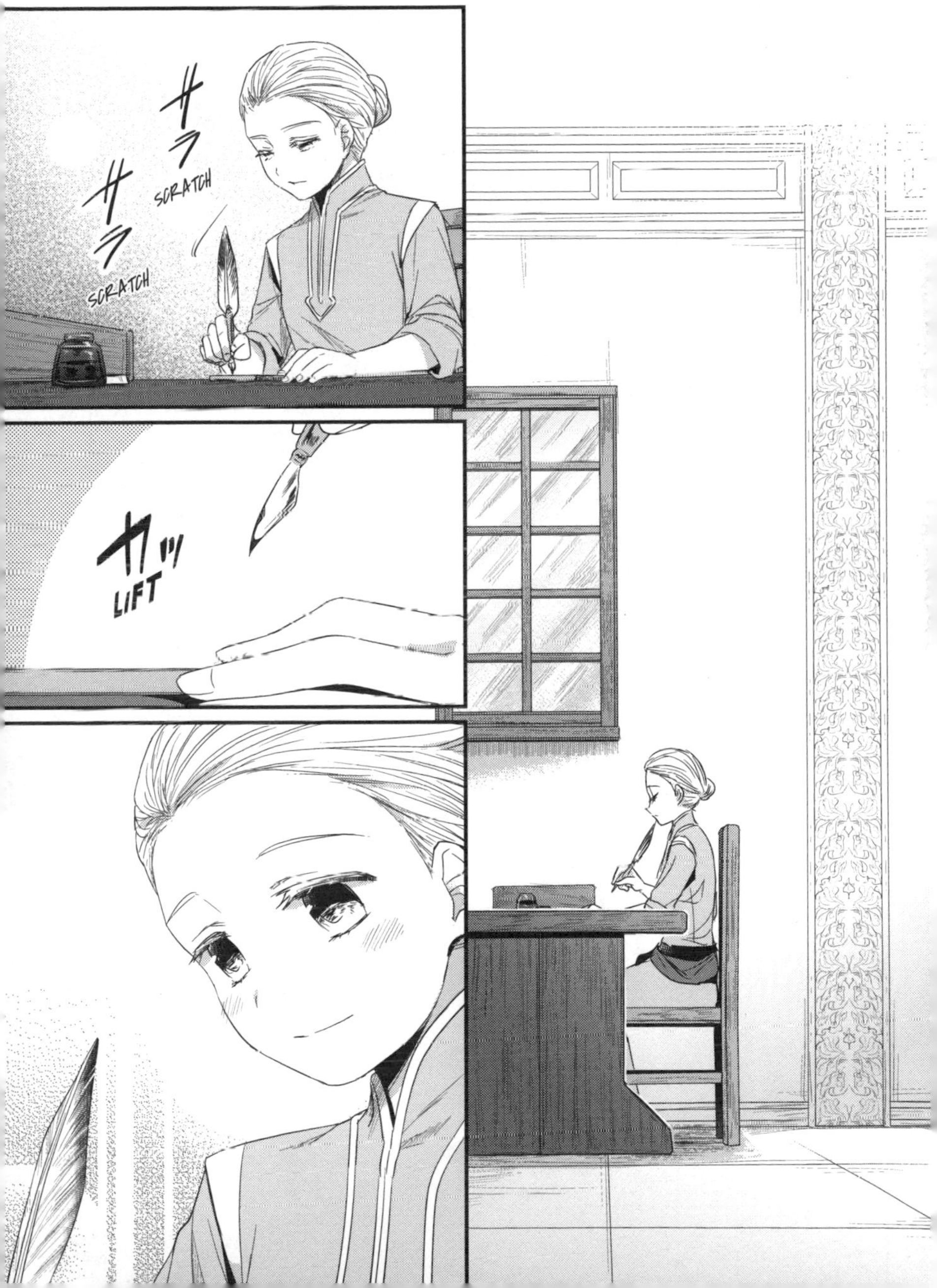
サラ
SCRATCH
サラ
SCRATCH
カッ
LIFT

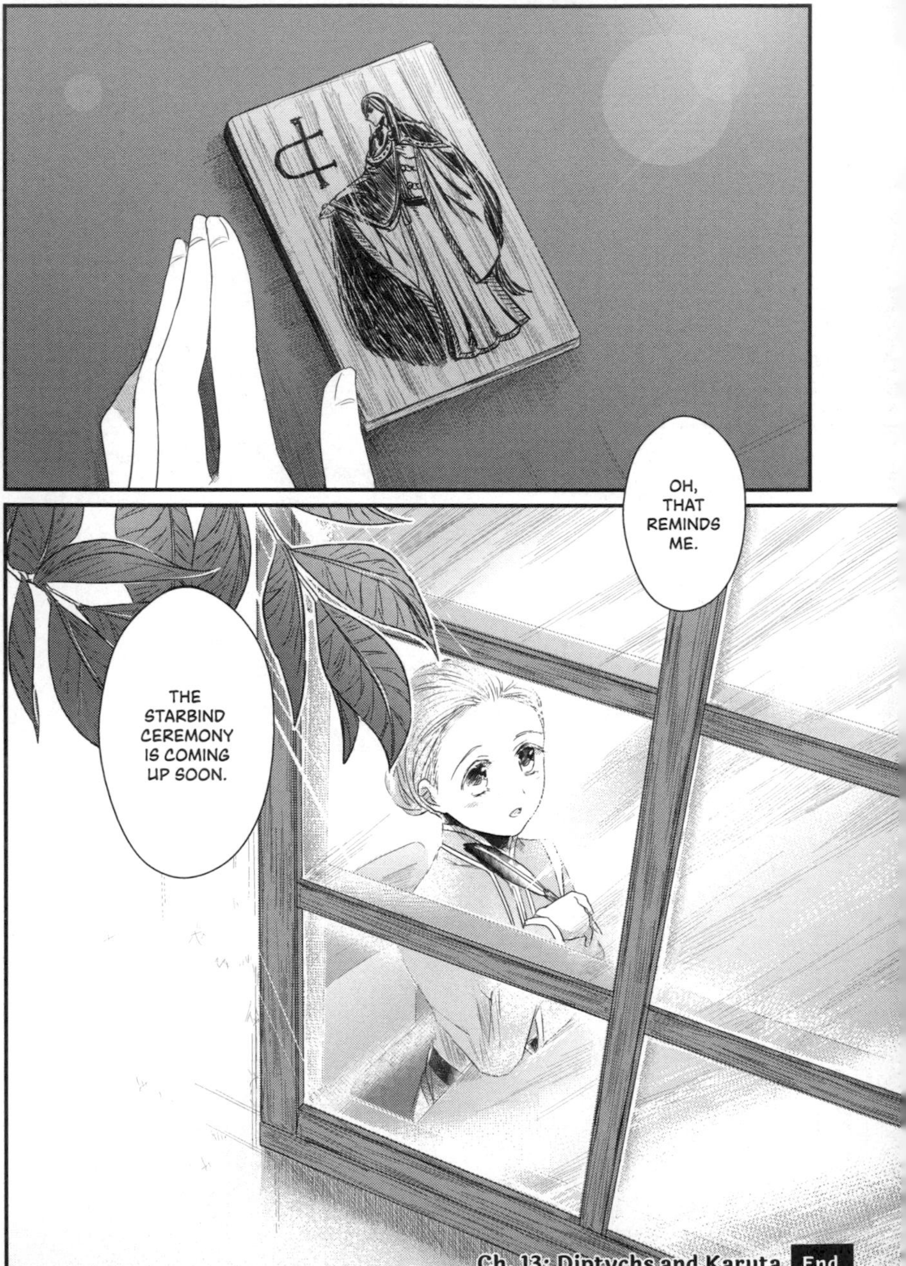
OH, THAT REMINDS ME.
THE STARBIND CEREMONY IS COMING UP SOON.
Ch. 13: Diptychs and Karuta End

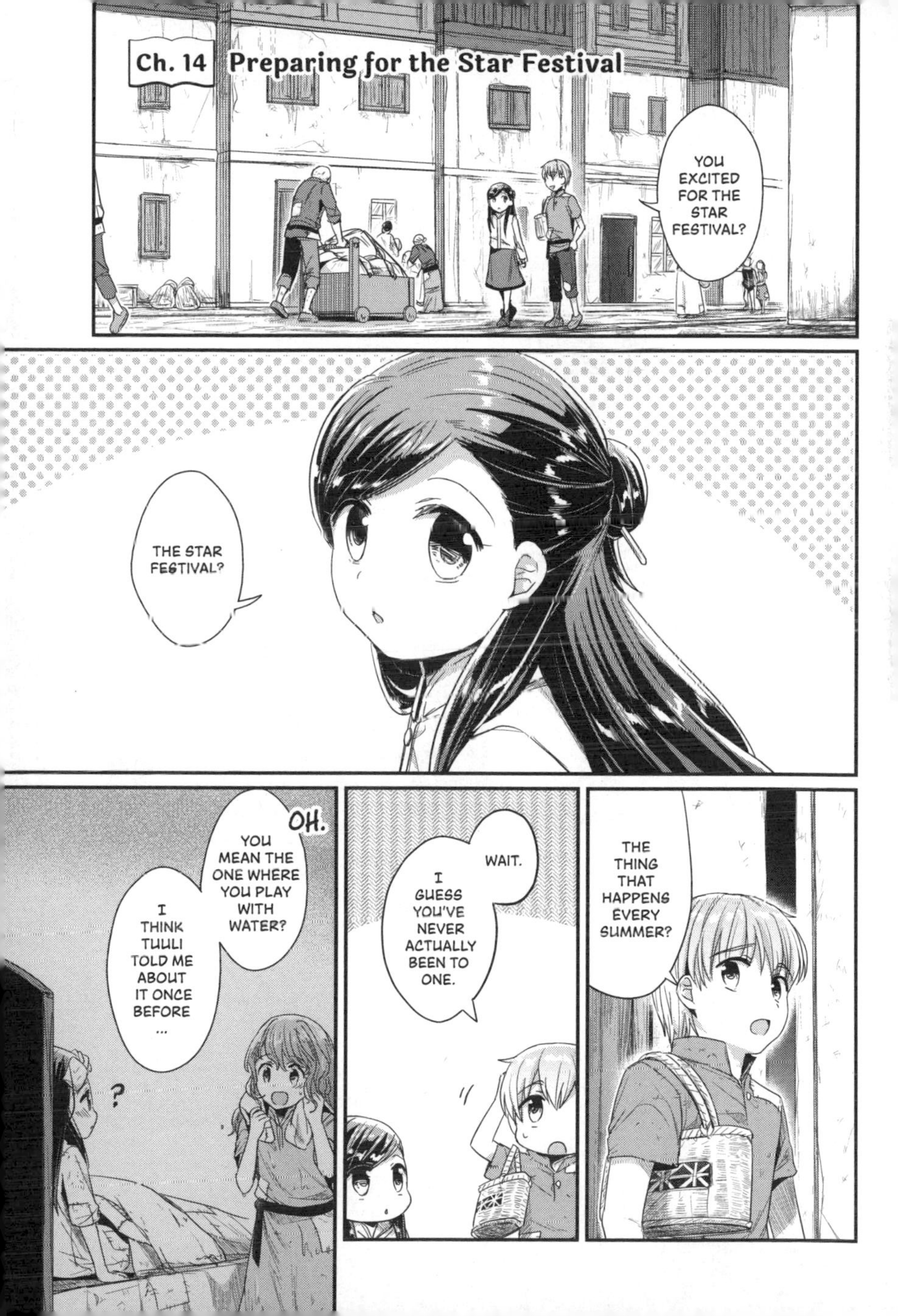
Ch. 14 Preparing for the Star Festival
YOU EXCITED FOR THE STAR FESTIVAL?
THE STAR FESTIVAL?
THE THING THAT HAPPENS EVERY SUMMER?
WAIT.
I GUESS YOU'VE NEVER ACTUALLY BEEN TO ONE.
OH.
YOU MEAN THE ONE WHERE YOU PLAY WITH WATER?
I THINK TUULI TOLD ME ABOUT IT ONCE BEFORE ...
?

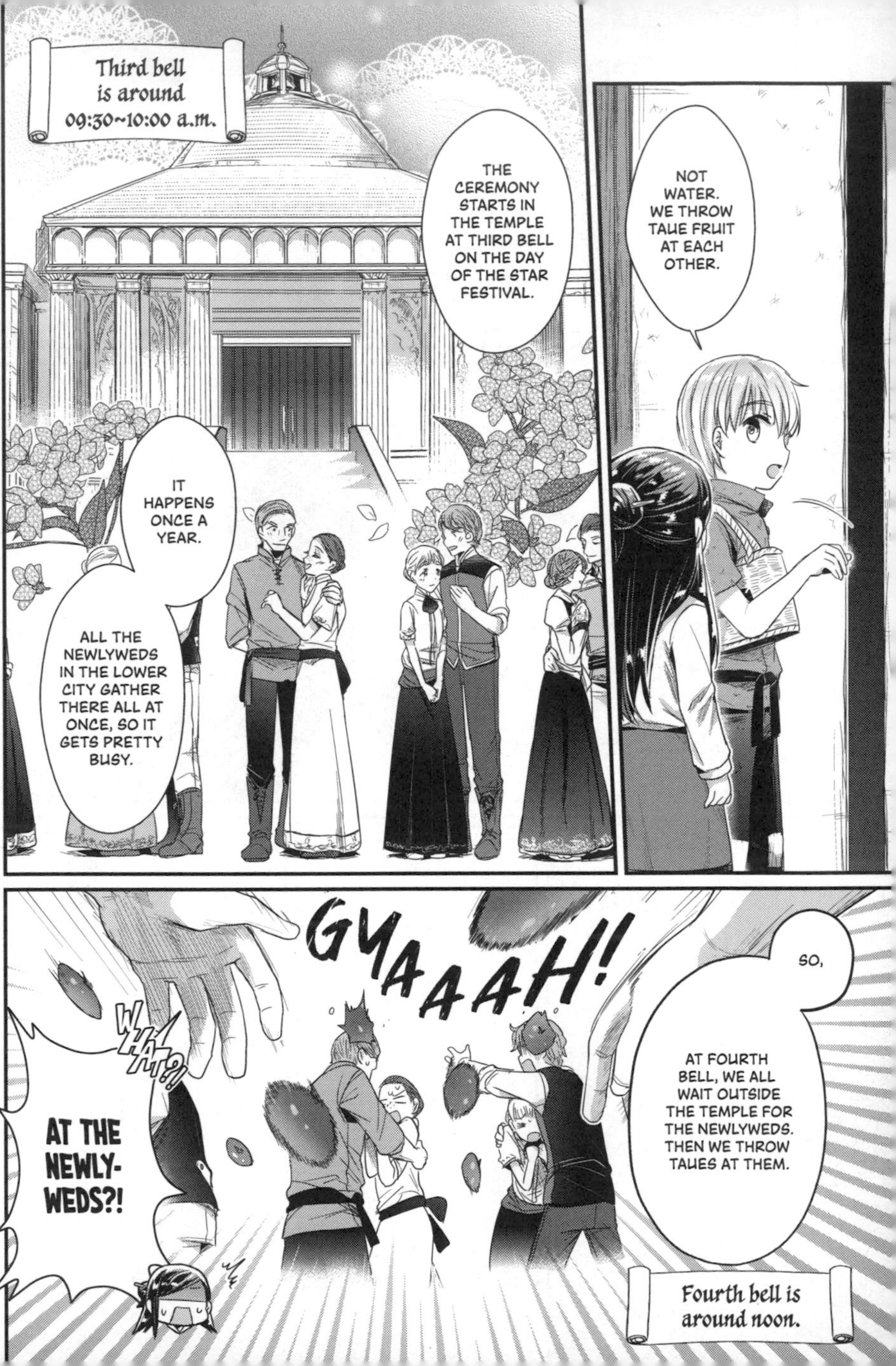
NOT WATER. WE THROW TAUE FRUIT AT EACH OTHER.
Third bell is around 09:30~10:00 a.m.
THE CEREMONY STARTS IN THE TEMPLE AT THIRD BELL ON THE DAY OF THE STAR FESTIVAL.
IT HAPPENS ONCE A YEAR.
ALL THE NEWLYWEDS IN THE LOWER CITY GATHER THERE ALL AT ONCE, SO IT GETS PRETTY BUSY.
SO,
AT FOURTH BELL, WE ALL WAIT OUTSIDE THE TEMPLE FOR THE NEWLYWEDS. THEN WE THROW TAUES AT THEM.
Fourth bell is around noon.
GYAAAAH!
WHAT?!
AT THE NEWLY-WEDS?!

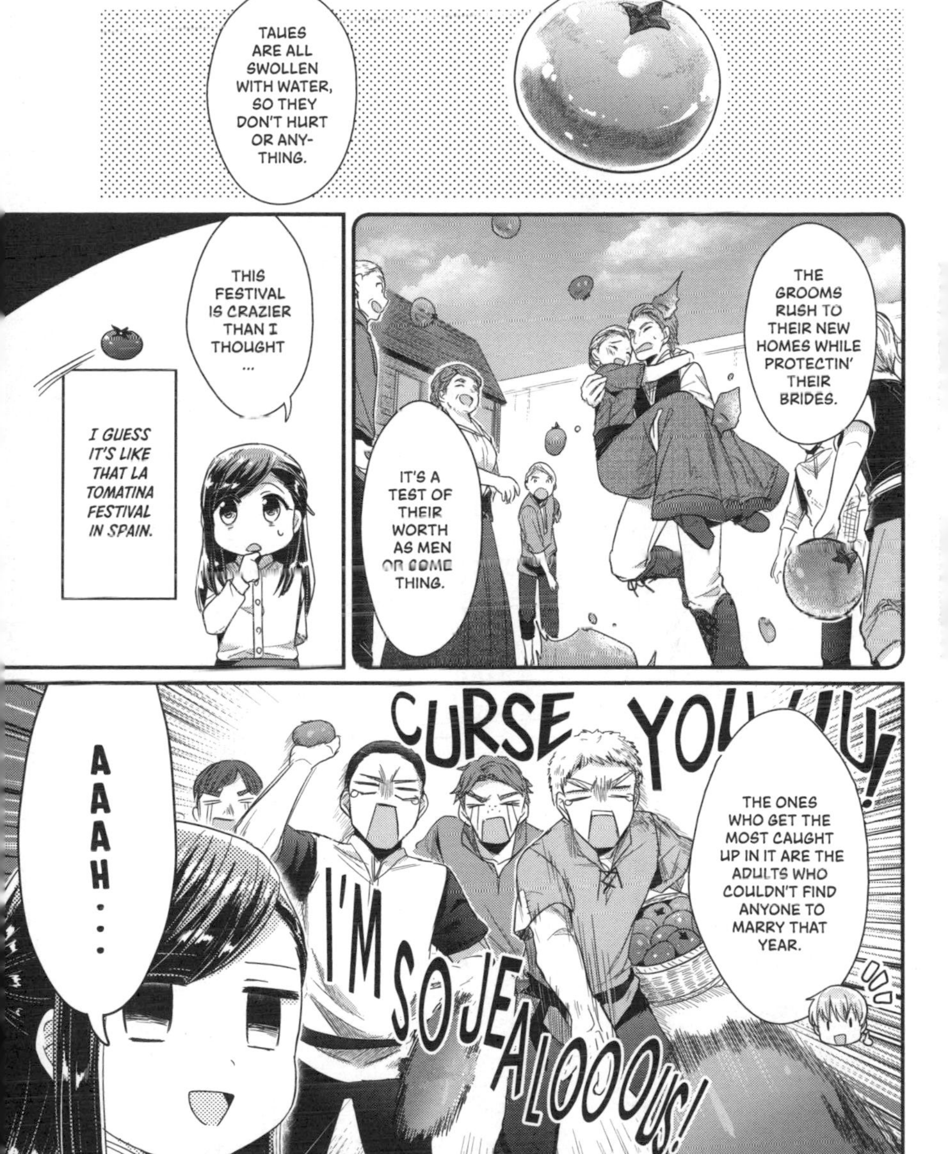
TAUES ARE ALL SWOLLEN WITH WATER, SO THEY DON'T HURT OR ANY-THING.
THE GROOMS RUSH TO THEIR NEW HOMES WHILE PROTECTIN' THEIR BRIDES.
IT'S A TEST OF THEIR WORTH AS MEN OR SOME THING.
THIS FESTIVAL IS CRAZIER THAN I THOUGHT ...
I GUESS IT'S LIKE THAT LA TOMATINA FESTIVAL IN SPAIN.
CURSE YOU
THE ONES WHO GET THE MOST CAUGHT UP IN IT ARE THE ADULTS WHO COULDN'T FIND ANYONE TO MARRY THAT YEAR.
I'M SO JEALOOOUS!
AAAH...

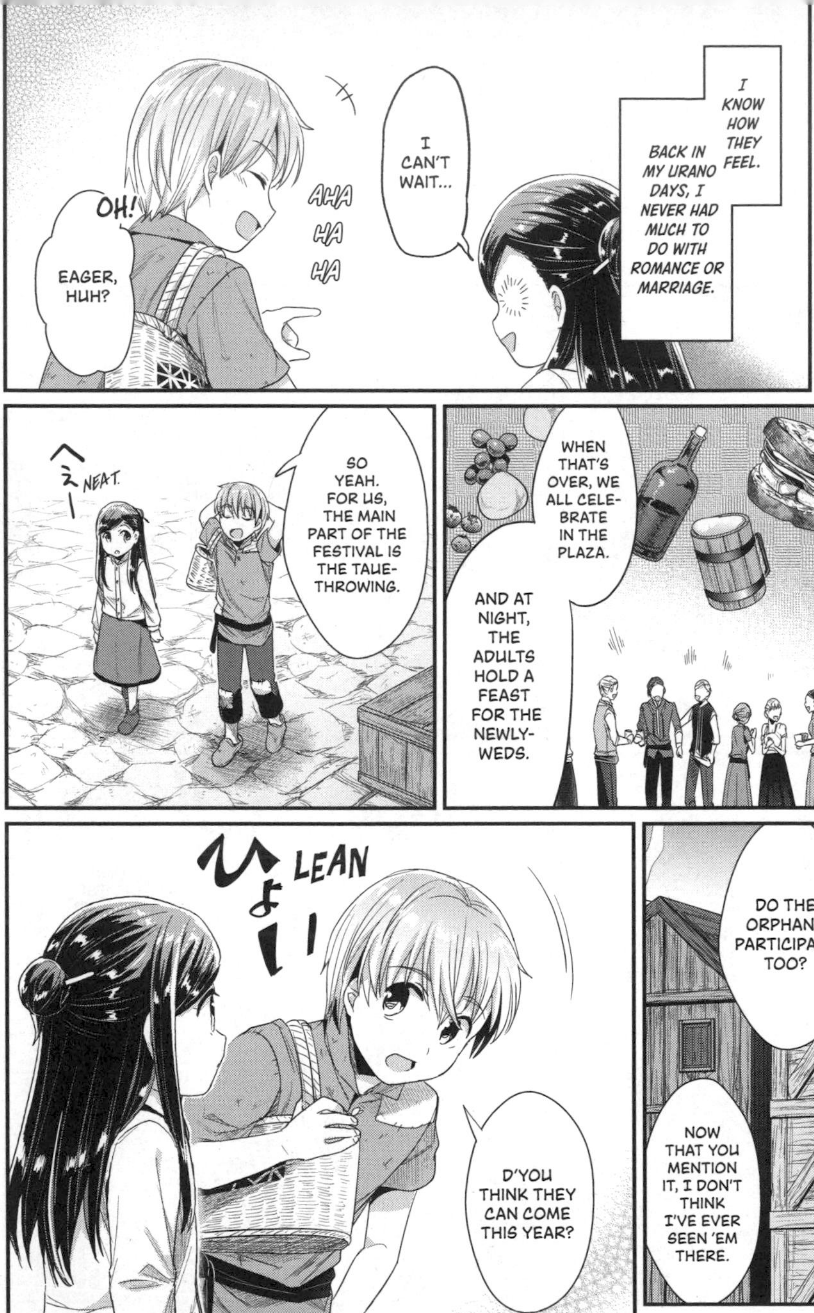
I KNOW HOW THEY FEEL.
BACK IN MY URANO DAYS, I NEVER HAD MUCH TO DO WITH ROMANCE OR MARRIAGE.
I CAN'T WAIT...
AHA HA HA
OH!
EAGER, HUH?
WHEN THAT'S OVER, WE ALL CELEBRATE IN THE PLAZA.
AND AT NIGHT, THE ADULTS HOLD A FEAST FOR THE NEWLYWEDS.
SO YEAH. FOR US, THE MAIN PART OF THE FESTIVAL IS THE TAUE-THROWING.
へえー NEAT.
DO THE ORPHANS PARTICIPATE TOO?
NOW THAT YOU MENTION IT, I DON'T THINK I'VE EVER SEEN 'EM THERE.
ひょい LEAN
D'YOU THINK THEY CAN COME THIS YEAR?

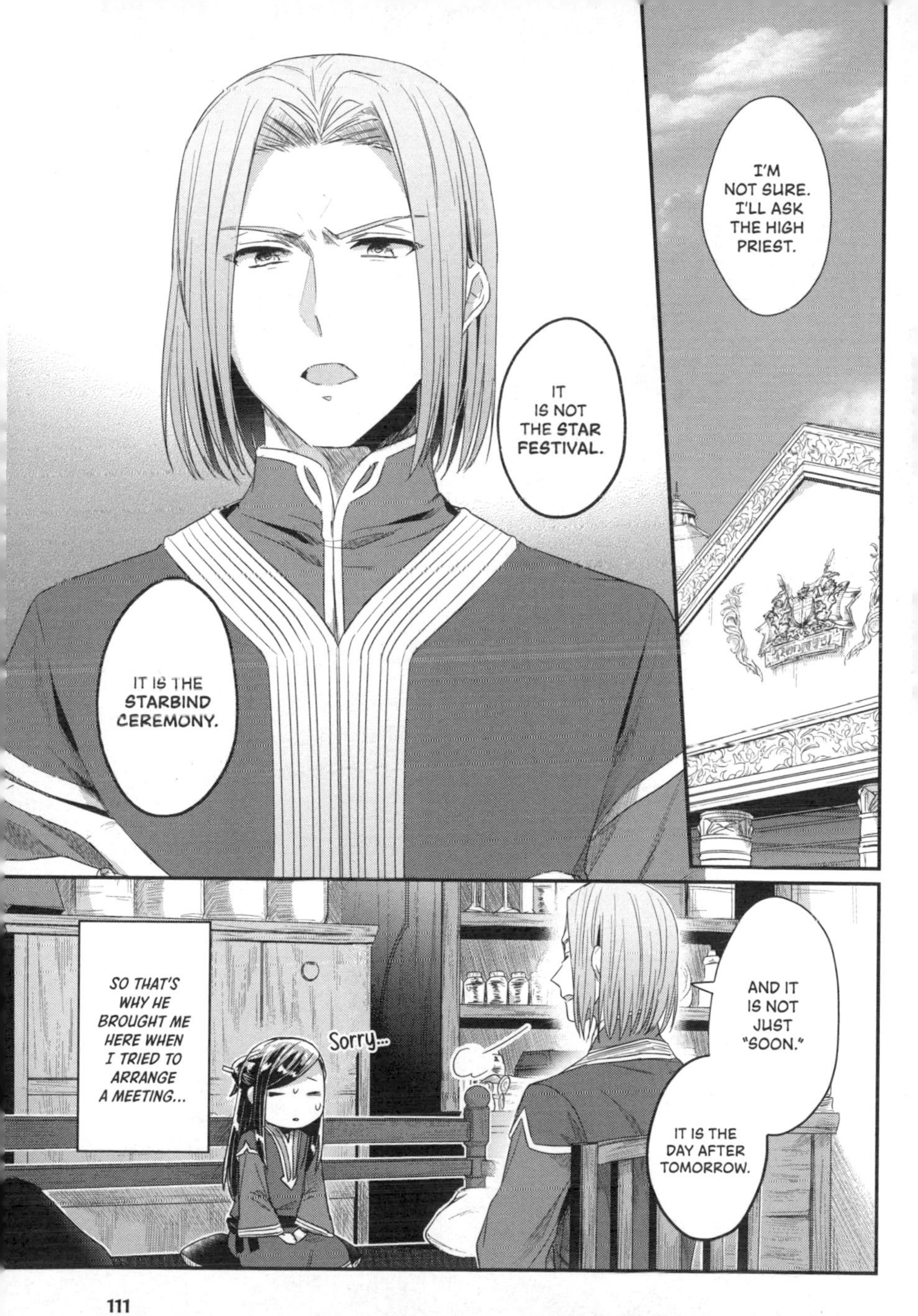
I'M NOT SURE. I'LL ASK THE HIGH PRIEST.
IT IS NOT THE STAR FESTIVAL.
IT IS THE STARBIND CEREMONY.
AND IT IS NOT JUST "SOON."
IT IS THE DAY AFTER TOMORROW.
Sorry...
SO THAT'S WHY HE BROUGHT ME HERE WHEN I TRIED TO ARRANGE A MEETING...

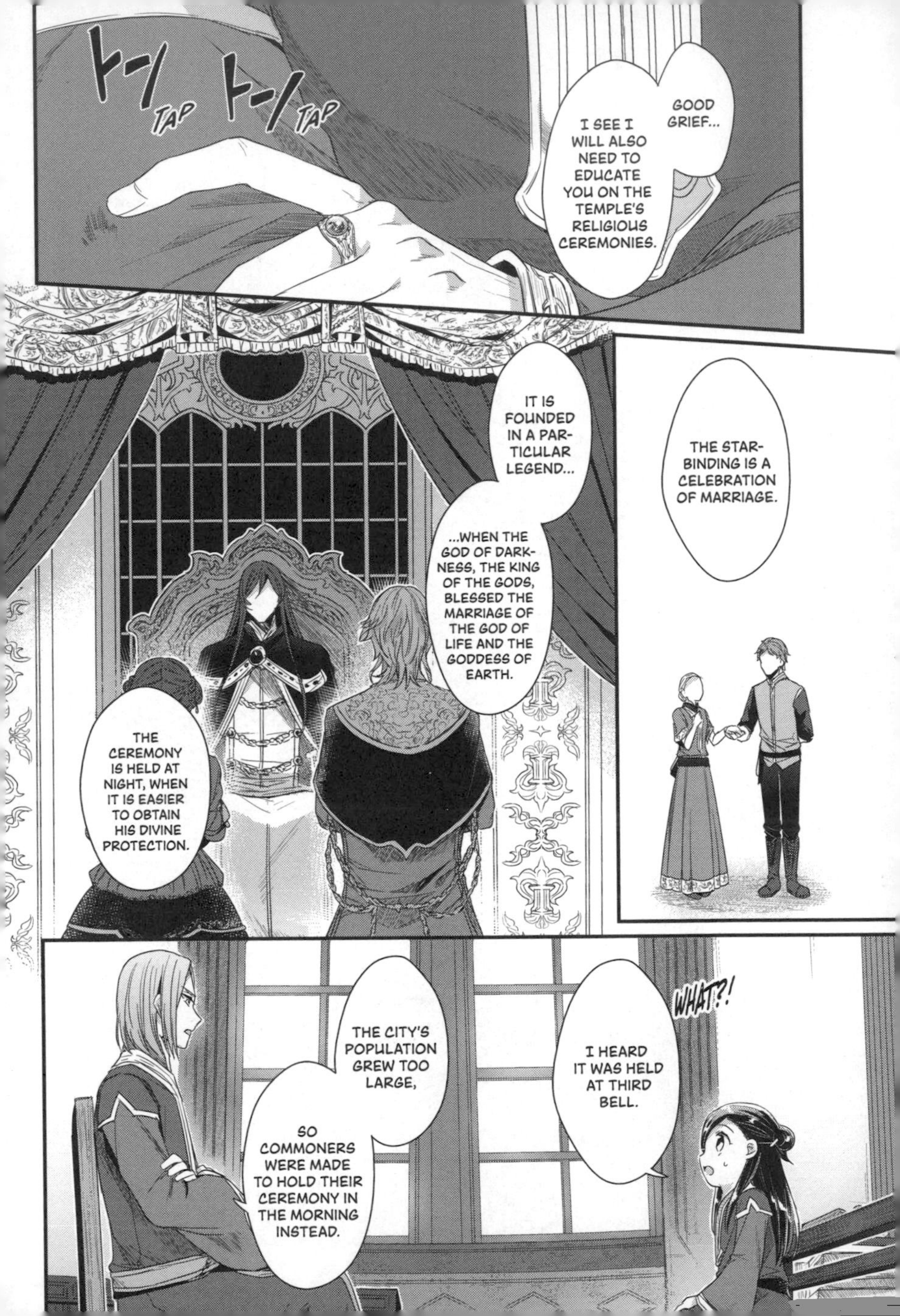

TAP
TAP
GOOD GRIEF...
I SEE I WILL ALSO NEED TO EDUCATE YOU ON THE TEMPLE'S RELIGIOUS CEREMONIES.
THE STAR-BINDING IS A CELEBRATION OF MARRIAGE.
IT IS FOUNDED IN A PAR-TICULAR LEGEND...
...WHEN THE GOD OF DARK-NESS, THE KING OF THE GODS, BLESSED THE MARRIAGE OF THE GOD OF LIFE AND THE GODDESS OF EARTH.
THE CEREMONY IS HELD AT NIGHT, WHEN IT IS EASIER TO OBTAIN HIS DIVINE PROTECTION.
WHAT?!
I HEARD IT WAS HELD AT THIRD BELL.
THE CITY'S POPULATION GREW TOO LARGE,
SO COMMONERS WERE MADE TO HOLD THEIR CEREMONY IN THE MORNING INSTEAD.

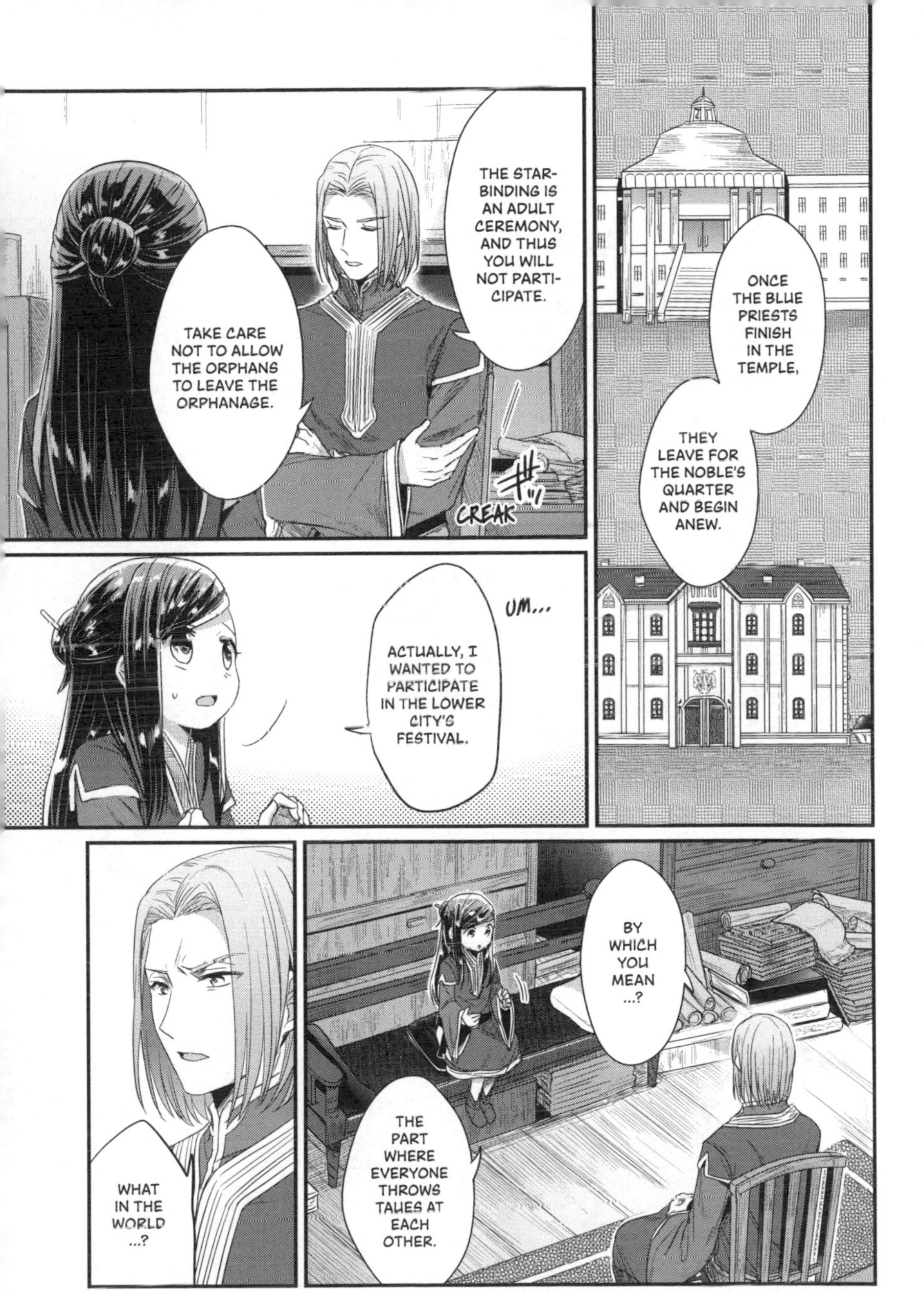
ONCE THE BLUE PRIESTS FINISH IN THE TEMPLE,
THEY LEAVE FOR THE NOBLE'S QUARTER AND BEGIN ANEW.
THE STAR-BINDING IS AN ADULT CEREMONY, AND THUS YOU WILL NOT PARTICIPATE.
TAKE CARE NOT TO ALLOW THE ORPHANS TO LEAVE THE ORPHANAGE.
CREAK
UM...
ACTUALLY, I WANTED TO PARTICIPATE IN THE LOWER CITY'S FESTIVAL.
BY WHICH YOU MEAN ...?
THE PART WHERE EVERYONE THROWS TAUES AT EACH OTHER.
WHAT IN THE WORLD ...?

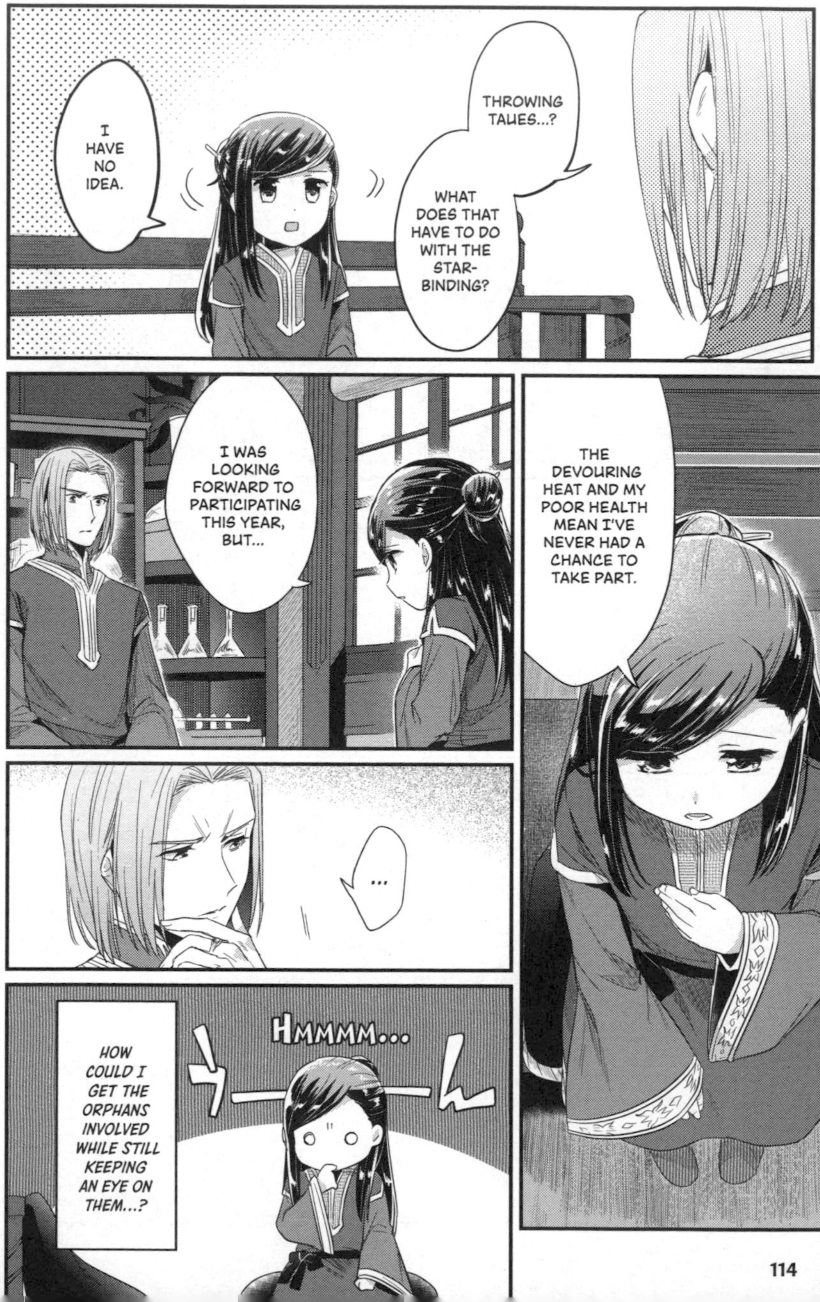
THROWING TAUES...?
WHAT DOES THAT HAVE TO DO WITH THE STAR-BINDING?
I HAVE NO IDEA.
THE DEVOURING HEAT AND MY POOR HEALTH MEAN I'VE NEVER HAD A CHANCE TO TAKE PART.
I WAS LOOKING FORWARD TO PARTICIPATING THIS YEAR, BUT...
...
HMMMM...
HOW COULD I GET THE ORPHANS INVOLVED WHILE STILL KEEPING AN EYE ON THEM...?

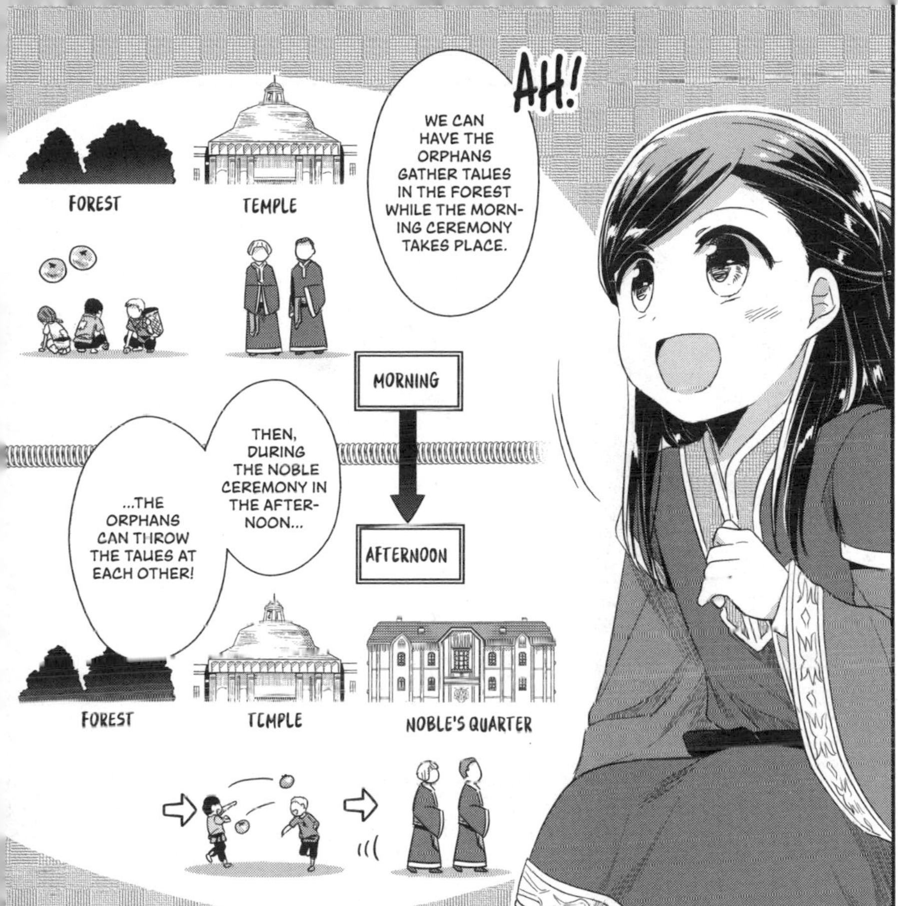
AH!
WE CAN HAVE THE ORPHANS GATHER TAUES IN THE FOREST WHILE THE MORNING CEREMONY TAKES PLACE.
TEMPLE
FOREST
MORNING
THEN, DURING THE NOBLE CEREMONY IN THE AFTERNOON...
...THE ORPHANS CAN THROW THE TAUES AT EACH OTHER!
AFTERNOON
NOBLE'S QUARTER
TEMPLE
FOREST
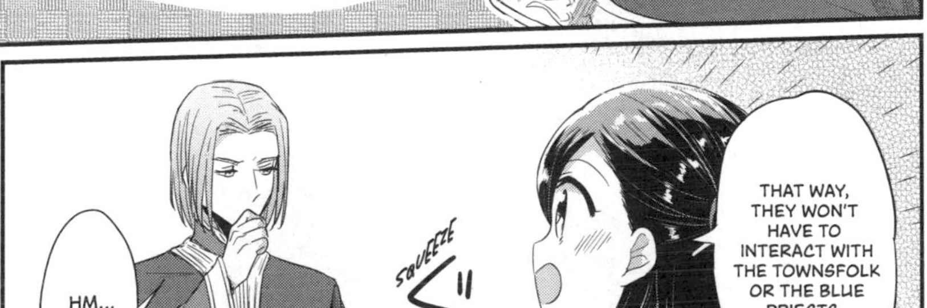
THAT WAY, THEY WON'T HAVE TO INTERACT WITH THE TOWNSFOLK OR THE BLUE PRIESTS.
SQUEEZE
HM...

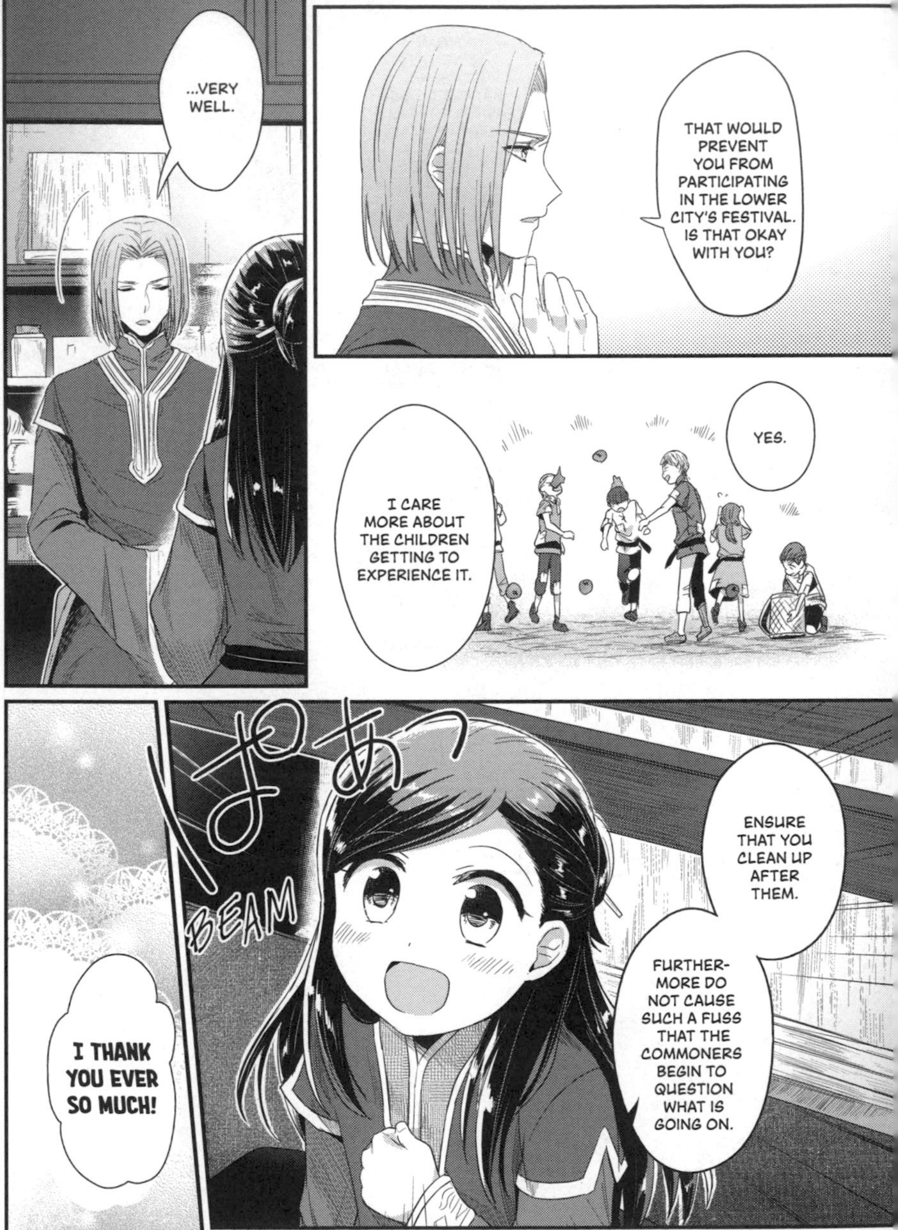
THAT WOULD PREVENT YOU FROM PARTICIPATING IN THE LOWER CITY'S FESTIVAL. IS THAT OKAY WITH YOU?
YES.
I CARE MORE ABOUT THE CHILDREN GETTING TO EXPERIENCE IT.
...VERY WELL.
ENSURE THAT YOU CLEAN UP AFTER THEM.
FURTHER-MORE DO NOT CAUSE SUCH A FUSS THAT THE COMMONERS BEGIN TO QUESTION WHAT IS GOING ON.
ぱあっ
BEAM
I THANK YOU EVER SO MUCH!

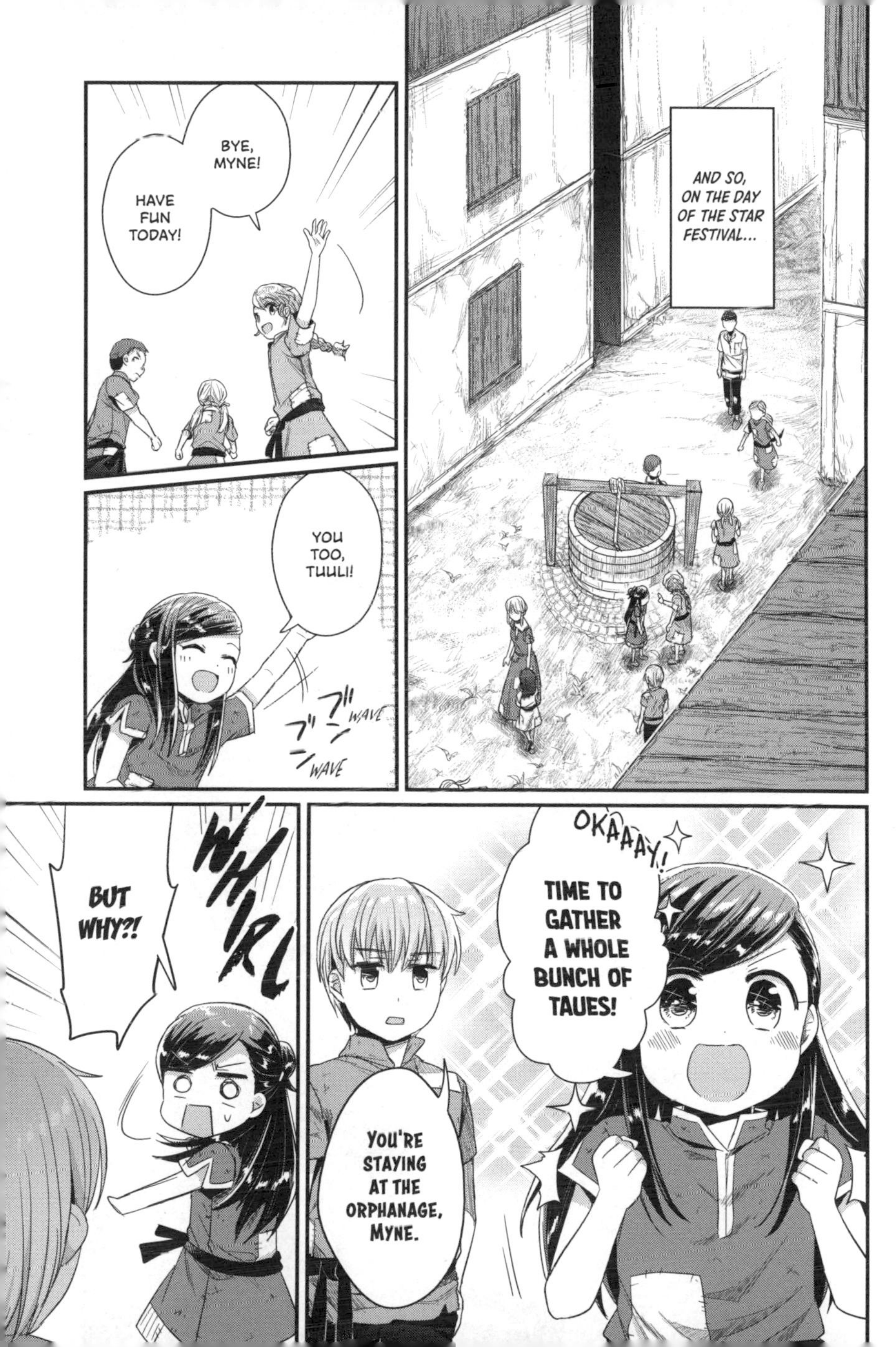
AND SO, ON THE DAY OF THE STAR FESTIVAL...
BYE, MYNE!
HAVE FUN TODAY!
YOU TOO, TUULI!
WAVE
WAVE
OKAAAY!
TIME TO GATHER A WHOLE BUNCH OF TAUES!
YOU'RE STAYING AT THE ORPHANAGE, MYNE.
WHIRL
BUT WHY?!

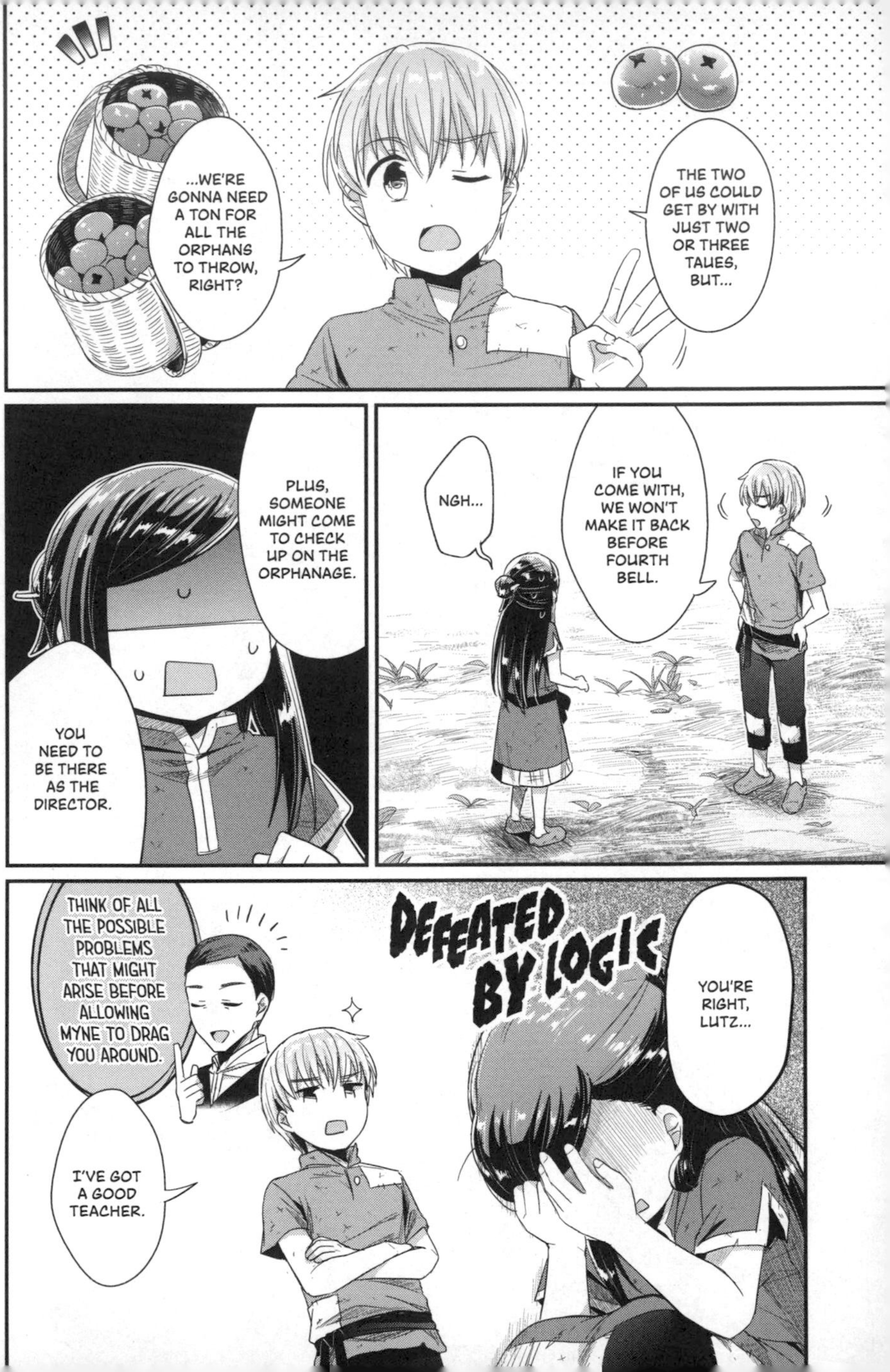
THE TWO OF US COULD GET BY WITH JUST TWO OR THREE TAUES, BUT...
...WE'RE GONNA NEED A TON FOR ALL THE ORPHANS TO THROW, RIGHT?
IF YOU COME WITH, WE WON'T MAKE IT BACK BEFORE FOURTH BELL.
NGH...
PLUS, SOMEONE MIGHT COME TO CHECK UP ON THE ORPHANAGE.
YOU NEED TO BE THERE AS THE DIRECTOR.
YOU'RE RIGHT, LUTZ...
DEFEATED BY LOGIC
THINK OF ALL THE POSSIBLE PROBLEMS THAT MIGHT ARISE BEFORE ALLOWING MYNE TO DRAG YOU AROUND.
I'VE GOT A GOOD TEACHER.

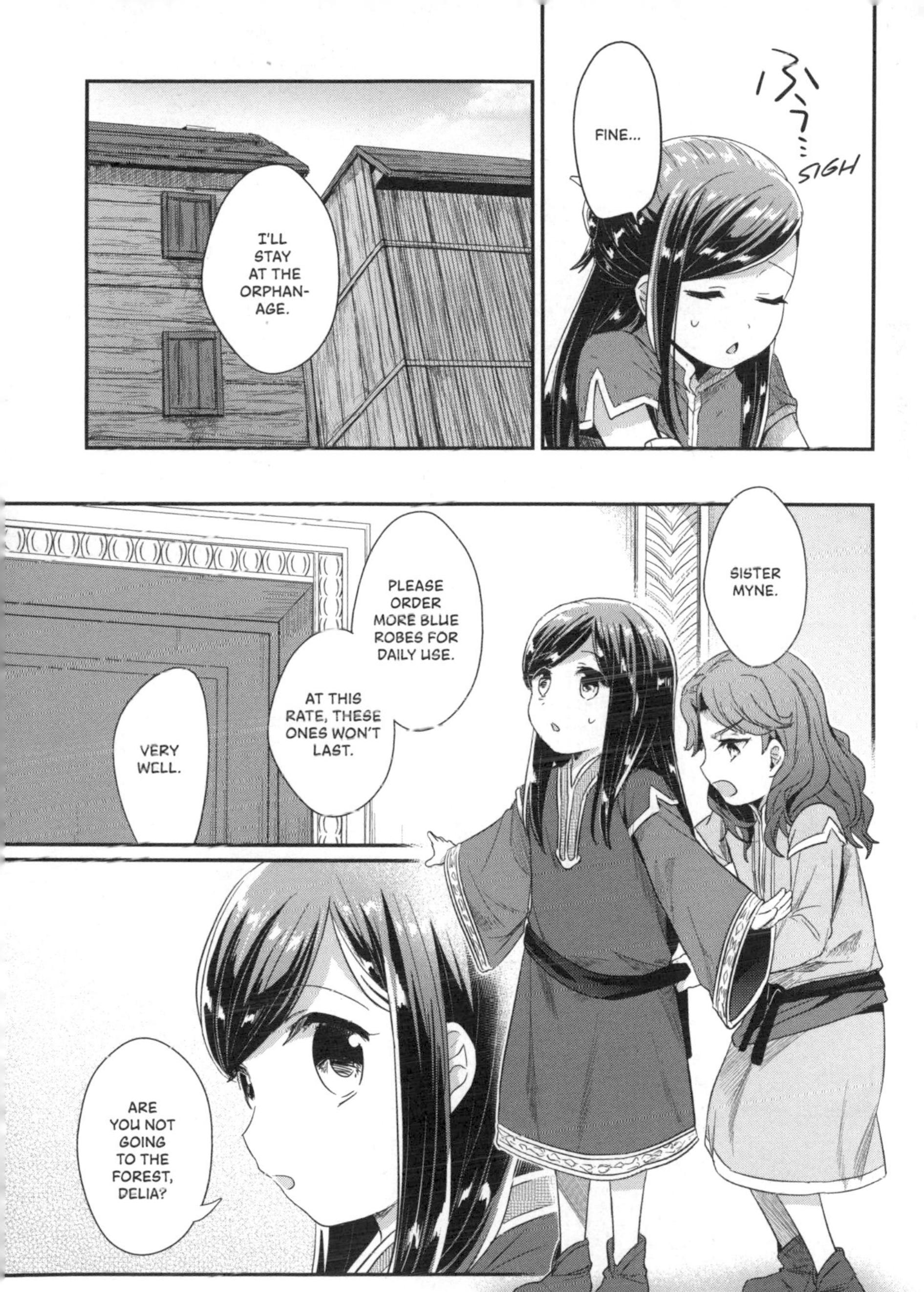
ふぅ
SIGH
FINE...
I'LL STAY AT THE ORPHAN-AGE.
SISTER MYNE.
PLEASE ORDER MORE BLUE ROBES FOR DAILY USE.
AT THIS RATE, THESE ONES WON'T LAST.
VERY WELL.
ARE YOU NOT GOING TO THE FOREST, DELIA?

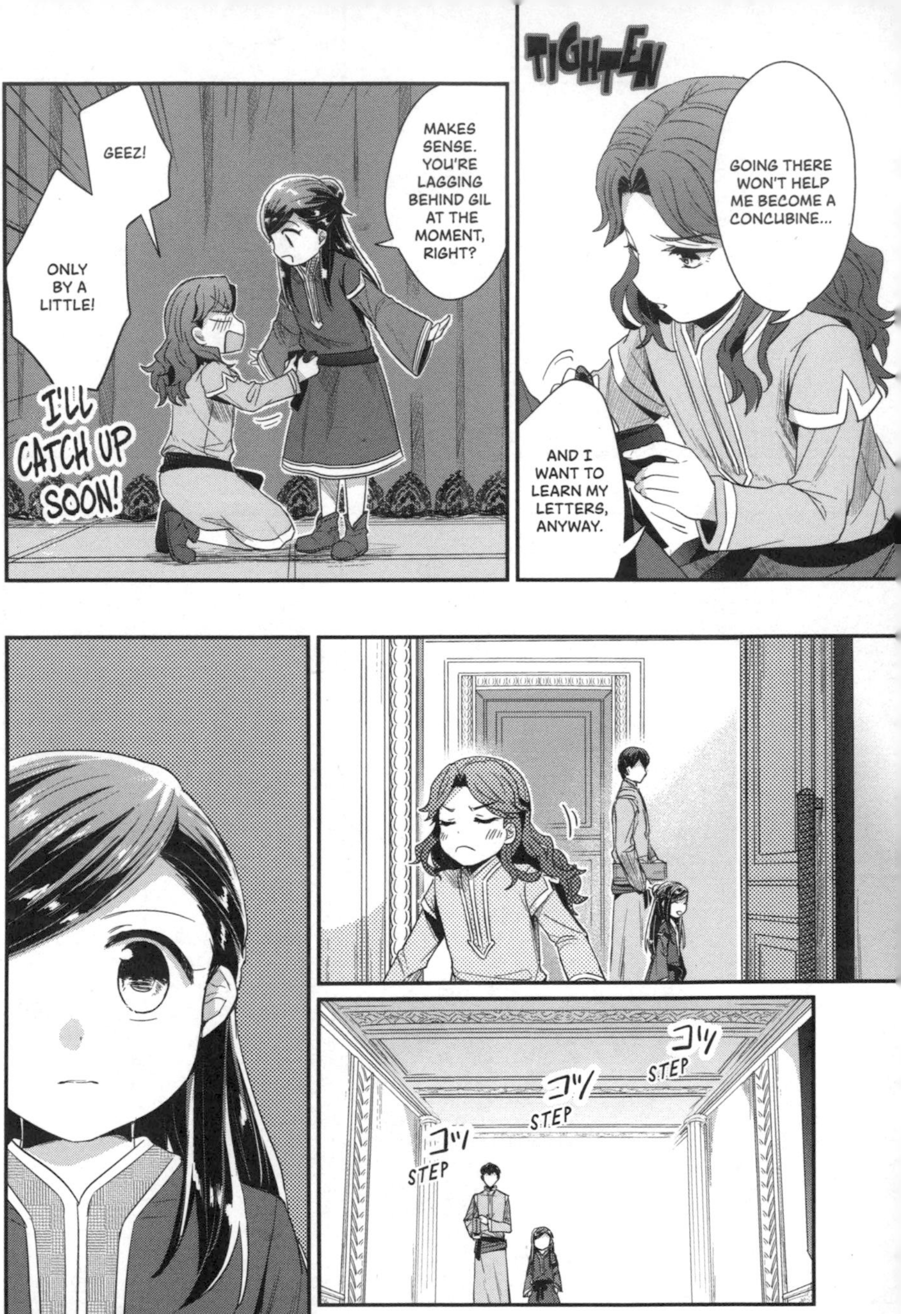
TIGHTEN
GOING THERE WON'T HELP ME BECOME A CONCUBINE...
AND I WANT TO LEARN MY LETTERS, ANYWAY.
MAKES SENSE. YOU'RE LAGGING BEHIND GIL AT THE MOMENT, RIGHT?
GEEZ!
ONLY BY A LITTLE!
I'LL CATCH UP SOON!
コッ
STEP
コッ
STEP
コッ
STEP

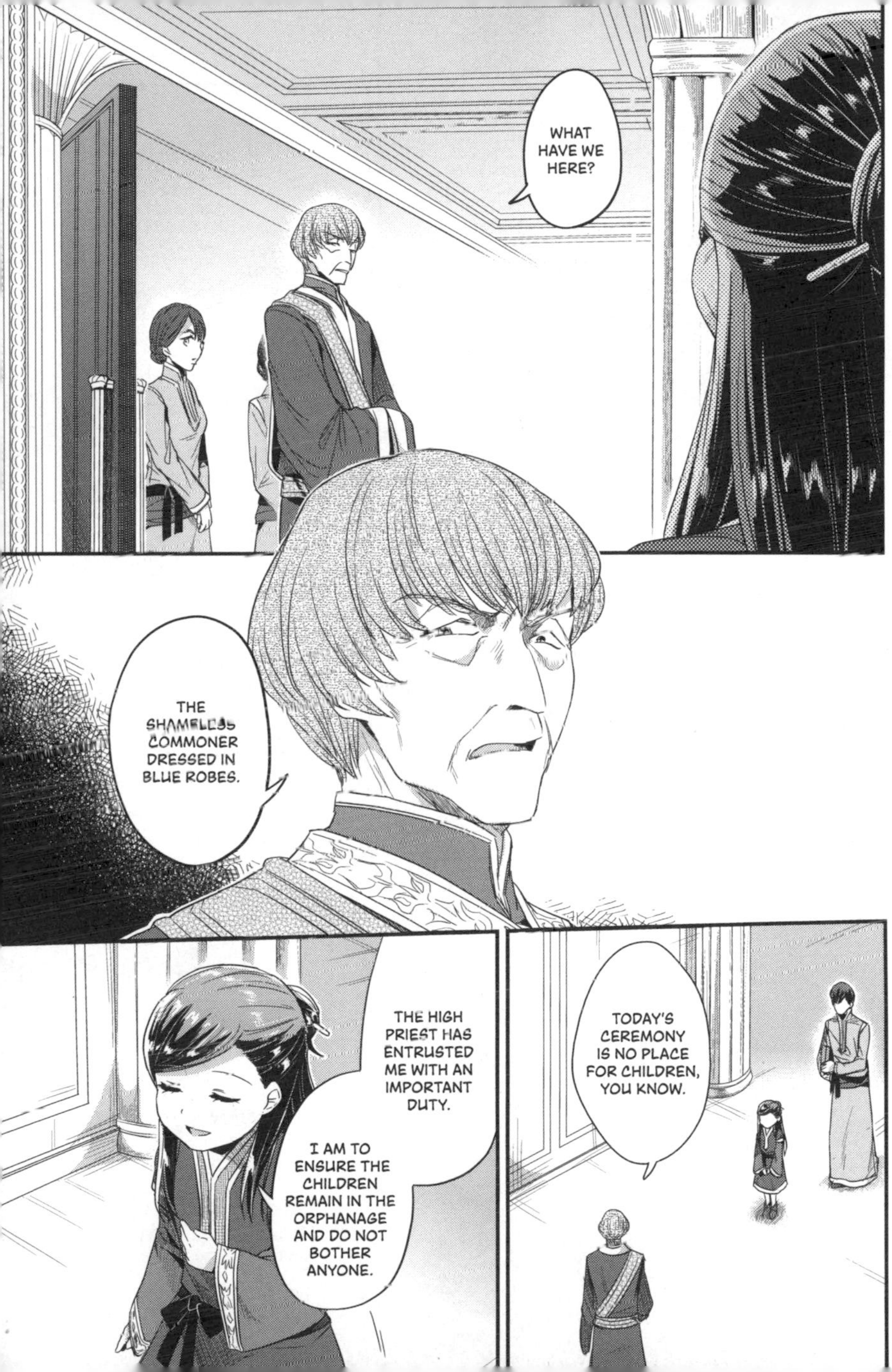
WHAT HAVE WE HERE?
THE SHAMELESS COMMONER DRESSED IN BLUE ROBES.
TODAY'S CEREMONY IS NO PLACE FOR CHILDREN, YOU KNOW.
THE HIGH PRIEST HAS ENTRUSTED ME WITH AN IMPORTANT DUTY.
I AM TO ENSURE THE CHILDREN REMAIN IN THE ORPHANAGE AND DO NOT BOTHER ANYONE.

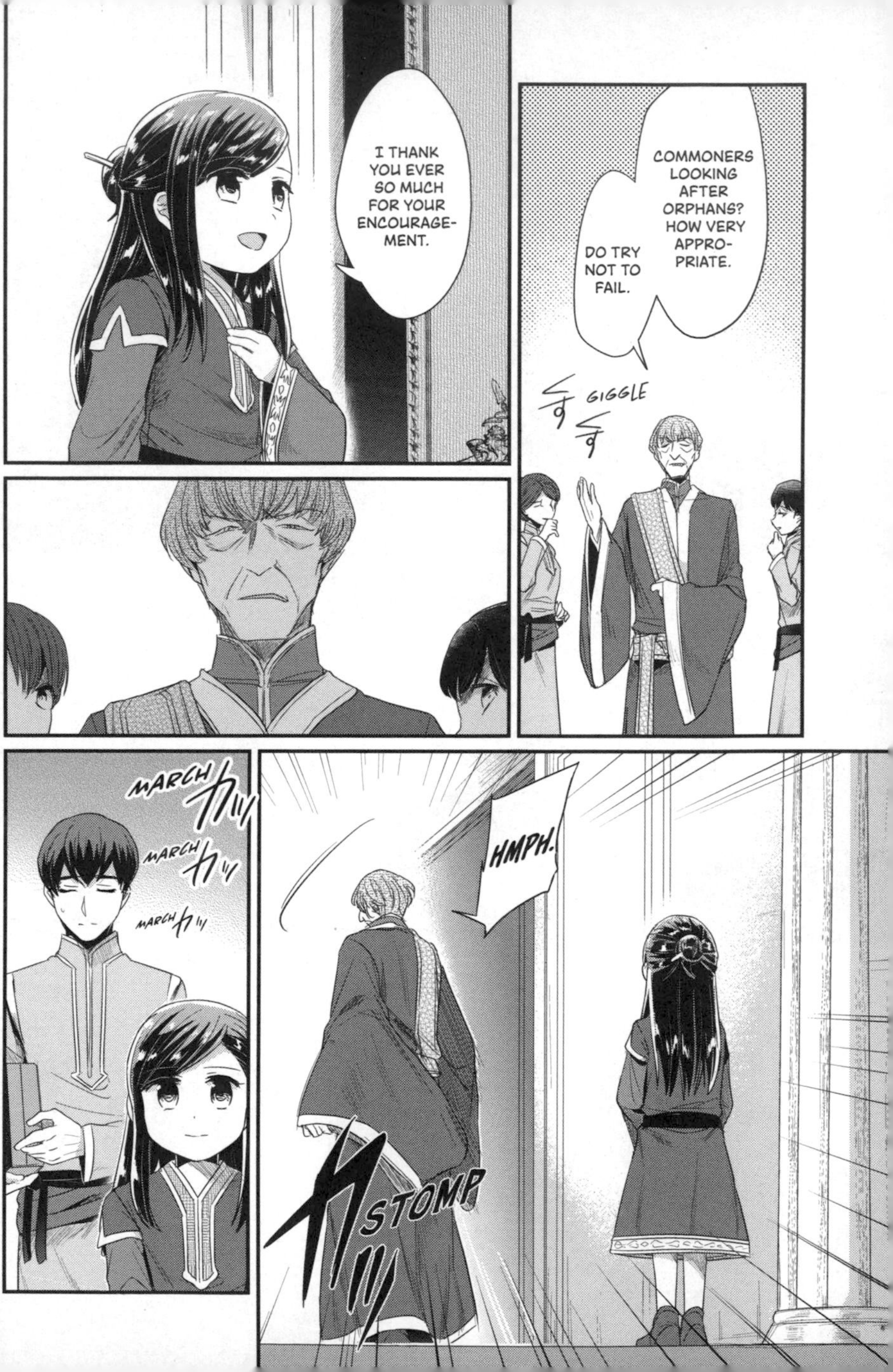
COMMONERS LOOKING AFTER ORPHANS? HOW VERY APPROPRIATE.
DO TRY NOT TO FAIL.
くす くす GIGGLE
I THANK YOU EVER SO MUCH FOR YOUR ENCOURAGE-MENT.
HMPH!
STOMP
MARCH
MARCH
MARCH

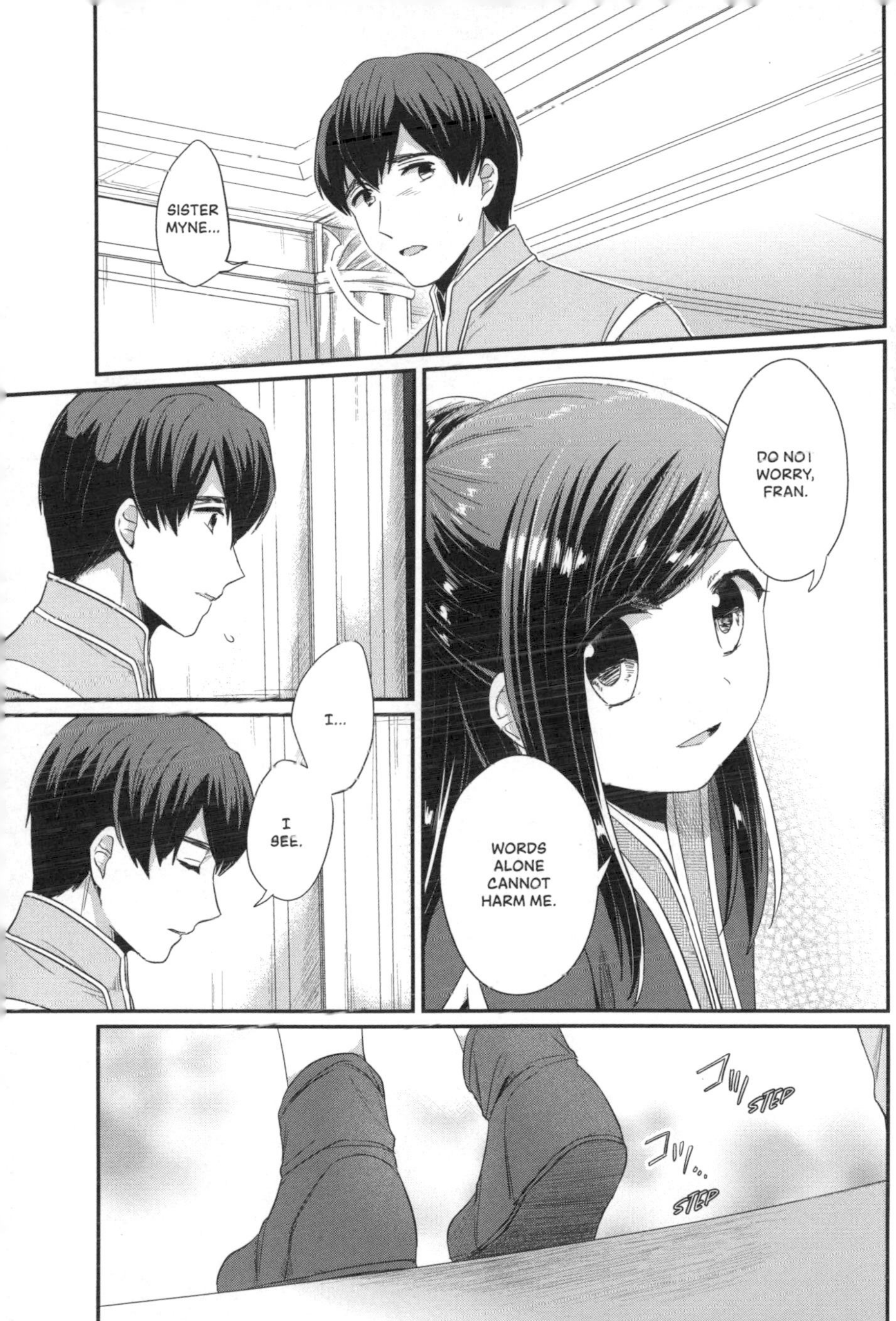
SISTER MYNE...
DO NOT WORRY, FRAN.
WORDS ALONE CANNOT HARM ME.
I...
I SEE.
ゴッ STEP
ゴッ... STEP

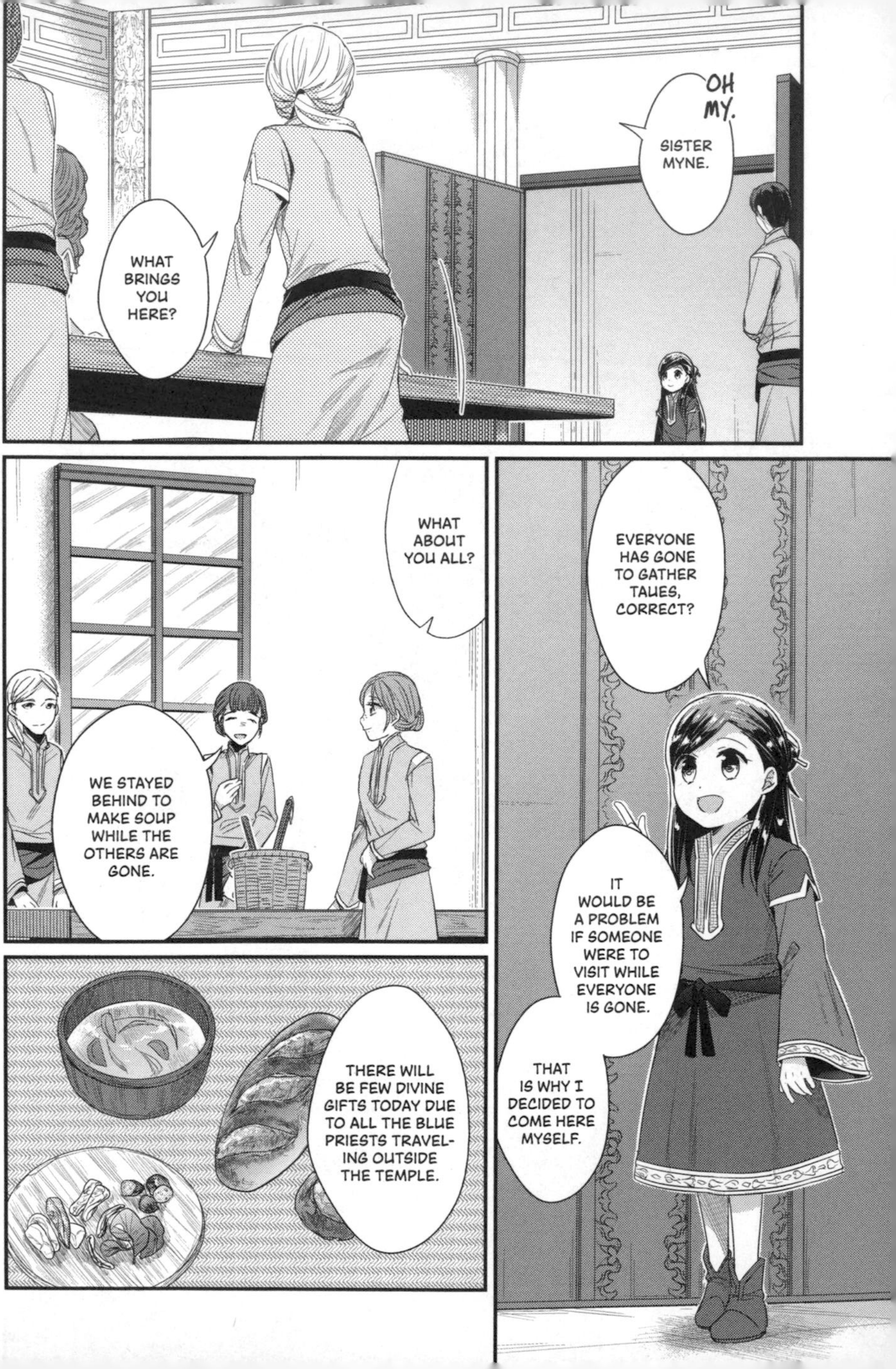
OH MY.
SISTER MYNE.
WHAT BRINGS YOU HERE?
EVERYONE HAS GONE TO GATHER TAUES, CORRECT?
IT WOULD BE A PROBLEM IF SOMEONE WERE TO VISIT WHILE EVERYONE IS GONE.
THAT IS WHY I DECIDED TO COME HERE MYSELF.
WHAT ABOUT YOU ALL?
WE STAYED BEHIND TO MAKE SOUP WHILE THE OTHERS ARE GONE.
THERE WILL BE FEW DIVINE GIFTS TODAY DUE TO ALL THE BLUE PRIESTS TRAVEL-ING OUTSIDE THE TEMPLE.

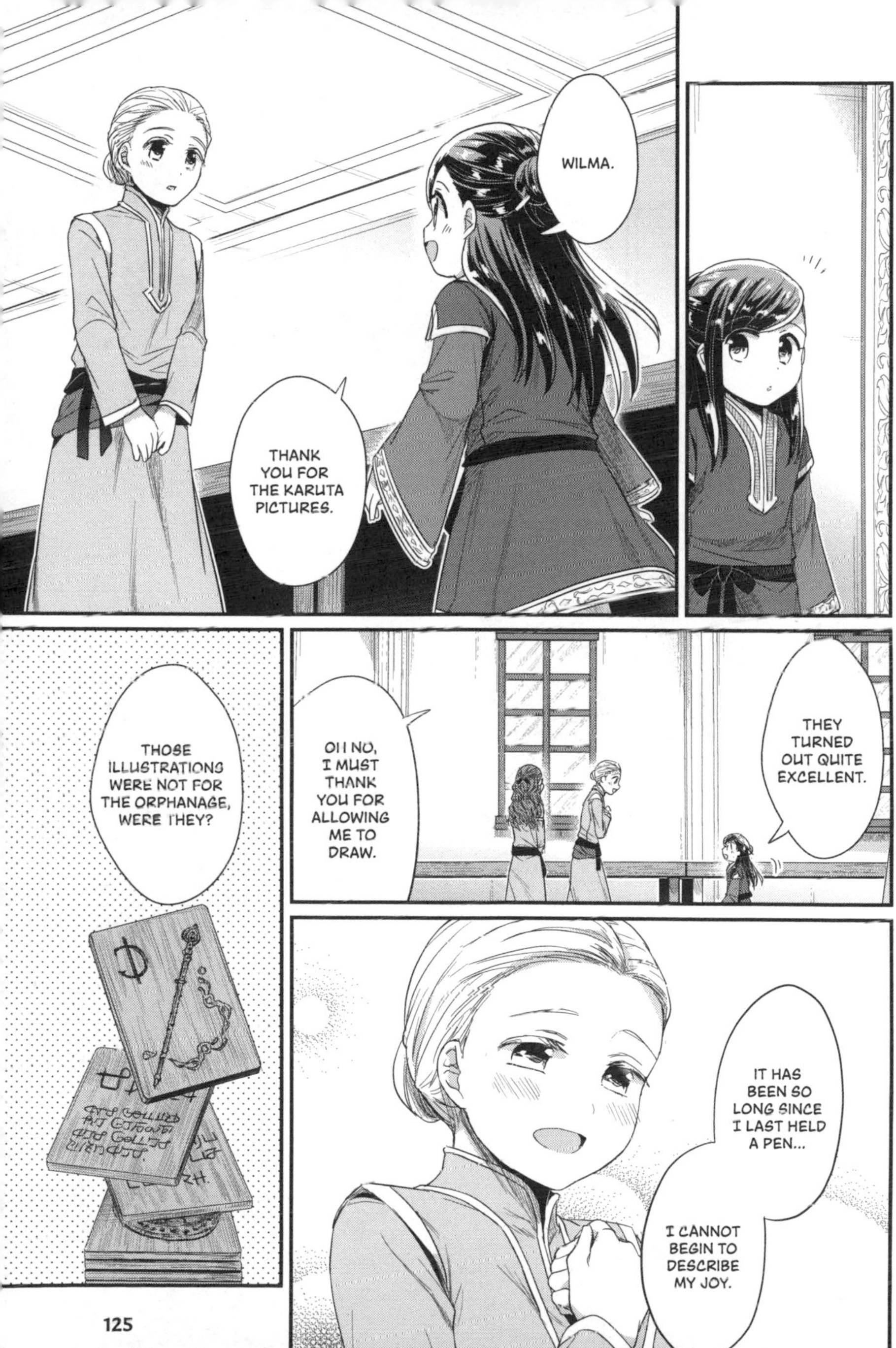
WILMA.
THANK YOU FOR THE KARUTA PICTURES.
THEY TURNED OUT QUITE EXCELLENT.
OH NO, I MUST THANK YOU FOR ALLOWING ME TO DRAW.
IT HAS BEEN SO LONG SINCE I LAST HELD A PEN...
I CANNOT BEGIN TO DESCRIBE MY JOY.
THOSE ILLUSTRATIONS WERE NOT FOR THE ORPHANAGE, WERE THEY?

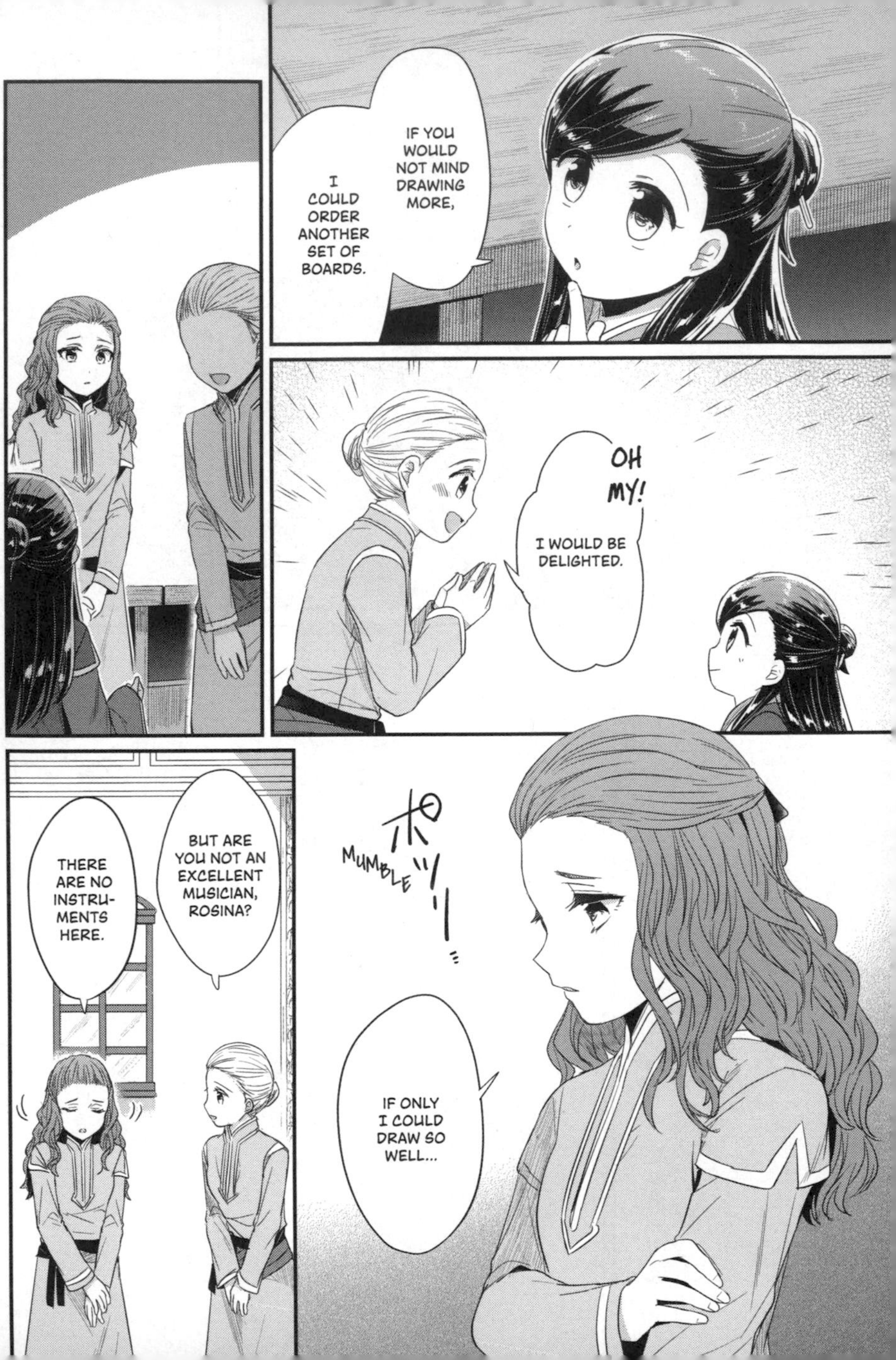
IF YOU WOULD NOT MIND DRAWING MORE,
I COULD ORDER ANOTHER SET OF BOARDS.
OH MY!
I WOULD BE DELIGHTED.
MUMBLE
IF ONLY I COULD DRAW SO WELL...
BUT ARE YOU NOT AN EXCELLENT MUSICIAN, ROSINA?
THERE ARE NO INSTRUMENTS HERE.

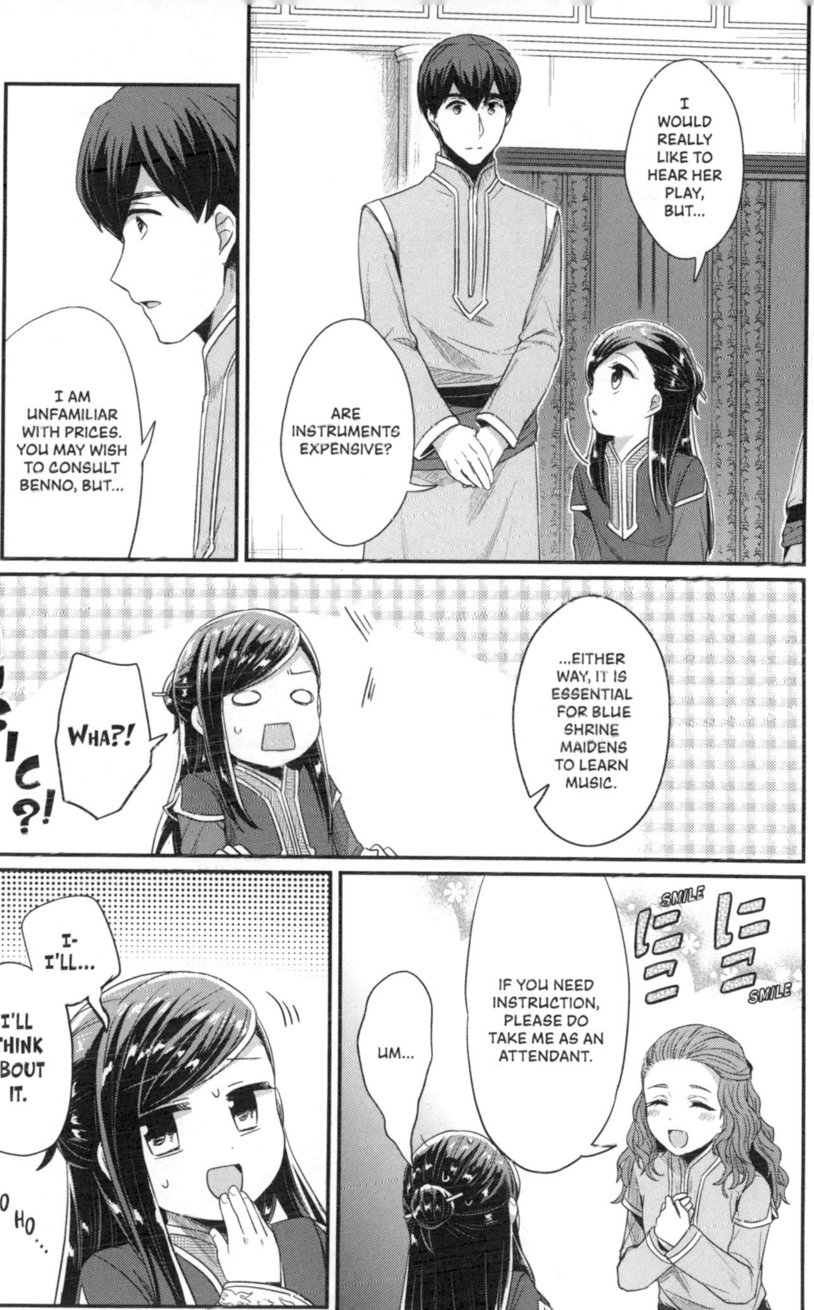
I WOULD REALLY LIKE TO HEAR HER PLAY, BUT...
ARE INSTRUMENTS EXPENSIVE?
I AM UNFAMILIAR WITH PRICES. YOU MAY WISH TO CONSULT BENNO, BUT...
...EITHER WAY, IT IS ESSENTIAL FOR BLUE SHRINE MAIDENS TO LEARN MUSIC.
WHA?!
MUSIC?!
SMILE
SMILE
IF YOU NEED INSTRUCTION, PLEASE DO TAKE ME AS AN ATTENDANT.
UM...
I- I'LL...
I'LL THINK ABOUT IT.
OHO HO HO...

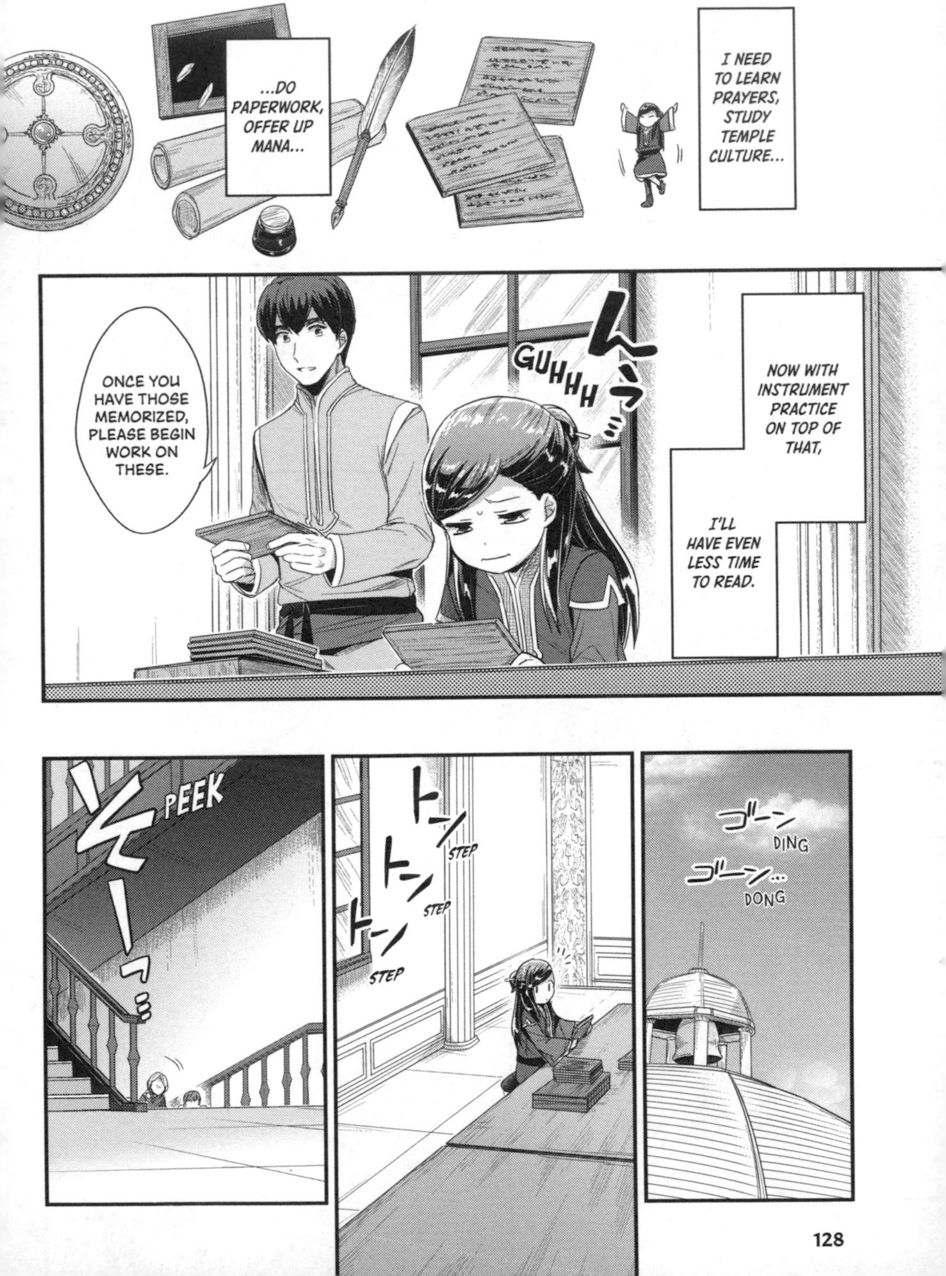
I NEED TO LEARN PRAYERS, STUDY TEMPLE CULTURE...
...DO PAPERWORK, OFFER UP MANA...
NOW WITH INSTRUMENT PRACTICE ON TOP OF THAT,
I'LL HAVE EVEN LESS TIME TO READ.
GUHHHH
ONCE YOU HAVE THOSE MEMORIZED, PLEASE BEGIN WORK ON THESE.
DING
DONG
STEP
STEP
STEP
PEEK

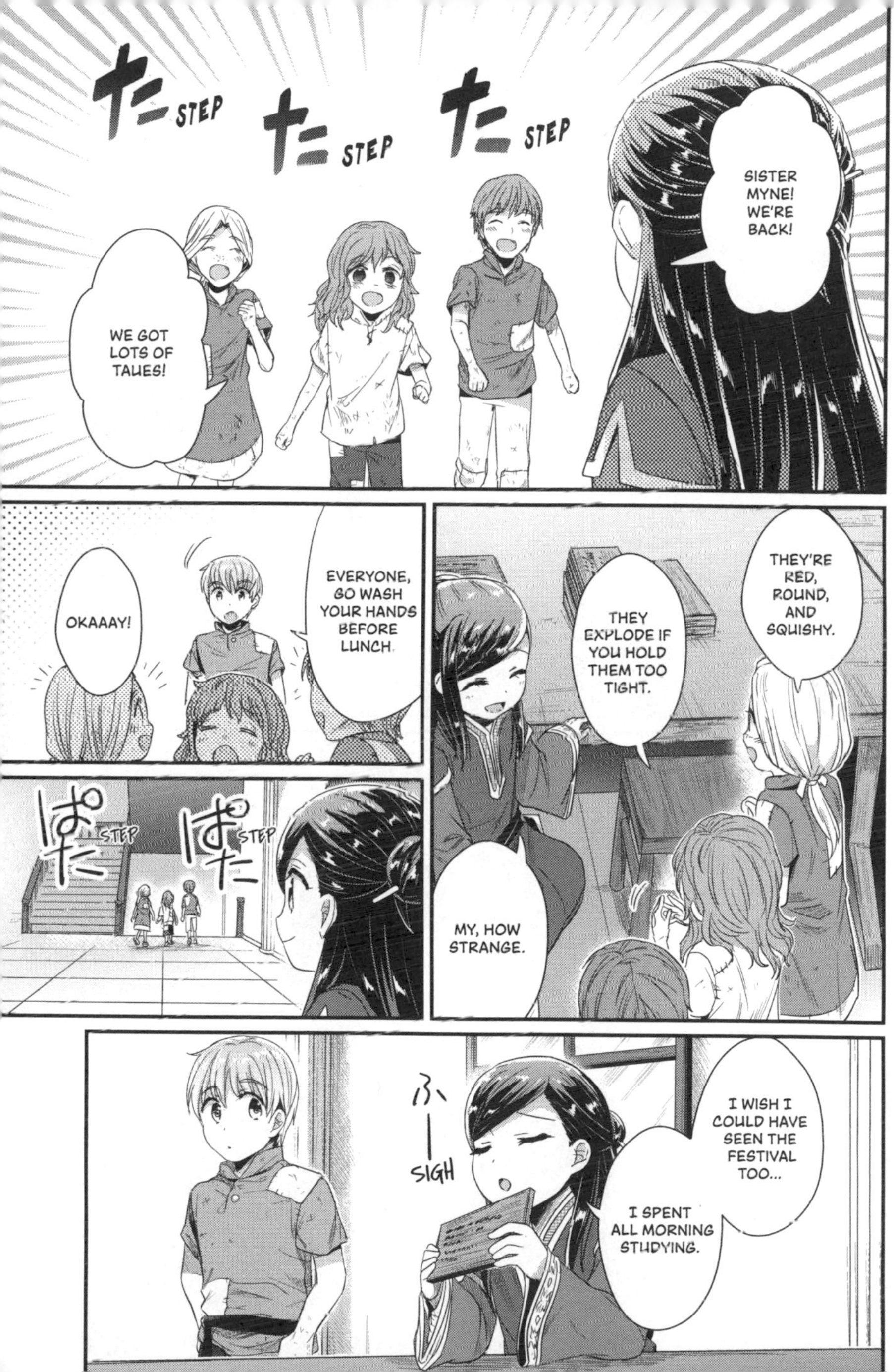
た STEP
た STEP
た STEP
SISTER MYNE! WE'RE BACK!
WE GOT LOTS OF TAUES!
THEY'RE RED, ROUND, AND SQUISHY.
THEY EXPLODE IF YOU HOLD THEM TOO TIGHT.
MY, HOW STRANGE.
EVERYONE, GO WASH YOUR HANDS BEFORE LUNCH.
OKAAAY!
ぱた STEP
ぱた STEP
I WISH I COULD HAVE SEEN THE FESTIVAL TOO...
I SPENT ALL MORNING STUDYING.
ふー SIGH

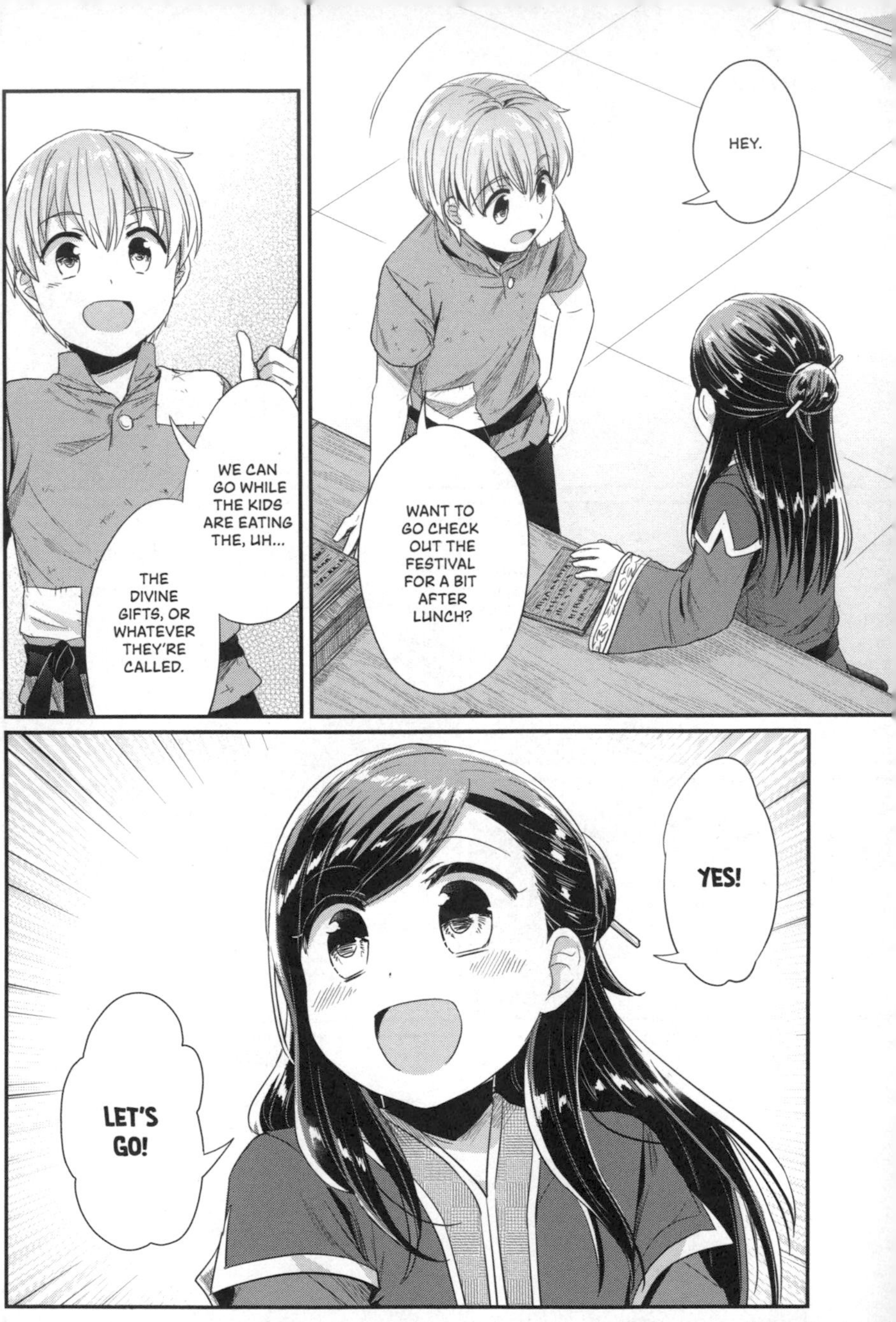
HEY.
WANT TO GO CHECK OUT THE FESTIVAL FOR A BIT AFTER LUNCH?
WE CAN GO WHILE THE KIDS ARE EATING THE, UH...
THE DIVINE GIFTS, OR WHATEVER THEY'RE CALLED.
YES!
LET'S GO!

Ch. 14: Preparing for the Star Festival **End**

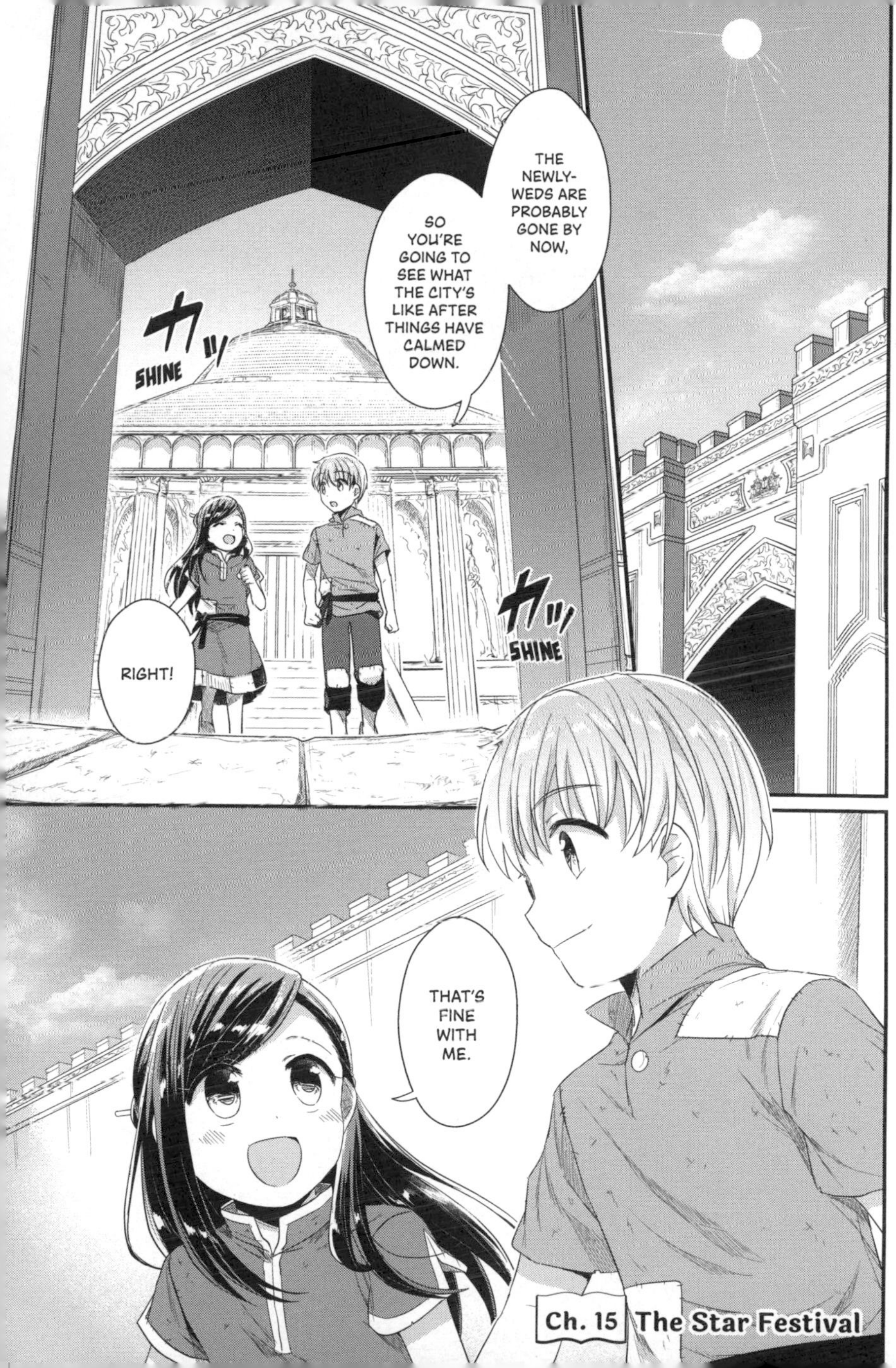
THE NEWLY-WEDS ARE PROBABLY GONE BY NOW,
SO YOU'RE GOING TO SEE WHAT THE CITY'S LIKE AFTER THINGS HAVE CALMED DOWN.
SHINE
SHINE
RIGHT!
THAT'S FINE WITH ME.

Ch. 15 The Star Festival

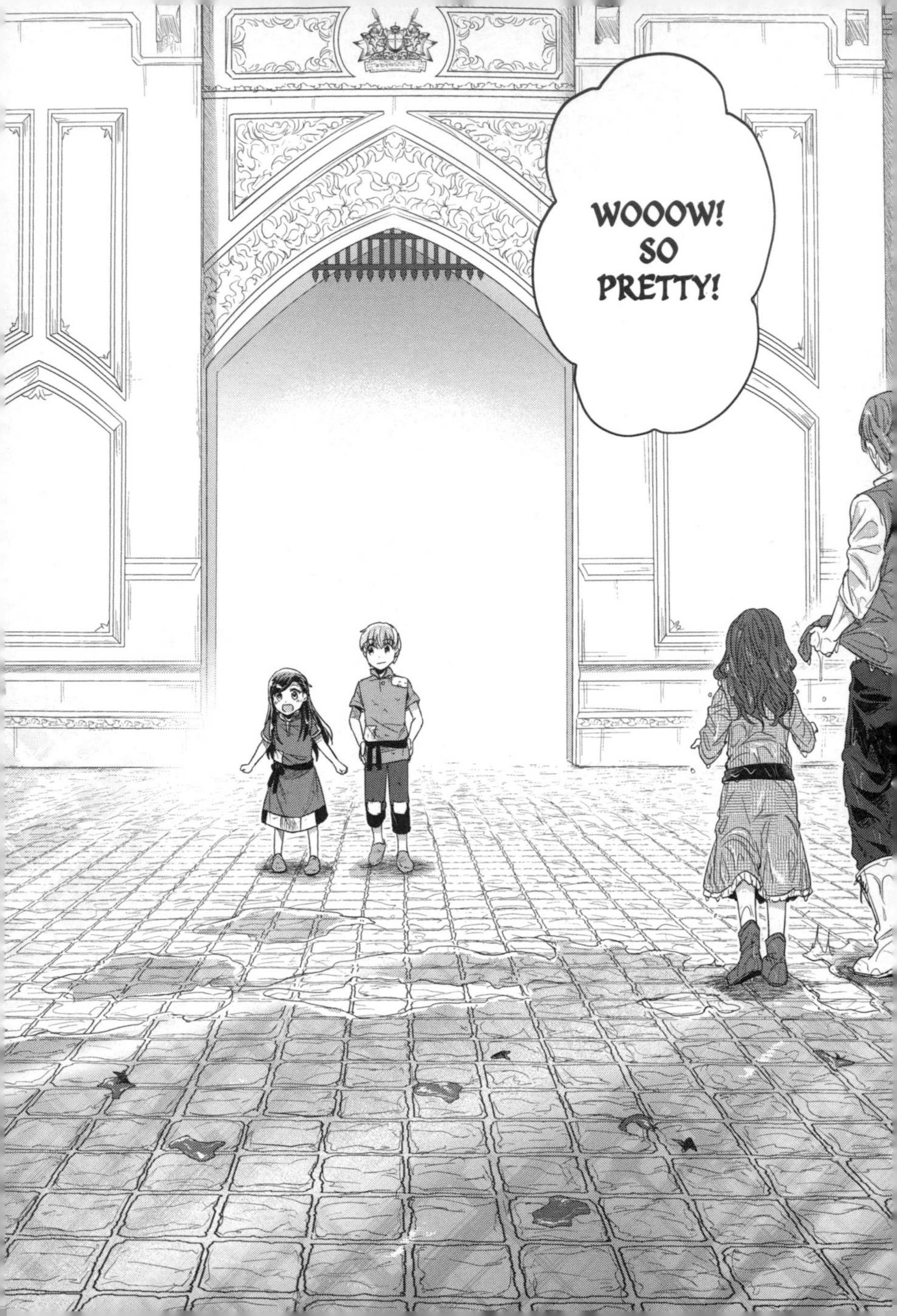
WOOOW! SO PRETTY!

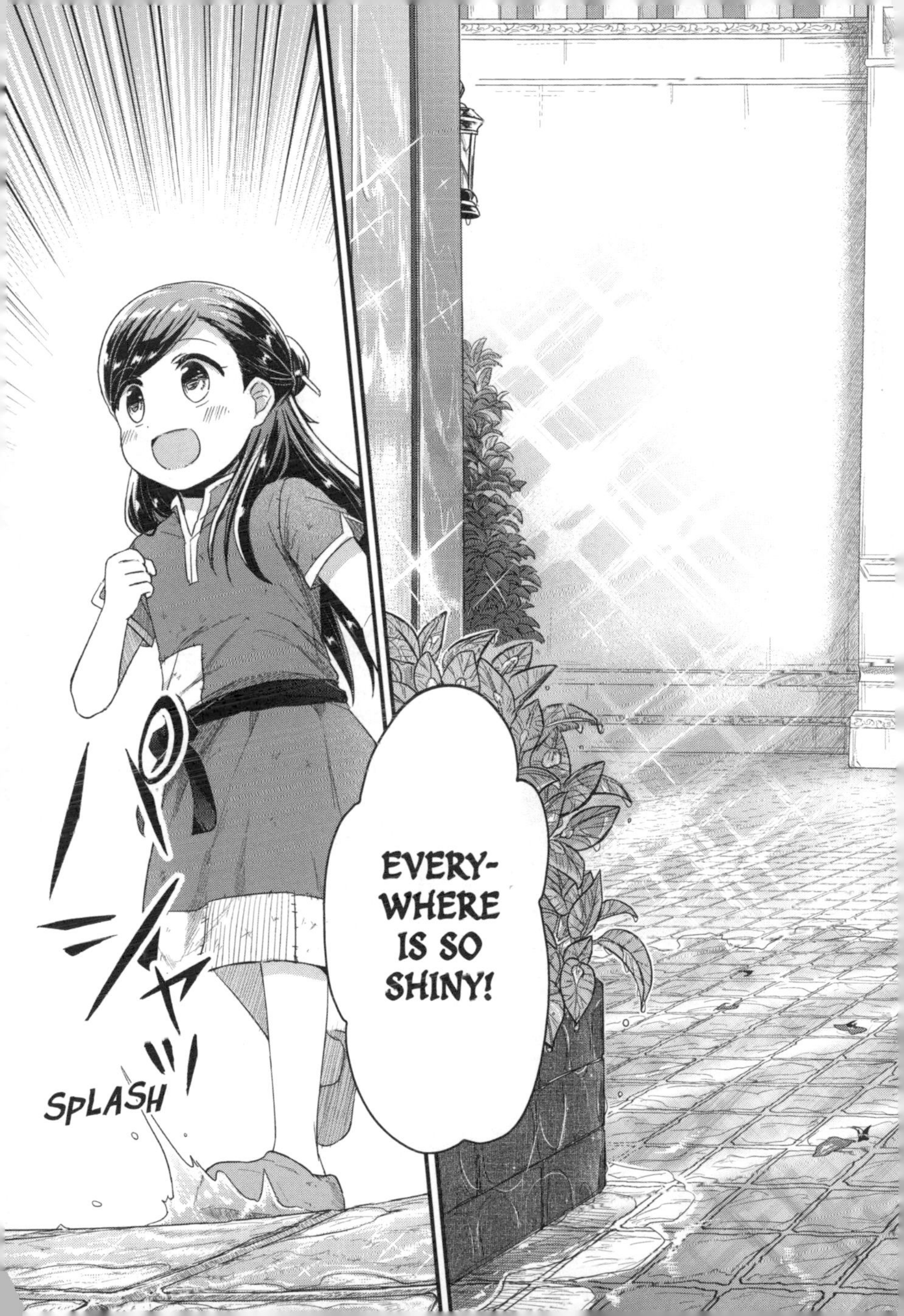
EVERY-WHERE IS SO SHINY!
SPLASH

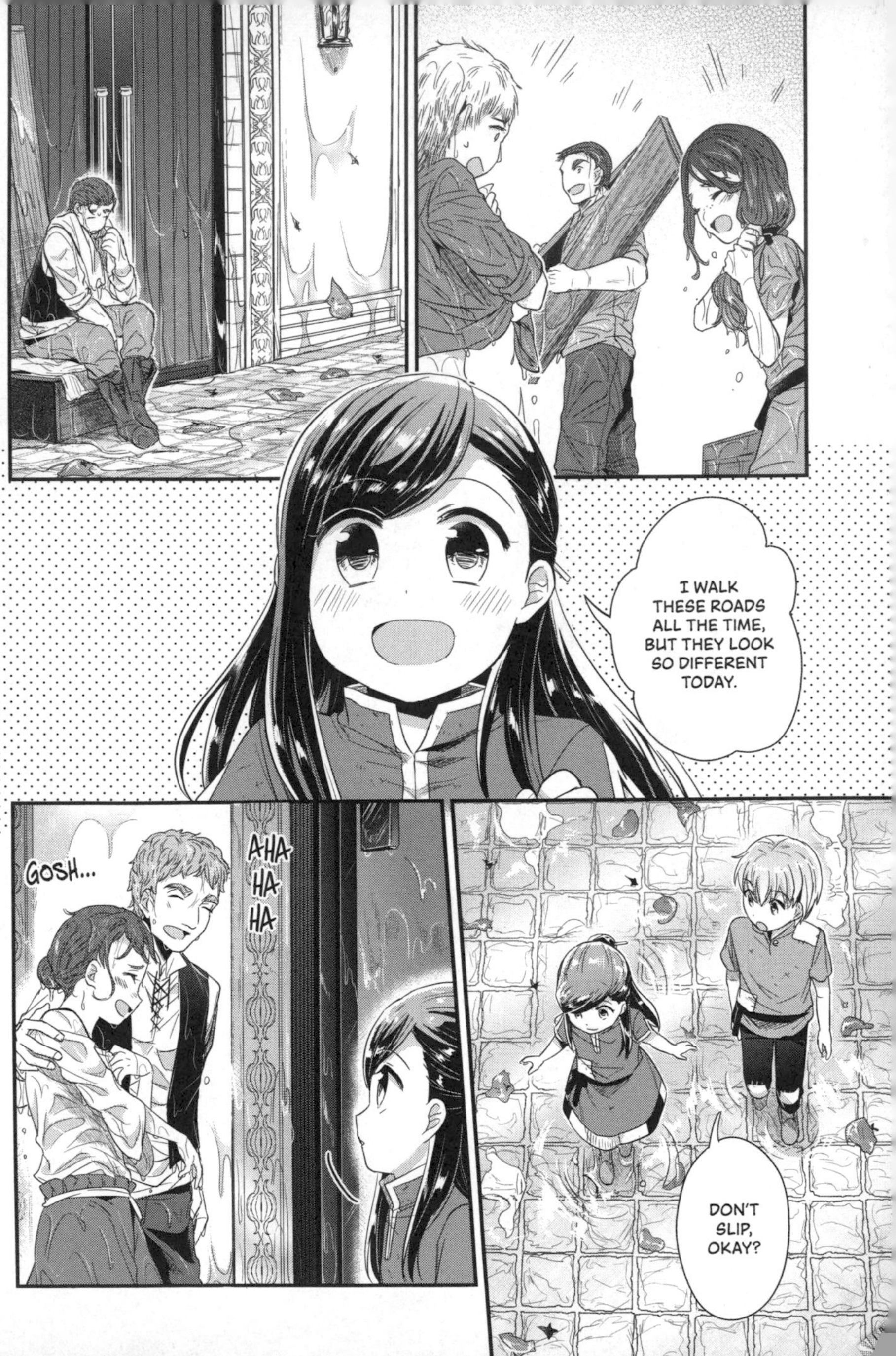
I WALK THESE ROADS ALL THE TIME, BUT THEY LOOK SO DIFFERENT TODAY.
DON'T SLIP, OKAY?
AHA HA HA
GOSH...

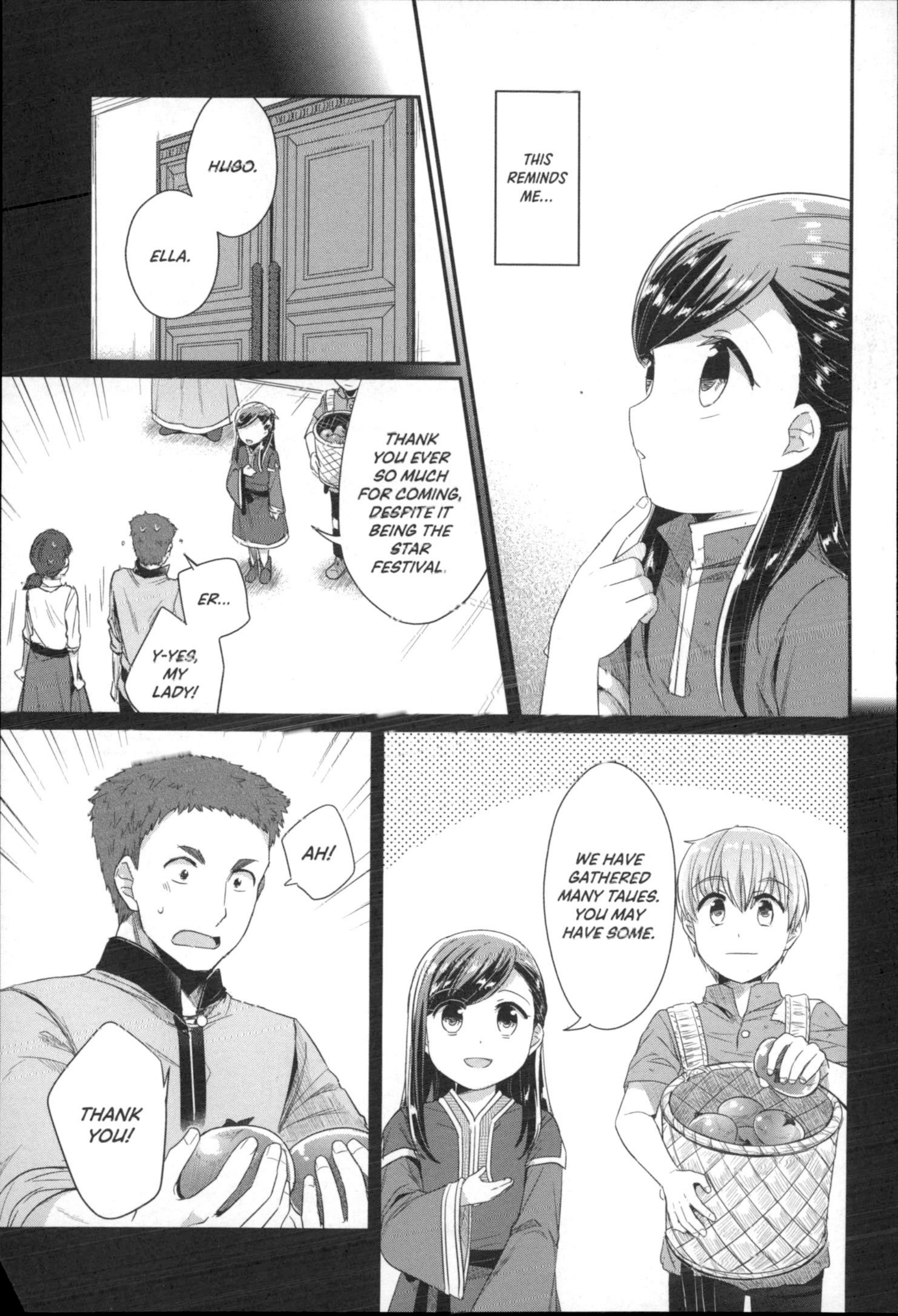
THIS REMINDS ME...
HUGO.
ELLA.
THANK YOU EVER SO MUCH FOR COMING, DESPITE IT BEING THE STAR FESTIVAL.
ER...
Y-YES, MY LADY!
WE HAVE GATHERED MANY TAUES. YOU MAY HAVE SOME.
AH!
THANK YOU!

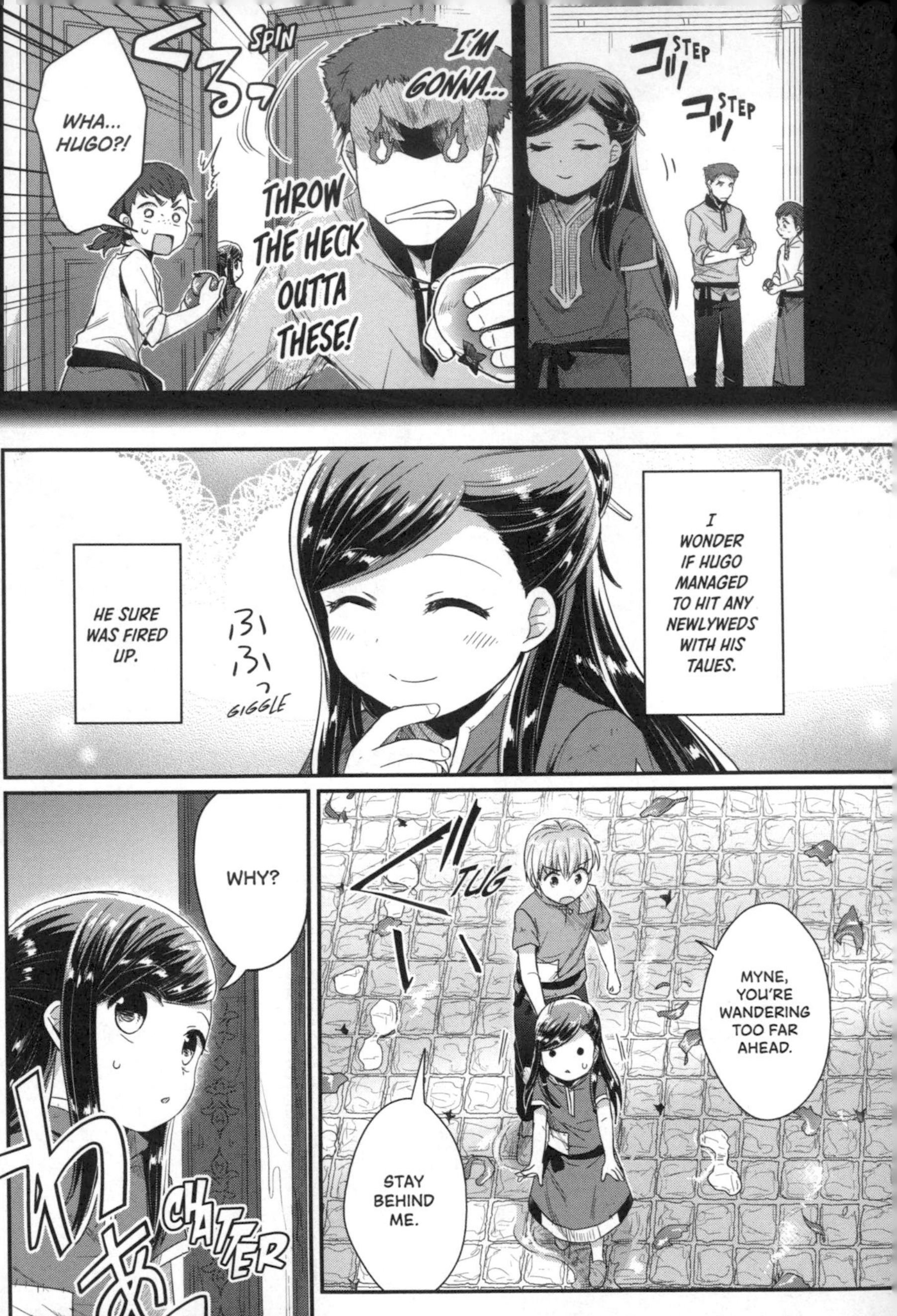

ゴッ STEP
ゴッ STEP
くるっ SPIN
I'M GONNA...
THROW THE HECK OUTTA THESE!
WHA... HUGO?!
I WONDER IF HUGO MANAGED TO HIT ANY NEWLYWEDS WITH HIS TAUES.
HE SURE WAS FIRED UP.
ふふっ GIGGLE
MYNE, YOU'RE WANDERING TOO FAR AHEAD.
ぐいっ TUG
STAY BEHIND ME.
WHY?
わあっ CHATTER

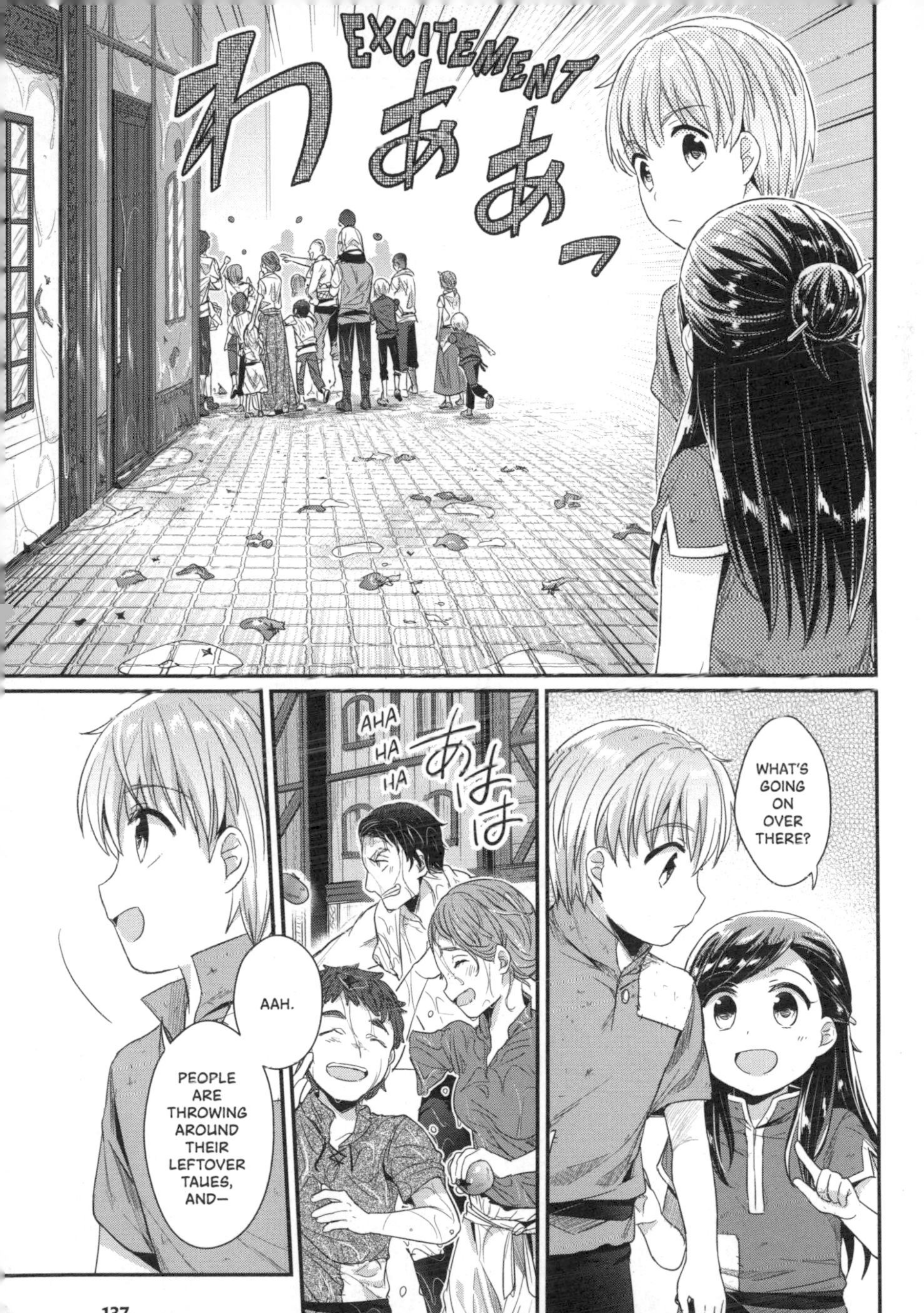
EXCITEMENT
わあああっ
WHAT'S GOING ON OVER THERE?
AHA HA HA
あはは
AAH.
PEOPLE ARE THROWING AROUND THEIR LEFTOVER TAUES, AND—

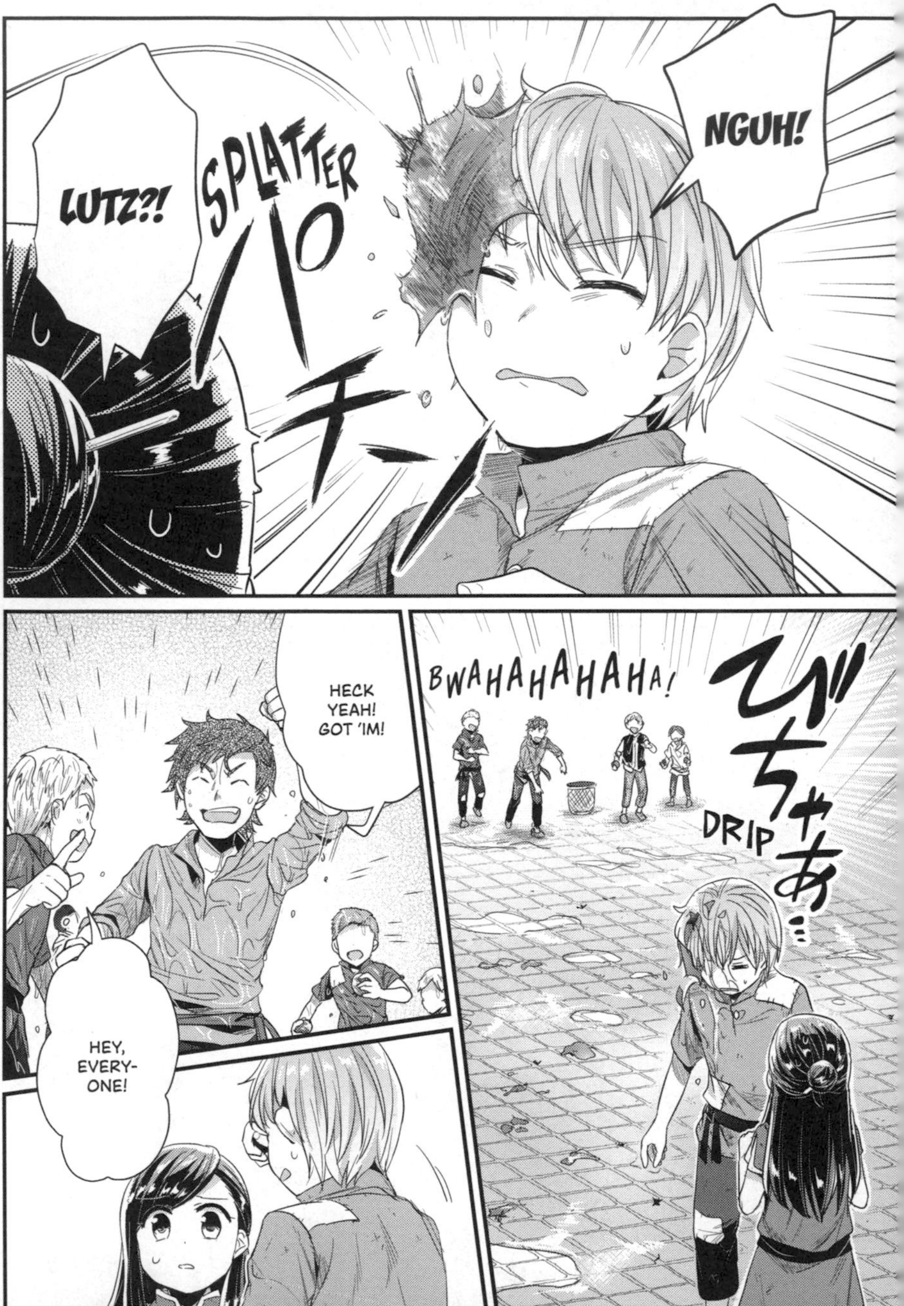
NGUH!
SPLATTER
パチーン
LUTZ?!
BWAHAHAHAHAHA!
びちゃあ…
DRIP
HECK YEAH! GOT 'IM!
HEY, EVERY-ONE!

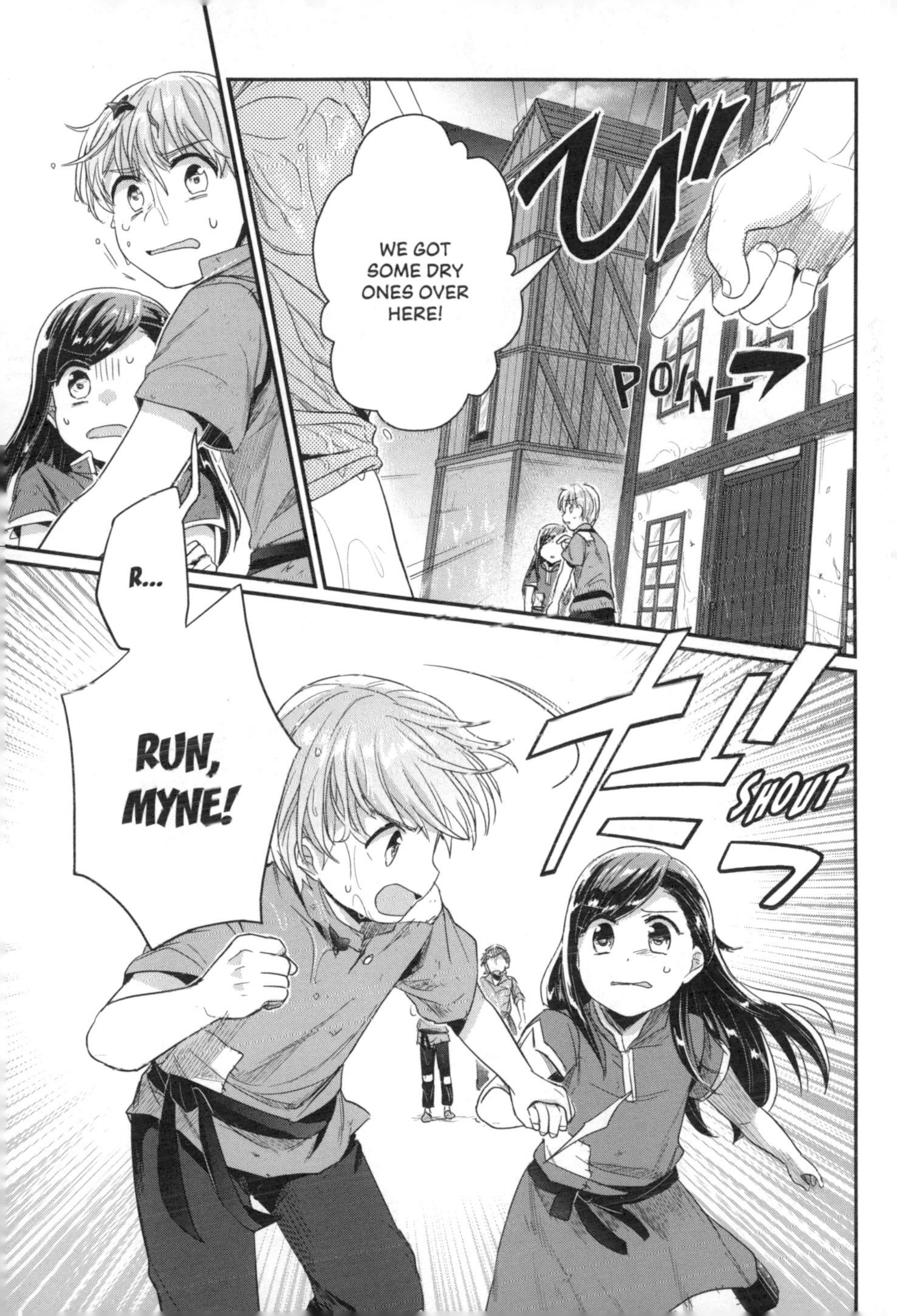
WE GOT SOME DRY ONES OVER HERE!
POINT
R...
RUN, MYNE!
SHOUT

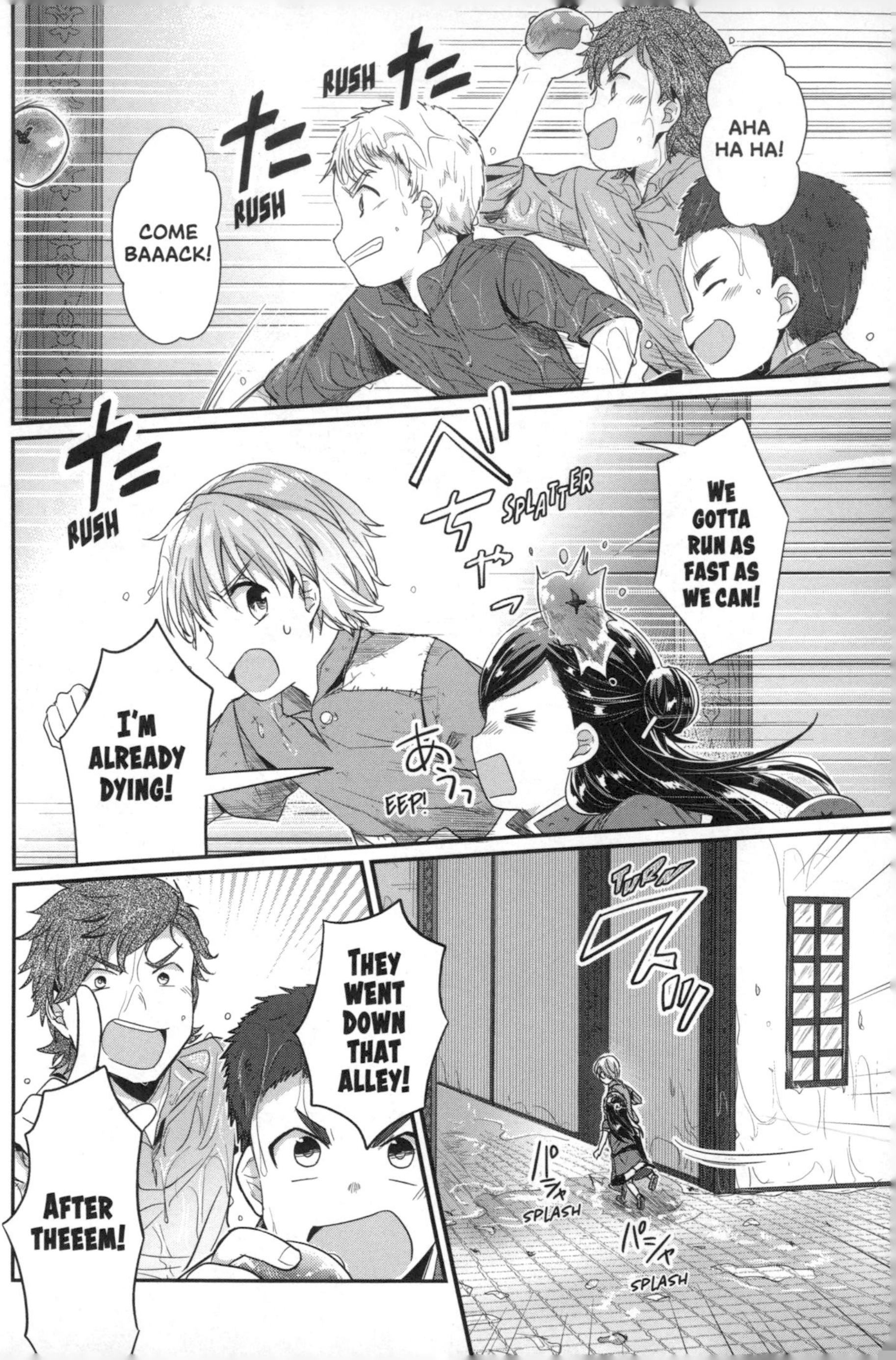
AHA HA HA!
RUSH
RUSH
COME BAAACK!
WE GOTTA RUN AS FAST AS WE CAN!
SPLATTER
EEP!
RUSH
I'M ALREADY DYING!
TURN
SPLASH
SPLASH
THEY WENT DOWN THAT ALLEY!
AFTER THEEEM!

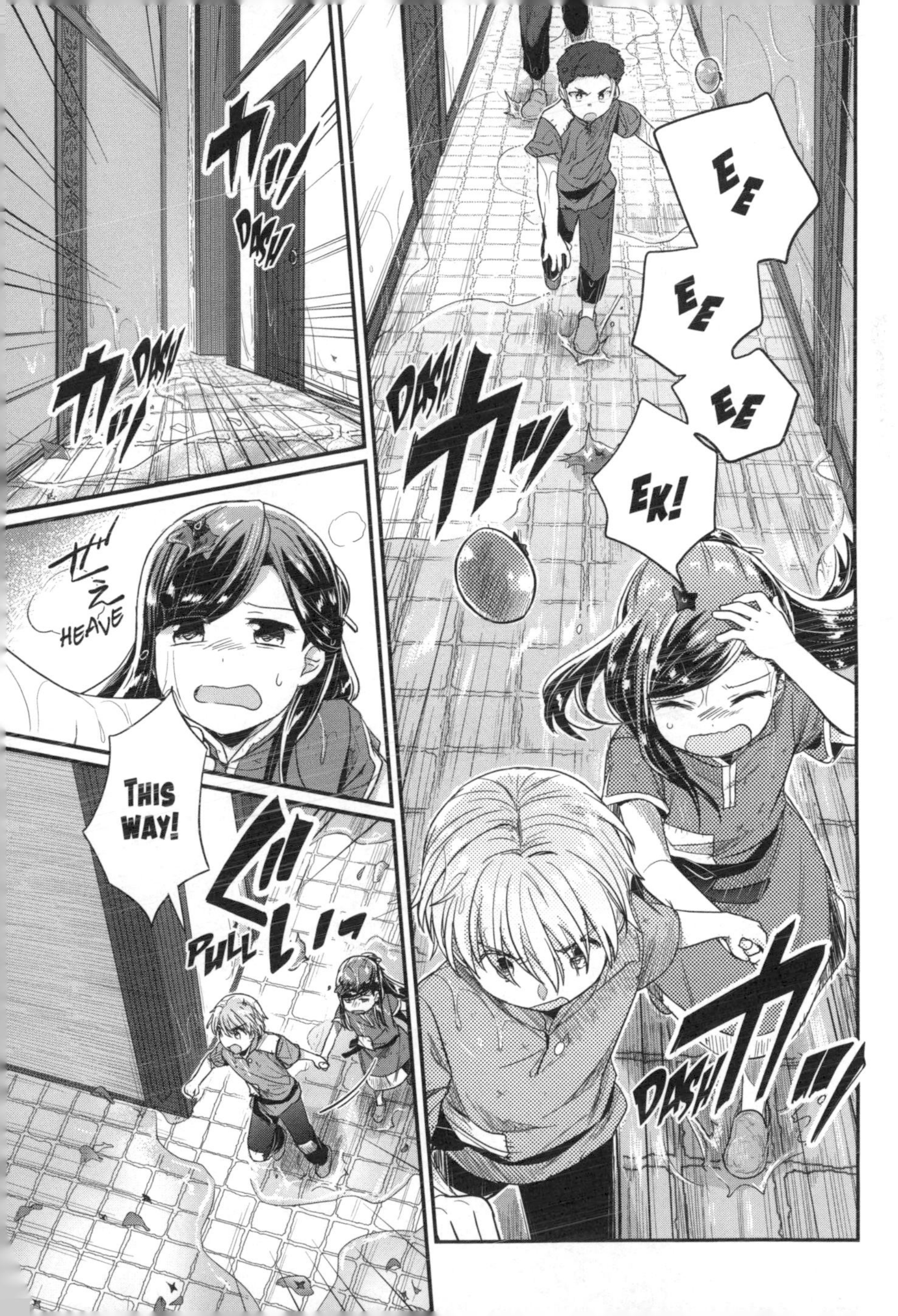
EE
EE
EE
EK!
DASH
DASH
DASH
DASH
HEAVE
THIS WAY!
PULL

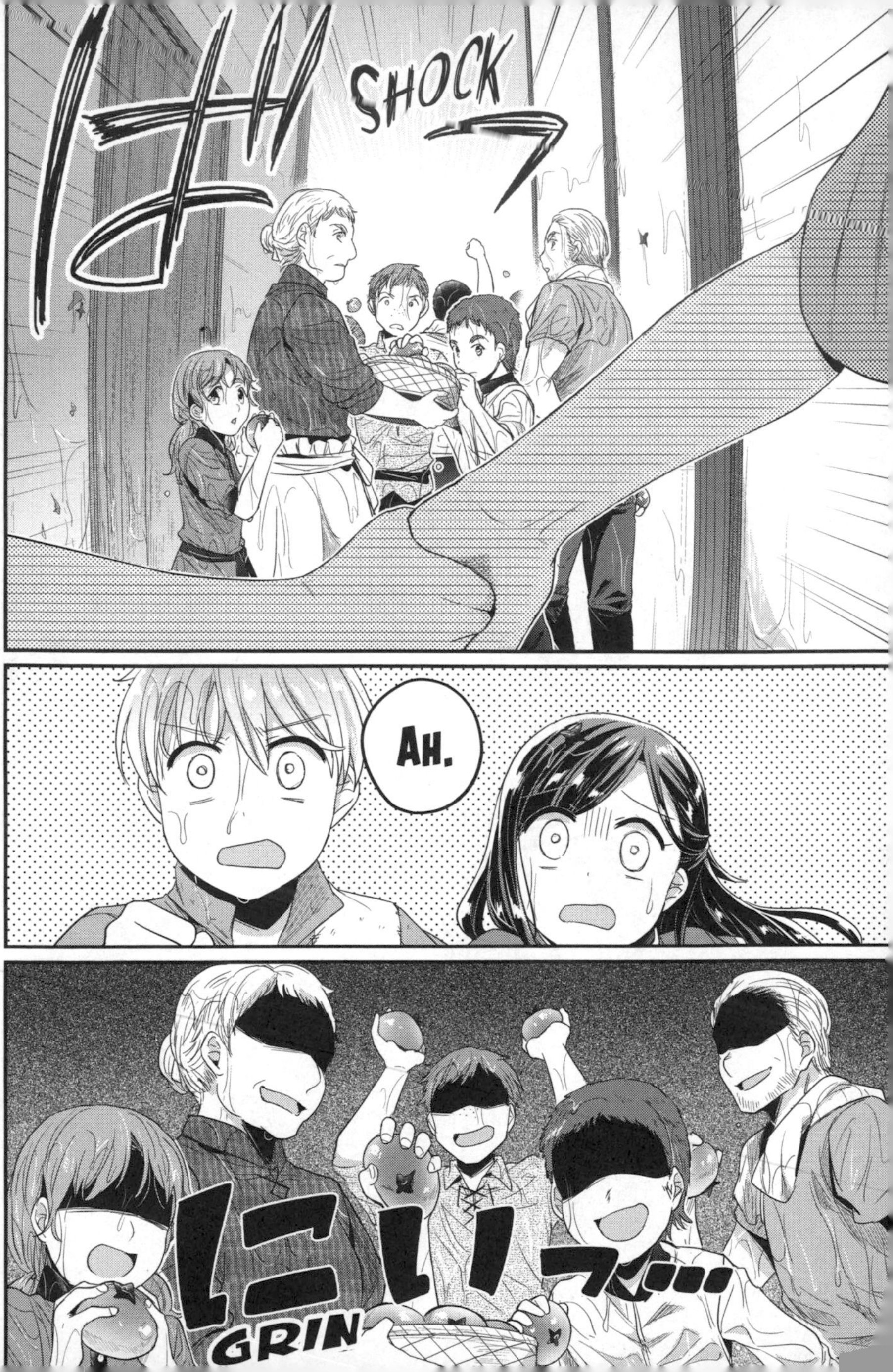
SHOCK
AH.
GRIN

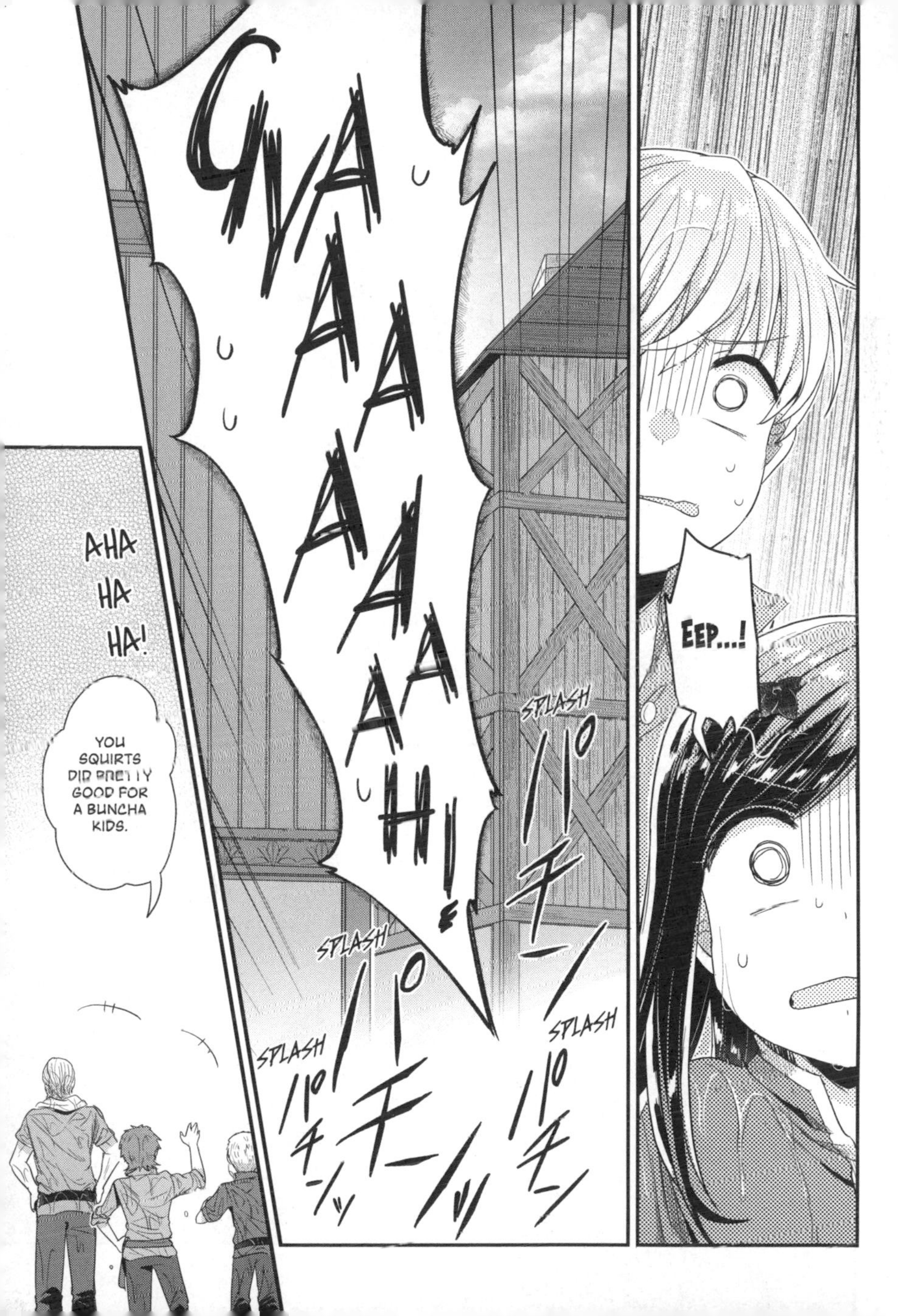
EEP...!
GYAAAAAAAH!
SPLASH
SPLASH
SPLASH
SPLASH
AHA HA HA!
YOU SQUIRTS DID PRETTY GOOD FOR A BUNCHA KIDS.

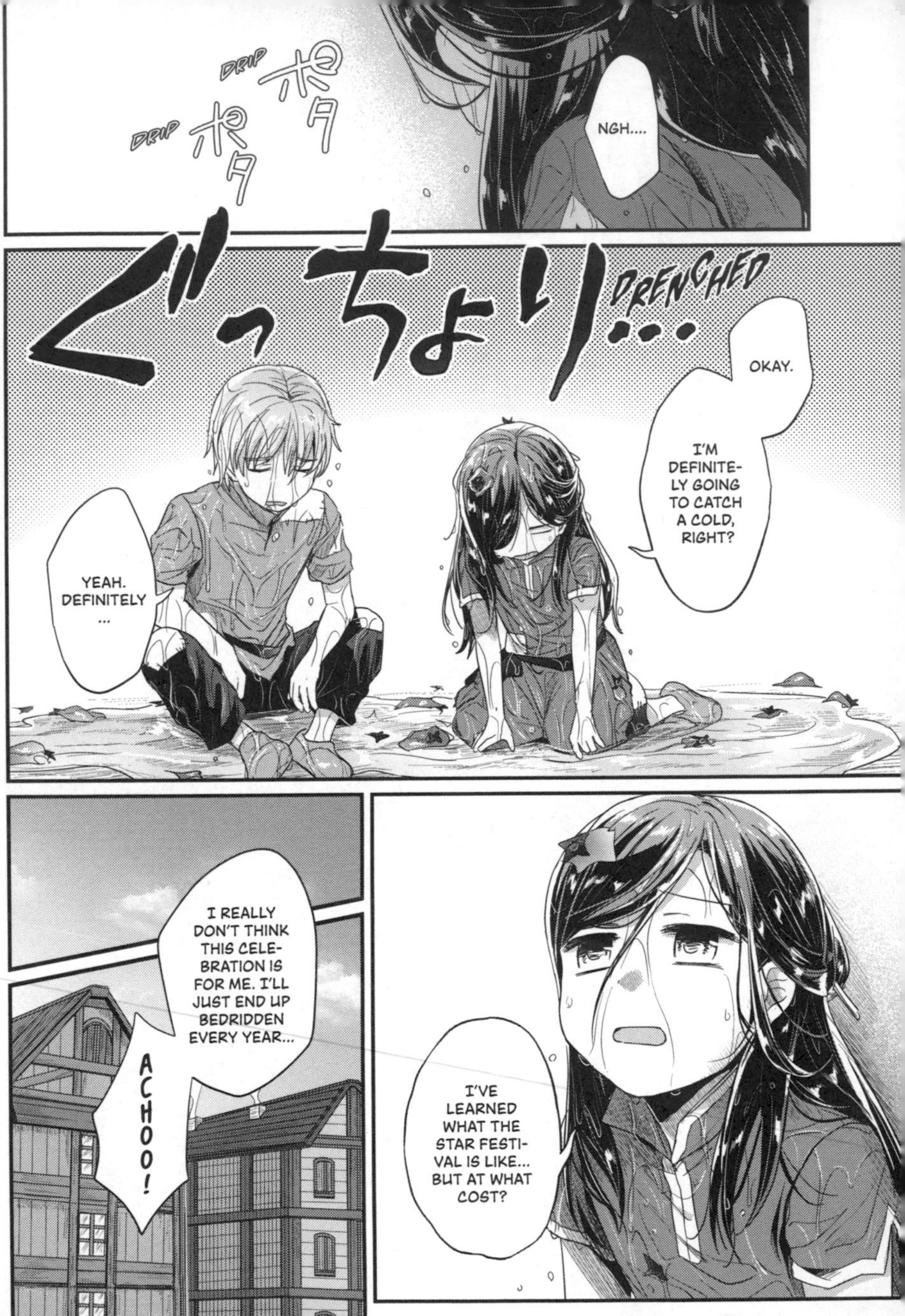
NGH....
DRIP ポタ
DRIP ポタ
ぐっちょり…
DRENCHED
OKAY.
I'M DEFINITE-LY GOING TO CATCH A COLD, RIGHT?
YEAH. DEFINITELY ...
I'VE LEARNED WHAT THE STAR FESTI-VAL IS LIKE... BUT AT WHAT COST?
I REALLY DON'T THINK THIS CELE-BRATION IS FOR ME. I'LL JUST END UP BEDRIDDEN EVERY YEAR...
ACHOO!

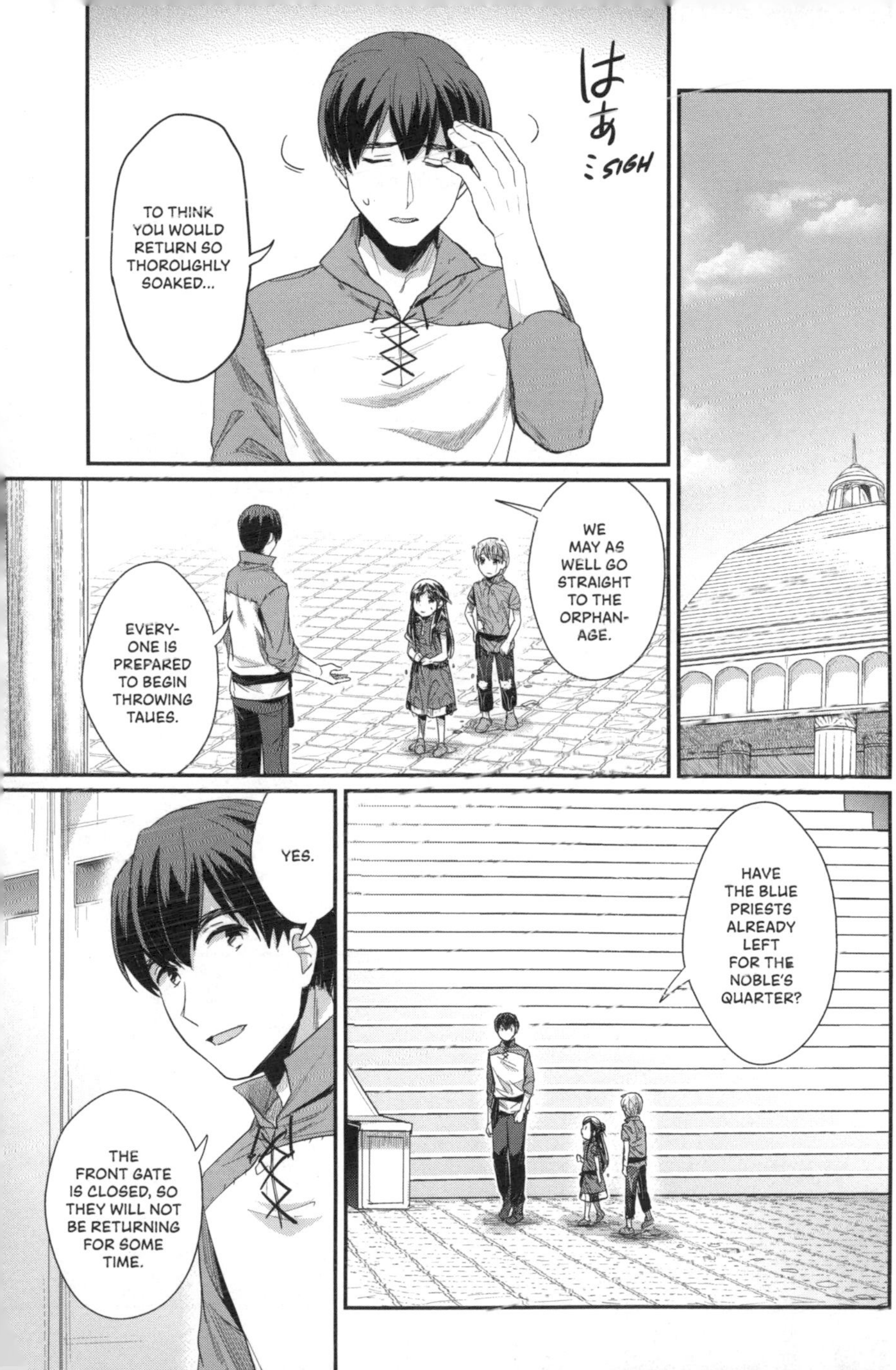
はあ
SIGH
TO THINK YOU WOULD RETURN SO THOROUGHLY SOAKED...
WE MAY AS WELL GO STRAIGHT TO THE ORPHAN-AGE.
EVERY-ONE IS PREPARED TO BEGIN THROWING TAUES.
HAVE THE BLUE PRIESTS ALREADY LEFT FOR THE NOBLE'S QUARTER?
YES.
THE FRONT GATE IS CLOSED, SO THEY WILL NOT BE RETURNING FOR SOME TIME.

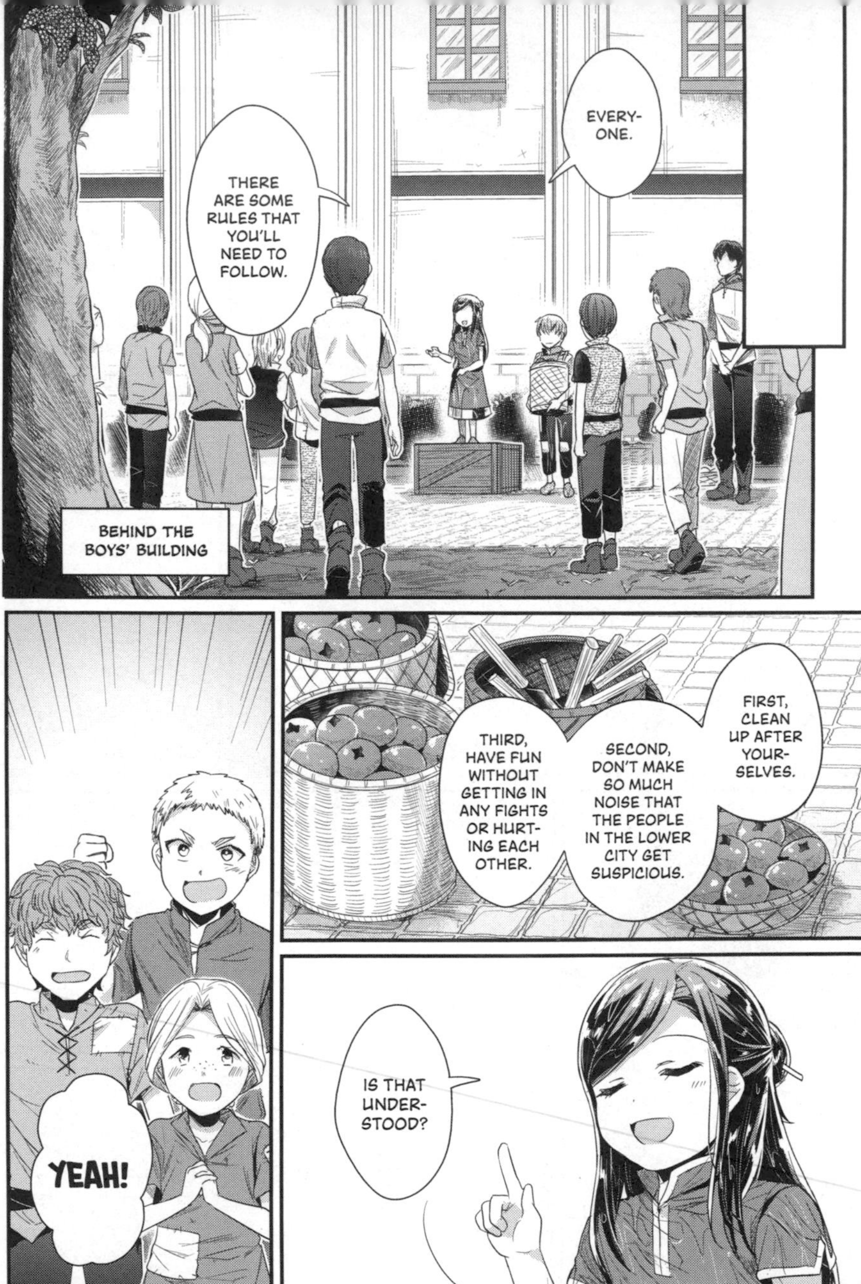
EVERY-ONE.
THERE ARE SOME RULES THAT YOU'LL NEED TO FOLLOW.
BEHIND THE BOYS' BUILDING
FIRST, CLEAN UP AFTER YOUR-SELVES.
SECOND, DON'T MAKE SO MUCH NOISE THAT THE PEOPLE IN THE LOWER CITY GET SUSPICIOUS.
THIRD, HAVE FUN WITHOUT GETTING IN ANY FIGHTS OR HURT-ING EACH OTHER.
IS THAT UNDER-STOOD?
YEAH!

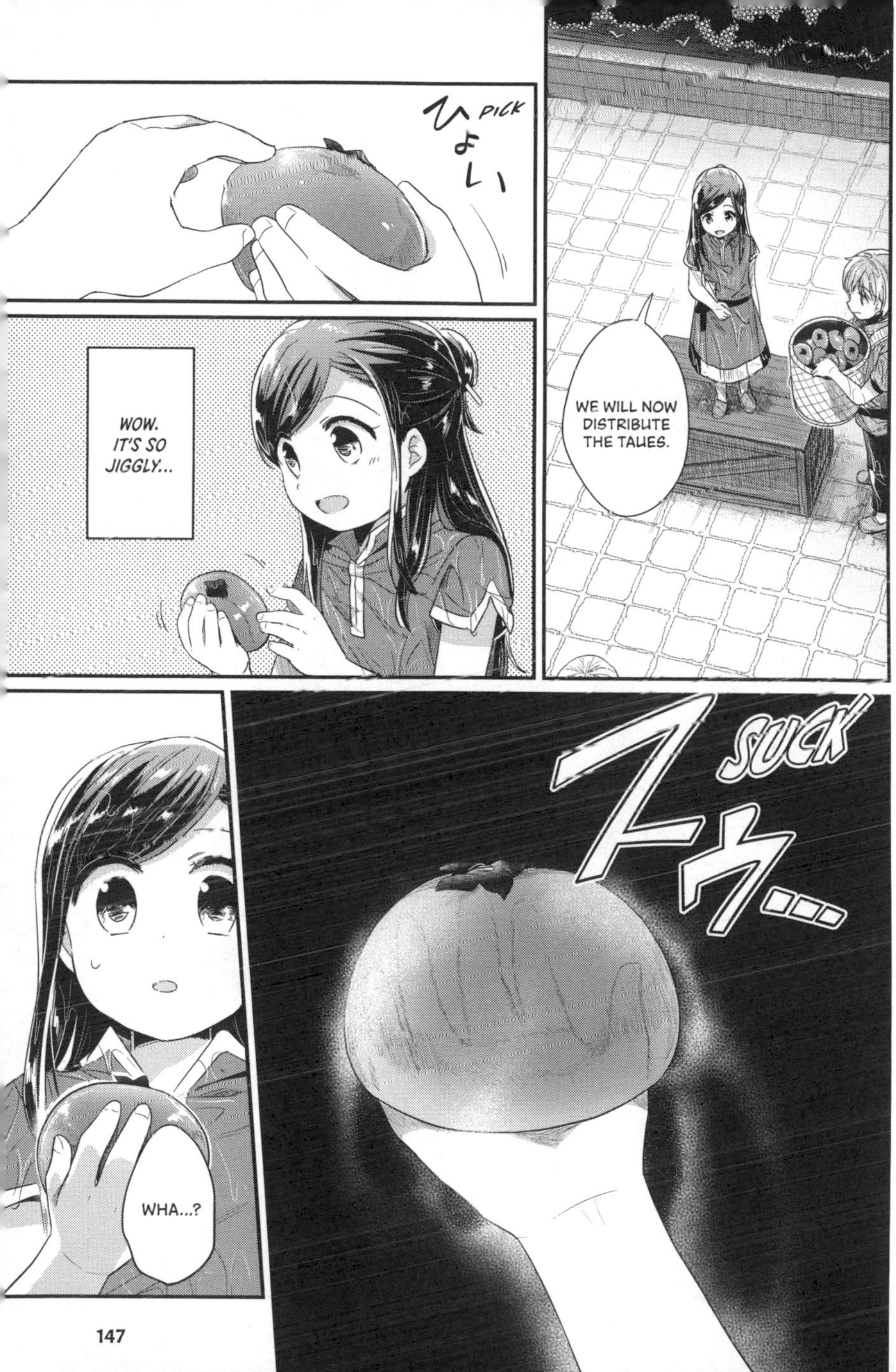
WE WILL NOW DISTRIBUTE THE TAUES.
ひょい
PICK
WOW. IT'S SO JIGGLY...
スゥ…
SUCK
WHA...?

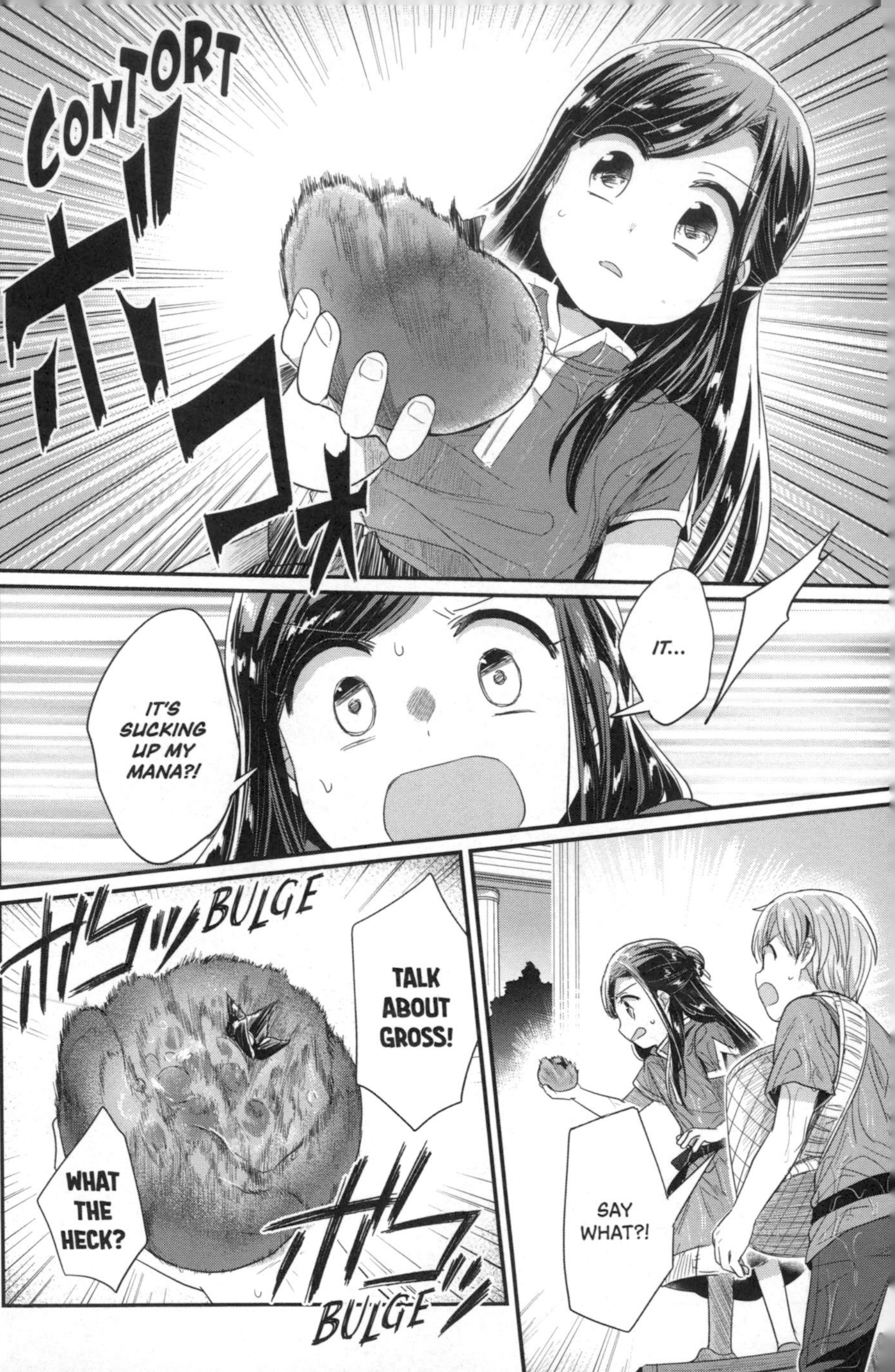
CONTORT
IT...
IT'S SUCKING UP MY MANA?!
SAY WHAT?!
BULGE
TALK ABOUT GROSS!
WHAT THE HECK?
BULGE

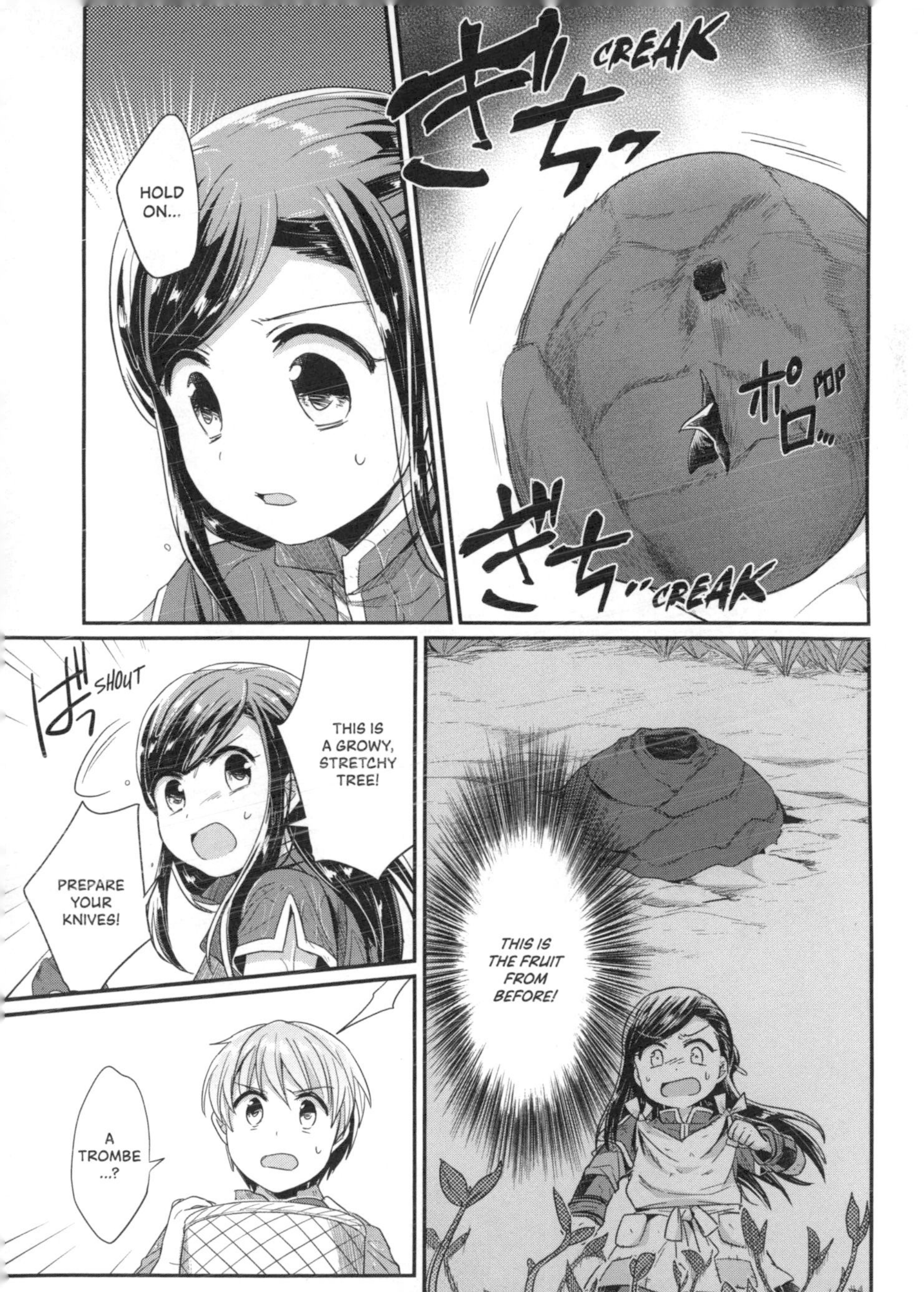
CREAK
POP
CREAK
HOLD ON...
THIS IS THE FRUIT FROM BEFORE!
SHOUT
THIS IS A GROWY, STRETCHY TREE!
PREPARE YOUR KNIVES!
A TROMBE ...?

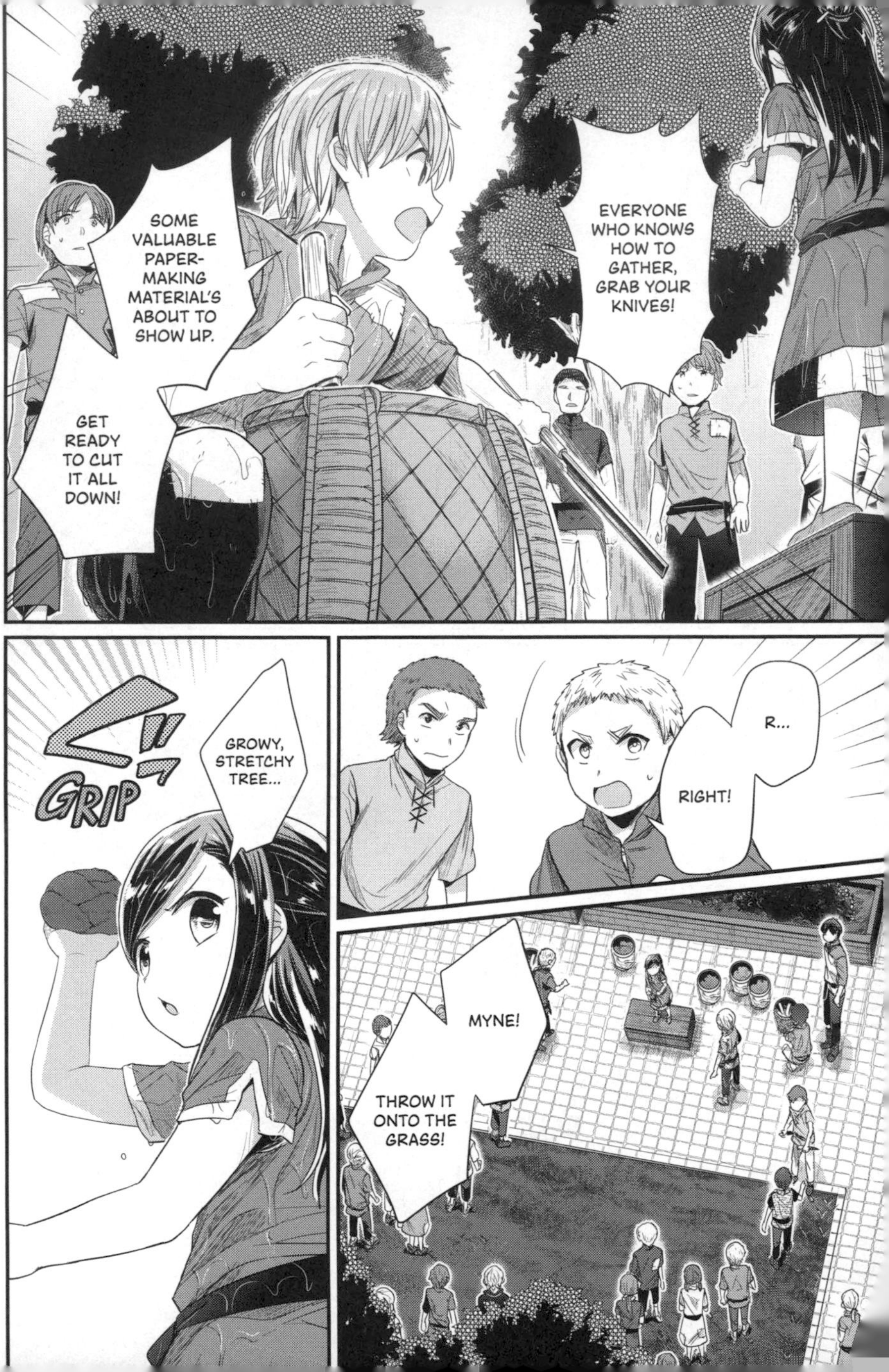
EVERYONE WHO KNOWS HOW TO GATHER, GRAB YOUR KNIVES!
SOME VALUABLE PAPER-MAKING MATERIAL'S ABOUT TO SHOW UP.
GET READY TO CUT IT ALL DOWN!
R...
RIGHT!
MYNE!
THROW IT ONTO THE GRASS!
GRIP
GROWY, STRETCHY TREE...

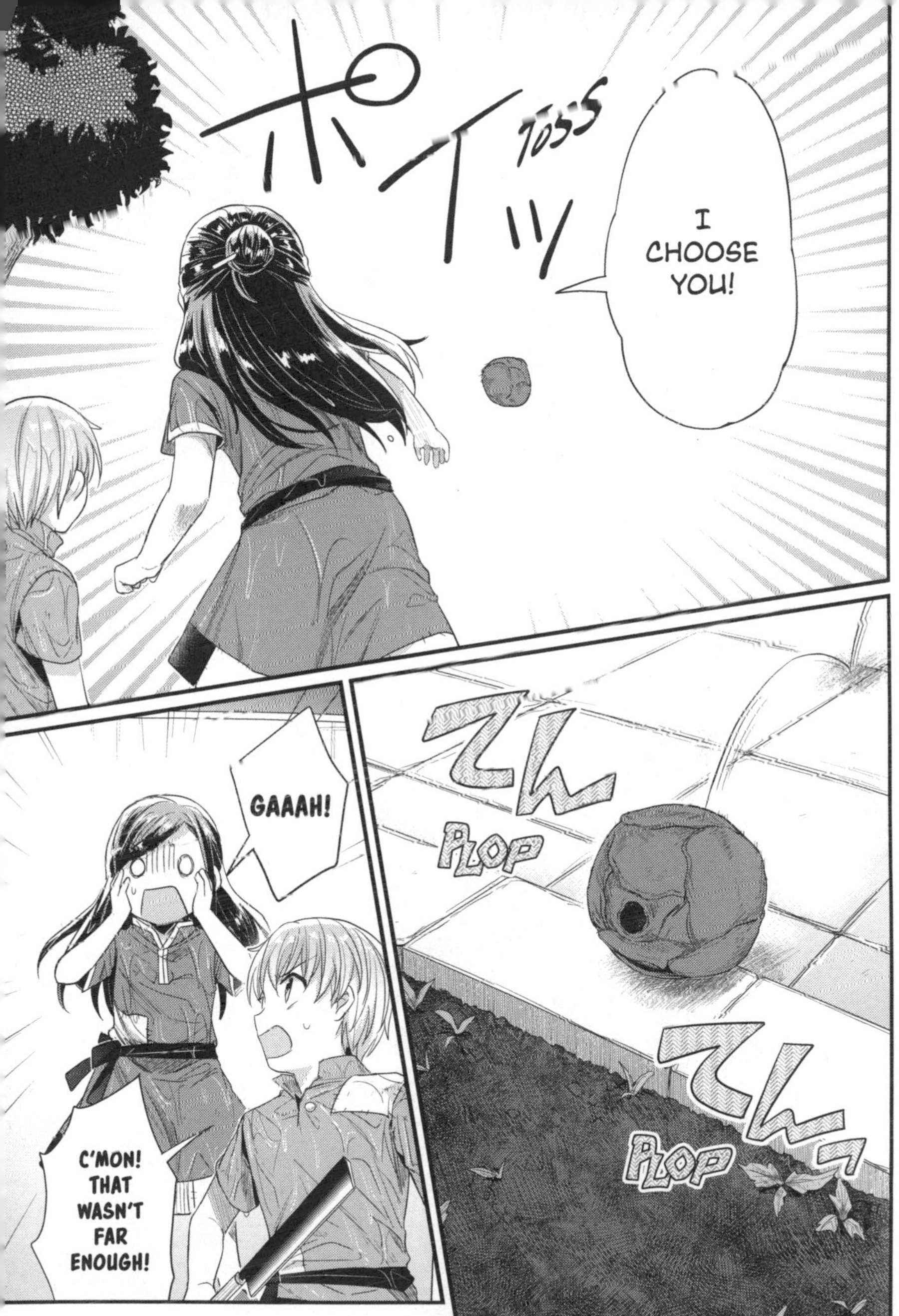
I CHOOSE YOU!
ポイッ
TOSS
てん
PLOP
てんっ
PLOP
GAAAH!
C'MON! THAT WASN'T FAR ENOUGH!

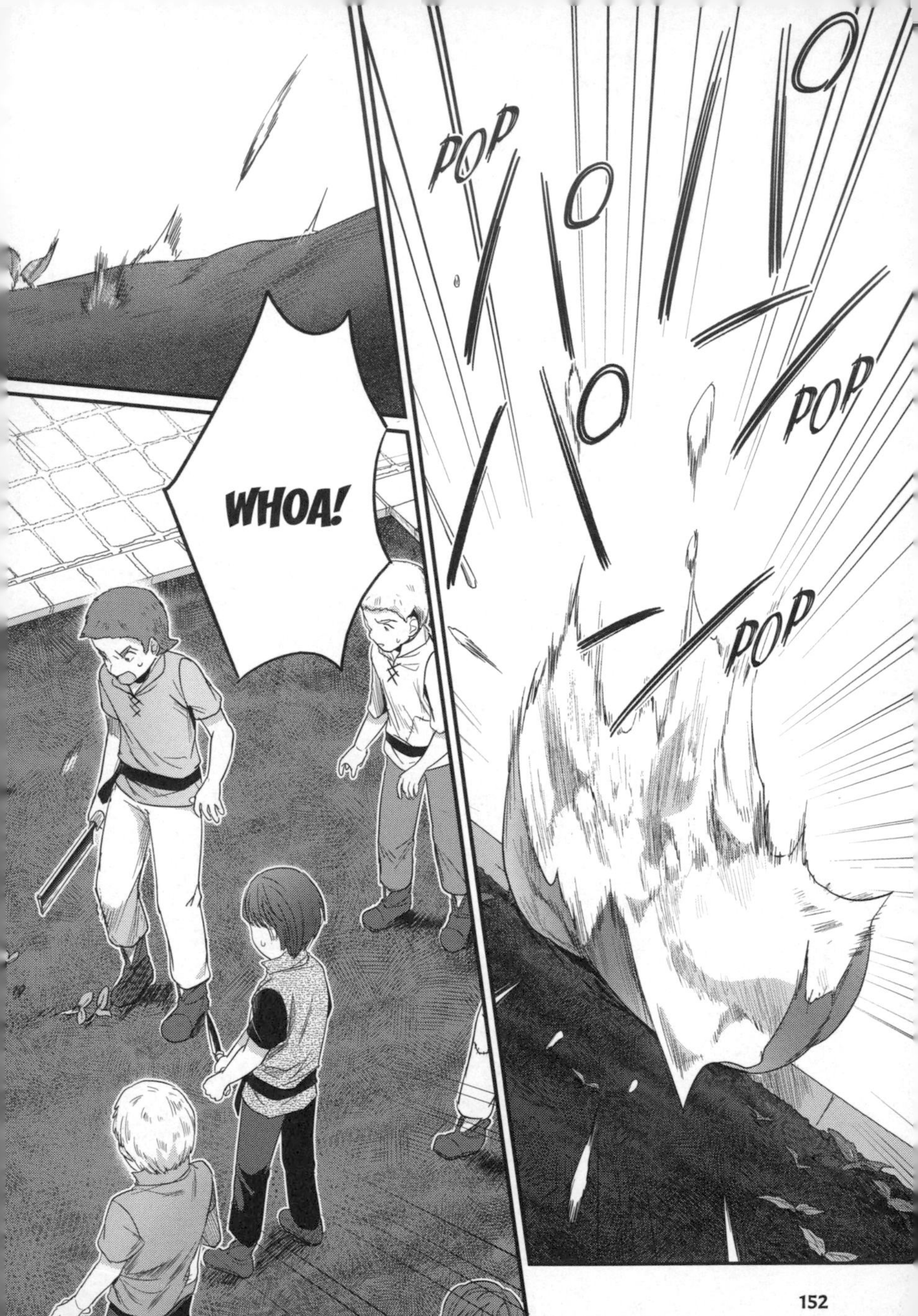
POP
POP
POP
WHOA!

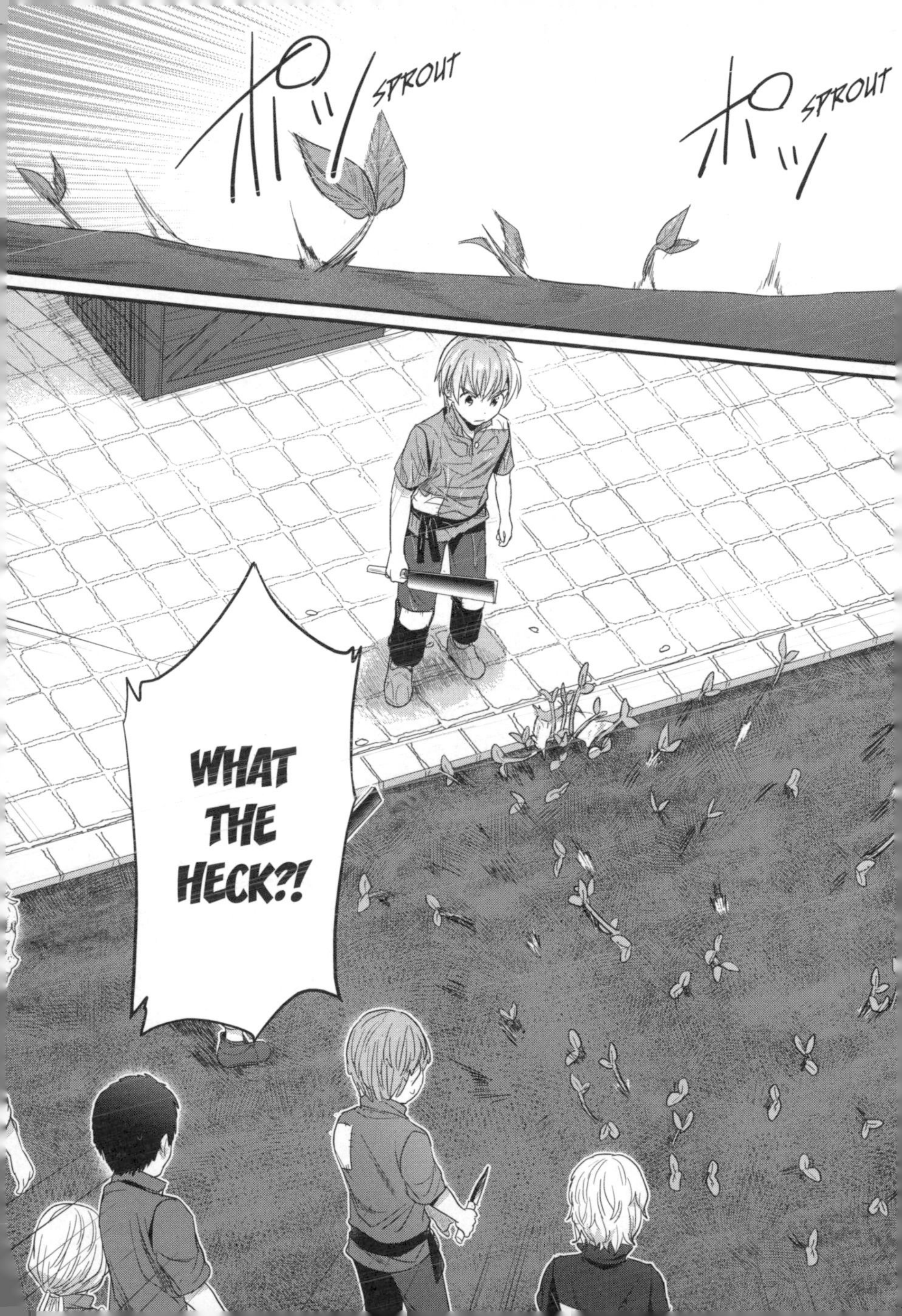
ポッ
SPROUT
ポッ
SPROUT
WHAT THE HECK?!

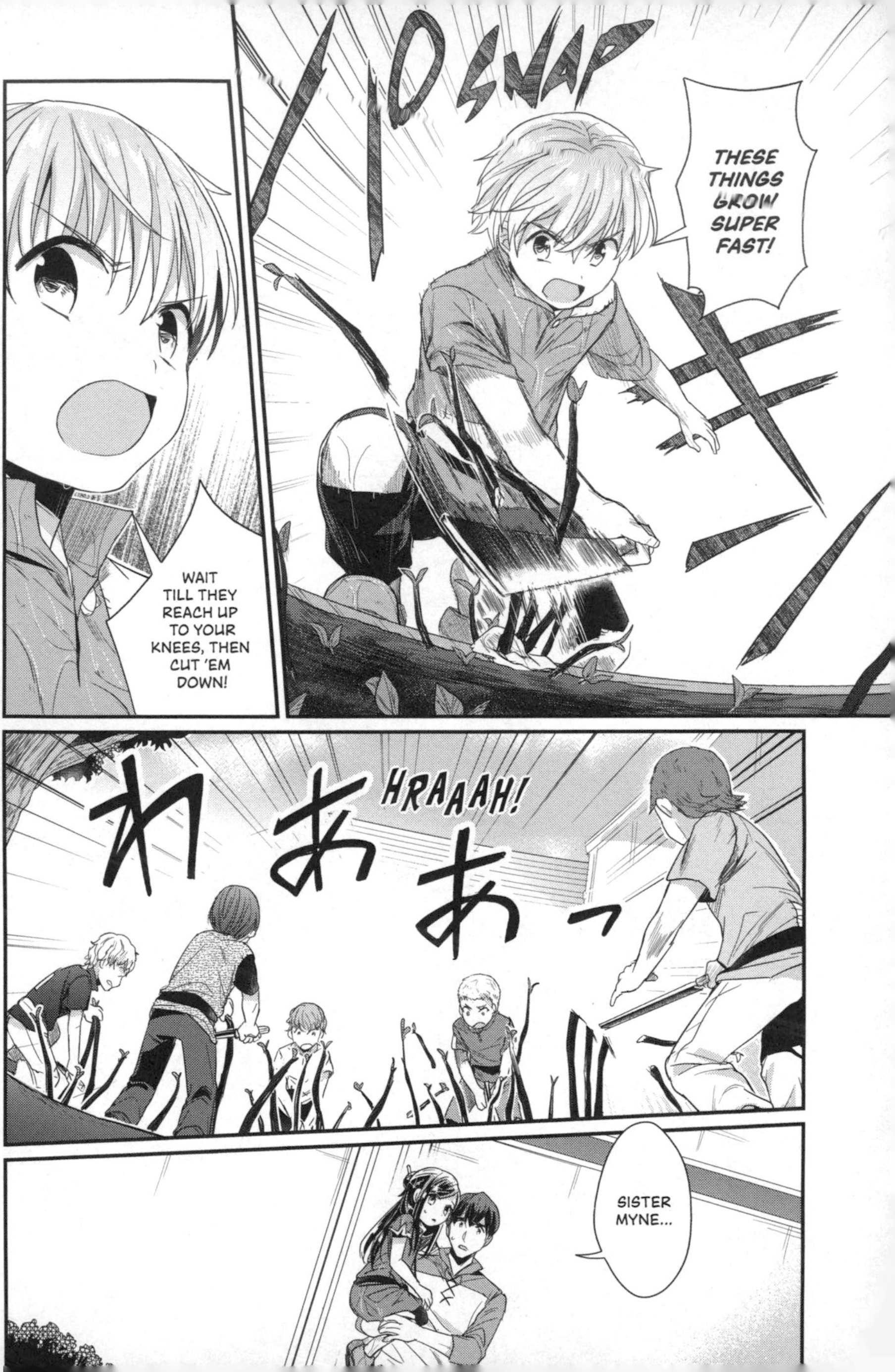
SNAP
THESE THINGS GROW SUPER FAST!
WAIT TILL THEY REACH UP TO YOUR KNEES, THEN CUT 'EM DOWN!
わああっ
HRAAAH!
SISTER MYNE...

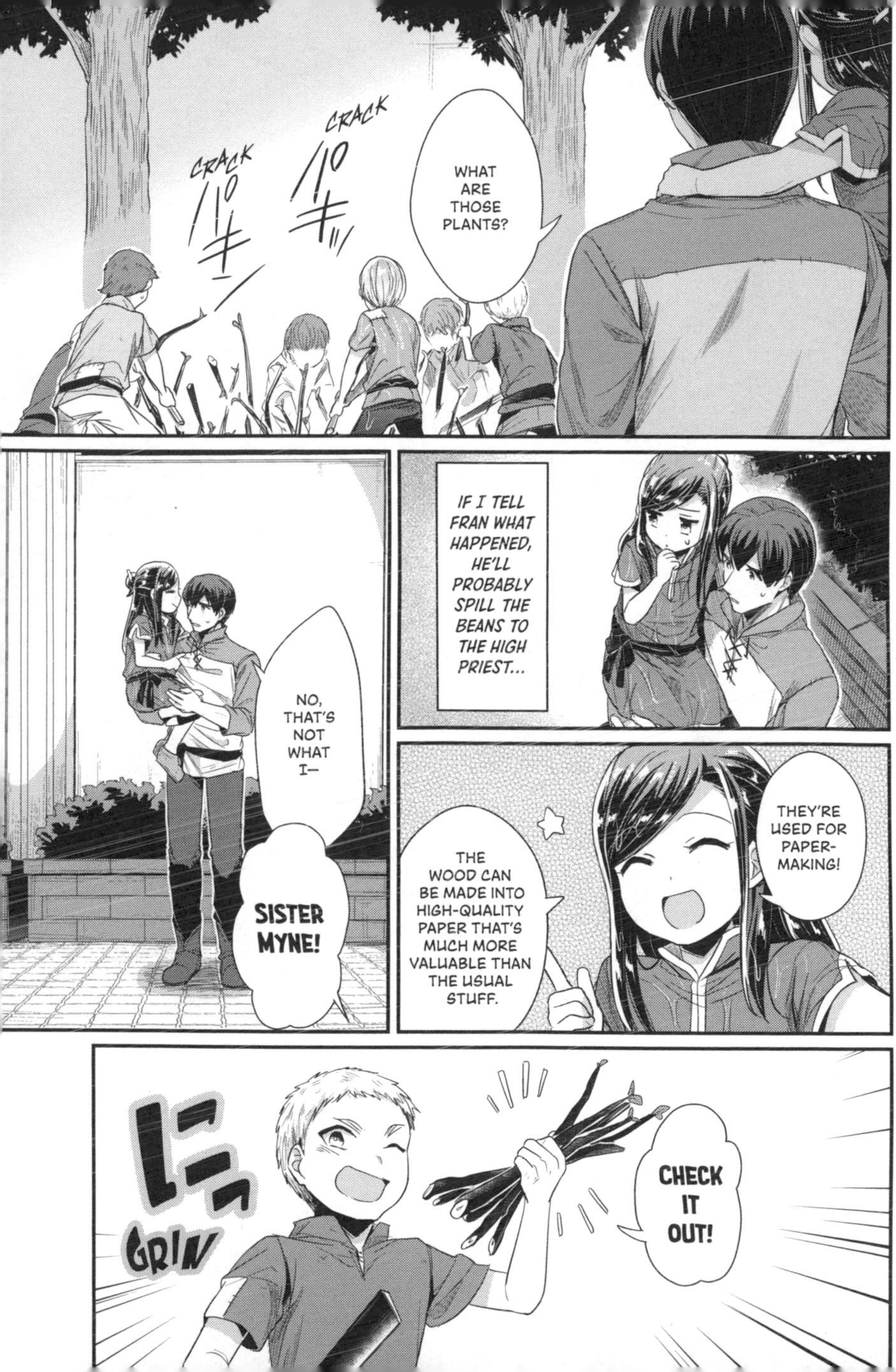
WHAT ARE THOSE PLANTS?
CRACK
CRACK
IF I TELL FRAN WHAT HAPPENED, HE'LL PROBABLY SPILL THE BEANS TO THE HIGH PRIEST...
THEY'RE USED FOR PAPER-MAKING!
THE WOOD CAN BE MADE INTO HIGH-QUALITY PAPER THAT'S MUCH MORE VALUABLE THAN THE USUAL STUFF.
NO, THAT'S NOT WHAT I—
SISTER MYNE!
CHECK IT OUT!
GRIN

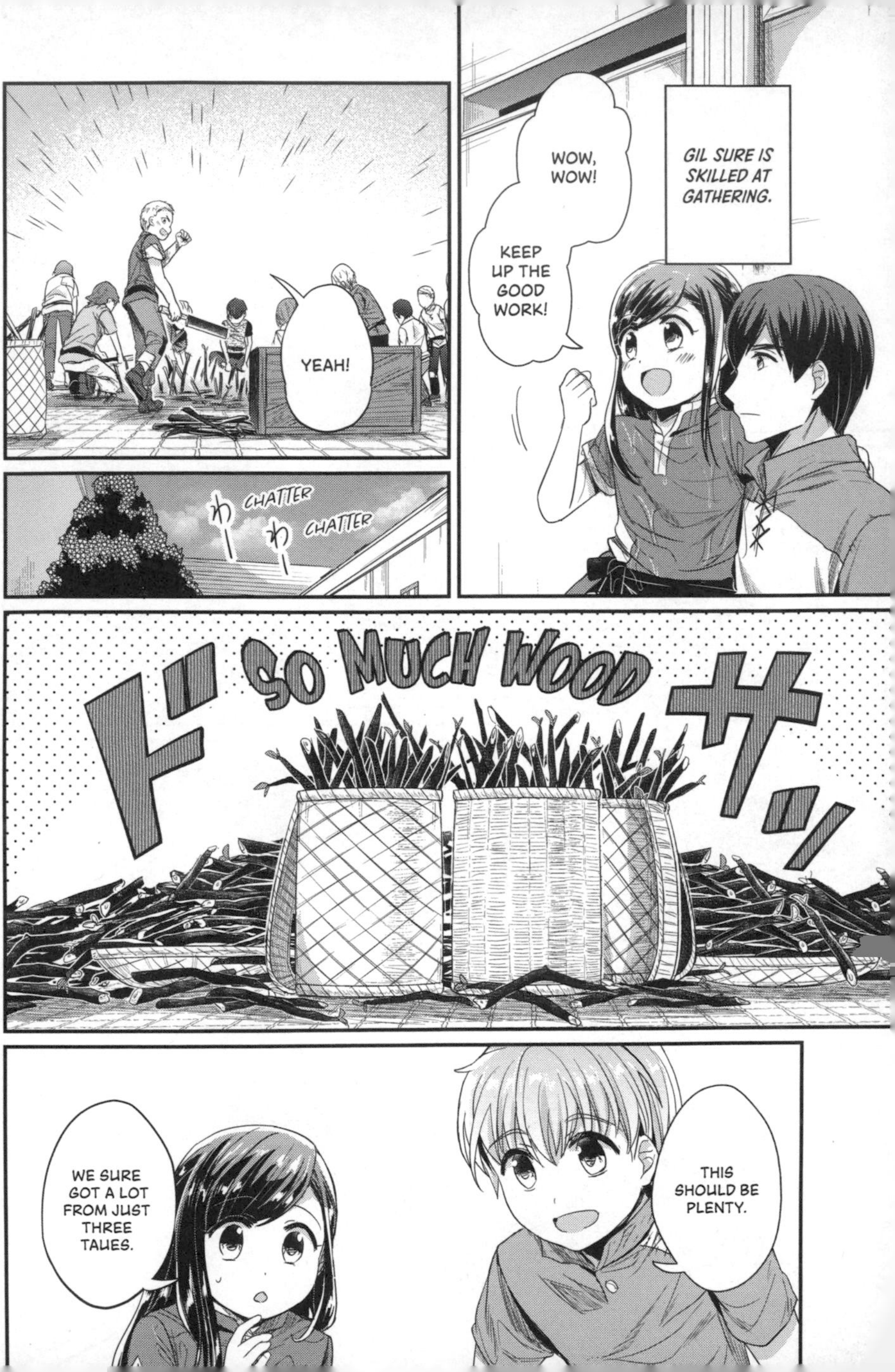
GIL SURE IS SKILLED AT GATHERING.
WOW, WOW!
KEEP UP THE GOOD WORK!
YEAH!
わ CHATTER
わ CHATTER
ド
SO MUCH WOOD
サッ
THIS SHOULD BE PLENTY.
WE SURE GOT A LOT FROM JUST THREE TAUES.

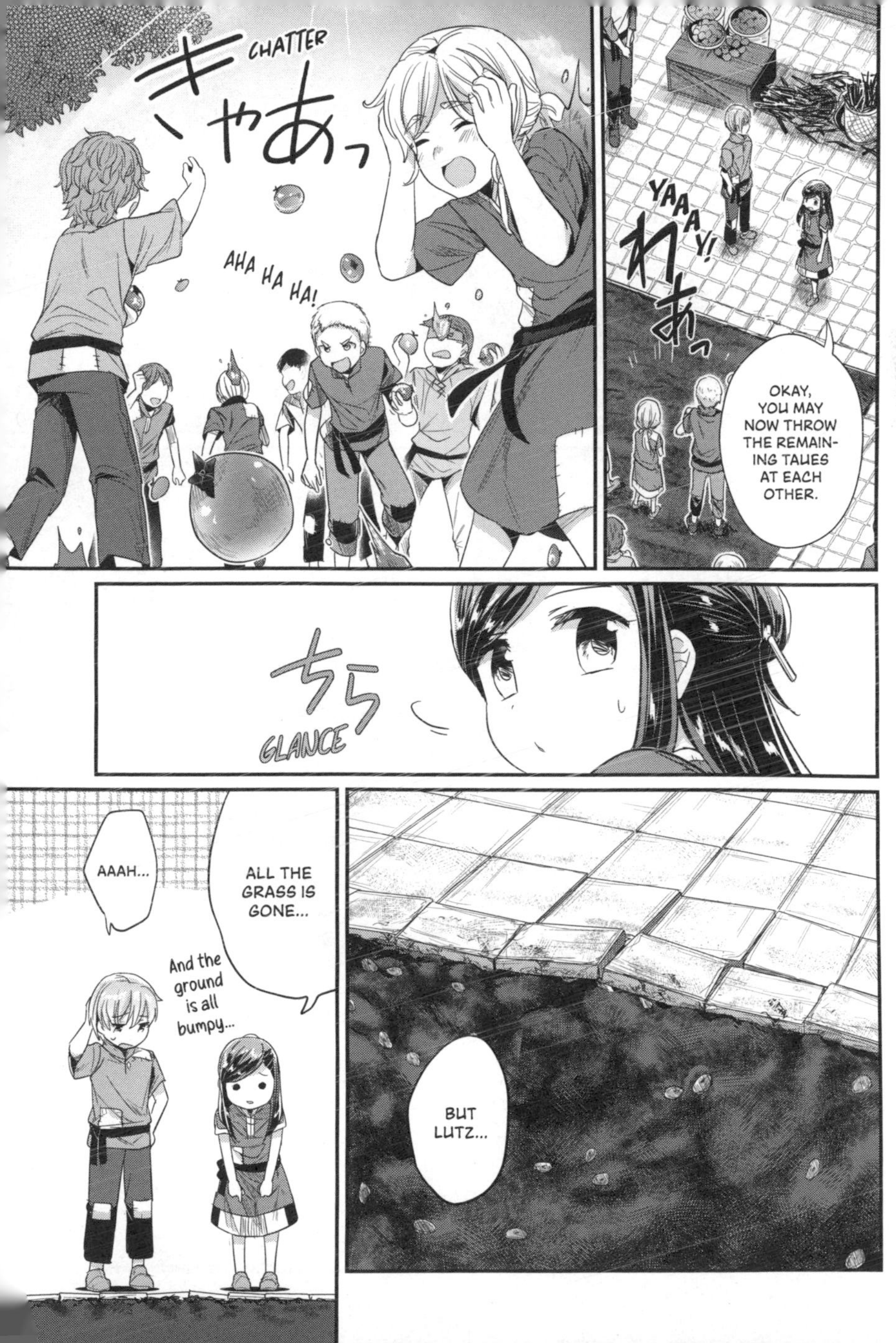
わあっ
YAAAY!
OKAY, YOU MAY NOW THROW THE REMAINING TAUES AT EACH OTHER.
ぎゃあっ
CHATTER
AHA HA HA!
ちら
GLANCE
BUT LUTZ...
ALL THE GRASS IS GONE...
AAAH...
And the ground is all bumpy...

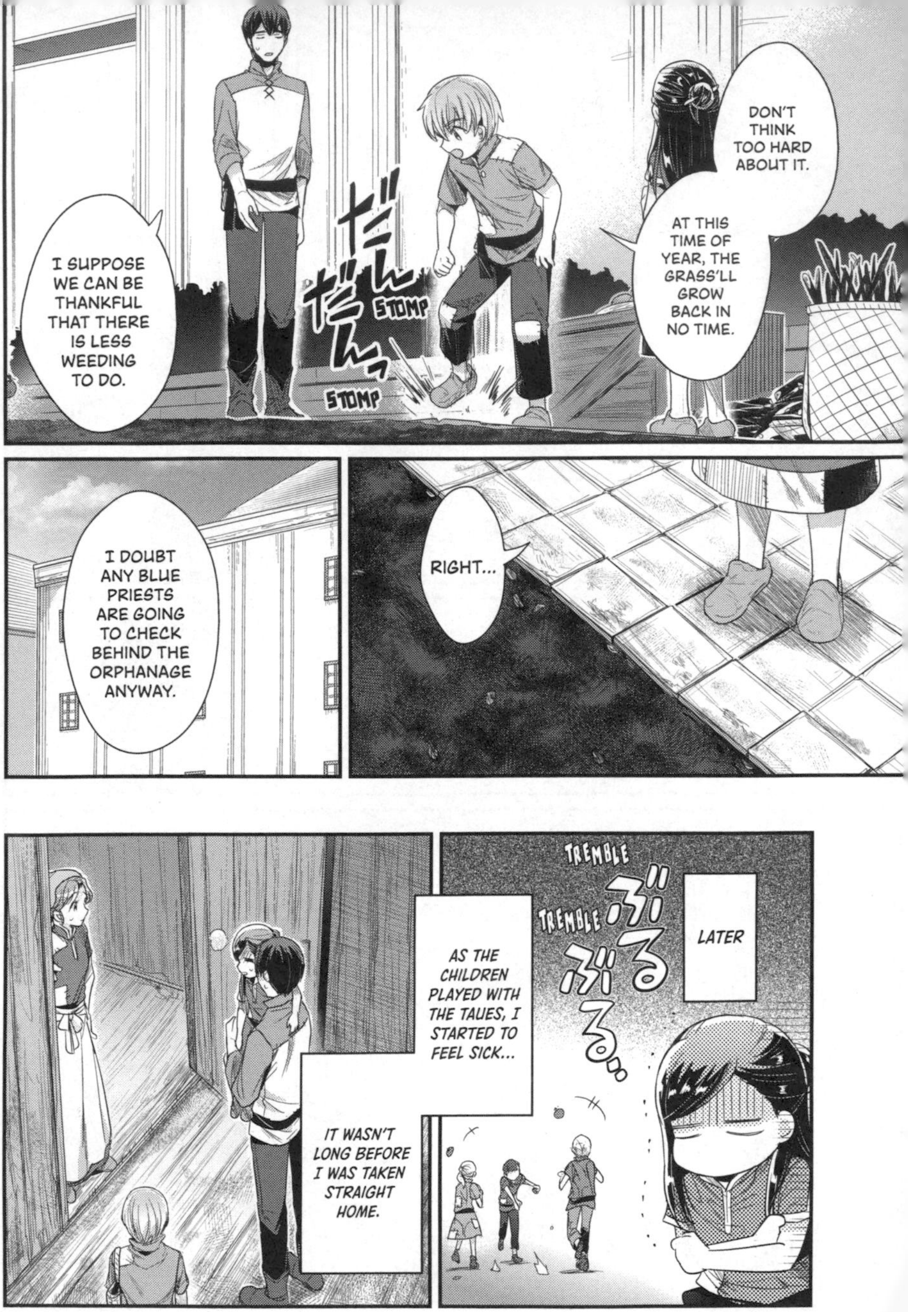
DON'T THINK TOO HARD ABOUT IT.
AT THIS TIME OF YEAR, THE GRASS'LL GROW BACK IN NO TIME.
だんだん
STOMP
STOMP
I SUPPOSE WE CAN BE THANKFUL THAT THERE IS LESS WEEDING TO DO.
RIGHT...
I DOUBT ANY BLUE PRIESTS ARE GOING TO CHECK BEHIND THE ORPHANAGE ANYWAY.
LATER
ぶるぶる…
TREMBLE
TREMBLE
AS THE CHILDREN PLAYED WITH THE TAUES, I STARTED TO FEEL SICK...
IT WASN'T LONG BEFORE I WAS TAKEN STRAIGHT HOME.

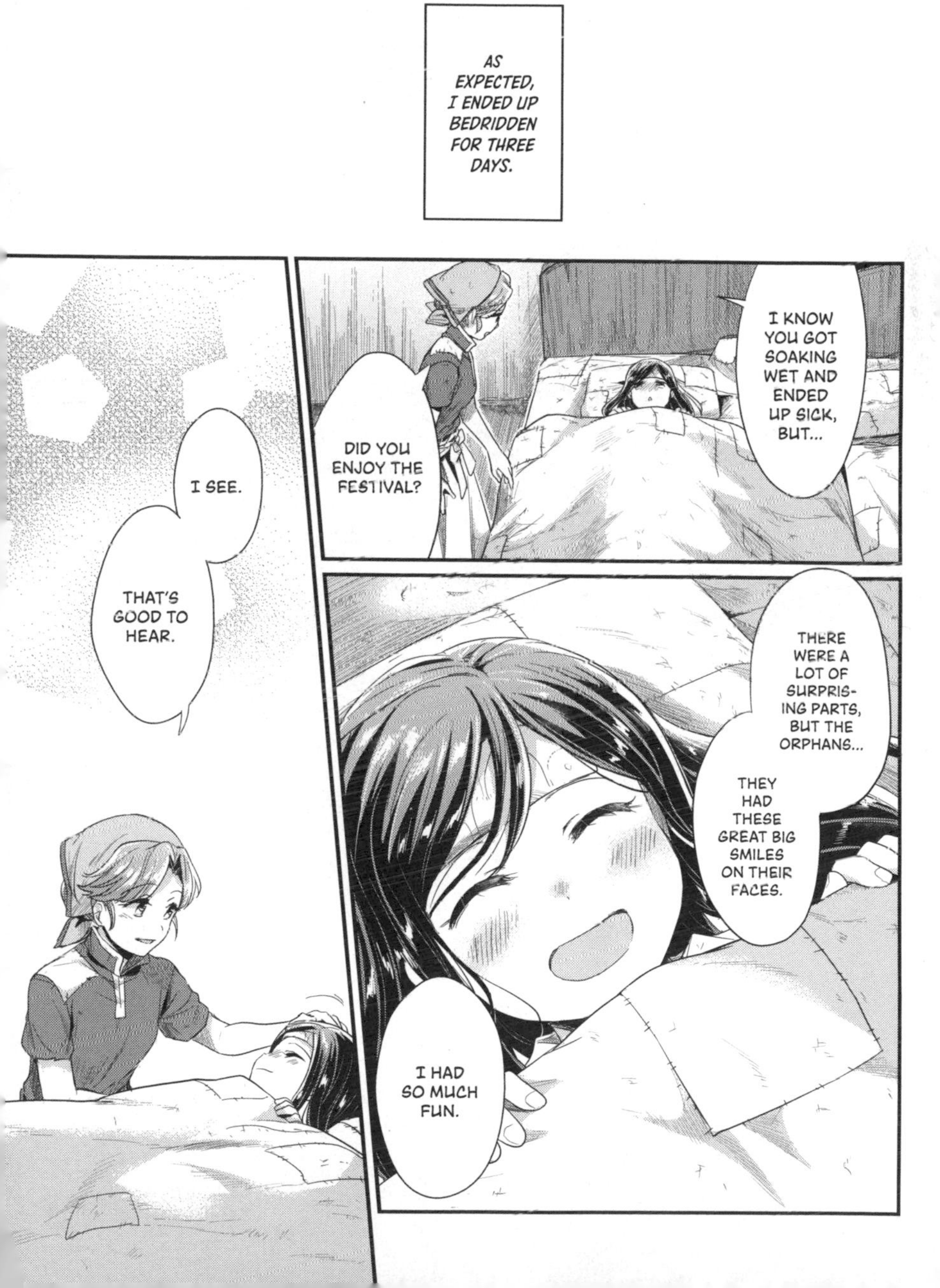
AS EXPECTED, I ENDED UP BEDRIDDEN FOR THREE DAYS.
I KNOW YOU GOT SOAKING WET AND ENDED UP SICK, BUT...
DID YOU ENJOY THE FESTIVAL?
THERE WERE A LOT OF SURPRIS-ING PARTS, BUT THE ORPHANS...
THEY HAD THESE GREAT BIG SMILES ON THEIR FACES.
I HAD SO MUCH FUN.
I SEE.
THAT'S GOOD TO HEAR.

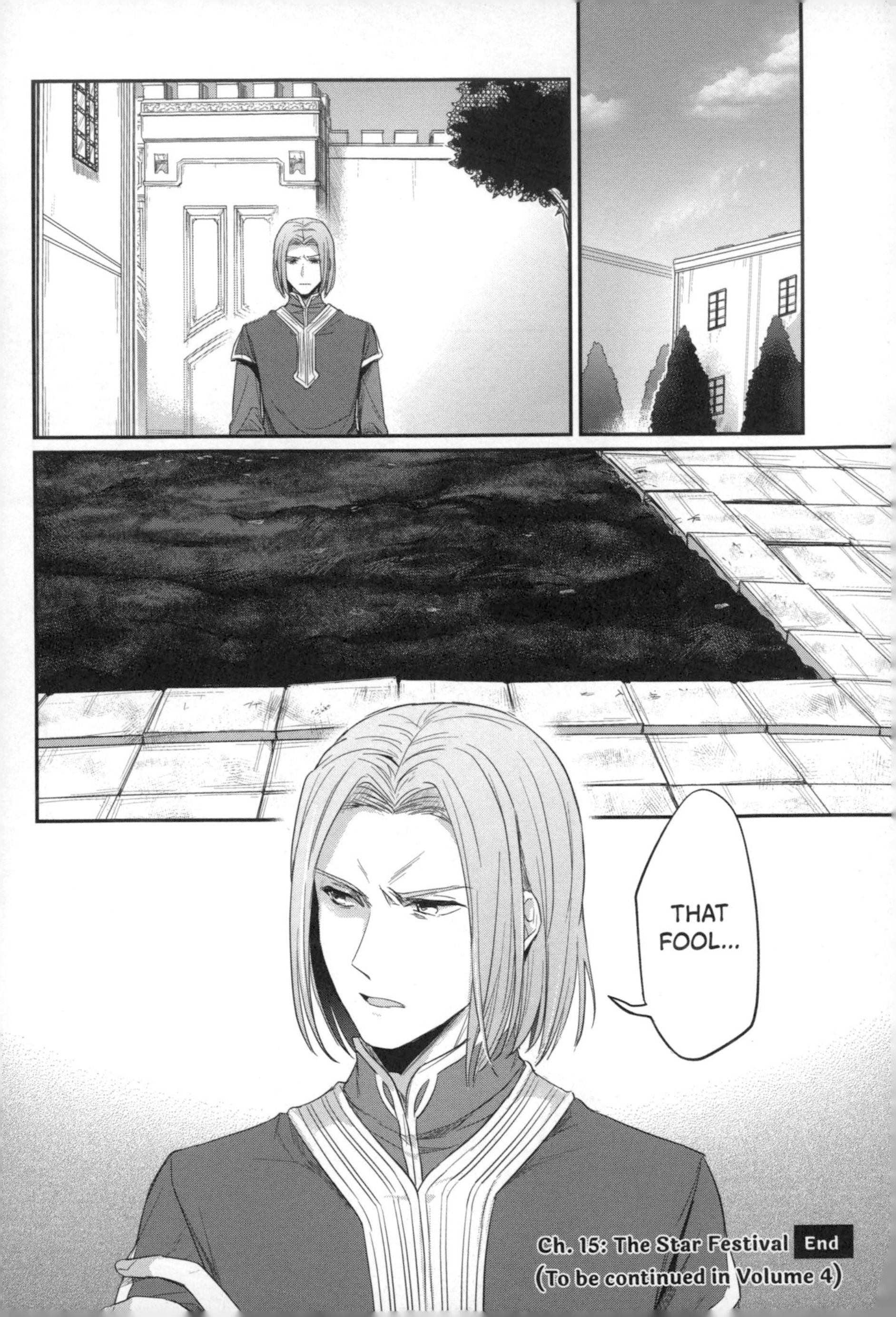
THAT FOOL...

Ch. 15: The Star Festival End
(To be continued in Volume 4)

ASCENDANCE
OF A
BOOKWORM

I'll do anything to
become a librarian!

Part 2 **I'll even join the
temple to read
books!**

Extra Ordering Ceremonial Robes

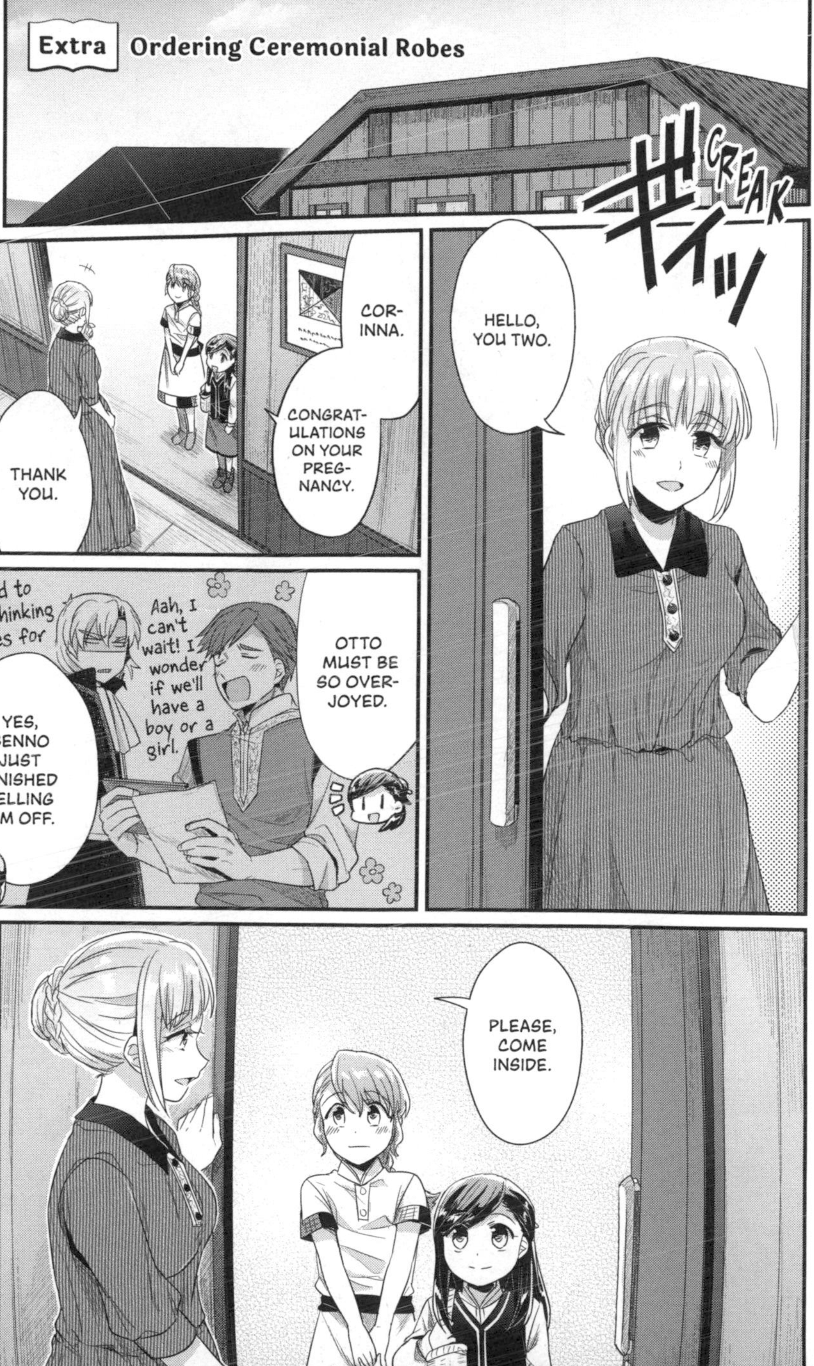
ギイッ
CREAK
HELLO, YOU TWO.
CORINNA.
CONGRATULATIONS ON YOUR PREGNANCY.
THANK YOU.
OTTO MUST BE SO OVERJOYED.
Aah, I can't wait! I wonder if we'll have a boy or a girl.
we need to start thinking of names for both!
YES, BENNO JUST FINISHED TELLING HIM OFF.
PLEASE, COME INSIDE.

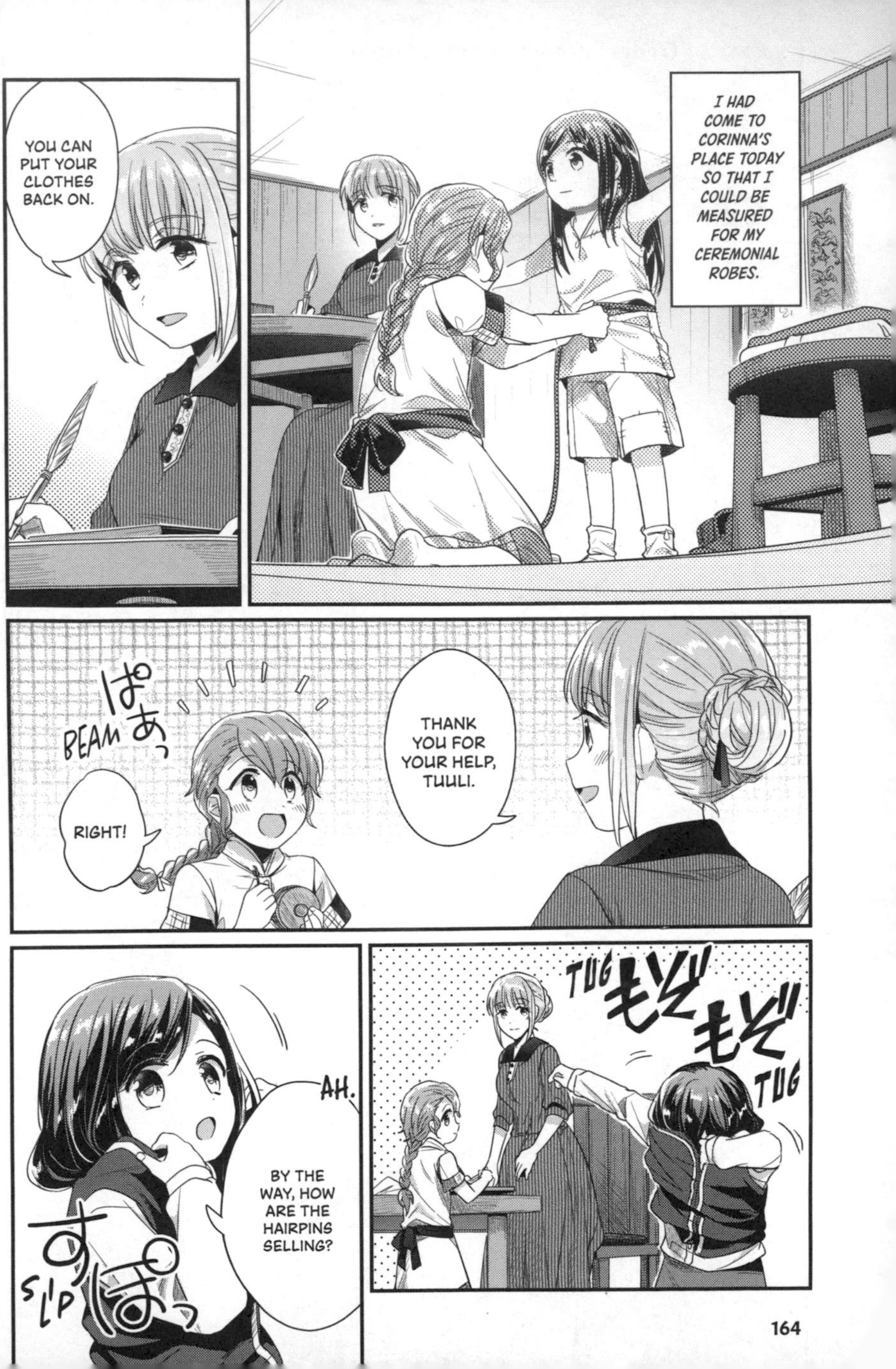
I HAD COME TO CORINNA'S PLACE TODAY SO THAT I COULD BE MEASURED FOR MY CEREMONIAL ROBES.
YOU CAN PUT YOUR CLOTHES BACK ON.
THANK YOU FOR YOUR HELP, TUULI.
ぱあっ
BEAM
RIGHT!
TUG
もぞもぞ
TUG
AH.
BY THE WAY, HOW ARE THE HAIRPINS SELLING?
すぽっ
SLIP

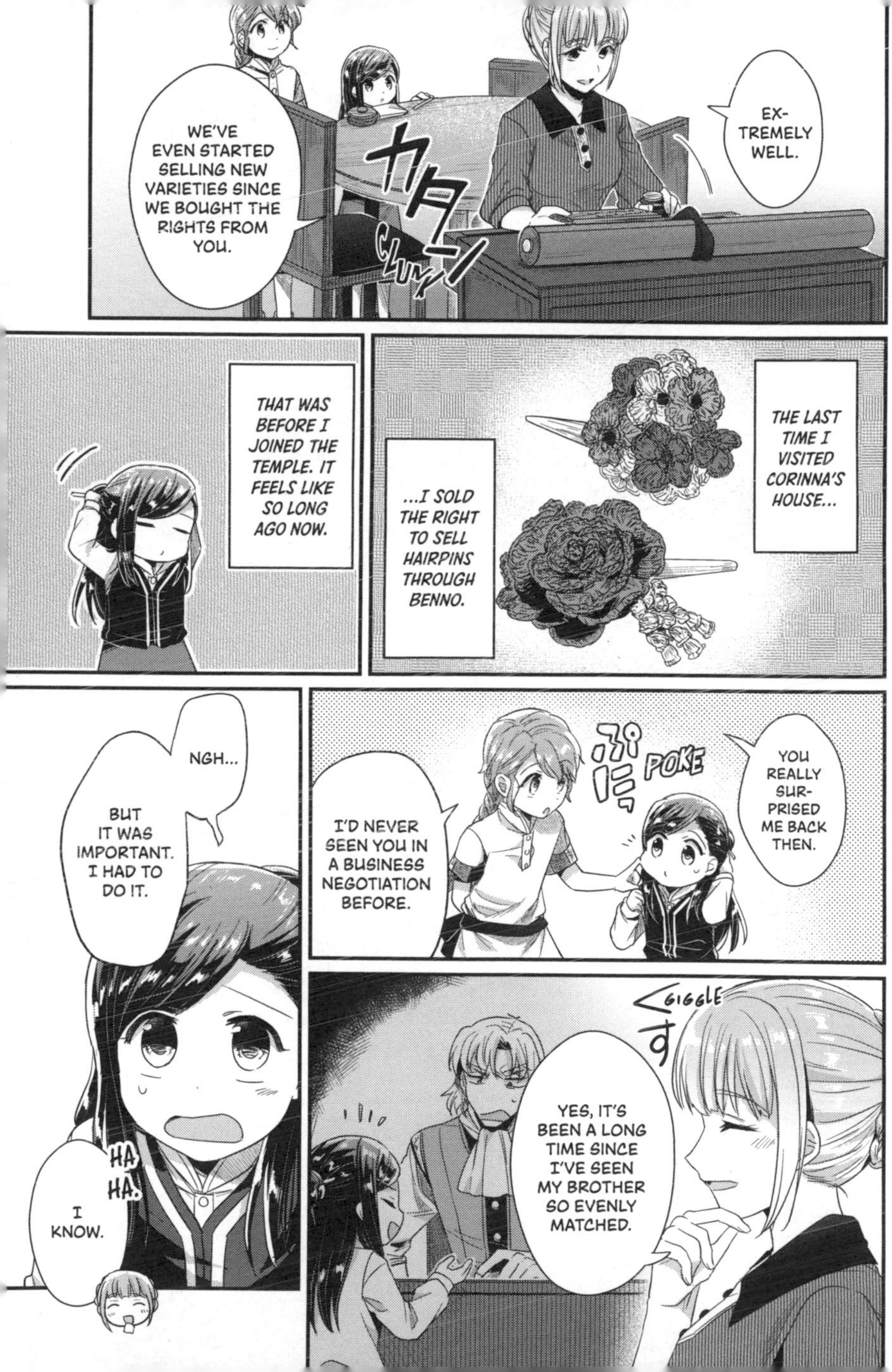
EX-TREMELY WELL.
WE'VE EVEN STARTED SELLING NEW VARIETIES SINCE WE BOUGHT THE RIGHTS FROM YOU.
CLUNK
THE LAST TIME I VISITED CORINNA'S HOUSE...
...I SOLD THE RIGHT TO SELL HAIRPINS THROUGH BENNO.
THAT WAS BEFORE I JOINED THE TEMPLE. IT FEELS LIKE SO LONG AGO NOW.
YOU REALLY SUR-PRISED ME BACK THEN.
POKE
I'D NEVER SEEN YOU IN A BUSINESS NEGOTIATION BEFORE.
GIGGLE
YES, IT'S BEEN A LONG TIME SINCE I'VE SEEN MY BROTHER SO EVENLY MATCHED.
NGH...
BUT IT WAS IMPORTANT. I HAD TO DO IT.
HA HA.
I KNOW.

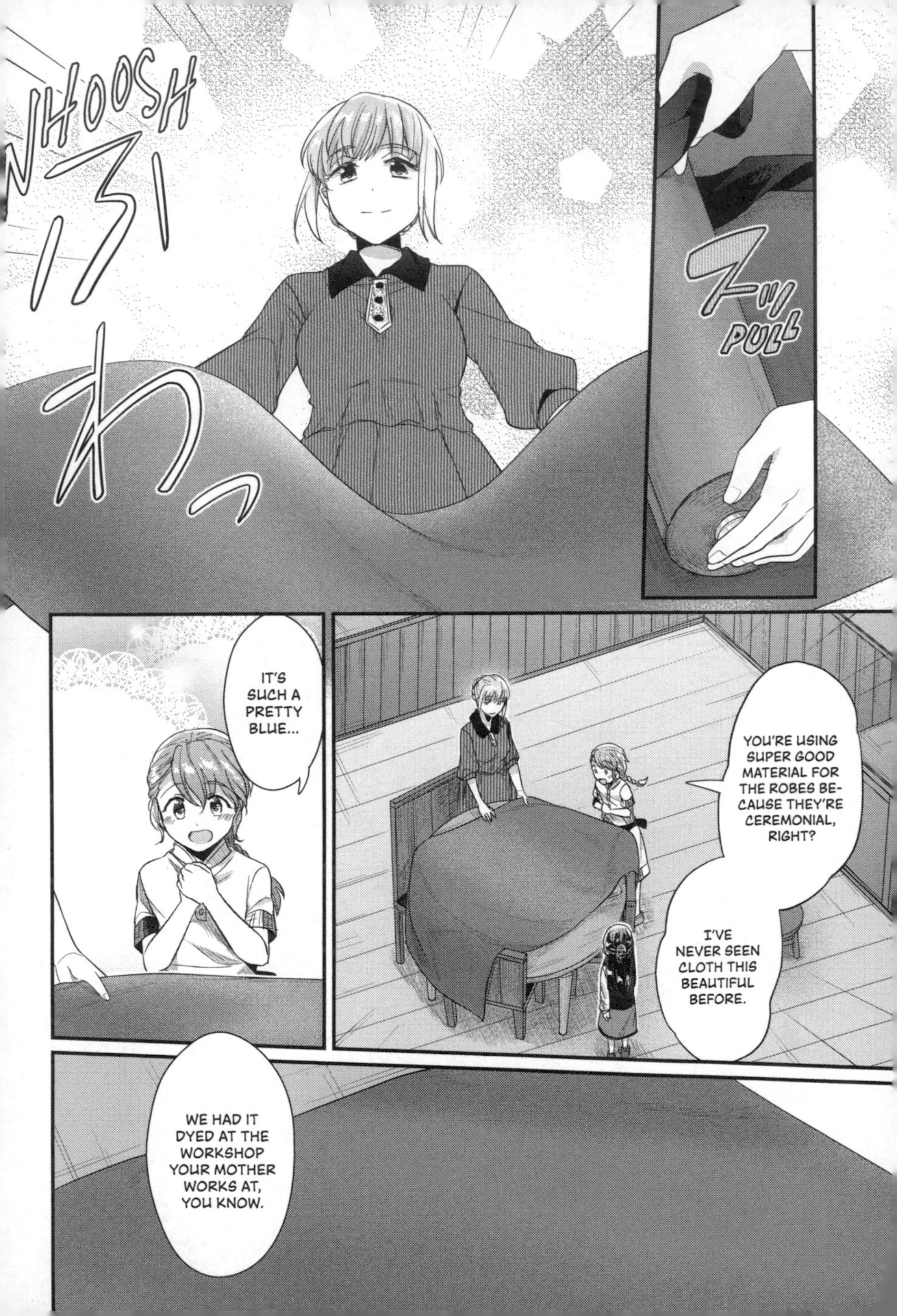
PULL
WHOOSH
わっ
YOU'RE USING SUPER GOOD MATERIAL FOR THE ROBES BECAUSE THEY'RE CEREMONIAL, RIGHT?
I'VE NEVER SEEN CLOTH THIS BEAUTIFUL BEFORE.
IT'S SUCH A PRETTY BLUE...
WE HAD IT DYED AT THE WORKSHOP YOUR MOTHER WORKS AT, YOU KNOW.

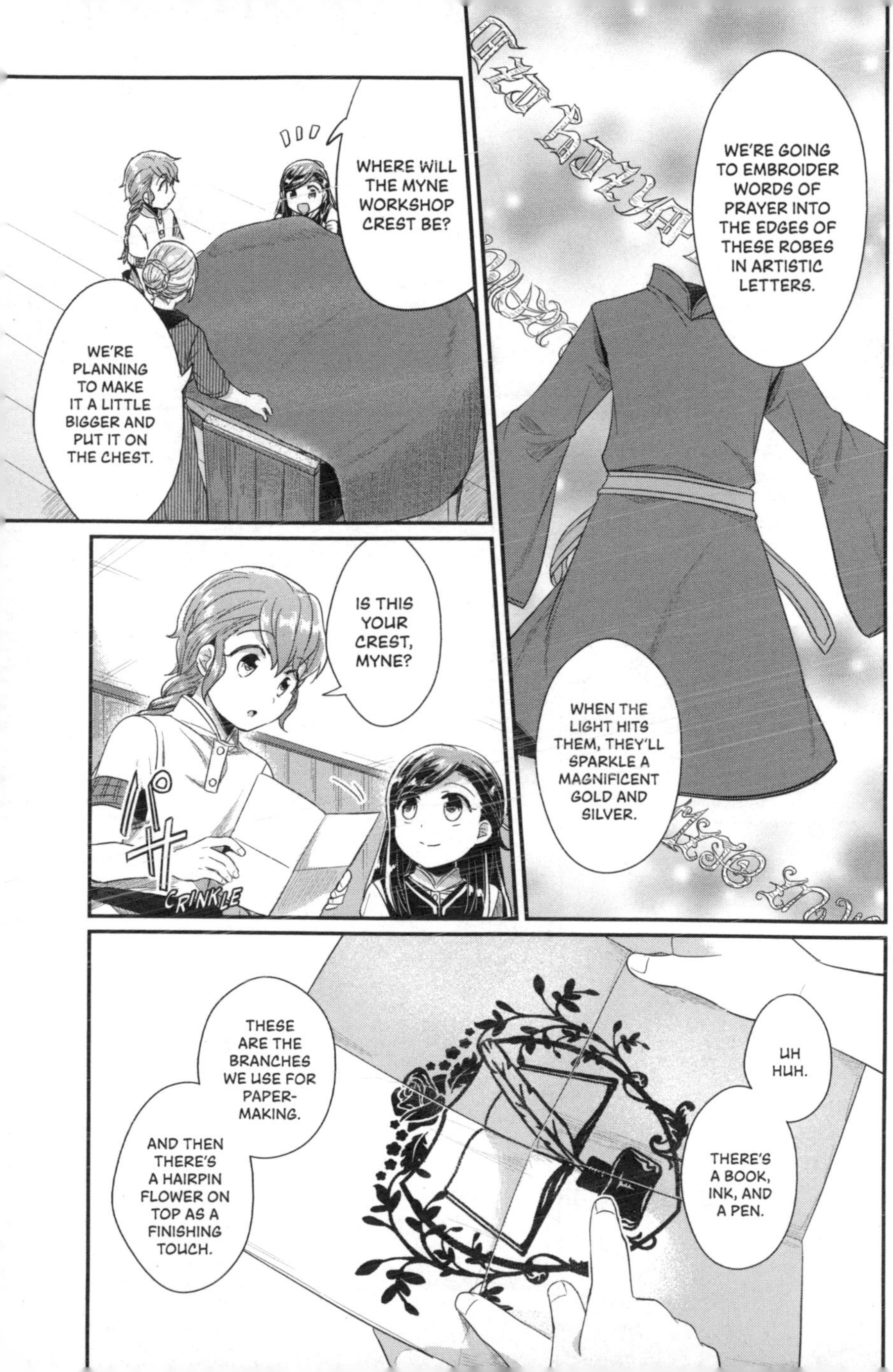
WE'RE GOING TO EMBROIDER WORDS OF PRAYER INTO THE EDGES OF THESE ROBES IN ARTISTIC LETTERS.
WHEN THE LIGHT HITS THEM, THEY'LL SPARKLE A MAGNIFICENT GOLD AND SILVER.
WHERE WILL THE MYNE WORKSHOP CREST BE?
WE'RE PLANNING TO MAKE IT A LITTLE BIGGER AND PUT IT ON THE CHEST.
IS THIS YOUR CREST, MYNE?
CRINKLE
UH HUH.
THERE'S A BOOK, INK, AND A PEN.
THESE ARE THE BRANCHES WE USE FOR PAPER-MAKING.
AND THEN THERE'S A HAIRPIN FLOWER ON TOP AS A FINISHING TOUCH.

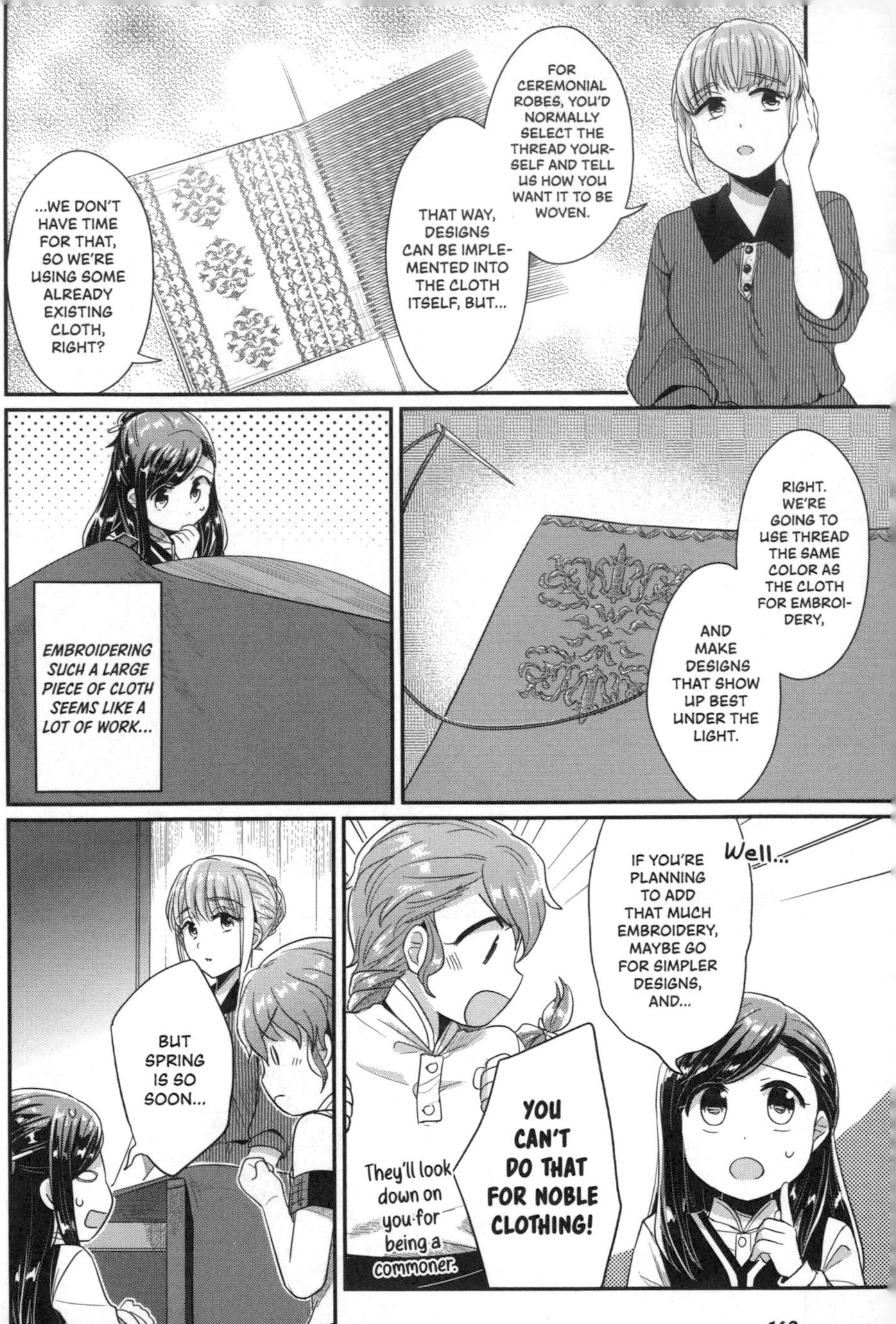

FOR CEREMONIAL ROBES, YOU'D NORMALLY SELECT THE THREAD YOURSELF AND TELL US HOW YOU WANT IT TO BE WOVEN.
THAT WAY, DESIGNS CAN BE IMPLEMENTED INTO THE CLOTH ITSELF, BUT...
...WE DON'T HAVE TIME FOR THAT, SO WE'RE USING SOME ALREADY EXISTING CLOTH, RIGHT?
RIGHT. WE'RE GOING TO USE THREAD THE SAME COLOR AS THE CLOTH FOR EMBROIDERY,
AND MAKE DESIGNS THAT SHOW UP BEST UNDER THE LIGHT.
EMBROIDERING SUCH A LARGE PIECE OF CLOTH SEEMS LIKE A LOT OF WORK...
Well...
IF YOU'RE PLANNING TO ADD THAT MUCH EMBROIDERY, MAYBE GO FOR SIMPLER DESIGNS, AND...
YOU CAN'T DO THAT FOR NOBLE CLOTHING!
They'll look down on you for being a commoner.
BUT SPRING IS SO SOON...

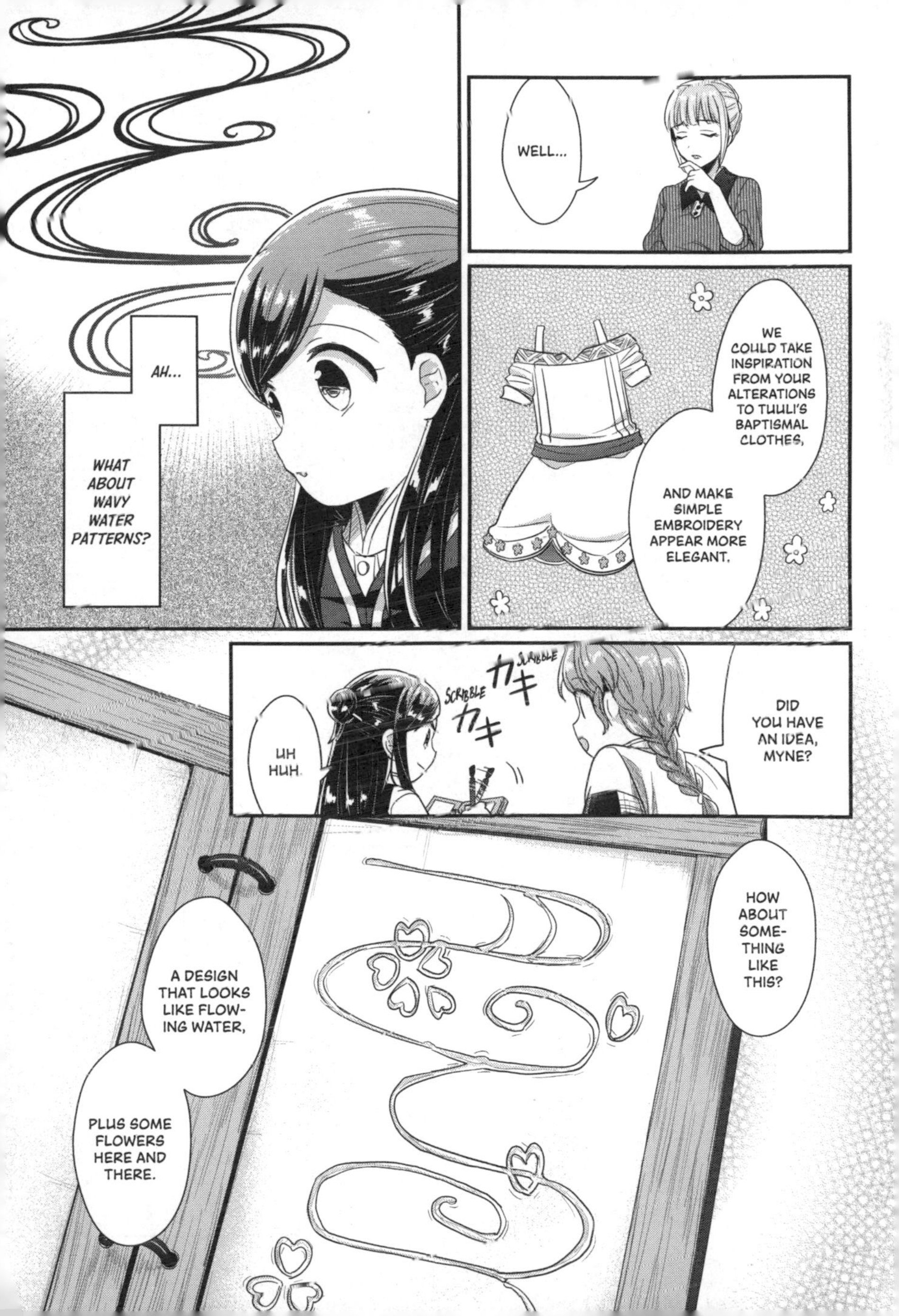
WELL...
WE COULD TAKE INSPIRATION FROM YOUR ALTERATIONS TO TUULI'S BAPTISMAL CLOTHES,
AND MAKE SIMPLE EMBROIDERY APPEAR MORE ELEGANT.
AH...
WHAT ABOUT WAVY WATER PATTERNS?
DID YOU HAVE AN IDEA, MYNE?
SCRIBBLE カキ
SCRIBBLE カキ
UH HUH.
HOW ABOUT SOME-THING LIKE THIS?
A DESIGN THAT LOOKS LIKE FLOW-ING WATER,
PLUS SOME FLOWERS HERE AND THERE.

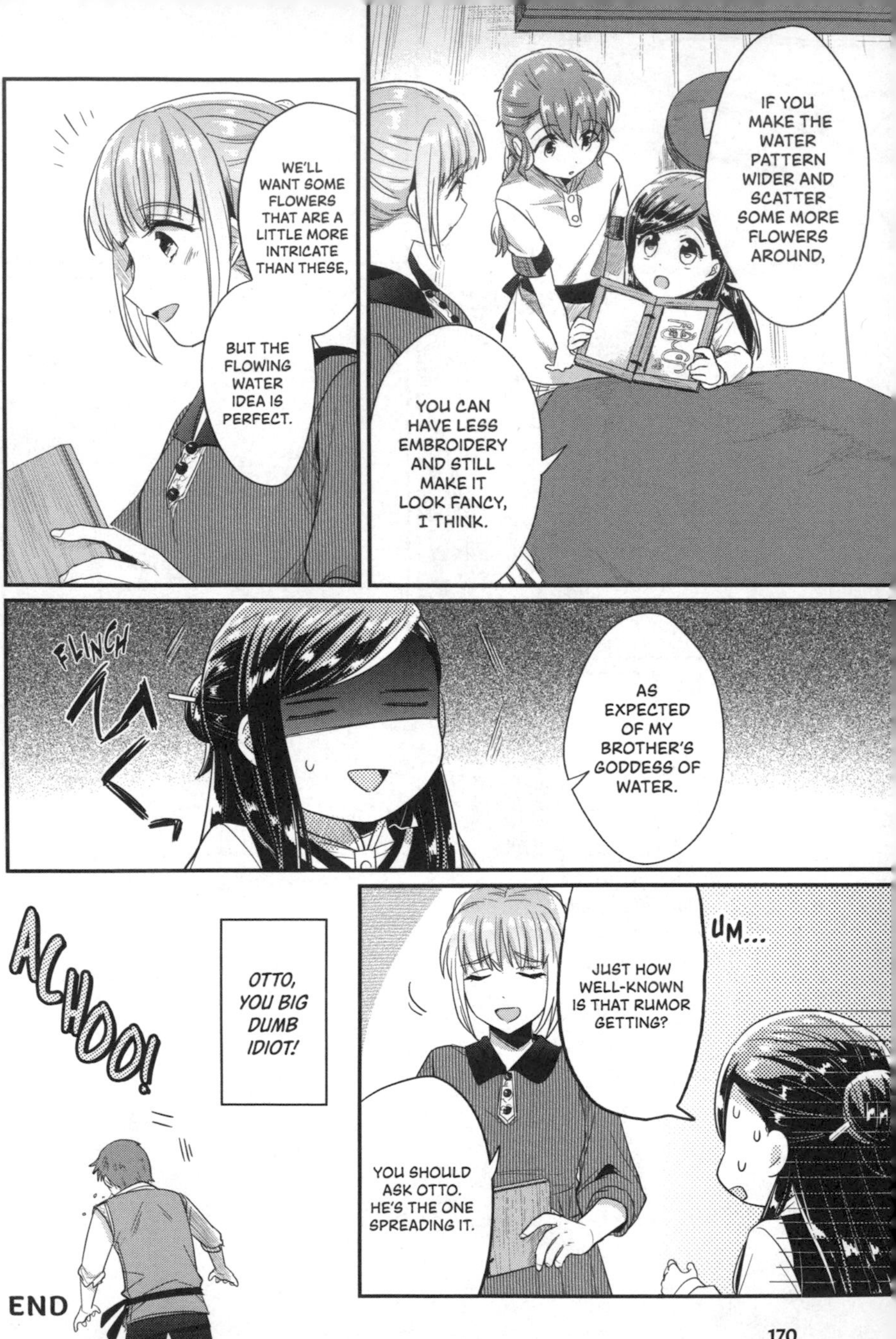
IF YOU MAKE THE WATER PATTERN WIDER AND SCATTER SOME MORE FLOWERS AROUND,
YOU CAN HAVE LESS EMBROIDERY AND STILL MAKE IT LOOK FANCY, I THINK.
WE'LL WANT SOME FLOWERS THAT ARE A LITTLE MORE INTRICATE THAN THESE,
BUT THE FLOWING WATER IDEA IS PERFECT.
AS EXPECTED OF MY BROTHER'S GODDESS OF WATER.
FLINCH
UM...
JUST HOW WELL-KNOWN IS THAT RUMOR GETTING?
YOU SHOULD ASK OTTO. HE'S THE ONE SPREADING IT.
OTTO, YOU BIG DUMB IDIOT!
ACHOO!
END

Gathering Taues

Gathering Taues

"Rico, are you ready? We shall be leaving as soon as Sister Myne returns to the temple."

"Indeed," I replied, patting the small box on my back to show the apprentice gray priest that I had all of the necessary gear.

Sister Myne's apprentice attendant, Gil, watched us with a grimace. "You two. Watch how you talk. We're going out to the forest, remember?"

"Oh, right..." We had been told to speak in a rougher and more casual manner in the lower city to avoid sticking out as much.

"Also, we're gonna need to be quieter this time," Gil continued. "Especially when going in and out of the orphanage."

"Yeah. We're going to walk with our hands over our mouths. I remember."

Today was the Starbind Ceremony, so the blue priests and their attendants would be going all the way to the chapel instead of staying holed up in the noble section of the temple as per usual. We couldn't let them see us leave no matter what, otherwise Sister Myne would get yelled at.

"Are we leaving earlier today 'cause of the ceremony?" I asked. "Second bell only just rang."

"Yeah. It's apparently called the Star Festival down in the lower city, where they treat it as a holiday of sorts. We'll need to get back by fourth bell this time. There won't be any taues left if we don't hurry... or so Lutz said, anyway."

"Hmm...?"

I only half understood myself, and it seemed that Gil didn't really understand either.

Were the Star Festival and the Starbind Ceremony the same thing? What exactly were taues? Neither of us could answer these questions.

"The lower city's filled with weird things," Gil said. "I'm not really an expert yet either."

"It's crazy. I'm still struggling to get over how different each floor of the temple is..."

During my time locked in the basement, we had had so little that one could count it all on two hands. There were the wooden frames we used as beds, the straw laid atop them, ragged blankets, tables, chairs, and water jugs.

"I couldn't believe it when you came through that other door," I said to Gil.

"Yeah, I bet. It can't be opened from the inside."

I hadn't even known the door existed, so to me, it was like the wall had suddenly opened up out of nowhere. From that point onward, Gil had started secretly bringing us divine gifts at Sister Myne's instruction, until eventually we were let out of the basement and given rooms on the first floor meant for apprentice shrine maidens.

"I had no idea what was going on, really."

"Hahaha... It took a lot of work for us to get the High Priest's permission."

"Oh, there's Sister Myne. Alright, time to go," Gil instructed. He had spoken to Fran at the back gate for a moment, and as Sister Myne entered the temple, we started toward the forest.

"Sister Myne seemed kind of sad."

"Did something happen?"

We tilted our heads, confused, but Lutz just gave a chuckle as he guided us. "Myne's just sad that she's stuck at the temple, 'cause she wanted to come to the forest with us," he explained. "Problem is, she's a slow walker and way too sickly, so she always collapses when going places. We can't risk that without Mr. Gunther here."

Sister Myne was apparently staying in the temple because Lutz couldn't look after her and us at the same time. I remembered that the gray priests stuck helping with the ceremony had looked sad about not being able to come with us too.

"In that case, I'll gather enough taues for Sister Myne. I promised to gather enough for the gray priests who had to stay behind too."

"Sounds good," Lutz replied. He reached out and mussed my hair with a grin. He was a bit rougher than Wilma, but it always felt nice for someone to smile at me like that.

I need to grab a ton of taues today. For Sister Myne too.

As I was pumping myself up, the ivory of the temple gave way to the mishmash of colors that made up the lower city. I was always surprised to see how vibrant it was down here—the buildings, the clothes of the people walking around, and even the ground seemed to vary so much in appearance. There were so many colors that I still wasn't used to them all.

"Huh? Nobody's here today," I said, noticing that there were far fewer people wandering about than usual. "Is it because of the Star Festival?"

The lower city felt notably different. Normally, whenever we went to the forest, the main street was always busy with carts, and there were people carrying boxes rushing around everywhere. Today, while I could sense people in the alleys, the city itself was like an empty shell.

"Where'd everyone go?" I asked.

"Right now, the people getting married are heading to meet their partners. Everyone else is cooking or going to the forest to gather taues," Lutz replied. He then went on to explain the ins and outs of the Star Festival to us. He knew more than the adult gray priests did.

"Lutz, what's the difference between the Star Festival and the Starbind Ceremony?"

"Everything. The ceremony is held in the temple, right? Well, the festival is about people gathering taues in the forest, throwing them in one big crazy event, and then spending the rest of the day enjoying a feast. The adults let loose even late into the night."

When Lutz put it like that, the Star Festival and the Starbind Ceremony really were completely unalike. Sister Myne had apparently negotiated with the High Priest so that we could play like those in the lower city did.

"Myne said she wanted to bring everyone to the lower city's festival, Rico, but the High Priest refused. Sorry about that. It might feel cramped at the temple, but I hope you'll still enjoy yourselves."

"Lutz, what does 'cramped' mean?" I had never heard that word before.

He blinked at me a few times. "Er, I mean..." he began, looking awkward.

"You're making things too complicated, Lutz," Gil interjected. "Hey, Rico. You're having more fun now than you were when you were stuck in the basement, right?"

"Uh huh! Way more fun!" I replied. The other kids who had been stuck in the basement all voiced their agreement too, which made Lutz and Gil give especially happy smiles.

We arrived in the forest to find a ton of people grabbing at things and fighting to get as many taues as they could. There were a lot of children here whom I hadn't seen before, and to my surprise, there were a lot of adults too.

"It feels like everyone in the lower city is here," I said.

"You're just seeing a small portion of them. The kids stay by the edge of the forest while most of the adults go deeper, so yeah. We're grabbing the red fruits today. Like that one," Lutz said, pointing at one that a nearby kid was picking up. We had been told not to touch those fruits the last time we had come to the forest; apparently they were taues.

"Oh, Lutz!" came a voice.

"Hiya, Tuuli. How's it going?"

Tuuli, a girl who sometimes came to the temple to teach us stuff, was waving so enthusiastically that her braided hair was bobbing around behind her head. Her basket was already filled more than halfway with taues. "You should probably start gathering more to the south. You'll need to hurry if you want to get any," she warned.

Following her advice, Lutz gestured us over to the southern part of the forest. We walked for a short while until we came across more of the red fruits.

"Let's hurry and get some!" Lutz yelled. "Don't let Tuuli beat us!"

We all cheered in response.

I rushed to grab the first red fruit I could find. It was squishy and jiggled about in my hand, as though it were brimming with water. I squeezed it a little, curious. Its skin was smooth and springy, and it felt good to rub against my cheek.

"I can imagine sleeping on a whole bed of these..." I murmured aloud, picturing a bed frame packed full of taues.

Lutz chuckled. "Taues are only this squishy for a few days. Once you take them from the earth, the water inside starts drying out and they end up hard as heck."

"Wow... Well, I'm sure I'd get a few good nights of sleep before then."

"Nah. No matter how light you are, Rico, you'd pop that bed in no time. Like this." Lutz demonstratively stepped on one of the taues, making it explode in a burst of water.

"Ah... I don't think Wilma would want me putting those on my bed." Wilma was a gray shrine maiden in the orphanage who looked after us the most. She was nice, but she made sure to scold us whenever we did anything bad.

"Who knows? My older brother actually tried to sleep on some taues himself, and my mom was ticked the heck off. He was given an ultimatum: he could sleep on the floor until everything dried, or he could go get some new straw for his mattress."

Based on Lutz's stories, I'd gathered that Mymom was someone from the lower city. She had a strange name and sounded much scarier than Wilma. Still, I didn't want Wilma to get mad at me.

Though the main reason I don't want to risk soaking my bed is because I don't want to sleep on the floor. Just the thought reminded me of my days in the basement, when there was nothing I could do but drag my shabby mattress as close to a table as possible and wait for divine gifts.

"I thought it was a good idea, but I guess not..." I said, promptly giving up on my bed of taues as I put the one in my hand into my basket.

We put our baskets of gathered taues in the basement of the boys' building and then snuck into the basement of the girls' building with our hands over our mouths.

Inside we found the gray shrine maidens preparing lunch. The aroma of soup was enough to make my stomach growl; I patted it a few times to ease its groans as we climbed the stairs to the second floor dining hall.

"Welcome back, everyone," Wilma said. "How was the forest? Did you collect many taues?"

We removed our hands from our mouths and all started speaking at once. "We got a lot for the gray priests and Sister Myne, since they had to stay behind," one kid said.

"I got the most out of everyone!" declared another.

Wilma listened with an amused smile as everyone began discussing the literal fruits of their labor. We talked because there was someone there to listen. Nobody had ever really conversed in the basement; none of us had the energy.

"I see," Wilma said. "It looks like you all worked very hard."

When I mentioned how Lutz had warned me not to put taues in my bed, Wilma giggled, saying that it really would have been hard for me to sleep if my bed had gotten soaked.

"Now, let us hurry and prepare for lunch. You are going to be throwing fruit in the afternoon, correct?"

"Will you join us, Wilma?" I asked. She never stepped outside the orphanage, but I thought she might be willing to join us just this once.

"It's just behind the orphanage!" one of the children chimed in.

"Yeah, we're only going to be throwing the taues around. Please join!"

We tried our best, but Wilma looked down sadly and shook her head. "I will be cleaning up the dishes so that all of you can have your fun. Do tell me how it went before bed, though."

Despite her kind smile, her eyes left no room for debate. This was an uncrossable line for her.

I hope we can go to the forest together someday...

A bowl of soup was set in front of me. Sister Myne had taught us how to make it, meaning we could prepare food for ourselves rather than relying on the divine blessings we had to wait to receive from the blue priests. It was something we couldn't have even dreamed of when we were living in the basement.

It was because of Sister Myne's kindness that we got to leave the basement. I'm sure that, if we ask her, she'll make it so Wilma can come to the forest with us one day...

Or so I thought while praying to the gods in appreciation of our meal.

"O mighty King and Queen of the endless skies who doth grace us with thousands upon thousands of lives to consume, O mighty Eternal Five who rule the mortal realm, I offer thanks and prayers to thee, and do take part in the meal so graciously provided."

Afterword

To all those who are new to the series and those who read the web or light novels: thank you very much for reading Part 2 Volume 3 of *Ascendance of a Bookworm*'s manga adaptation.

The great orphanage cleanup-slash-revolution has begun. Myne just gives orders, of course, given her status in the temple and weak constitution. She's sad that she can't work with the others, but such is life for an apprentice blue shrine maiden—not everything can go as one wishes. She faces money problems too. Aah, life sure is hard...

However, Myne meets a lot of people in the midst of all this. Among the newly introduced characters are Johann the apprentice smith and Wilma. Johann's overly meticulous attention to detail makes him unpopular with clients, but he's exceedingly talented at his job. Wilma looks after the kids in the orphanage, but she's also an excellent artist who manages to draw some beautiful-looking karuta. Keep an eye on her future appearances.

Both the manga and the anime have been working on their Part 2 adaptations simultaneously, so it's been quite a challenge managing how Suzuka-san and the anime squad represent buildings, animals, background characters in the orphanage, and the like... Before sending character designs to the anime squad, Suzuka-san would send them to me and ask whether they were okay. The tight deadlines led to me sometimes giving Suzuka-san my approval before they were done, which led to some characters looking and acting differently between the manga and the anime. Hahaha. As a result, there are some characters who share nothing but a name. Please do compare the two and discover them for yourselves.

The bonus short story for this volume is "Gathering Taues," which is told from Rico's perspective. He was the tiniest of all the orphans in the basement, and without Myne's help, he would have died before his baptism. I envisioned him when the anime was underway and they asked me for an orphan with a name.

I wrote this short story per Suzuka-san's request, as she wanted to see how the lives of the pre-baptism orphans changed after Myne saved them from the basement, as well as how it felt when they went to the forest and the Star Festival for the first time.

As one last note, the *Bookworm* anime will resume in April with the start of Part 2. Unlike Part 1, there are going to be more scenes with the High Priest, as well as new characters like Fran, Gil, and Delia. They have actual voices, and you'll get to see them move around on screen! Please enjoy life in the temple, animated.

Miya Kazuki

AFTERWORD

Thank you for buying Part 2 Volume 3 of the *Ascendance of a Bookworm* manga! This is Suzuka, the artist.

At the end of the second volume, I said to look forward to the anime for Part 1. Now I'm saying to look forward to the anime for Part 2! The anime for Part 1 came out after the manga adaptation was finished, and I was surprised to see how carefully they included all sorts of tiny details from it.

Part 2 is going to have completely original scripts and more direction from the anime staff, so I'll be watching as a fan myself.

Also, this volume is the tenth one in the series so far. I'm so moved! I'm glad to have been allowed to spend so long with a single work. It's all thanks to the support of you, the readers.

I hope you're looking forward to the next volume!

Suzuka

Special Thanks

Author: Miya Kazuki-sensei
Character Design: You Shiina-sensei
Cover Coloring: Aine-san and also to Sachiko-san, Ryo Namino-sensei, Mio Hattori-san, and my bosses at Tinami and TO Books!

BATHING IN THE TEMPLE

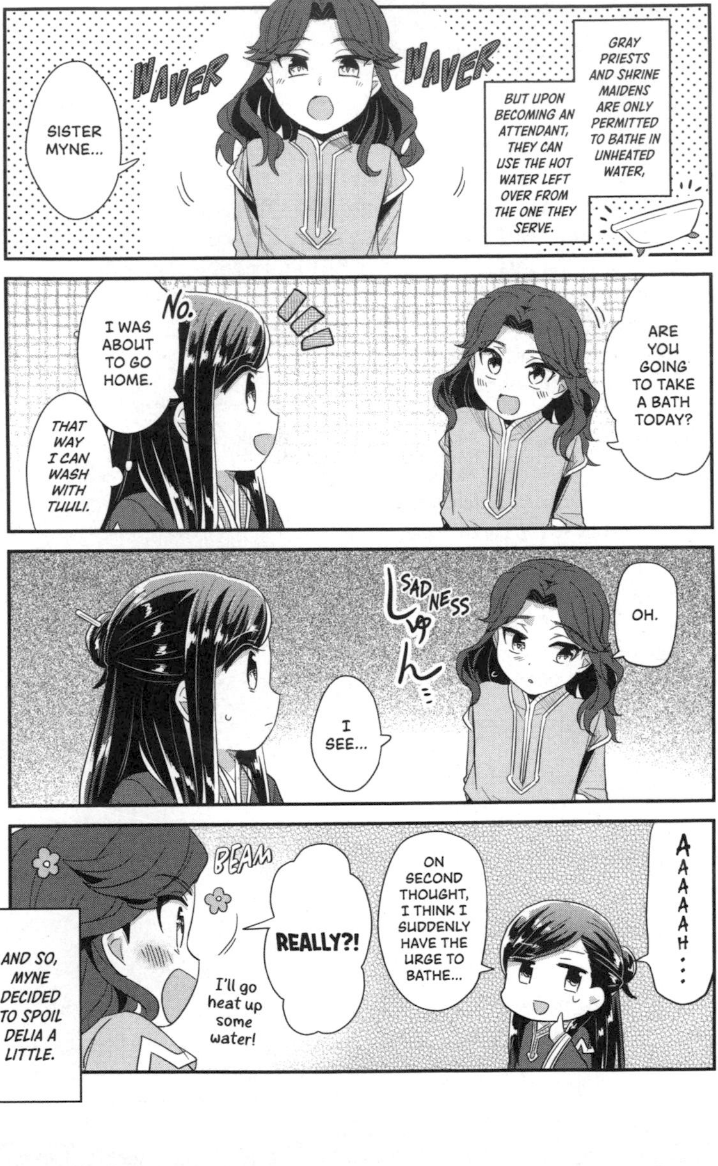
GRAY PRIESTS AND SHRINE MAIDENS ARE ONLY PERMITTED TO BATHE IN UNHEATED WATER,
BUT UPON BECOMING AN ATTENDANT, THEY CAN USE THE HOT WATER LEFT OVER FROM THE ONE THEY SERVE.
WAVER
WAVER
SISTER MYNE...
ARE YOU GOING TO TAKE A BATH TODAY?
NO.
I WAS ABOUT TO GO HOME.
THAT WAY I CAN WASH WITH TUULI.
OH.
SADNESS
しゅん
I SEE...
AAAAAH...
ON SECOND THOUGHT, I THINK I SUDDENLY HAVE THE URGE TO BATHE...
BEAM
REALLY?!
I'll go heat up some water!
AND SO, MYNE DECIDED TO SPOIL DELIA A LITTLE.

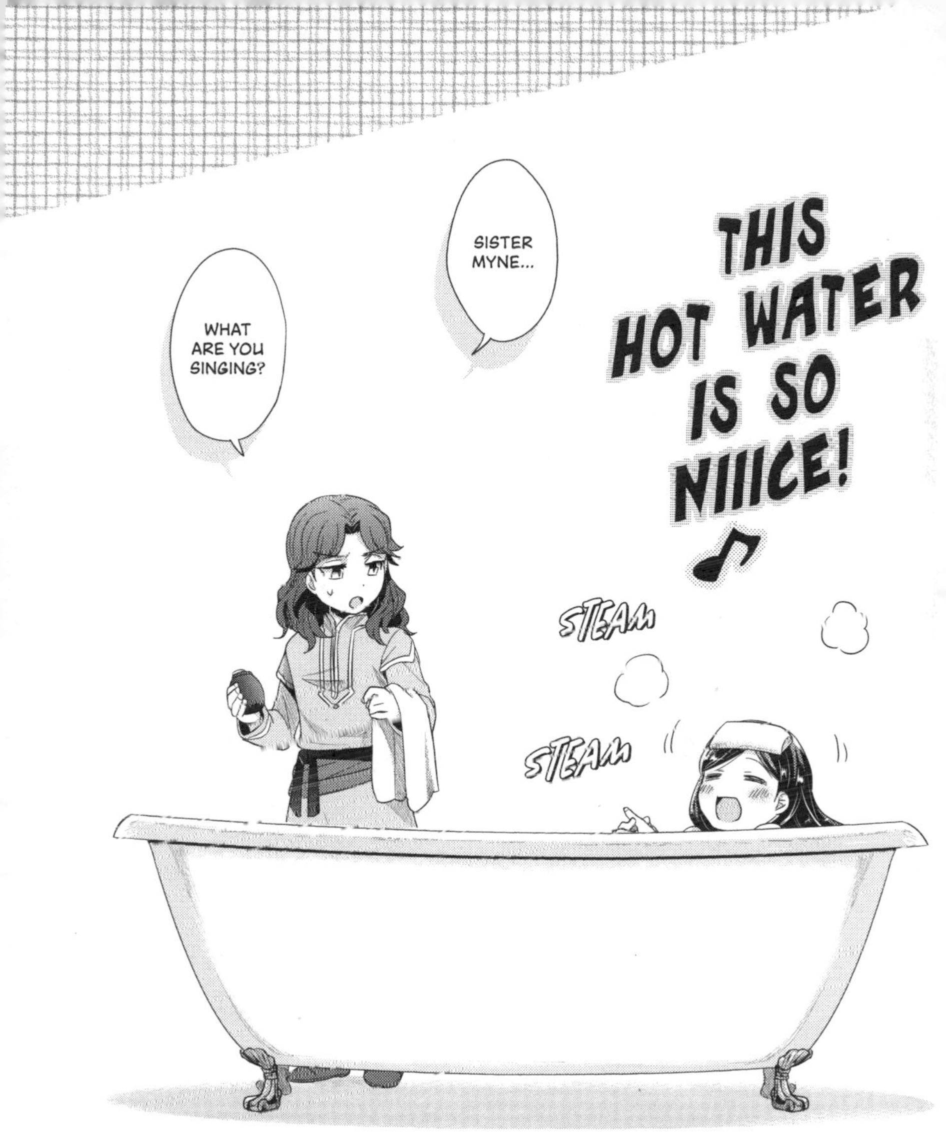
THIS HOT WATER IS SO NIIICE! ♪
STEAM
STEAM
SISTER MYNE...
WHAT ARE YOU SINGING?

ASCENDANCE OF A BOOKWORM (MANGA) PART 2 VOLUME 3
by Miya Kazuki (story) and Suzuka (artwork)
Original character designs by You Shiina

Translated by quof
Edited by Kieran Redgewell
Lettered by Nicole Roderick

First published in Japan in 2020 by TO Books, Tokyo.
Publication rights for this English edition arranged through TO Books, Tokyo.

Managing Director: Samuel Pinansky
Manga Line Manager: J. Collis
Managing Editor: Jan Mitsuko Cash
Managing Translator: Kristi Fernandez
QA Manager: Hannah N. Carter
Marketing Manager: Stephanie Hii

ISBN: 978-1-7183-7259-7
Printed in Korea
First Printing: June 2022
10 9 8 7 6 5 4 3 2 1

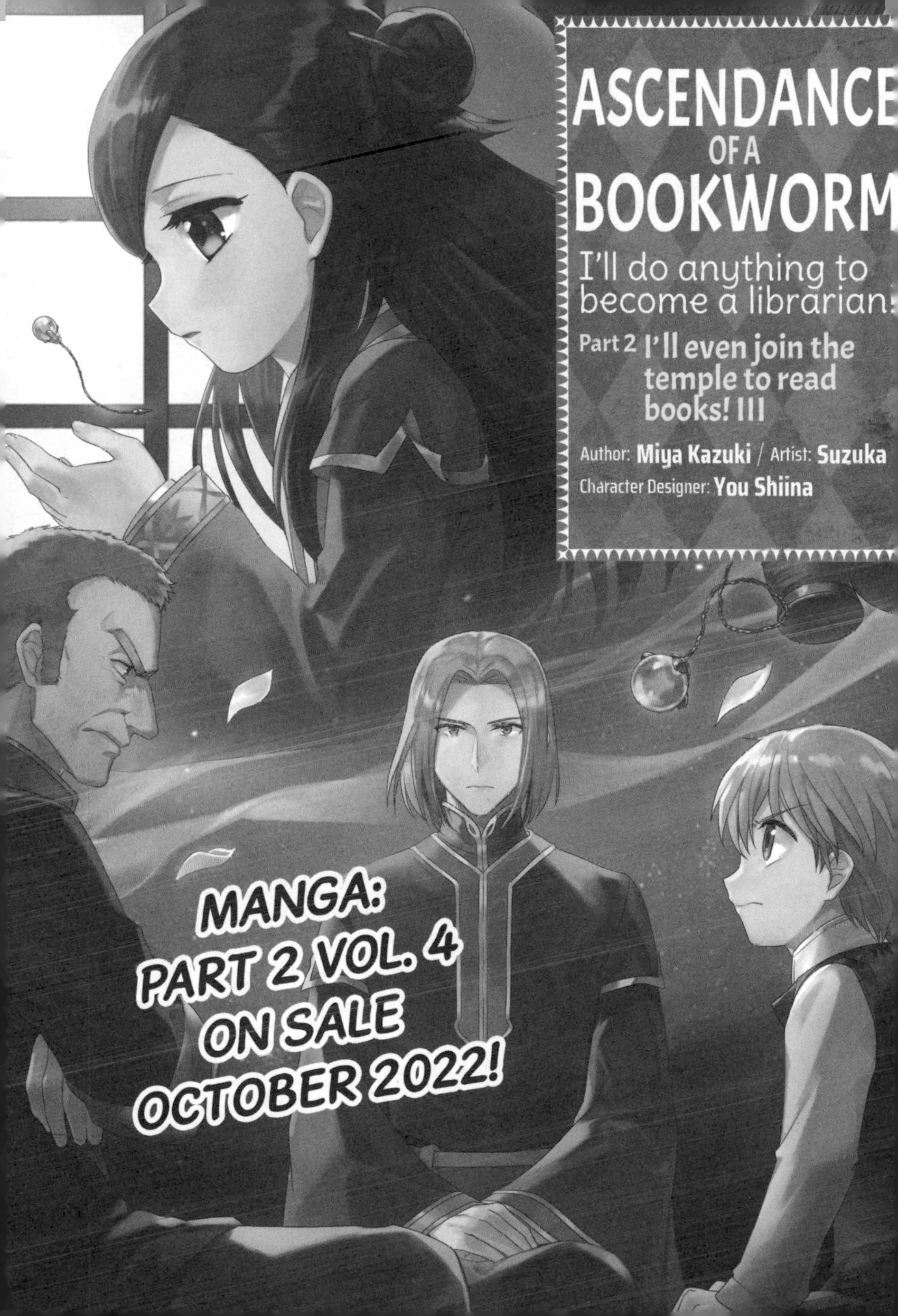
ASCENDANCE OF A BOOKWORM
I'll do anything to become a librarian!
Part 2 I'll even join the temple to read books! III
Author: Miya Kazuki / Artist: Suzuka
Character Designer: You Shiina
MANGA: PART 2 VOL. 4 ON SALE OCTOBER 2022!

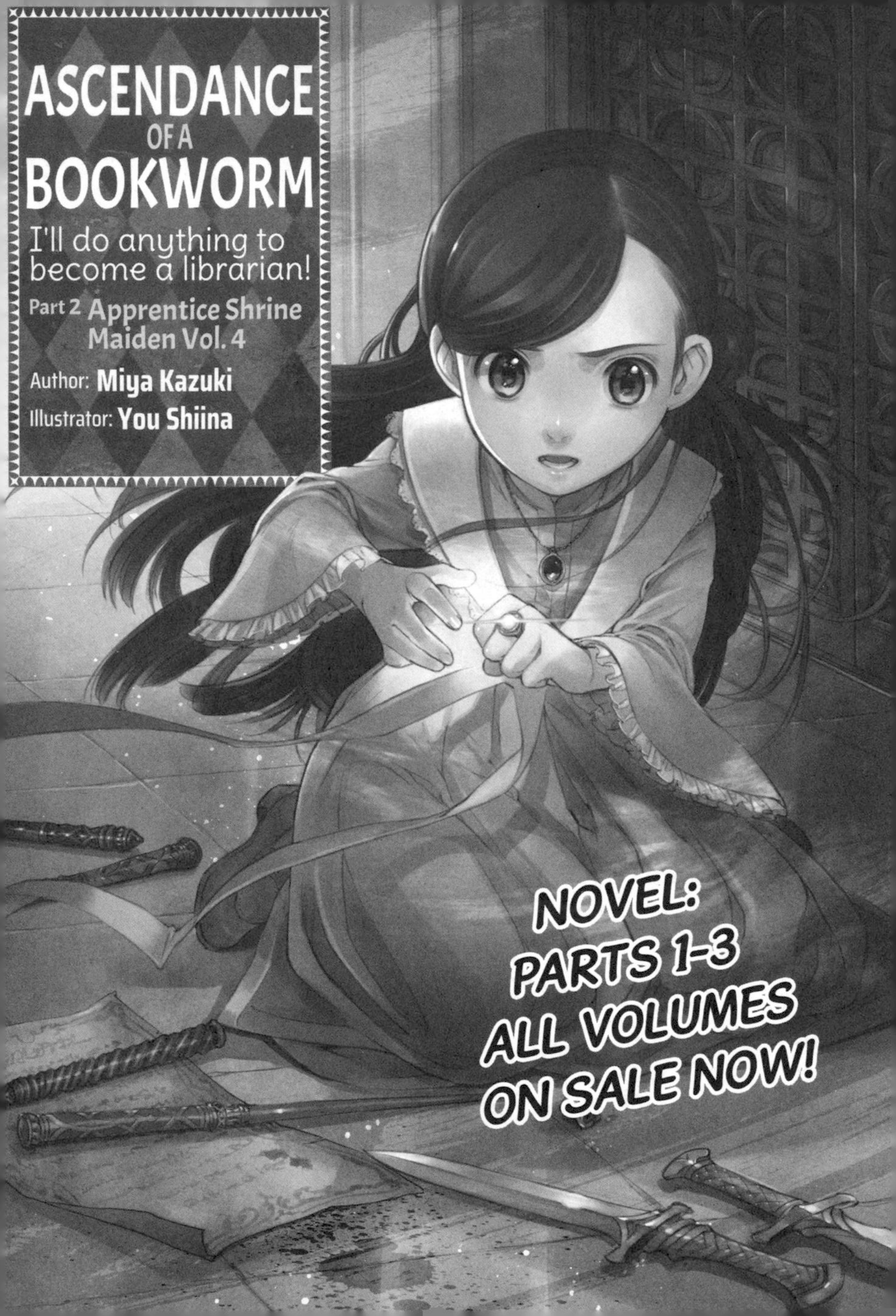
ASCENDANCE OF A BOOKWORM
I'll do anything to become a librarian!
Part 2 Apprentice Shrine Maiden Vol. 4
Author: Miya Kazuki
Illustrator: You Shiina
NOVEL:
PARTS 1-3
ALL VOLUMES
ON SALE NOW!

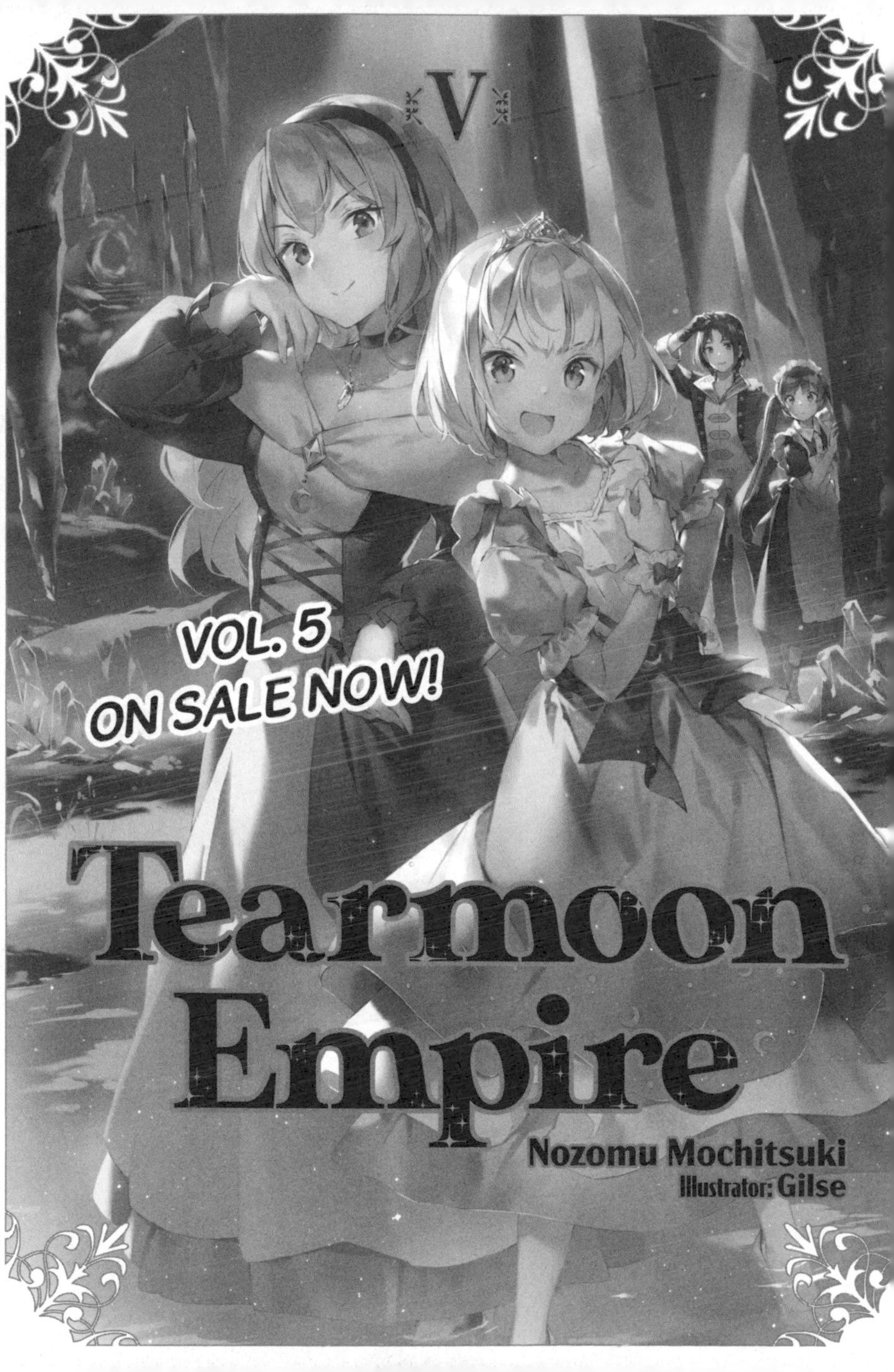
V
VOL. 5
ON SALE NOW!
Tearmoon
Empire
Nozomu Mochitsuki
Illustrator: Gilse

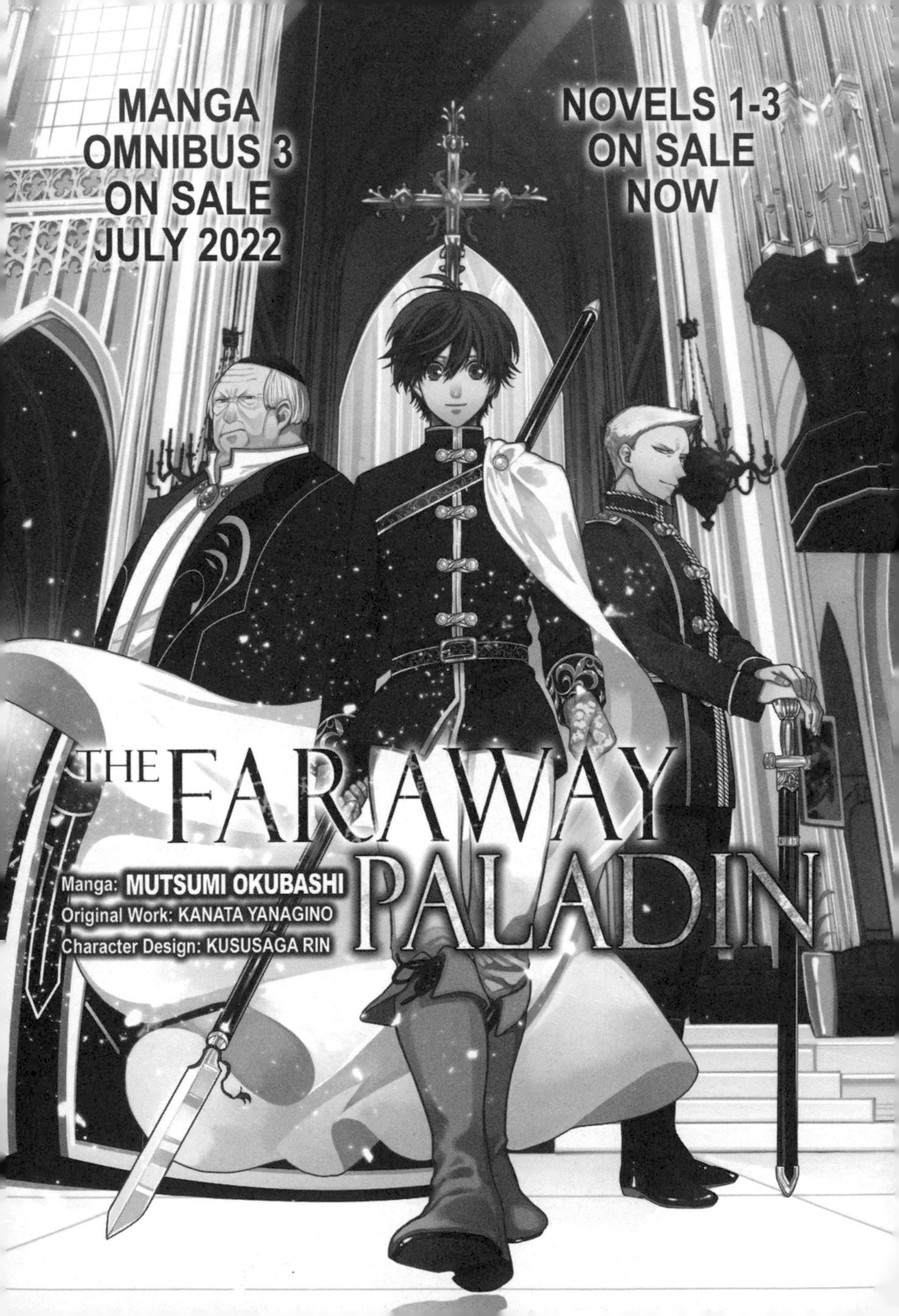

MANGA
OMNIBUS 3
ON SALE
JULY 2022
NOVELS 1-3
ON SALE
NOW
THE FARAWAY PALADIN
Manga: MUTSUMI OKUBASHI
Original Work: KANATA YANAGINO
Character Design: KUSUSAGA RIN

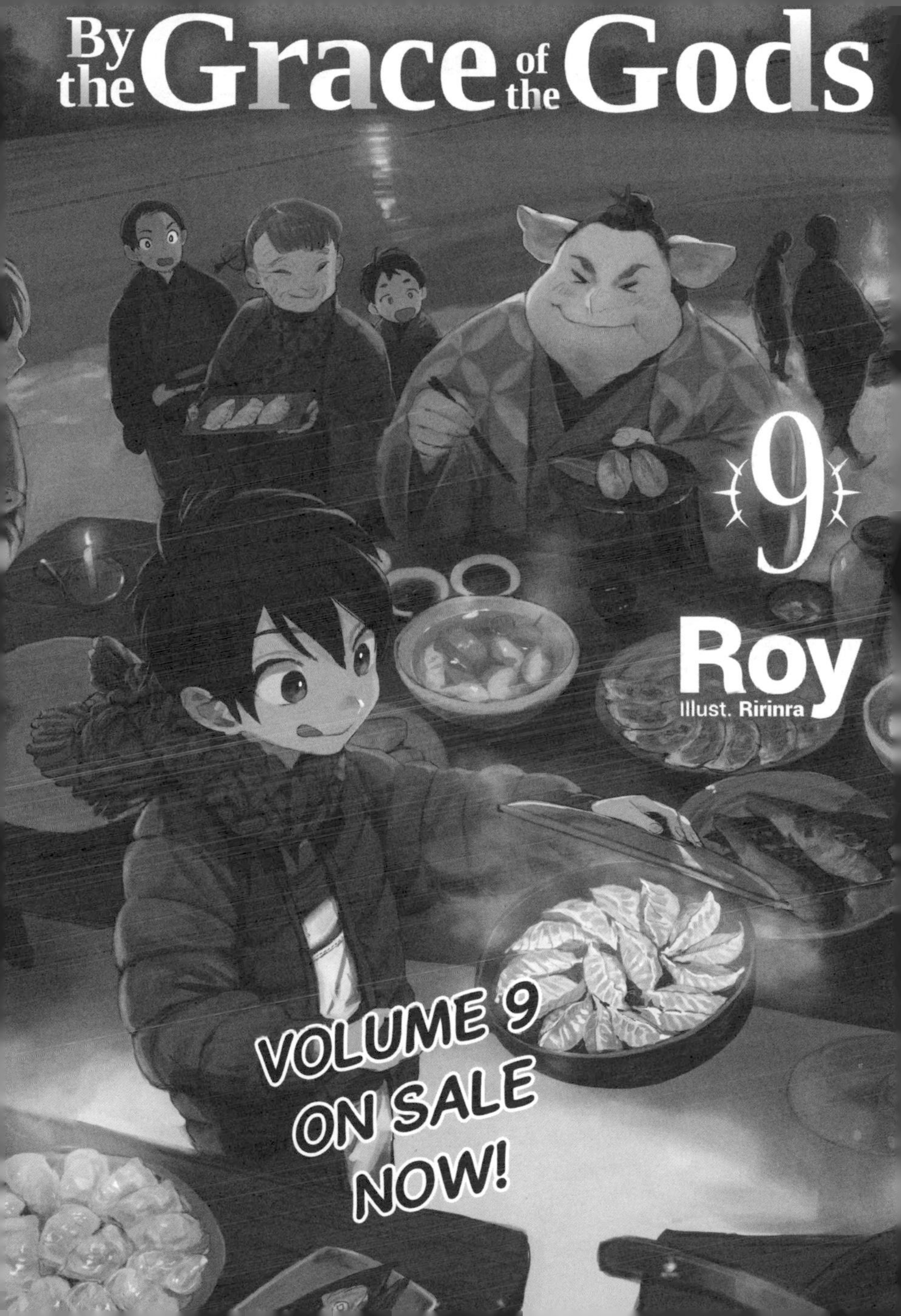
By the Grace of the Gods
9
Roy
Illust. Ririnra
VOLUME 9 ON SALE NOW!

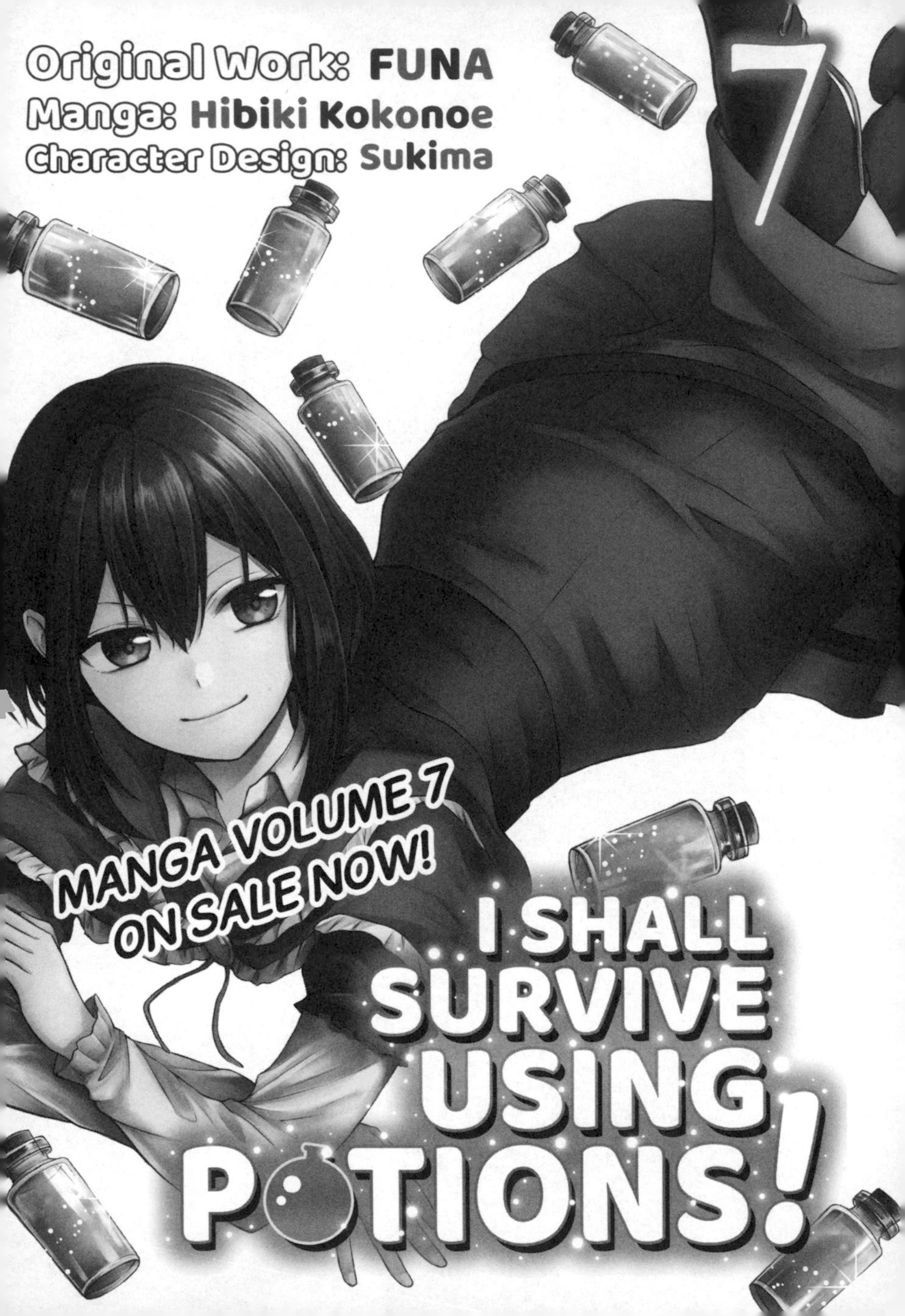
Original Work: FUNA
Manga: Hibiki Kokonoe
Character Design: Sukima
7
MANGA VOLUME 7
ON SALE NOW!
I SHALL SURVIVE USING POTIONS!

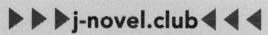

J-Novel Club Lineup

Latest Ebook Releases Series List

Altina the Sword Princess
Amagi Brilliant Park
Animeta!**
The Apothecary Diaries
An Archdemon's Dilemma:
    How to Love Your Elf Bride*
Are You Okay With a Slightly Older
    Girlfriend?
Arifureta: From Commonplace
    to World's Strongest
Arifureta Zero
Ascendance of a Bookworm*
Banner of the Stars
Bibliophile Princess*
Black Summoner*
The Bloodline
By the Grace of the Gods
Campfire Cooking in Another
    World with My Absurd Skill*
Can Someone Please Explain
    What's Going On?!
Chillin' in Another World with
    Level 2 Super Cheat Powers
The Combat Baker and Automaton
    Waitress
Cooking with Wild Game*
Culinary Chronicles of the Court
    Flower
Dahlia in Bloom: Crafting a Fresh
    Start with Magical Tools
Deathbound Duke's Daughter
Demon Lord, Retry!*
Der Werwolf: The Annals of Veight*
Dragon Daddy Diaries: A Girl
    Grows to Greatness
Dungeon Busters
The Emperor's Lady-in-Waiting Is
    Wanted as a Bride*
Endo and Kobayashi Live! The
    Latest on Tsundere Villainess
    Lieselotte
The Faraway Paladin*
Full Metal Panic!
Full Clearing Another World under
    a Goddess with Zero Believers*
Fushi no Kami: Rebuilding
    Civilization Starts With a Village
Goodbye Otherworld, See You
    Tomorrow
The Great Cleric
The Greatest Magicmaster's
    Retirement Plan

Girls Kingdom
Grimgar of Fantasy and Ash
Hell Mode
Her Majesty's Swarm
Holmes of Kyoto
How a Realist Hero Rebuilt the
    Kingdom*
How NOT to Summon a Demon
    Lord
I Shall Survive Using Potions!*
I'll Never Set Foot in That House
    Again!
The Ideal Sponger Life
If It's for My Daughter, I'd Even
    Defeat a Demon Lord
In Another World With My
    Smartphone
Infinite Dendrogram*
Invaders of the Rokujouma!?
Jessica Bannister
JK Haru is a Sex Worker in Another
    World
John Sinclair: Demon Hunter
A Late-Start Tamer's Laid-Back Life
Lazy Dungeon Master
A Lily Blooms in Another World
Maddrax
The Magic in this Other World is
    Too Far Behind!*
The Magician Who Rose From
    Failure
Mapping: The Trash-Tier Skill That
    Got Me Into a Top-Tier Party*
Marginal Operation**
The Master of Ragnarok & Blesser
    of Einherjar*
Min-Maxing My TRPG Build in
    Another World
Monster Tamer
My Daughter Left the Nest and
    Returned an S-Rank Adventurer
My Friend's Little Sister Has It
    In for Me!
My Instant Death Ability is So
    Overpowered, No One in This
    Other World Stands a Chance
    Against Me!*
My Next Life as a Villainess: All
    Routes Lead to Doom!
Otherside Picnic
Outbreak Company
Perry Rhodan NEO

Private Tutor to the Duke's
    Daughter
Reborn to Master the Blade: From
    Hero-King to Extraordinary
    Squire ♀*
Record of Wortenia War*
Reincarnated as the Piggy Duke:
    This Time I'm Gonna Tell Her
    How I Feel!
The Reincarnated Princess Spends
    Another Day Skipping Story
    Routes
Seirei Gensouki: Spirit Chronicles*
Sexiled: My Sexist Party Leader
    Kicked Me Out, So I Teamed Up
    With a Mythical Sorceress!
She's the Cutest... But We're
    Just Friends!
The Sidekick Never Gets the Girl,
    Let Alone the Protag's Sister!
Slayers
The Sorcerer's Receptionist
Sorcerous Stabber Orphen*
Sweet Reincarnation**
The Tales of Marielle Clarac*
Tearmoon Empire
Teogonia
The Underdog of the Eight Greater
    Tribes
The Unwanted Undead
    Adventurer*
Villainess: Reloaded! Blowing
    Away Bad Ends with
    Modern Weapons*
Welcome to Japan, Ms. Elf!*
The White Cat's Revenge as
    Plotted from the Dragon King's
    Lap
A Wild Last Boss Appeared!
The World's Least Interesting
    Master Swordsman

...and more!
* Novel and Manga Editions
** Manga Only
Keep an eye out at j-novel.club
    for further new title
    announcements!